The Haute Noblesse
A Novel

by

George Manville Fenn

The Haute Noblesse
A Novel
by George Manville Fenn

ISBN: 978-93-59954-17-2

Published by

DOUBLE 9 BOOKS

2/13-B, Ansari Road
Daryaganj, New Delhi – 110002
info@double9books.com
www.double9books.com
Tel. 011-40042856

ABOUT THE AUTHOR

George Manville Fenn was a very productive author of novels, a writer, an editor, and an educator from England. He was born on January 3, 1831, in Pimlico, London. He mostly learned on his own; he taught himself Italian, French, and German. During the years 1851-1854, he went to Battersea Training College for Teachers and then became the head of a state school in Alford, Lincolnshire. In the early 1850s, Fenn started to write short stories and pieces for newspapers and magazines. The Old Forest Ranger, his first book, came out in 1856. Afterward, he wrote more than 100 books, many of them for teenagers and young adults. He was one of the most famous writers of his time, and his books were well-liked and read by many people. I also worked as a reporter and writer for Fenn. Among the newspapers and magazines, he worked for was The Boy's Own Paper, which he ran from 1866 to 1874. He worked hard to make children's books better and was a strong supporter of education and reading. The Englishman Fenn passed away on August 26, 1909, in Isleworth.

CONTENTS

Chapter One
"In the West Countree" 11

Chapter Two
Elements of a Whole 19

Chapter Three
Discords 31

Chapter Four
A Thunderbolt 40

Chapter Five
Poison and Antidote 48

Chapter Six
Harry Vine Speaks Plainly; So Does His Friend 57

Chapter Seven
Chez Van Heldre 65

Chapter Eight
Uncle Luke Speaks His Mind 72

Chapter Nine
In Office Hours 79

Chapter Ten
Harry Vine has a Want 88

Chapter Eleven
Aunt Marguerite studies a Comedy 94

Chapter Twelve
Uncle Luke's Spare Cash 99

Chapter Thirteen
To Reap the Wind 108

Chapter Fourteen
Diogenes in his Tub 112

Chapter Fifteen
My Aunt's Bête Noire... 123

Chapter Sixteen
In a West Coast Gale.. 130

Chapter Seventeen
The News 137

Chapter Eighteen
Harry Vine Shows His Bright Side 142

Chapter Nineteen
A Bad Night's Work 149

Chapter Twenty
In the Black Shadow 157

Chapter Twenty One
Harry Looks the Fact in the Face 163

Chapter Twenty Two
The Punishment Begins.. 166

Chapter Twenty Three
Uncle Luke Grows Harder... 176

Chapter Twenty Four
The Trifle that Tells Tales.. 181

Chapter Twenty Five
On the Rack... 184

Chapter Twenty Six
Leslie Makes a Declaration 192

Chapter Twenty Seven
A Brother's Appeal 200

Chapter Twenty Eight
In Defence of his Young 205

Chapter Twenty Nine
On His Behalf 209

Chapter Thirty
In the Queen's Name 217

Chapter Thirty One
"Oh! Absalom, My Son, My Son" 220

Chapter Thirty Two
"The Lord Gave, and..." 225

Chapter Thirty Three
At the Granite House... 233

Chapter Thirty Four
George Vine Asks for Help... 240

Chapter Thirty Five
The Old Watchdog... 245

Chapter Thirty Six
Crampton Reports Progress 248

Chapter Thirty Seven
A Title of Honour... 255

Chapter Thirty Eight
Poll Perrow goes a-Begging... 261

Chapter Thirty Nine
A Meeting in Pain 271

Chapter Forty
Duncan Leslie Speaks Out... 276

Chapter Forty One
Aunt Marguerite Makes Plans 281

Chapter Forty Two
A Startling Visitation... 287

Chapter Forty Three
For Liberty and Life... 294

Chapter Forty Four
A Place of Refuge 299

Chapter Forty Five
The Horror in the Zorn 304

Chapter Forty Six
The Friend of Adversity 312

Chapter Forty Seven
Brother—Lover 317

Chapter Forty Eight
The Plant Aunt Marguerite Grew 326

Chapter Forty Nine
After the Great Sorrows 333

Chapter Fifty
The Discovery 338

Chapter Fifty One
Broken with the Fight 352

Chapter Fifty Two
A Strange Summons 359

Chapter Fifty Three
Her Defender 363

Chapter Fifty Four
Aunt Marguerite Finds a Friend 367

Chapter Fifty Five
Half Converted 373

Chapter Fifty Six
Hard Test 378

Chapter Fifty Seven
An Old Friend—or Enemy? 386

Chapter Fifty Eight
The Needle in a Bundle of Hay 390

Chapter Fifty Nine
Pradelle is Pricked 392

Chapter Sixty
The Dog Bites 396

Chapter Sixty One
Diogenes Discovers 402

Chapter Sixty Two
Uncle Luke Turns Prophet... 409

Chapter Sixty Three
Leslie Makes an Announcement.. 414

Chapter Sixty Four
Harry's Message.. 419

Chapter Sixty Five
Uncle Luke has a Word 424

Chapter Sixty Six
Tried in the Fire.. 432

Chapter One
"In the West Countree"

"Take care, Mr Luke Vine, sir. There's a big one coming."

The thin, little, sharp-featured, grey-haired man on a rock looked sharply round, saw the "big one coming," stooped, picked up a large basket, and, fishing-rod in hand, stepped back and climbed up a few feet, just as a heavy swell, which seemed to glide along rapidly over the otherwise calm sea, heaved, flooded the rock, on which he had been standing, ran right up so high as to bathe his feet, then sank back in a series of glittering falls which sparkled in the glorious sunshine; there was a hissing and sighing and sucking noise among the rocks, and the wave passed on along the rugged coast, leaving the sea calm and bright once more.

"Many a poor lad's been took like that, Mr Luke, sir," said the speaker, "and never heard of again. Why, if I hadn't called out, it would have took you off your legs, and the current's so strong here you'd have been swept away."

"And there'd been an end of me, Polly, and nobody a bit the worse, eh?"

The last speaker seemed to fill his sharp, pale face full of tiny wrinkles, and reduced his eyes to mere slits, as he looked keenly at the big robust woman at his side. She was about fifty, but with her black hair as free from grey as that of a girl, her dark eyes bright, and her sun-tanned face ruddy with health, as she bent forward with a great fish-basket supported on her back by means of a broad leather strap passed over her print sun-bonnet and across her forehead.

"Nobody the worse, Mr Luke, sir?" cried the woman. "What a shame to talk like that! You aren't no wife, nor no child, but there's Miss Louise."

"Louisa, woman, Louisa," said the fisher sharply.

"Well, Louisa, sir. I only want to be right; but it was only yes'day as old Miss Vine, as stood by when I was selling her some hake, shook her finger at me and said I was to say Miss Louise."

"Humph! Never mind what my sister says. Christened Louisa.—That ought to fetch 'em."

"Yes, sir; that ought to fetch 'em," said the woman in a sing-song way, as the elderly man gave the glistening bait at the end of his running line a deft swing and sent it far out into the bright sea. "I've seen the water boiling sometimes out there with the bass leaping and playing. What, haven't you caught none, sir?"

"No, Polly, not one; so just be off about your business, and don't worry me with your chatter."

"Oh, I'm a-going, sir," said the woman good-humouredly; "only I see you a-fishing, and said to myself, 'maybe Mr Luke Vine's ketched more than he wants, and he'd like to sell me some of 'em for my customers.'"

"And I haven't seen a bass this morning, so be off."

"To be sure, Mr Luke Vine, sir; and when are you going to let me come up and give your place a good clean? I says to my Liza up at your brother's, sir, only yes'day—"

"Look here, Polly Perrow," cried the fisher viciously, "will you go, or must I?"

"Don't be criss-cross, sir, I'm going," said the woman, giving her basket a hitch. "Here's Miss Louise—isa—coming down the rocks with Miss Madlin."

"Hang her confounded chatter!" snarled the fisher, as he drew out his bait, unwound some more line, and made another throw, "bad as those wretched stamps."

He cast an angry glance up at the mining works high on the cliff-side, whose chimney shaft ran along the sloping ground till it reared itself in air on the very top of the hill, where in constant repetition the iron-shod piles rose and fell, crushing the broken ore to powder. "A man might have thought he'd be free here from a woman's tongue."

He gave another glance behind him, along the rocky point which jutted out several hundred yards and formed a natural breakwater to the estuary, which ran, rock-sheltered, right up into the land, and on either side of which were built rugged flights of natural steps, from the bright water's edge to where, five hundred feet above, the grey wind-swept masses of granite looked jagged against the sky.

Then he watched his great pointed float, as it ran here and there in the eddies of the tremendous Atlantic currents which swept along by the point. The sea sparkled, the sun shone, and the grey gulls floated above the deep blue transparent water, uttering a querulous cry from time to time, and then dipping down at the small shoals of fry which played upon the surface.

Far away seaward a huge vessel was going west, leaving behind a trail of smoke; on his right a white-sailed yacht or two glistened in the sun. In another direction, scattered here and there, brown-sailed luggers were passing slowly along; while behind the fisher lay the picturesque straggling old town known as East and West Hakemouth, with the estuary of the little river pretty well filled with craft, from the fishing luggers and trawlers up to the good-sized schooners and brigs which traded round the coast or adventured across the Bay of Storms, by Spain and through the Straits, laden with cargoes of pilchards for the Italian ports.

"Missed him," grumbled the fisher, withdrawing his line to rebait with a pearly strip of mackerel. "Humph! now I'm to be worried by those chattering girls."

The worry was very close at hand, for directly after balancing themselves on the rough rocks, and leaping from mass to mass, came two bright-looking girls of about twenty, their faces flushed by exercise, and more than slightly tanned by the strong air that blows health-laden from the Atlantic.

As often happens in real life as well as in fiction, the companions were dark and fair; and as they came laughing and talking, full of animation, looking a couple of as bonny-looking English maidens as the West Country could produce, their aspect warranted, in reply to the greetings of "Ah, Uncle Luke!" "Ah, Mr Vine!" something a little more courteous than—

"Well, Nuisance?" addressed with a short nod to the dark girl in white serge, and "Do, Madelaine?" to the fair girl in blue.

The gruffness of the greeting seemed to be taken as a matter of course, for the girls seated themselves directly on convenient masses of rock, and busied themselves in the governance of sundry errant strands of hair which were playing in the breeze.

The elderly fisher watched them furtively, and his sour face seemed a little less grim, and as if there was something after all pleasant to look upon in the bright youthful countenances before him.

"Well, uncle, how many fish?" said the dark girl.

"Bah! and don't chatter, or I shall get none at all. How's dad?"

"Quite well. He's out here somewhere."

"Dabbling?"

"Yes."

The girl took off her soft yachting cap, and fanned her face; then ceased and half closing her eyes and throwing back her head, let her red lips part slightly as she breathed in full draughts of the soft western breeze.

"If he ever gives her a moment's pain," said the old man to himself as he jerked a look up at the mining works, "I'll kill him." Then, turning sharply to the fair girl, he said aloud: — "Well, Madelaine, how's the *bon père*?"

"Quite well and very busy seeing to the lading of the *Corunna*," said the girl with animation.

"Humph! Old stupid. Worrying himself to death money grubbing. Here, Louie, when's that boy going back to his place?"

"To-morrow, uncle."

"Good job too. What did he want with a holiday? Never did a day's work in his life. Here! Hold her, Louie. She's going to peck," he added in mock alarm, and with a cynical sneering laugh, as he saw his niece's companion colour slightly, and compress her lips.

"Well, it's too bad of you, uncle. You are always finding fault about Harry."

"Say Henri, pray, my child, and with a good strong French accent," cried the old man with mock remonstrance. "What would Aunt Marguerite say?"

"Aunt Margaret isn't here, uncle," cried the girl merrily; "and it's of no use for you to grumble and say sour things, because we know you by heart, and we don't believe in you a bit."

"No," said the fisherman grimly, "only hate me like poison, for a sour old crab. Never gave me a kiss when you came."

"How could I without getting wet?" said the girl with a glance at the tiny rock island on which the fisher stood.

"Humph! Going back to-morrow, eh? Good job too. Why, he has been a whole half-year in his post."

"Yes, uncle, a whole half-year!"

"And never stayed two months before at any of the excellent situations your father and I worried ourselves and our friends to death to get for him."

"Now, uncle — "

"A lazy, thoughtless, good-for-nothing young vag— There, hold her again, Louie. She's going to peck."

"And you deserve it, uncle," cried the girl, with a smile at her companion, in whose eyes the indignant tears were rising.

"What! for speaking the truth, and trying to let that foolish girl see my lord in his right colours?"

"Harry's a good affectionate brother, and I love him very dearly," said Louise, firmly; "and he's your brother's son, uncle, and in your heart, you love him too, and you're proud of him, as proud can be."

"You're a silly, young goose, and as feather-brained as he is. Proud of him? Bah! I wish he'd enlist for a soldier, and get shot."

"For shame, uncle!" cried Louise indignantly; and her face flushed too as she caught and held her companion's hand.

"Yes. For shame! It's all your aunt's doing, stuffing the boy's head full of fantastic foolery about his descent, and the disgrace of trade. And now I am speaking, look here," he cried, turning sharply on the fair girl, and holding his rod over her as if it were a huge stick which he was about to use. "Do you hear, Madelaine?"

"I'm listening, Mr Vine," said the girl, coldly.

"I've known you ever since you were two months old, and your silly mother must insist upon my taking hold of you—you miserable little bit of pink putty, as you were then, and fooled me into being godfather. How I could be such an ass, I don't know—but I am, and I gave you that silver cup, and I've wanted it back ever since."

"Oh, uncle, what a wicked story!" cried Louise, laughing.

"It's quite true, miss. Dead waste of money. It has never been used, I'll swear."

"No, Mr Vine, never," said Madelaine, smiling now.

"Ah, you need not show your teeth at me because you're so proud they're white. Lots of the fisher-girls have got better. That's right, shut your lips up, and listen. What I've got to say is this; if I see any more of that nonsense there'll be an explosion."

"I don't know what you mean," said Madelaine, colouring more deeply.

"Yes, you do, miss. I saw Harry put his arm round your waist, and I won't have it. What's your father thinking about? Why, that boy's no more fit to be your husband than that great, ugly, long brown-bearded Scotchman who poisons the air with his copper mine, is to be Louie's."

"Uncle, you are beyond bearing to-day."

"Am I? Well then be off. But you mind, Miss Maddy, I won't have it. You'll be silly enough to marry some day, but when you do, you shall marry a man, not a feather-headed young ass, with no more brains than that bass. Ah, I've got you this time, have I?"

He had thrown in again, and this time struck and hooked a large fish, whose struggles he watched with grim satisfaction, till he drew it gasping and quivering on to the rock—a fine bass, whose silver sides glistened like those of a salmon, and whose sharp back fin stood up ready to cut the unwitting hand.

"Bad for him, Louie," said the old man with a laugh; "but one must have dinners, eh? What a countenance!" he continued, holding up his fish, "puts me in mind of that fellow you have up at the house, what's his name, Priddle, Fiddle?"

"Pradelle, uncle."

"Ah, Pradelle. Of course he's going back too."

"Yes, uncle."

"Don't like him," continued Uncle Luke, rebaiting quickly and throwing out; "that fellow has got scoundrel written in his face."

"For shame! Mr Vine," said Madelaine, laughing. "Mr Pradelle is very gentlemanly and pleasant."

"Good-looking scoundrels always are, my dear. But he don't want you. I watched him. Going to throw over the Scotchman and take to Miss Louie?"

"Uncle, you've got a bite," said the girl coolly.

"Eh? So I have. Got him, too," said the old man, striking and playing his fish just as if he were angling in fresh water. "Thumper."

"What pleasure can it give you to say such unpleasant things, uncle?" continued the girl.

"Truths always are unpleasant," said the old man, laughing. "Don't bother me, there's a shoal off the point now, and I shall get some fish."

"Why you have all you want now, uncle."

"Rubbish! Shall get a few shillings' worth to sell Mother Perrow."

"Poor Uncle Luke!" said the girl with mock solemnity; "obliged to fish for his living."

"Better than idling and doing nothing. I like to do it, and—There he is again. Don't talk."

He hooked and landed another fine bass from the shoal which had come up with the tide that ran like a millstream off the point, when as he placed the fish in the basket he raised his eyes.

"Yah! Go back and look after your men. I thought that would be it. Maddy, look at her cheeks."

"Oh, uncle, if I did not know you to be the best and dearest of—"

"Tchah! Carney!" he cried, screwing up his face. "Look here, I want to catch a few fish and make a little money, so if that long Scot is coming courting, take him somewhere else. Be off!"

"If Mr Duncan Leslie is coming to say good-day, uncle, I see no reason why he should not say it here," said Louise, calmly enough now, and with the slight flush which had suffused her cheeks fading out.

"Good-day. A great tall sheepish noodle who don't know when he's well off," grumbled the fisher, throwing out once more as a tall gentlemanly-looking young fellow of about eight-and-twenty stepped actively from rock to rock till he had joined the group, raising his soft tweed hat to the ladies and shaking hands.

"What a lovely morning!" he said eagerly. "I saw you come down. Much sport, Mr Vine?" he added, as he held out his hand.

"No," said Uncle Luke, nodding and holding tightly on to his rod. "Hands full. Can't you see?"

"Oh, yes, I see. One at you now."

"Thankye. Think I couldn't see?" said the old man, striking and missing his fish. "Very kind of you to come and see how I was getting on."

"But I didn't," said the new-comer, smiling. "I knew you didn't want me."

"Here, Louie, make a note of that," said Uncle Luke, sharply. "The Scotch are not so dense as they pretend they are."

"Uncle!"

"Oh, pray, don't interpose, Miss Vine. Your uncle and I often have a passage of arms together."

"Well, say what you've got to say, and then go back to your men. Has the vein failed?"

"No, sir; it grows richer every day."

"Sorry for it. I suppose you'll be burrowing under my cottage and burying me one of these days before my time?"

"Don't be alarmed, sir."

"I'm not," growled Uncle Luke.

"Uncle is cross, because he is catching more fish than he wants this morning," said Louise quietly.

"Hear that, Maddy, my dear?" said the old man, sharply. "Here's a problem for you:—If my niece's tongue is as keen-edged as that before she is twenty, what will it be at forty?"

The girl addressed laughed and shook her head.

"Any one would think it would be a warning to any sensible man to keep his distance."

"Uncle! Pray!" whispered the niece, looking troubled; but the old man only chuckled and hooked another fish.

"Going to make a fortune out of the old mine, Leslie?" he said.

"Fortune? No, sir. A fair income, I hope."

"Which with prudence and economy—Scottish prudence and economy," he added, meaningly, "would keep you when you got to be an old man like me. Bah!"

He snatched out his line and gave an impatient stamp with his foot.

"What is the matter, uncle?"

"What's the matter? It was bad enough before. Look there?"

Chapter Two
Elements of a Whole

Madelaine Van Heldre had seen the object of Uncle Luke's vexation before he called attention to it; and at the first glance her eyes had lit up with pleasure, but only to give place to an anxious, troubled look, and faint lines came across her brow.

"Why, it is only Harry with his friend," said Louise quietly.

"Yes: flopping and splashing about in the boat. There will not be a fish left when they've done."

"I'll tell them to land at the lower stairs," said Louise eagerly.

"No; let 'em come and do their worst," said the old man, with quite a snarl. "Why doesn't Harry row, instead of letting that miserable cockney fool about with an oar?"

"Miserable cockney!" said Duncan Leslie to himself; and his face, which had been overcast, brightened a little as he scanned the boat coming from the harbour.

"Mr Pradelle likes exercise," said Louise quietly.

Duncan's face grew dull again.

"Then I wish he would take it in London," said the old man, "jumping over his desk or using his pen, and not come here."

The water glistened and sparkled with the vigorous strokes given by the two young men who propelled the boat, and quickly after there was a grating noise as the bows ground against the rocks of the point and a young man in white flannels leaped ashore, while his companion after awkwardly laying in his oar followed the example, balancing himself as he stepped on to the gunwale, and then after the fashion of a timid horse at a gutter, making a tremendous bound on to the rocks.

As he did this his companion made a quick leap back into the bows to seize the chain, when he had to put out an oar once more and paddle close up to the rock, the boat having been sent adrift by the force of the other's leap.

"What a fellow you are, Pradelle!" he said, as he jumped on to a rock, and twisted the chain about a block.

"Very sorry, dear boy. Didn't think of that."

"No," said the first sourly, "you didn't."

He was a well-knit manly fellow, singularly like his sister, while his companion, whom he had addressed as Pradelle, seemed to be his very opposite in every way, though on the whole better looking; in fact, his features were remarkably handsome, or would have been had they not been marred by his eyes, which were set close together, and gave him a shifty look.

"How are you, uncle? How do, Leslie?" said Harry, as he stood twirling a gold locket at the end of his chain, to receive a grunt from the fisherman, and a friendly nod from the young mine-owner. "So here you are then," he continued; "we've been looking for you everywhere. You said you were going along the west walk."

"Yes, but we saw uncle fishing, and came down to him."

"Well, come along now."

"Come? Where?"

"Come where? Why for a sail. Wind's just right. Jump in."

Duncan Leslie looked grave, but he brightened a little as he heard what followed.

"Oh no, Harry."

As she spoke, Louise Vine glanced at her companion, in whose face she read an eager look of acquiescence in the proposed trip, which changed instantly to one of agreement with her negative.

"There, Vic. Told you so. Taken all our trouble for nothing."

"But, Harry—"

"Oh, all right," he cried, interrupting her, in an ill-used tone. "Just like girls. Here's our last day before we go back to the confounded grindstone. We've got the boat, the weather's lovely; we've been looking for you everywhere, and it's 'Oh no, Harry!' And Madelaine looking as if it would be too shocking to go for a sail."

"We don't like to disappoint you," said Madelaine, "but—"

"But you'd rather stay ashore," said the young man shortly. "Never mind, Vic, old chap, we'll go alone, and have a good smoke. Cheerful, isn't it? I say, Uncle Luke, you're quite right."

"First time you ever thought so then," said the old man shortly.

"Perhaps Miss Vine will reconsider her determination," said the young man's companion, in a low soft voice, as he went toward Louise, and seemed to Duncan Leslie to be throwing all the persuasion possible into his manner.

"Oh, no, thank you, Mr Pradelle," she replied hastily, and Duncan Leslie once more felt relieved and yet pained, for there was a peculiar consciousness in her manner.

"We had brought some cans with us and a hammer and chisel," continued Pradelle. "Harry thought we might go as far as the gorns."

"Zorns, man," cried Harry.

"I beg pardon, zorns, and get a few specimens for Mr Vine."

"It was very kind and thoughtful of Harry," said Louise hastily, "and we are sorry to disappoint him—on this his last day—but—"

"Blessed *but!*" said Harry, with a sneer; and he gave Madelaine a withering look, which made her bite her lip.

"And the fish swarming round the point," said Uncle Luke impatiently. "Why don't you go with them, girls?"

"Right again, uncle," said Harry.

The old man made him a mocking bow.

"Go, uncle?" said Louise eagerly, and then checking herself.

Duncan Leslie's heart sank like an ingot of his own copper dropped in a tub.

"Yes, go."

"If you think so, uncle—"

"Well, I do," he said testily, "only pray go at once."

"There!" cried Harry. "Come, Maddy."

He held out his hand to his sister's companion, but she hesitated, still looking at Louise, whose colour was going and coming as she saw Pradelle take off his cap and follow his friend's example, holding out his hand to help her into the boat.

"Yes, dear," she said to Madelaine gravely. "They would be terribly disappointed if we did not go."

The next moment Madelaine was in the boat, Louise still hanging back till, feeling that it would be a slight worse than the refusal to go if she ignored the help extended to her, she laid her hand in Pradelle's and stepped off the rock into the gently rising and falling boat.

"Another of my mistakes," said Duncan Leslie to himself; and then he started as if some one had given him an electric shock.

"Hullo!" cried the old man, "You're going too?"

"I? going?"

"Yes, of course! To take care of them. I'm not going to have them set off without some one to act as ballast to those boys."

Louise mentally cast her arms round the old man's neck and kissed him.

Harry, in the same manner, kicked his uncle into the sea, and Pradelle's eyes looked closer together than usual, as he turned them upon the young mine-owner.

"I should only be too happy," said the latter, "if—"

"Oh, there's plenty of room, Mr Leslie," cried the girls in duet. "Pray come."

The invitation was so genuine that Leslie's heart seemed to leap.

"Oh, yes, plenty of room," said Harry, "only if the wind drops, you'll have to pull an oar."

"Of course," said Leslie, stepping in.

Harry raised the boat-hook, and thrust the little vessel away, and then began to step the mast.

"Lay hold of the rudder, Leslie," he cried. "Send us up some fish for tea, uncle."

"I'll wait and see first whether you come back," said the old man. "Good-bye, girls. Don't be uneasy. I'll go and tell the old people if you're drowned."

"Thank you," shouted back the young man as he hoisted the little sail, which began to fill at once, and by the time he had it sheeted home, the boat was swiftly running eastward with the water pattering against her bows, and a panorama of surpassing beauty seeming to glide slowly by them on the left.

"There!" cried Harry to his friend, who had seated himself rather sulkily forward, the order to take the tiller having placed Leslie between Louise and Madelaine. "Make much of it, Vic: Paddington to-morrow night, hansom cab or the Underground, and next morning the office. Don't you feel happy?"

"Yes, now," said Pradelle, with a glance at Louise.

"Easy, Leslie, easy," cried Harry; "where are you going?"

"I beg pardon," said the young man hastily, for he had unwittingly changed the course of the boat.

"That's better. Any one would think you wanted to give Uncle Luke the job he talked about."

Madelaine looked up hastily.

"No; we will not do that, Miss Van Heldre," said Leslie smiling. "Shall I hold the sheet, Vine?"

"No need," said the young man, making the rope fast.

"But—"

"Oh, all right. I know what you're going to say—puff of wind might lay us over as we pass one of the combes. Wasn't born here for nothing."

Leslie said no more, but deferred to the opinion of the captain of the boat.

"Might as well have brought a line to trail. You'd have liked to fish, wouldn't you, Vic?"

"Only when we are alone," said Pradelle. "Can you tell me the name of that point, Miss Vine?"

"Brea," said Louise quietly.

"And that little valley?"

"Tol Du. The old Cornish names must sound strange to any one from London."

"Oh, no," he said, bending forward to engage her in conversation. "This place is very interesting, and I shall regret going," he added with a sign, and a thoughtful look toward the picturesque little group of houses on either side of the estuary.

"I should think you will," said Harry. "Never mind, we've had a very jolly time. I say, Maddy," he whispered, "you will write to a fellow, won't you?"

"No," she said quietly; "there is no need."

"No need?"

"Louie will be writing to you every week, and you will answer her. I shall hear how you are getting on."

Harry whistled and looked angrily at his sister, who was replying to some remark made by Leslie.

"Here, Vic," he said, "she's too heavy forward. Come and sit by my sister. That's better. A little more over to the side, Leslie. Always trim your boat."

The changes were made, and the little yawl sped rapidly on past the headland of grey granite hoary and shaggy with moss; past black frowning masses of slaty shale, over and amongst which the waves broke in sparkling foam, and on and on by ferny hollows and rifts, down which trickled tiny streams. The day was glorious, and the reflection of the sapphire sky dyed the sea tint of a blue that seemed amethystine in its richer transparent hue. The grey gulls floated overhead, and the tiny fish they pursued made the sea flash as they played about and showed their silvery sides.

But the conversation flagged. Possibly the fact of its being the last day of a pleasant sojourn acted upon the spirits of two of the party, while the third of the male occupants of the boat rather welcomed the restraint and silence, for it gave him an opportunity to sit and think and wonder what was to be his future, and what the animated countenance of Louise Vine meant as she answered the questions of her brother's friend.

He was a visitor as well as her brother's companion; he had been staying at Mr Vine's for a fortnight. They had had endless opportunities for conversation and—in short, Duncan Leslie felt uncomfortable.

It was then with a feeling of relief that was shared by both the ladies, that after a few miles' run Henry Vine stood up in the bows, and, keeping a sharp look out for certain rocks, shouted his orders to Leslie as to the steering of the boat, and finally, as they neared the frowning cliffs, suddenly lowered the sail and took up the oars.

They were abreast of a large cave where the swift grey-winged pigeons flew in and out over the swelling waves which seemed to glide slowly on and on, to rush rapidly after the birds and disappear in the gloom beneath the arch. Then there was a low echoing boom as the wave struck far away in the cave, and came back hissing and whispering to be merged in the next.

"Going to row close in?" said Leslie, scanning the weird, forbidding place rather anxiously.

"Going to row right in," said Harry, with a contemptuous smile. "Not afraid, are you?"

"Can't say," replied Leslie. "A little perhaps. The place does not look tempting. Do you think it is safe to go in?"

"Like to land on the rock till we come back?" said Harry instead of answering the question.

"No," said Leslie quietly; "but do you think it wise to row in there?"

"You're not afraid, are you, girls?"

"I always feel nervous till we are outside again," said Louise quietly.

"But you will be very careful, Harry," said Madelaine.

"Think I want to drown myself?" he said bitterly. "I might just as well p'r'aps, as go back to that dismal office in London, to slave from morning till night."

He rested upon his oars for a minute or two, and perhaps from the reflection of the masses of ferns which fringed the arch of the cavern, and which were repeated in the clear waters, Victor Pradelle's face seemed to turn of a sickly green while one hand grasped the edge of the boat with spasmodic force.

"Now then, hold tight," said the rower, as a swell came from seaward, running right in and raising the boat so that by skilful management she was borne forward, right beneath the arch and then away into the depths of the cavern, leaving her rocking upon the watery floor, while it sped on away into the darkness where it broke with a booming noise which echoed, and whispered, and died away in sobs and sighs, and strange hisses and gasps, as if the creatures which made the cavern their lair had been disturbed, and were settling down again to sleep.

"There, Vic," cried Harry, "what do you think of this?"

Pradelle was holding tightly by the side of the boat, and gazing uneasily round.

"Think? Yes: very wild and wonderful," he said huskily.

"Wonderful? I should think it is. Goes in ever so far, only it isn't wide enough for the boat."

Leslie looked back at the mouth, fringed with the fronds of ferns, and at the lovely picture it frame a of sunny amethystine sea; then at the rocky sides, dripping with moisture, and here of a rich metallic green, there covered with glistening weeds of various shades of olive-green and brown.

"Ahoy—oy!" shouted Harry with all his might, and at the same moment he let his oars splash in the water.

Pradelle leaped to his feet as there came a strange echo and a whirring rush, and a dozen pigeons swept past their heads from out of the depths of the water cave, and away into the brilliant sunshine.

"Oh, if I had a gun," cried Pradelle, to hide his confusion.

"What for—to make a miss?" sneered Harry. "Now then, out with those cans. Fill every one, and I'll try and knock off a few anemones for the governor."

As he spoke he laid in his oars, picked a hammer and chisel from out of the locker in the forepart of the boat, and then worked it along by the side of the great cave, as from out of the clefts and crannies above and beneath the water he searched for the semi-gelatinous sea-anemones that clustered among barnacles, and the snail-like whorl molluscs whose home was on the weedy rocks.

The girls aided all they could, pointing out and receiving in the tins a many-rayed creature, which closed up till it resembled a gout of blood; now, still adhering to the rock which Harry chipped off, a beautiful *Actinia* of olive-green with gem-like spots around the mouth and amid its fringe of turquoise blue.

Duncan Leslie eagerly lent his help; and, not to be behindhand, Pradelle took up the boat-hook and held on, but with the smoothness and care of a sleek tom-cat, he carefully avoided wetting his hands.

"Nothing very new here," said Harry at last, as the waves that kept coming in made the boat rise and fall gently; "there's another better cave than this close by. Let's go there; or what do you say to stopping here and having a smoke till the tide has risen and shut us in?"

"Is there any risk of that?" said Pradelle anxiously.

"Oh, yes, plenty."

Leslie glanced at Louise and thought that it would be very pleasant to play protector all through the darkness till the way was open and daylight shone again. He caught her eyes more than once and tried to read them as he wondered whether there was hope for him; but so surely as she found him gazing rather wistfully at her, she hurriedly continued the collecting, pointing out one of the beautiful objects they sought beneath the surface, and asking Pradelle to shift the boat a little farther along.

"All my vanity and conceit," said Leslie to himself with a sigh; "and why should I worry myself about a woman? I have plenty to do without thinking of love and marriage. If I did, why not begin to dream about pleasant, straightforward Madelaine Van Heldre? There can be nothing more than a friendly feeling towards Master Harry here."

"Now then, sit fast," cried the latter object of his thoughts; "and if we are capsized, girls, I'll look after you, Maddy. Pradelle here will swim out with Louie, and I shall leave you to bring out the boat, Leslie. You can swim, can't you?"

"A little," said the young man drily.

Pradelle looked rather more green, for the light within the cave was of a peculiar hue, and he began to think uneasily of bathing out of a machine at Margate, holding on to a rope, and also of the effort he once made to swim across a tepid bath in town. But he laughed heartily directly after as he realised that it was all banter on his friend's part, while, in spite of himself, he gave a sigh of relief as, riding out on the crest of a broken wave, they once more floated in the sunshine.

Ten minutes' careful rowing among the rocks, which were now four or five feet beneath the water, now showing their weedy crests above, brought them to the mouth of another cave, only approachable from the sea, and sending the boat in here, the collection went on till it was deemed useless to take more specimens, when they passed out again, greatly to Pradelle's satisfaction.

"How's time?" said Harry. "Half-past four? Plenty of time. High tea at six. What shall we do—sail right out and tack, or row along here in the smooth water among the rocks?"

"Row slowly back," said Louise: and Pradelle took an oar.

At the end of half a mile he ceased rowing.

"Tired?" said Harry.

"No; I have a blister on my hand; that's all."

"Come and pull, Leslie," said Harry. "You'd better steer, Louie, and don't send us on to a rock."

The exchange of places was made, and once more they began to progress with the boat, travelling far more swiftly as they glided on close in to the mighty cliff which rose up overhead, dappled with mossy grey and patches of verdure, dotted with yellow and purple blooms.

"To go on like this for ever!" thought Leslie as he swung to and fro, his strong muscles making the water foam as he dipped his oar, watching Louise as she steered, and seemed troubled and ready to converse with Pradelle whenever she caught his eye.

"Starn all!" shouted Harry suddenly, as about three miles from home they came abreast of a narrow opening close to the surface of the water.

The way of the boat was checked, and Harry looked at the hole into which the tide ran and ebbed as the swell rose and fell, now nearly covering the opening, now leaving it three or four feet wide.

"Bound to say there are plenty of good specimens in there," he said. "What do you say, Vic, shall we go in?"

"Impossible."

"Not it. Bound to say that's the opening to quite a large zorn. I've seen the seals go in there often."

"Has it ever been explored?" said Leslie, who felt interested in the place.

"No; it's nearly always covered. It's only at low tides like this that the opening is bared. If the girls were not here I'd go in."

"How?" said Pradelle.

"How?—why swim in."

"And be shut up by the tide and drowned," said Louise.

"Good thing too," said Harry, with the same look of a spoiled boy at Madelaine. "I don't find life go very jolly. Boat wouldn't pass in there."

He had risen from his seat and was standing with one foot on the gunwale, the other on the thwart, gazing curiously at the dark orifice some forty yards away, the boat rising and falling as it swayed here and there on the waves, which ran up to the face of the cliff and back, when just as the attention of all was fixed upon the little opening, from which came curious hissing and rushing noises, the boat rose on a good-sized swell, and as it sank was left upon the top of a weedy rock which seemed to rise like the shaggy head of a huge sea-monster beneath the keel.

There was a bump, a grinding, grating noise, a shout and a heavy splash, and the boat, after narrowly escaping being capsized, floated once more in deep water; but Harry had lost his balance, gone overboard, and disappeared.

Madelaine uttered a cry of horror, and then for a few moments there was a dead silence, during which Louise sat with blanched face, parted lips, and dilated eyes, gazing at the spot where her brother had disappeared. Pradelle held on by the side of the boat, and Leslie sprang up, rapidly stripped off coat and vest, and stood ready to plunge in.

Those moments seemed indefinitely prolonged, and a terrible feeling of despair began to attack the occupants of the boat as thought after thought, each of the blackest type, flashed through their brains. He had been sucked down by the undertow, and was being carried out to sea—he was entangled in the slimy sea-wrack, and could not rise again—he had struck his head against the rocks, stunned himself, and gone down like a stone, and so on.

Duncan Leslie darted one glance at the pale and suffering face of the sister, placed a foot on the gunwale, and was in the act of gathering himself up to spring from the boat, when Harry's head rose thirty yards away.

"Ahoy!" he shouted, as he began to paddle and tread water. "Hallo, Leslie, ready for a bathe? Come out! Water's beautiful. Swim you back to the harbour."

There was a long-drawn breath in the boat which sounded like a groan, as the terrible mental pressure was removed, and the young man began to swim easily and slowly towards his friends.

"Mind she doesn't get on another rock, Leslie," he cried.

"Here, catch hold of this," cried Pradelle, whose face was ashy, and he held out the boat-hook as far as he could reach.

"Thank ye," said Harry mockingly, and twenty yards away. "Little farther, please. What a lovely day for a swim!"

"Harry, pray come into the boat," cried Louise excitedly.

"What for? Mind the porpoise."

He gave a few sharp blows on the water with his hands, raising himself up and turning right over, dived, his legs just appearing above the surface, and then there was an eddy where he had gone down.

"Don't be frightened," whispered Madelaine, whose voice sounded a little husky.

"Here we are again!" cried Harry, reappearing close to the boat and spluttering the water from his lips, as with all the gaiety of a boy he looked mirthfully at the occupants of the boat. "Any orders for pearls, ladies?"

"Don't be foolish, Harry," said Louise, as he swam close to them.

"Not going to be. I say, Leslie, take the boat-hook away from that fellow, or he'll be making a hole in the bottom of the boat."

As he spoke, he laid a hand upon the gunwale and looked merrily from one to the other.

"Don't touch me, girls. I'm rather damp," he said. "I say, what a capital bathing dress flannels make!"

"Shall I help you in?" said Leslie.

"No, thank ye, I'm all right. As I am in, I may as well have a swim."

"No, no, Harry, don't be foolish," cried Louise.

"There, you'd better hitch a rope round me, and tow me behind, or I shall swamp the boat."

"Harry! what are you going to do?" cried Madelaine, as he loosened his hold of the gunwale, and began to swim away.

"Wait a bit and you'll see," he cried. "Leslie, you take care of the boat. I shan't be long."

"But Harry—"

"All right, I tell you."

"Where are you going?"

"In here," he shouted back, and he swam straight to the low opening at the foot of the massive granite cliff, paddled a little at the mouth till the efflux of water was over, and then as the fresh wave came, he took a few strokes, gave a shout, and to the horror of the two girls seemed to be sucked right into the opening.

As he disappeared, he gave another shout, a hollow strange echoing "Good-bye," and a few moments after there was a run back of the water and a hollow roar, and it needed very little exercise of the imagination to picture the rugged opening as the mouth of some marine monster into which the young man had passed.

Chapter Three
Discords

"Don't be alarmed," said Leslie quietly, "I daresay it is like one of the zorns yonder, only the mouth is too narrow for a boat."

"But it is so foolish," said Louise, giving him a grateful look.

"Yes, but he swims so easily and well, there is nothing to mind. What are you going to do, Mr Pradelle?"

"Work the boat close up so as to help him," said Pradelle shortly.

"No, don't do that. We have had one escape from a capsize. We must keep out here in deep water."

Pradelle frowned.

"I think I know what I'm about, sir," he said sharply; "do you suppose I am going to sit here when my friend may be in danger?"

"I have no doubt you know what you are about in London, sir," said Leslie quietly, "but this is not a pavement in the Strand, and it is not safe to take the boat closer in."

Pradelle was about to make some retort, but Louise interposed.

"Try if you can get nearer the mouth of that dreadful place, Mr Leslie," she said, "I am getting terribly alarmed."

Leslie seated himself, took the oars, turned the boat, and backed slowly and cautiously in, holding himself ready to pull out again at the slightest appearance of danger. For the sea rushed against the rocky barrier with tremendous force, while even on this calm day, the swing and wash and eddy amongst the loose rocks was formidable.

By skilful management Leslie backed the boat to within some thirty feet of the opening; but the position was so perilous that he had to pull out for a few yards to avoid a couple of rocks, which in the movement of the clear water seemed to be rising toward them from time to time, and coming perilously near.

Then he shouted, but there was no answer. He shouted again and again, but there was no reply, and a chill of horror, intensifying from moment to moment, came upon all.

"Harry! Harry!" cried Louise, now raising her voice, as Madelaine crept closer to her and clutched her hand.

But there was no reply. No sound but the rush and splash and hiss of the waters as they struck the rocks, and came back broken from the attack.

"What folly!" muttered Leslie, with his face growing rugged. Then quickly, "I don't think you need feel alarmed; I dare say he has swum in for some distance, and our voices do not reach him. Stop a moment."

He suddenly remembered a little gold dog-whistle at his watch-chain, and raising it to his lips he blew long and shrilly, till the ear piercing note echoed along the cliff, and the gulls came floating lazily overhead and peering wonderingly down.

"I say, Harry, old man, come out now," cried Pradelle, and then rising from his seat, he placed his hands on either side of his lips, and uttered the best imitation he could manage of the Australian call, "Coo-ey! Coo-ey!"

There were echoes and whispers, and the rush and hiss of the water. Then two or three times over there came from out of the opening a peculiar dull hollow sound, such as might be made by some great animal wallowing far within.

"Mr Leslie," said Louise in a low appealing voice, "what shall we do?"

"Oh, wait a few minutes, my dear Miss Vine," interposed Pradelle, hastily. "He'll be out directly. I assure you there is no cause for alarm."

Leslie frowned, but his face coloured directly, for his heart gave a great throb.

Louise paid not the slightest heed to Pradelle's words, but kept her limpid eyes fixed appealingly upon Leslie's, as if she looked to him for help.

"I hardly know what to do," he said in a low business-like tone. "I dare not leave you without some one to manage the boat, or I would go in."

"Yes, yes, pray go!" she said excitedly, "Never mind us."

"We could each take an oar and keep the boat here," said Madelaine quickly, "we can both row."

"No, really; I'll manage the boat," said Pradelle.

"I think you had better leave it to the ladies, Mr Pradelle," said Leslie coldly. "They know the coast."

"Well really, sir, I—"

"This is no time for interference," cried Madelaine with a flush of excitement, and she caught hold of an oar. "Louie dear, quick!"

The other oar was resigned, and as Leslie passed aft, he gave Louise one quick look, reading in her face, as he believed, trust and thankfulness and then dread.

"No, no, Mr Leslie, I hardly dare let you go," she faltered.

Plash!

The boat was rolling and dancing on the surface, relieved of another burden, and Duncan Leslie was swimming toward the opening.

The two girls dipped their oars from time to time, for their seaside life had given them plenty of experience of the management of a boat; and as Pradelle sat looking sulky and ill-used, they watched the swimmer as he too timed his movements, so that he gradually approached, and then in turn was sucked right into the weird water-way, which might lead another into some terrible chasm from which there was no return.

A low hoarse sigh, as if one had whispered while suffering pain the word "Hah!" And then with dilated eyes the two girls sat watching the black opening for what seemed a terrible interval of time, before, to their intense relief, there came a shout of laughter, followed by the appearance of Leslie, who swam out looking stern, and closely followed by Harry.

"It is not the sort of fun I can appreciate, Mr Vine," said Leslie, turning as he reached the stern of the boat.

"Well, I know that," cried Harry mockingly. "Scotchmen never can appreciate a joke."

"There, ladies, what did I tell you?" cried Pradelle triumphantly.

There was no reply, and the visitor from London winced, for his presence in the boat seemed to be thoroughly *de trop*.

"Miss Vine—Miss Van Heldre," said Leslie quietly, "will you change places now? Get right aft and we will climb in over the bows."

"But the boat?" faltered Louise, whose emotion was so great that she could hardly trust herself to speak.

"We'll see to that," said Leslie. "Your brother and I will row back."

It did not seem to trouble him now that the two girls took their places, one on either side of Pradelle, while as soon as they were seated he climbed in streaming with water, seating himself on the gunwale, Harry climbing in on the other side.

"Harry, how could you?" cried Louise, now, with an indignant look.

"Easily enough," he said, seating himself calmly. "Thought you'd lost me?"

He looked at Madelaine as he spoke, but she turned her face away biting her lips, and it was Louise who replied:

"I did not think you could have been so cruel."

"Cruel be hanged!" he retorted. "Thought I'd find out whether I was of any consequence after all. You people seem to say I'm of none. Did they begin to cry, Vic?"

"Oh, I'm not going to tell tales," said Pradelle with a smile.

"I should have had a pipe in there, only my matches had got wet."

"Ha-ha-ha!" laughed Pradelle, and the mirth sounded strange there beneath the rocks, and a very decided hiss seemed to come from out of the low rugged opening.

"Try again, Vic," said Harry mockingly, but his friend made no reply, for he was staring hard and defiantly at Leslie, who, as he handled his oar, gave him a calmly contemptuous look that galled him to the quick.

"Ready, Leslie?" said Harry.

"Yes."

The oars dipped, Leslie pulling stroke, and the boat shot out from its dangerous position among the rocks, rose at a good-sized swelling wave, topped it, seemed to hang as in a balance for a moment, and then glided down and went forward in response to a few vigorous strokes.

"Never mind the tiller, Vic," said Harry; "let it swing. We can manage without that. All right, girls?"

There was no reply.

"Sulky, eh? Well, I'd a good mind to stop in. Sorry you got so wet, Leslie."

Still no reply.

"Cheerful party, 'pon my word!" said Harry, with a contemptuous laugh. "Hope no one objects to my smoking."

He looked hard at Madelaine, but she avoided his gaze, and he uttered a short laugh.

"Got a cigar to spare, Vic?"

"Yes, dear boy, certainly."

"Pass it along then and the lights. Hold hard a minute, Leslie."

The latter ceased rowing as Pradelle handed a cigar and the matches to his friend.

"Will you take one, Mr Leslie?" said Pradelle.

"Thanks, no," said Leslie quietly, and to the would-be donor's great relief, for he had only two left. Then once more the rowing was resumed, Pradelle striking a match to light a cigar for himself, and then recollecting himself and throwing the match away.

"Well, we're enjoying ourselves!" cried Harry after they had proceeded some distance in silence. "I say, Vic, say something!"

Pradelle had been cudgelling his brains for the past ten minutes, but the more he tried to find something à propos the more every pleasant subject seemed to recede.

In fact it would have been difficult just then for the most accomplished talker to have set all present at their ease, for Harry's folly had moved his sister so that she feared to speak lest she should burst into a hysterical fit of weeping, and Madelaine, as she sat there with her lips compressed, felt imbued with but one desire, which took the form of the following words:

"Oh, how I should like to box his ears!"

"Getting dry, Leslie?" said Harry after a long silence.

"Not very," was the reply.

"Ah well, there's no fear of our catching cold pulling like this."

"Not the slightest," said Leslie coldly; then there was another period of silence, during which the water seemed to patter and slap the bows of the boat, while the panorama of rock and foam and glittering cascade, as the crags were bathed by the Atlantic swell, and it fell back broken, seemed perfectly fresh and new as seen from another point of view.

At last Harry, after trying two or three times more to start a conversation, said shortly —

"Well, this is my last day at home, and I think I ought to say, 'Thank goodness!' This is coming out for a pleasant sail, and having to row back like a galley-slave! Oh, I beg your pardon, ladies! All my mistake. I am highly complimented. All this glumminess is because I am going away."

He received such a look of reproach that he uttered an angry ejaculation and began to pull so hard that Leslie had to second his movement to keep the boat's head straight for the harbour, whose farther point soon after came in sight, with two figures on the rocks at the end.

"Papa along with Uncle Luke," said Louise softly.

"Eh?" said Harry sharply; "the old man still fishing?"

"Yes," said Louise rather coldly; "and, Maddy, dear, is not that Mr Van Heldre?"

Madelaine shaded her eyes from the western sun, where it was sinking fast, and nodded.

"Where shall we land you?" said Harry sulkily now, "at the point, or will you go up the harbour?"

"If there is not too much sea on, at the point," said Louise gravely.

"Oh, I dare say we can manage that without wetting your plumes," said the young man contemptuously; and after another ten minutes' pulling they reached the harbour mouth and made for the point, where Uncle Luke stood leaning on his rod watching the coming boat, in company with a tall grey man with refined features, who had taken off the straw hat he wore to let the breeze play through his closely-cut hair, while from time to time he turned to speak either to Uncle Luke or to the short thick set man who, with his pointed white moustache and closely clipped peaked beard, looked in his loose holland blouse like a French officer taking his vacation at the seaside.

"Mind how you come," said the latter in a sharp, decided way. "Watch your time, Leslie. Back in, my lad. Can you manage it, girls?"

"Oh, yes," they cried confidently. "Sit still then till the boat's close in, then one at a time. You first, my dear."

This to Louise, as he stepped actively down the granite rocks to a narrow natural shelf, which was now bare, now several inches deep in water.

"If we manage it cleverly we can get you ashore without a wetting."

The warnings were necessary, for the tide ran fast, and the Atlantic swell made the boat rise and fall, smooth as the surface was.

"Now then," cried the French-looking gentleman, giving his orders as if he were an officer in command, "easy, Harry Vine; back a little, Mr Leslie. Be ready, Louie, my dear. That's it: a little more. I have you. Bravo!"

The words came slowly, and with the latter there was a little action; as he took the hands outstretched to him, when the boat nearly grazed the rock, there was a light spring, the girl was on the narrow shelf, and the boat, in answer to a touch of the oars, was half-a-dozen yards away rising and falling on the swell.

"Give me your hand, my dear," said the tall grey gentleman, leaning down.

"Oh, I can manage, papa," she cried, and the next moment she was by his side. Looking back, "Thank you, Mr Van Heldre," she said.

"Eh? All right, my child. Now, Maddy. Steady, my lads. Mind that ledge; don't get her under there. Bravo! that's right. Now, my girl. Well done."

Madelaine leaped to his side, and was in turn assisted to the top, she accepting the tall gentleman's help, while Uncle Luke, with his hands resting on his rod, which he held with the butt on the rock, stood grimly looking down at the boat.

"I think I'll land here," said Leslie. "You don't want my help with the boat."

"Oh, no; we can manage," said Harry sourly; and Leslie gave up his oar and leaped on to the rock as the boat was again backed in.

"That chap looks quite green," said Uncle Luke with a sneering laugh. "Our London friend been poorly, Louie?"

Before she could answer the tall gentleman cried to those in the boat—

"Don't be long, my boy. Tea will be waiting."

"All right, dad. Lay hold of this oar, Vic, and let's get her moored."

"Why, you're wet, Mr Leslie," said the tall gentleman, shaking hands.

"Only sea-water, sir. It's nothing."

"But," said the former speaker, looking quickly from one to the other, and his handsome thoughtful face seemed troubled, "has there been anything wrong?"

"Harry fell in," said Louise, speaking rather quickly and excitedly; "and, Mr Leslie—"

"Ah!" ejaculated the tall gentleman excitedly.

"It was nothing, sir," said Leslie hastily. "He swam in among the rocks— into a cave, and he was a long time gone, and I went after him; that's all."

"But, my dear boy, you must make haste and change your things."

"I shall not be hurt, Mr Vine."

"And—and—look here. Make haste and come on then to us. There will be a meal ready. It's Harry's last day at home."

"Oh, thank you, Mr Vine; I don't think I'll come to-night."

"But you have been one of the party so far, and I should—Louie, my dear—"

"We shall be very glad if you will come, Mr Leslie," said Louise, in response to her father's hesitating words and look, and there was a calm, ingenious invitation in her words that made the young man's heart throb.

"I, too, shall be very glad," he said quietly.

"That's right, that's right," said Mr Vine, laying one of his long thin white hands on the young man's arm: and then changing its position, so that he could take hold of one of the buttons on his breast. Then turning quickly: "Madelaine's coming, of course."

"Louie says so," said the girl quietly.

"To be sure; that's right, my dear; that's right," said the old man, beaming upon her as he took one of her hands to hold and pat it in his. "You'll come too, Van?"

"I? No, no. I've some bills of lading to look over."

"Yah!" ejaculated Uncle Luke with a snarl.

"Yes; bills of lading, you idle old cynic. I can't spend my time fishing."

"Pity you can't," said Uncle Luke. "Money, money, always money."

"Hear him, Mr Leslie?" said Van Heldre smiling. "Are you disposed to follow his teachings?"

"I'm afraid not," said Leslie.

"Not he," snarled Uncle Luke.

"But you will come, Van?" said Mr Vine.

"My dear fellow, I wish you would not tempt me. There's work to do. Then there's my wife."

"Bring Mrs Van Heldre too," said Louise, laying her hand on his.

"Ah, you temptress," he cried merrily.

"It's Harry's last evening," said Mr Vine.

"Look here," said Van Heldre, "will you sing me my old favourite if I come, Louie?"

"Yes; and you shall have a duet too."

"Ah, never mind the duet," said Van Heldre laughingly; "I can always hear Maddy at home. There, out of pocket again by listening to temptation. I'll come."

"Come and join us too, Luke," said Mr Vine.

"No!" snapped the old fisher.

"Do, uncle," said Louise.

"Shan't," he snarled, stooping to pick up his heavy basket.

"But it's Harry's last—"

"Good job too," snarled the old man.

"I'm going your way, Mr Luke Vine," said Leslie. "Let me carry the basket?"

"Thank ye; I'm not above carrying my own fish," said the old man sharply; and he raised and gave the basket a swing to get it upon his back, but tottered with the weight, and nearly fell on the uneven rocks.

"There, it is too heavy for you," said Leslie, taking possession of the basket firmly; and Louise Vine's eyes brightened.

"Be too heavy for you when you get as old as I am," snarled the old man.

"I daresay," said Leslie quietly; and they went off together.

"Luke's in fine form this afternoon," said Van Heldre, nodding and smiling.

"Yes," said the brother, looking after him wistfully. "We shall wait till you come, Mr Leslie," he shouted, giving vent to an afterthought.

The young man turned and waved his hand.

"Rather like Leslie," said Van Heldre. "Maddy, you'll have to set your cap at him."

Madelaine looked up at him and laughed.

"Yes, poor Luke!" said Mr Vine thoughtfully, as he stooped and picked up a small net and a tin can, containing the treasures he had found in sundry rock pools. "I'm afraid we are a very strange family, Van," he added, as they walked back towards the little town.

"Very, old fellow," said his friend smiling. "I'll be with you before Leslie gets back, wife and the necessary change of dress permitting."

Chapter Four
A Thunderbolt

George Vine, gentleman, as he was set down in the parish books and the West-Country directory, lived in a handsome old granite-built residence that he had taken years before, when, in obedience to his sister's wish, he had retired from the silk trade a wealthy man. But there he had joined issue with the lady in question, obstinately refusing to make France his home and selecting the house above named in the old Cornish port for two reasons: one, to be near his old friend Godfrey Van Heldre, a well-to-do merchant who carried on rather a mixed business, dealing largely in pilchards, which he sent in his own ships to the Italian ports, trading in return in such produce of the Levant as oranges, olives, and dried fruit; the other, so that he could devote himself to the branch of natural history, upon which he had grown to be an authority so great that his work upon the Actiniadae of our coast was looked forward to with no little expectation by a good many people, in addition to those who wrote F.Z.S. at the end of their names.

The pleasant social meal known as high tea was spread in the long low oak-panelled dining-room, whose very wide bay window looked right over the town from its shelf upon the huge granite cliffs, and far away westward from whence came the gales which beat upon the old mansion, whose granite sides and gables had turned them off for the past two hundred years.

It was a handsomely furnished room, thoroughly English, and yet with a suggestion of French in the paintings of courtly-looking folk, which decorated the panels above the old oak sideboard and dressers, upon which stood handsome old chased cups, flagons and salvers battered and scratched, but rich and glistening old silver all the same, and looking as if the dents and scratches were only the natural puckers and furrows such venerable pieces of plate should possess.

There was another suggestion of the foreign element, too, in the glazing of the deeply embayed window, for right across and between all the mullions, the leaden lattice panes gave place, about two-thirds of the way up, to a series of artistically painted armorial bearings in stained glass, shields and helmets with their crests and supporters, and beneath the escutcheon in the middle, a ribbon with triple curve and fold bearing the words *Roy et Foy.*

The furniture had been selected to be thoroughly in keeping with the antiquity of the mansion, and the old oak chairs and so much of the table as could be seen for the long fine white linen cloth, was of the oldest and darkest oak.

The table was spread with the abundant fare dear to West-Country folk; fruit and flowers gave colour, and the thick yellow cream and white sugar were piled high in silver bowls. The great tea urn was hissing upon its stand, the visitors had arrived, and the host was dividing his time between fidgeting to and fro from the door to Van Heldre, who was leaning up against one of the mullions of the great bay window talking to Leslie upon subjects paramount in Cornwall—fish and the yielding of the mines.

The young people were standing about talking, Louise with her hand resting on the chair where sat a pleasant-looking, rosy little woman with abundant, white hair, and her mittened hands crossed over the waist of her purple velvet gown enriched with good French lace.

"Margaret Vine's keeping us waiting a long time this evening," she said.

"Mamma!" said Madelaine reproachfully.

"Well, my dear, it's the simple truth. And so you go back to business to-morrow, Harry?"

"Yes, Mrs Van Heldre. Slave again."

"Nonsense, my boy. Work's good for every one. I'm sure your friend, Mr Pradelle, thinks so," she continued, appealing to that gentleman.

"Well," he said, with an unpleasant laugh, "nobody left me a fortune, so I'm obliged to say yes."

"Ah, here she is!" said Mr Vine, with a sigh of relief, as the door opened, and with almost theatrical effect a rather little sharp-looking woman of about sixty entered, gazing quickly round and pausing just within the room to make an extremely formal old-fashioned courtesy—sinking nearly to the ground as if she were a telescopic figure disappearing into the folds of the stiff rich brocade silk dress, of a wonderful pattern of pink and green, and cut in a fashion probably popular at Versailles a hundred years ago. She did not wear powder, but her white hair turned up and piled upon her head after the fashion of that blooming period, produced the same effect; and as she gave the fan she held a twitch which spread it open with a loud rattling noise, she seemed, with her haughty carriage, handsome aquiline face with long chin, that appeared to have formed the pattern for her stomacher, like one of the paintings on the panelled wall suddenly come to life, and feeling strange at finding herself among that modern company.

"I hope you have not waited for me," she said, smiling and speaking in a high-pitched musical voice. "Louise, my child, you should not. Ah!" she continued, raising her gold-rimmed eye-glass to her thin arched nose and dropping it directly, "Mrs Van Heldre, Mr Van Heldre, pray be seated. Mr Victor Pradelle, will you be so good?"

The young man had gone through the performance several times before, and he was in waiting ready to take the tips of the gloved fingers extended to him, and walking over the thick Turkey carpet with the lady to the other end of the room in a way that seemed to endow him with a court suit and a sword, and suggested the probability of the couple continuing their deportment walk to the polished oak boards beyond the carpet, and then after sundry bows and courtesies going through the steps of the *menuet de la cour.*

As a matter of fact, Pradelle led the old girl, as he called her, to the seat she occupied at the end of the table, when she condescended to leave her room; the rest of the company took their seats, and the meal began.

Harry had tried to ensconce himself beside Madelaine, but that young lady had made a sign to Duncan Leslie, who eagerly took the chair beside her, one which he coveted, for it was between her and Louise, now busy with the tea-tray; and in a sulky manner, Harry obeyed the motion of the elderly lady's fan.

"That's right, Henri, *mon cher,*" she said, smiling, "come and sit by me. I shall miss you so, my darling, when you are gone back to that horrible London, and that wretched business."

"Don't, don't, don't, Margaret, my dear," said Mr Vine, good-humouredly. "You will make him unhappy at having to leave home."

"I hope so, George," said the lady with dignity, and pronouncing his Christian name with the softness peculiar to the French tongue; "and," she added with a smile, "especially as we have company, will you oblige me — Marguerite, if you please?"

"Certainly, certainly, my dear."

"Is that Miss Van Heldre?" said the lady, raising her glass once more. "I beg your pardon, my child: I hope you are well."

"Quite well, thank you, Miss Marguerite Vine," said Madelaine quietly, and her bright young face looked perfectly calm, though there was a touch of sarcasm in her tone.

"Louise, dearest, my tea a little sweeter, please."

The meal progressed, and the stiffness produced by the *entrée* of the host's sister—it was her own term for her appearance—soon wore off, the lady being very quiet as she discussed the viands placed before her with a very excellent appetite. Mrs Van Heldre prattled pleasantly on, with plenty of homely commonsense, to her host. Van Heldre threw in a word now and then, joked Louise and his daughter, and made a wrinkle on his broad forehead, which was his way of making a note.

The note he made was that a suspicion which had previously entered his brain was correct.

"He's taken with her," he said to himself, as he glanced at Louise and then at Duncan Leslie, who seemed to be living in a dream. As a rule he was an energetic, quick, and sensible man; on this occasion he was particularly silent, and when he spoke to either Madelaine or Louise, it was in a softened voice.

Van Heldre looked at his daughter.

Madelaine looked at her father, and they thoroughly read each other's thoughts, the girl's bright grey eyes saying to him as plainly as could be—

"You are quite right."

"Well," said Van Heldre to himself, as he placed a spoonful of black currant jam on his plate, and then over that two piled-up table-spoonfuls of clotted cream—"she's as nice and true-hearted a girl as ever stepped, and Leslie's a man, every inch of him. I'd have said *yes* in a moment if he had wanted my girl. I'm glad of it; but, poor fellow, what he'll have to suffer from that terrible old woman!"

He had just thought this, and was busy composing a *nocturne* or a *diurne*—probably the latter from its tints of red and yellow—upon his plate, which flowed with jam and cream, when Aunt Marguerite, who had eaten all she wished, began to stir her tea with courtly grace, and raised her voice in continuation of something she had been saying, but it was twenty-four hours before.

"Yes, Mr Pradelle," she said, so that everyone should hear: "my memories of the past are painful, and yet a delight. We old Huguenots are proud of our past."

"You must be, madam."

"And you too," said the lady. "I feel sure that if you will take the trouble you will find that I am right. The Pradelles must have been of our people."

"I'll look into it as soon as I get back to town," said the young man.

Harry gave him a very vulgar wink.

"Do," said Aunt Marguerite. "By the way, I don't think I told you that though my brother persists in calling himself Vine, our name is des Vignes, and we belong to one of the oldest families in Auvergne."

"Yes, that's right, Mr Pradelle," said the host, nodding pleasantly; "but when a cruel persecution drove us over here, and old England held out her arms to us, and we found a kindly welcome—"

"My dear George!" interposed Aunt Marguerite.

"Let me finish, my dear," said Mr Vine, good-temperedly. "It's Mr Pradelle's last evening here."

"For the present, George, for the present."

"Ah, yes, of course, for the present, and I should like him to hear my version too."

Aunt Marguerite tapped the back of her left hand with her fan impatiently.

"We found here a hearty welcome and a home," continued Mr Vine, "and we said we can never—we will never—return to the land of fire and the sword; and then we, some of us poor, some of us well-to-do, settled down among our English brothers, and thanked God that in this new Land of Canaan we had found rest."

"And my dear Mr Pradelle," began Aunt Marguerite, hastily; but Mr Vine was started, and he talked on.

"In time we determined to be, in spite of our French descent, English of the English, for our children's sake, and we worked with them, and traded with them; and, to show our faith in them, and to avoid all further connection and military service in the country we had left, we even anglicised our names. My people became Vines; the D'Aubigneys, Daubney or Dobbs; the Boileaus, Drinkwater; the Guipets, Guppy. Vulgarising our names, some people say; but never mind, we found rest, prosperity and peace."

"Quite right, Mr Pradelle," said Van Heldre, "and in spite of my name and my Huguenot descent, I say, thank Heaven I am now an Englishman."

"No, no, no, no. Mr Van Heldre," said Aunt Marguerite throwing herself back, and looking at him with a pitying smile. "You cannot prove your Huguenot descent."

"Won't contradict you, ma'am," said Van Heldre. "Capital jam this, Louise."

"You must be of Dutch descent," said Aunt Marguerite.

"I went carefully over my father's pedigree, Miss Marguerite," said Madelaine quietly.

"Indeed, my child?" said the lady, raising her brows.

"And I found without doubt that the Venelttes fled during the persecutions to Holland, where they stayed for half a century, and changed their names to Van Heldre before coming to England."

"Quite right," said Van Heldre in a low voice. "Capital cream."

"Ah, yes," said Aunt Margaret; "but, my dear child, such papers are often deceptive."

"Yes," said Van Heldre, smiling, "often enough, so are traditions and many of our beliefs about ancestry; but I hope I have enough of what you call the *haute noblesse* in me to give way, and not attempt to argue the point."

"No, Mr Van Heldre," said Aunt Margaret, with a smile of pity and good-humoured contempt; "we have often argued together upon this question, but I cannot sit in silence and hear you persist in that which is not true. No: you have not any Huguenot blood in your veins."

"My dear madam, I feel at times plethoric enough to wish that the old-fashioned idea of being blooded in the spring were still in vogue. I have so much Huguenot blood in my veins, that I should be glad to have less."

Aunt Margaret shook her head, and tightened her lips.

"Low Dutch," she said to herself, "Low Dutch."

Van Heldre read her thoughts in the movement of her lips.

"Don't much matter," he said. "Vine, old fellow, think I shall turn over a new leaf."

"Eh? New leaf?"

"Yes; get a good piece of marsh, make a dam to keep out the sea and take to keeping cows. What capital cream!"

"Yes, Mr Pradelle," continued Aunt Margaret; "we are Huguenots of the Huguenots, and it is the dream of my life that Henri should assert his right to the title his father repudiates, and become Comte des Vignes."

"Ah!" said Pradelle.

"Vigorous steps have only to be taken to wrest the family estates in Auvergne from the usurpers who hold them. I have long fought for this, but so far, I grieve to say, vainly. My brother here has mistaken notions about the respectability of trade, and is content to vegetate."

"Oh, you miserable old vegetable!" said Van Heldre to himself, as he gave his friend a droll look, and shook his head.

"To vegetate in this out-of-the-way place when he should be watching over the welfare of his country, and as a nobleman of that land, striving to stem the tide of democracy. He will not do it; but if I live my nephew Henri shall, as soon as he can be rescued from the degrading influence of trade, and the clerk's stool in an office. Ah, my poor boy, I pity you and I say out boldly that I am not surprised that you should have thrown up post after post in disgust, and refused to settle down to such sordid wretchedness."

"My dear Marguerite! our visitors."

"I must speak, George. Mr Van Heldre loves trade."

"I do, ma'am."

"Therefore he cannot feel with me."

"Well, never mind, my dear. Let some one else be Count des Vignes, only let me be in peace, and don't fill poor Harry's head with that stuff just before he's leaving home to go up to the great city, where he will I am sure redeem the follies of the past, and prove himself a true man. Harry, my dear boy, we'll respect Aunt Margaret's opinion; but we will not follow them out. Van, old fellow, Leslie, Mr Pradelle, a glass of wine. We'll drink Harry's health. All filled? That's right. Harry, my boy, a true honest man is nature's nobleman. God speed you, my boy; and His blessing be upon all your works. Health and happiness to you, my son!"

"Amen," said Van Heldre; and the simple old-fashioned health was drunk.

"Eh, what's that—letters?" said Vine, as a servant entered the room and handed her master three.

"For you, Mr Pradelle; for you, Harry, and for me. May we open them. Mrs Van Heldre? They may be important."

"Of course, Mr Vine, of course."

Pradelle opened his, glanced at it, and thrust it into his pocket.

Harry did likewise.

Mr Vine read his twice, then dropped it upon the table.

"Papa!—father!" cried Louise, starting from her place, and running round to him as he stood up with a fierce angry light in his eyes, and the table was in confusion.

"Tidings at last of the French estates, Mr Pradelle," whispered Aunt Margaret.

"Papa, is anything wrong? Is it bad news?" cried Louise.

"Wrong! Bad news!" he cried, flashing up from the quiet student to the stern man, stung to the quick by the announcement he had just received. "Van Heldre, old friend, you know how I strove among our connections and friends to place him where he might work and rise and prove himself my son."

"Yes, yes, old fellow, but be calm."

"Father, hush!" whispered Louise, as she glanced at Leslie's sympathetic countenance. "Hush! be calm!"

"How can I be calm!" cried the old man fiercely. "The des Vignes! The family estates! The title! You hear this, Margaret. Here is a fine opportunity for the search to be made—the old castle and the vineyards to be rescued from the occupiers."

"George—brother, what do you mean?" cried the old lady indignantly, and she laid her hand upon her nephew's shoulder, as he sat gazing straight down before him at his plate.

"What do I mean?" cried the indignant father tossing the letter towards her. "I mean that my son is once more dismissed from his situation in disgrace."

Chapter Five
Poison and Antidote

"Now, sir, have the goodness to tell me what you mean to do."

Harry Vine looked at his father, thrust his hands low down into his pockets, leaned back against the mantelpiece, and was silent.

Vine senior leaned over a shallow glass jar, with a thin splinter of wood in his hand, upon which he had just impaled a small fragment of raw, minced periwinkle, and this he thrust down to where a gorgeous sea-anemone sat spread open upon a piece of rock—chipped from out of one of the caverns on the coast.

The anemone's tentacles bristled all around, giving the creature the aspect of a great flower; and down among these the scrap of food was thrust till it touched them, when the tentacles began to curve over, and draw the scrap of shell-fish down toward the large central mouth, in which it soon began to disappear.

Vine senior looked up.

"I have done everything I could for you in the way of education. I have, I am sure, been a most kind and indulgent father. You have had a liberal supply of money, and by the exercise of my own and the personal interests of friends, I have obtained for you posts among our people, any one of which was the beginning of prosperity and position, such as a youth should have been proud to win."

"But they were so unsuitable, father. All connected with trade."

"Shame, Harry! As if there was anything undignified in trade. No matter whether it be trade or profession by which a man honestly earns his subsistence, it is an honourable career. And yet five times over you have been thrown back on my hands in disgrace."

"Well, I can't help it, father; I've done my best."

"Your best!" cried Vine senior, taking up a glass rod, and stirring the water in another glass jar. "It is not true."

"But it's so absurd. You're a rich man."

"If I were ten times as well off, I would not have you waste your life in idleness. You are not twenty-four, and I am determined that you shall take some post. I have seen too much of what follows when a restless, idle young man sits down to wait for his father's money. There, I am busy now. Go and think over what I have said. You must and shall do something. It is now a month since I received that letter. What is Mr Pradelle doing down here again?"

"Come for a change, as any other gentleman would."

"Gentleman?"

"Well, he has a little income of his own, I suppose. If I've been unlucky, that's no reason why I should throw over my friends."

The father looked at the son in a perplexed way, and then fed another sea-anemone, Harry looking on contemptuously.

"Well, sir, you have heard what I said. Go and think it over."

"Yes, father."

The young man left the business-like study, and encountered his sister in the hall.

"Well, Harry?"

"Well, Lou."

"What does papa say?"

"The old story. I'm to go back to drudgery. I think I shall enlist."

"For shame! and you professing to care as you do for Madelaine."

"So I do. I worship her."

"Then prove it by exerting yourself in the way papa wishes. I wonder you have not more spirit."

"And I wonder you have not more decency towards my friends."

Louise coloured slightly.

"Here you profess to believe in my going into trade and drudging behind a counter."

"I did not know that a counter had ever been in question, Harry," said his sister sarcastically.

"Well, a clerk's desk; it's all the same. I believe you would like to see me selling tea and sugar."

"I don't think I should mind."

"No; that's it. I'm to be disgraced while you are so much of the fine lady that you look down on, and quite insult my friend Pradelle."

"Aunt Margaret wishes to speak to you, dear," said Louise gravely. "I promised to tell you as soon as you left the study."

"Then hang it all! why didn't you tell me? Couldn't resist a chance for a lecture. There's only one body here who understands me, and that's aunt. Why even Madelaine's turning against me now, and I believe it is all your doing."

"I have done nothing but what is for your good, Harry."

"Then you own to it? You have been talking to Maddy."

"She came and confided in me, and I believe I spoke the truth."

"Yes, I knew it!" cried Harry warmly. "Then look here, my lady, I'm not blind. I've petted you and been the best of brothers, but if you turn against me I shall turn against you."

"Harry, dear!"

"Ah, that startles you, does it? Then I shall tell the truth, and I'll back up Aunt Margaret through thick and thin."

"What do you mean?"

"What Aunt Margaret says. That long Scotch copper-miner is no match for you."

"Harry!"

"And I shall tell him this, if he comes hanging about here where he sees he is not wanted, and stands in the way of a gentleman of good French Huguenot descent, I'll horsewhip him. There!"

He turned on his heel, and bounded up the old staircase three steps at a time.

"Oh!" ejaculated Louise, as she stood till she heard a sharp tap at her aunt's door and her brother enter and close it after him. "Mr Pradelle, too, of all people in the world!"

"Ah, my darling," cried Aunt Margaret, looking up from the tambour-frame and smoothing out the folds of her antique flowered peignoir. "Bring that stool, and come and sit down here."

Harry bent down and kissed her rather sulkily. Then in a half-contemptuous way he fetched the said stool, embroidered by the lady herself, and placed it at her feet.

"Sit down, my dear."

Harry lowered himself into a very uncomfortable position, while Aunt Margaret placed one arm about his neck, struck a graceful pose, and began to smooth over the young man's already too smooth hair.

"I want to have another very serious talk to you, my boy," she said. "Ah, yes," she continued, raising his chin and looking down in his disgusted face; "how every lineament shows your descent! Henri, I do not mean to die until I have seen you claim your own, and you are received with acclamation as Comte Henri des Vignes."

"I say, aunt, I've just brushed my hair," he protested.

"Yes, dear, but you should not hide your forehead. It is the brow of the des Vignes."

"Oh, all right, auntie, have it your own way. But, I say, have you got any money?"

"Alas! no, my boy."

"I don't mean now. I mean haven't you really got any to leave me in your will?"

There was a far-off look in Aunt Margaret's eyes as she slowly shook her head.

"You will leave me what you have, aunt?"

"If I had hundreds of thousands, you should have all, Henri; but, alas, I have none. I had property once."

"What became of it?"

"Well, my dear, it is a long story and a sad one. I could not tell it to you even in brief, but you are a man now, and must know the meaning of the word love."

"Oh; yes, I know what that means; but I say, don't fidget my hair about so."

"I could not tell you all, Henri. It was thirty years ago. He was a French gentleman of noble descent. His estates had been confiscated, and I was only too glad to place my little fortune at his disposal to recover them."

"And did he?"

"No, my dear. Those were terrible times. He lost all; and with true nobility, he wrote to me that he loved me too well to drag me down to poverty—to share his lot as an exile. I have never seen him since. But I would have shared his lot."

"Humph! Lost it? Then if I had money and tried for our family estates, I might lose it too."

"No, no, my boy; you would be certain to win. Did you do what I told you?"

"Yes, aunt; but I can't use them down here."

"Let me look, my dear; and I do not see why not. You must be bold; and proud of your descent."

"But they'd laugh."

"Let them," said Aunt Margaret grandly. "By-and-by they will bow down. Let me see."

The young man took a card-case from his pocket, on which was stamped in gold a French count's coronet.

"Ah! yes; that is right," said the old lady, snatching the case with trembling fingers, opening it, and taking out a card on which was also printed a coronet. "*Comte Henri des Vignes*," she read, in an excited manner, and with tears in her eyes. "My darling boy! that will carry conviction with it. I am very glad it is done."

"Cost a precious lot, aunt; made a regular hole in your diamond ring."

"Did you sell it?"

"No; Vic Pradelle pawned it for me."

"Ah! he is a friend of whom you may be proud, Henri."

"Not a bad sort of fellow, aunt. He got precious little on the ring, though, and I spent it nearly all."

"Never mind the ring, my boy, and I'm very glad you have the cards. Now for a little serious talk about the future."

"Wish to goodness there was no future," said Harry glumly.

"Would you like to talk about the past, then?" said the old lady playfully.

"Wish there was no past neither," grumbled Harry.

"Then we will talk about the present, my dear, and about—let me whisper to you—love!"

She placed her thin lips close to her nephew's ear, and then held him at arm's length and smiled upon him proudly.

"Love! Too expensive a luxury for me, auntie. I say, you are ruffling my hair so."

"Too expensive, Henri? No, my darling boy; follow my advice, and the richest and fairest of the daughters of France shall sue for your hand, and be proud to take your noble name."

"I say, auntie," he said laughingly, "aren't you laying on the colour rather thick?"

"Not a bit, my darling; and that's why I want to talk to you about your sister's friend."

"What, Maddy?" he said eagerly; "then you approve of it."

"Approve! Bah! you are jesting, my dear. I approve of your making an alliance with a fat Dutch fraülein!"

"Oh, come, aunt!" said Harry, looking nettles; "Madelaine is not Dutch, nor yet fat."

"I know better, my boy. Dutch! Dutch! Dutch! Look at her father and her mother! No, my boy, you could not make an alliance with a girl like that. She might do for a kitchen-maid."

"Auntie, she's a very charming girl."

"Silly boy! Go and travel, and see the daughters of France."

"And she'll be rich some day."

"If she were heiress to millions she could not marry you. As some writer says, eagles do not mate with plump Dutch ducklings. No, Henri, my boy, you must wait."

Harry frowned, but Aunt Margaret paid no heed.

"That is a boyish piece of nonsense, unworthy the Comte des Vignes, my dear boy. But tell me—you have been with your father—what does he say now?"

"The old story. I'm to choose what I will do. I must go to work."

"Poor George!" sighed Aunt Margaret; "always so sordid in his ideas in early life; now that he is wealthy, so utterly wanting in aspirations! Always dallying over some miserable shrimp. He has no more ambition than one of those silly fish over which he sits and dreams. Oh, Henri, my boy, when I look back at what our family has been—right back into the distant ages of French history—valorous knights and noble ladies; and later on, how they graced the court at banquet and at ball, I weep the salt tears of misery to see my brother sink so low, and so careless about the welfare of his boy."

"Ah! well, it's of no use, aunt. I must go and turn somebody's grindstone again."

"No, Henri, it shall not be," cried the old lady, with flashing eyes. "We must think; we must plot and plan. You must get money somehow, so as to carry on the war; and we will have back the estate in Auvergne; and a noble future shall be yours; and—"

"If you please, ma'am, I've brought your lunch," said a voice; and Liza, the maid, who bore a strong resemblance to the fish-woman who had accosted Uncle Luke at the mouth of the harbour, set down a delicately-cooked cutlet and bit of fish, and spread on a snowy napkin, with the accompaniments of plate, glass, and a decanter of sherry.

"Ah! yes, my lunch," said Aunt Margaret, with a sigh. "Go, and think over what I have said, my dear, and we will talk again another time."

"All right, auntie," said the young man, rising slowly; "but it seems to me as if the best thing I could do would be to jump into the sea."

"No, no, Henri," said Aunt Margaret, taking up a silver spoon and shaking it slowly at her nephew, "a des Vignes was ready with his sword in defence of his honour, and to advance his master's cause; but he never dreamed of taking his own life. That, my dear, would be the act of one of the low-born *canaille*. Remember who you are, and wait. I am working for you, and you shall triumph yet. Consult your friend."

"Sometimes I think it's all gammon," said Harry, as he went slowly down-stairs, and out into the garden, "and sometimes it seems as if it would be very jolly. I dare say the old woman is right, and—"

"What are you talking about—muttering aside like the wicked man on the stage?"

"Hullo, Vic! You there?"

"Yes, dear boy. I'm here for want of somewhere better."

"Consult your friend!" Aunt Margaret's last words.

"Been having a cigar?"

"I've been hanging about here this last hour. How is it she hasn't been for a walk?"

"Louie? Don't know. Here, let's go down under the cliff, and find a snug corner, and have a talk over a pipe."

"The latter, if you like; never mind the former. Yes, I will: for I want a few words of a sort."

"What about?" said Harry, as they strolled away.

"Everything. Look here, old fellow; we've been the best of chums ever since you shared my desk."

"Yes, and you shared my allowance."

"Well, chums always do. Then I came down with you, and it was all as jolly as could be, and I was making way fast, in spite of that confounded red-headed porridge-eating fellow. Then came that upset, and I went away. Then you wrote to me in answer to my letter about having a good thing on, and said 'Come down.'"

"And you came," said Harry thoughtfully, "and the good thing turned out a bad thing, as every one does that I join in."

"Well, that was an accident; speculators must have some crust as well as crumb."

"But I get all crust."

"No, I seem to be getting all crust now from your people. Your aunt's right enough, but your father casts his cold shoulder and stale bread at me whenever we meet; and as for a certain lady, she regularly cut me yesterday."

"Well, I can't help that, Vic. You know what I said when you told me you were on that. I said that I couldn't do anything, and that I wouldn't do anything if I could: but that I wouldn't stand in your way if you liked to try."

"Yes, I know what you said," grumbled Pradelle, as they strolled down to the shore, went round the rocks, and then strolled on over and amongst the shingle and sand, till—a suitable spot presenting itself, about half a mile from the town—they sat down on the soft sand, tilted their hats over their eyes, leaned their backs against a huge stone, and then lit up and began to smoke.

"You see, it's like this," said Pradelle; "I know I'm not much of a catch, but I like her, and that ought to make up for a great deal."

"Yes," said Harry, whose mind was wandering elsewhere, and he was hesitating as to whether he should take his friend into his counsels or not.

"She don't know her own mind, that's about it," continued Pradelle; "and a word from you might do a deal."

"Got any money, Vic?"

"Now there's a mean sort of a question to ask a friend! Have I got any money? As if a man must be made of money before he may look at his old chum's sister."

"I wasn't thinking about her, but of something else," said Harry hastily.

"Ah, well, I wasn't. I've got a little bit of an income, a modest one I suppose you'd call it, and—but look there!"

"What at?" said Harry, whose eyes were shut, and his thoughts far away.

"Them. They're going for a walk. Why, Hal, old chap, they saw us come down here."

Harry started into wakefulness, and realised the fact that his sister and Madelaine Van Heldre were passing before them, but down by the water's edge, while the young men were close up under the towering cliff.

"Let's follow them," said Pradelle eagerly.

"Wait a moment."

Harry waited to think, and scraps of his aunt's remarks floated through his brain respecting the fair daughters of France, who would fall at the feet of the young count when he succeeded to his property, and the castle in the air which she reconstructed for him to see mentally.

Harry cogitated. The daughters of France were no doubt very lovely, but they were imaginative; and though Madelaine Van Heldre might, as his aunt said, not be of the pure Huguenot blood, still that fact did not seem to matter to him. For that was not imagination before him, but the bright, natural, clever girl whom he had known from childhood, his old playfellow, who had always seemed to supply a something wanting in his mental organisation, the girl who had led him and influenced his career, and whom he now told himself he loved very dearly, principally because he felt bound to look up to her and submit to all she said.

It was a very raw, green, and acrid kind of love, though Harry Vine was not aware of the fact, and he leaped to his feet.

"Bother Aunt Marguerite!" he said to himself, and then a loud, "Come along!" in happy ignorance of the fact that his good genius had prepared for him an antidote for the poison of vanity lately administered by his aunt.

Chapter Six
Harry Vine Speaks Plainly; So Does His Friend

In perfect ignorance of their presence, Louise and Madelaine went on down by the water's edge, picking their way among the rocks with an activity that would have startled some of their contemporaries, whose high heeled shoes and non perpendicular walk would have rendered such progress impossible. They were in profound ignorance of the fact that they were followed at a distance of about a couple of hundred yards, for Harry kept back his more eager friend, partly from a peculiar shrinking of a duplex nature, relating as it did to whether he was doing right in letting Pradelle make such very pronounced approaches to his sister, and the reception his own words would have upon Madelaine.

The two friends female were then in profound ignorance of the fact that they were watched, so were the two friends male.

For some time past the owner of the mine high up on the cliff, whose engine shaft went trailing along the ground like a huge serpent, higher and higher, till it reared its head for a landmark on the hill overlooking the sea, had for some time past been awakening to the fact that he had a heart, and that this heart was a good deal moved by Louise Vine. Till now he had been a thoroughly energetic man of business, but after the first introduction to the Vine family his business energy seemed to receive an impetus. He was working for her, everything might be for her.

Then came Pradelle upon the scene, and the young Scot was not long in seeing that the brother's London friend was also impressed, and that his advances found favour with Harry. Whether they did with the sister he could not tell.

The consequence was that there was a good deal of indecision on Duncan Leslie's part, some neglect of his busy mine, and a good deal of use of a double glass, which was supposed to be kept in a room, half office, half study and laboratory, for the purpose of scanning the shipping coming into port.

On the day in question the glass was being applied to a purpose rather reprehensible, perhaps, but with some excuse of helping Duncan Leslie's affair of the heart. From his window he could see the old granite-built house, and with interruptions, due to rocks and doublings and jutting pieces of cliff, a great deal of the winding and zig-zag path, half steps, which led down to the shore.

As, then, was frequently the case, the glass was directed toward the residence of the Vines, and Duncan Leslie saw Louise and Madelaine go down to the sea, stand watching the receding tide, and then go off west.

After gazing through the glass for a time he laid it down, with his heart beating faster than usual, as he debated within himself whether he should go down to the shore and follow them.

It was a hard fight, and inclination was rapidly mastering etiquette, when two figures, hitherto concealed came into view from beneath the cliff and began to follow the ladies.

Duncan Leslie's eyes flashed as he caught up the glass again, and after looking through it for a few minutes he closed it and threw it down.

"I'm making a fool of myself," he said bitterly. "Better attend to my business and think about it no more."

The desire was upon him to focus the glass again and watch what took place, but he turned away with an angry ejaculation and put the glass in its case.

"I might have known better," he said, "and it would be like playing the spy."

He strode out and went to his engine-house, forcing himself to take an interest in what was going on, and wishing the while that he had not used that glass in so reprehensible a way.

Oddly enough, just at that moment Uncle Luke was seated outside the door of his little cottage in its niche of the cliff below the mine, and wishing for this very glass.

His was a cottage of the roughest construction, which he had bought some years before of an old fisherman; and his seat—he could not afford chairs, he said—was a rough block of granite, upon which he was very fond of sunning himself when the weather was fine.

"I've a good mind to go and ask Leslie to lend me his glass," muttered the old man. "No. He'd only begin asking favours of me. But all that ought to be stopped. Wonder whether George knows. What's Van Heldre about? As for those two girls, I'll give them such a talking to—the gipsies! There they go, pretending they can't see that they are followed, and those two scamps making after them, and won't close up till they're round the point. Bah! it's no business of mine! I'm not going to marry."

Uncle Luke was quite right. Harry Vine and his friend were waiting till the jutting mass of cliff was passed—about a quarter of a mile to the westward, and they overtook the objects of their pursuit just as a consultation was taking place as to whether they should sit down and rest.

"Yes, let's sit down," said Madelaine, turning round. "Oh!"

"What is it? sprained your ankle?"

"No. Mr Pradelle and Harry are close by."

"Let's walk on quickly then, and go round back by the fields."

"But it will be six miles."

"Never mind if it's sixteen," said Louise, increasing her pace.

"Hallo, girls," cried Harry, and they were obliged to face round.

There was no warm look of welcome from either, but Pradelle was too much of the London man of the world to be taken aback, and he stepped forward to Louise's side, smiling.

"You have chosen a delightful morning for your walk, Miss Vine."

"Yes, but we were just going back."

"No; don't go back yet," said Harry quickly, for he had strung himself up. "Vic, old boy, you walk on with my sister. I want to have a chat with Miss Van Heldre."

The girls exchanged glances, each seeming to ask the other for counsel.

Then, in a quiet, decisive way, Madelaine spoke.

"Yes, do, Louie dear; I wanted to speak to your brother, too."

There was another quick look passing between the friends, and then Louise bowed and walked on, Pradelle giving Harry a short nod which meant, according to his judgment, "It's all right."

Louise was for keeping close to her companion, but her brother evidently intended her to have a *tête-à-tête* encounter with his friend, and she realised directly that Madelaine did not second her efforts. In fact the latter yielded at once to Harry's manoeuvres, and hung back with him, while Pradelle pressed forward, so that before many minutes had elapsed, the couples, as they walked west, were separated by a space of quite a couple of hundred yards.

"Now I do call that good of you, Maddy," said Harry eagerly. "You are, and you always were, a dear good little thing."

"Do you think so?" she said directly, and her pleasant bright face was now very grave.

"Do I think so! You know I do. There, I want a good talk to you, dear. It's time I spoke plainly, and that we fully understood one another."

"I thought we did, Harry."

"Well, yes, of course, but I want to be more plain. We're no boy and girl now."

"No, Harry, we have grown up to be man and woman."

"Yes, and ever since we were boy and girl, Maddy, I've loved you very dearly."

Madelaine turned her clear searching eyes upon him in the most calm and untroubled way.

"Yes, Harry, you have always seemed to."

"And you have always cared for me very much?"

"Yes, Harry. Always."

"Well, don't say it in such a cold, serious way, dear."

"But it is a matter upon which one is bound to be cool and very serious."

"Well, yes, of course. I don't know that people are any the better for showing a lot of gush."

"No, Harry, it is not so deep as the liking which is calm and cool and enduring."

"I s'pose not," said the young man very disconcertedly. "But don't be quite so cool. I know you too well to think you would play with me."

"I hope I shall always be very sincere, Harry."

"Of course you will. I know you will. We began by being playmates—almost like brother and sister."

"Yes, Harry."

"But I always felt as I grew older that I should some day ask you to be my darling little wife, and, come now, you always thought so too?"

"Yes, Harry, I always thought so too."

"Ah, that's right, dear," said the young man flushing. "You always were the dearest and most honest and plain-spoken girl I ever met."

"I try to be."

"Of course; and look yonder, there's old Pradelle, the dearest and best friend a fellow ever had, talking to Louise as I'm talking to you."

"Yes, I'm afraid he is."

"Afraid? Oh, come now, don't be prejudiced. I want you to like Victor."

"That would be impossible."

"Impossible! What, the man who will most likely be Louie's husband?"

"Mr Pradelle will never be Louie's husband."

"What! Why, how do you know?"

"Because I know your sister's heart too well."

"And you don't like Pradelle?"

"No, Harry; and I'm sorry you ever chose him for a companion."

"Oh, come, dear, that's prejudice and a bit of jealousy. Well, never mind about that now. I want to talk about ourselves."

"Yes, Harry."

"I want you to promise to be my little wife. I'm four-and-twenty, and you are nearly twenty, so it's quite time to talk about it."

Madelaine shook her head.

"Oh, come!" he said merrily, "no girl's coyness; we are too old friends for that, and understand one another too well. Come, dear, when is it to be?"

She turned and looked in the handsome flushed face beside her, and then said in the most cool and matter-of-fact way:

"It is too soon to talk like that. Harry."

"Too soon? Not a bit of it. You have told me that you will be my wife."

"Some day; perhaps."

"Oh, nonsense, dear! I've been thinking this all over well. You see, Maddy, you've let my not sticking to business trouble you."

"Yes, Harry, very much."

"Well, I'm very sorry, dear; and I suppose I have been a bit to blame, but I've been doing distasteful work, and I've been like a boat swinging about without an anchor. I want you to be my anchor to hold me fast. I've wanted something to steady me—something to work for; and if I've got you for a wife I shall be a different man directly."

Madelaine sighed.

"Aunt Marguerite won't like it, because she is not very fond of you."

"No," said Madelaine, "she does not like fat Dutch fraüleins—Dutch dolls."

"Get out! What stuff! She's a prejudiced old woman full of fads. She never did like you."

"Never, Harry."

"Well, that doesn't matter a bit."

"No. That does not matter a bit."

"You see I've had no end of thinks about all this, and it seems to me that if we're married at once, it will settle all the worries and bothers I've had lately. The governor wants me to go to business again; but what's the use of that? He's rich, and so is your father, and they can easily supply us with all that we should want, and then we shall be as happy as can be. Of course I shall work at something. I don't believe in a fellow with nothing to do. You don't either?"

"No, Harry."

"Of course not, but all that toiling and moiling for the sake of money is a mistake. Never mind what Aunt Marguerite says. I'll soon work her round, and of course I can do what I like with the governor. He's so fond of you that he'll be delighted, and he knows it will do me good. So now there's nothing to do but for me to go and see your father and ask his permission. I did think of letting you coax him round; but that would be cowardly, wouldn't it."

"Yes, Harry, very cowardly, and lower you very much in my eyes."

"Of course; but, I say, don't be so serious. Well, it's a bitter pill to swallow, for your governor will be down on me tremendously. I'll face him, though. I'll talk about our love and all that sort of thing, and it will be all right. I'll go to him to-day."

"No, Harry," said Madelaine, looking him full in the face, "don't do that."

"Why?"

"Because it would expose you to a very severe rebuff."

"Will you speak to him then? No; I'll do it."

"No. If you did my father would immediately speak to me, and I should have to tell him what I am going to tell you."

"Well. Out with it."

"Do you suppose," said Madelaine, once more turning her clear frank eyes upon the young man, and speaking with a quiet decision that startled him; "do you suppose I could be so wanting in duty to those at home, so wanting in love to you, Harry, that I could consent to a marriage which would only mean fixing you permanently in your present thoughtless ways? You talk like a foolish boy, and not like the Harry Vine whom I have always looked forward to being my protector through life."

"Madelaine!"

"Let me finish, Harry, and tell what has been on my lips for months past, but which you have never given me the opportunity to say to you till now. I am younger by several years than you, but do you think I am so wanting in worldly experience that I am blind to your reckless folly, or the pain you are giving father and sister by your acts?"

"Why, Maddy," he cried, in a voice full of vexation, which belied the mocking laugh upon his lips, "I didn't think you could preach like that."

"It is time to preach, Harry, when I see you so lost to self-respect, and find that you are ready to place yourself and the girl you wish to call wife, in a dependent position, instead of proudly and manfully making yourself your own master."

"Well, this is pleasant," cried Harry, as soon as he had recovered somewhat from his astonishment, "and am I to understand that you throw me over?"

"No, Harry," said Madelaine sadly, "you are to understand that I care for you too much to encourage you in a weak folly."

"A weak folly—to ask you what you have always expected I should ask!"

"Yes, to ask it at such a time when, after being placed in post after post by my father's help, and losing them one by one by your folly, you—"

"Oh, come, that will do," cried the young man angrily; "if it's to be like this it's a good job that we came to an explanation at once. So this is gentle, amiable, sweet-tempered Madelaine, eh! Hallo! You?"

He turned sharply, for during the latter part of the conversation they had been standing still, and Louise and Pradelle had come over a stretch of sand with their footsteps inaudible.

"It is quite time we returned, Madelaine," said Louise gravely; and without another word the two girls walked away.

"'Pon my word," cried Harry with a laugh, "things are improving. Well, Vic, how did you get on?"

"How did I get on indeed!" cried Pradelle angrily. "Look here, Harry Vine, are you playing square with me?"

"What do you mean?"

"What I say; are you honest, or have you been setting her against me?"

"Why you—no, I won't quarrel," cried Harry.

"What did she say to you?"

"Say to me? I was never so snubbed in my life. Any one would think I had been the dirt under her feet; but I've not done yet. Her ladyship doesn't know me if she thinks I'm going to give up like that."

"There, that'll do, Vic. No threats, please."

"Oh, no; I'm not going to threaten. I can wait."

"Yes," said Harry, thoughtfully; "we chose the wrong time. We mustn't give up, Vic; we shall have to wait."

And they went back to their old nook beneath the cliff to smoke their pipes, while as the thin blue vapour arose, Harry's hot anger grew cool, and he began to think of his aunt's words, of Comte Henri des Vignes, and of the fair daughters of France—a reverie from which he was aroused by his companion, as he said suddenly—

"I say, Harry lad, I want you to lend me a little coin."

Chapter Seven
Chez Van Heldre

The two friends parted at the gate, Madelaine refusing to go in.

"No," she said; "they will be expecting me at home."

They kissed, and then stood holding one another's hands, both wanting to relieve their full hearts, but dreading to begin. Hardly a word had been spoken on their way back, and such words as had been said were upon indifferent subjects.

But now the moment for parting had come, and they gazed wistfully in each other's eyes.

Louise was the first to break the painful since.

"Maddy, dear, ought we not to confide in each other?"

"Ah!" exclaimed Madelaine, with a sigh of relief that the constraint was over. "Yes, dear. Did Mr Pradelle propose to you?"

"Yes."

"And you told him it was impossible?"

"Yes. What did my brother want to say?"

"That we ought to be married now, and it would make him a better man."

"And you told him it was impossible?"

"Yes."

There was another sigh as if of relief on both sides, and the two girls kissed again and parted.

It was a brisk quarter of an hour's walk to the Van Heldre's, which lay at the end of the main street up the valley down which the little river ran; and on entering the door, with a longing upon her to go at once to her room and sit down and cry, Madelaine uttered a sigh full of misery, for she saw that it was impossible.

As she approached the great stone porch leading into the broad hall, which was one of the most attractive looking places in the house, filled as it was with curiosities and other objects brought by the various captains from the Mediterranean, and embracing cabinets from Constantinople with rugs and pipes, little terra-cotta figures from Sardinia, and pictures and pieces of statuary from Rome, Naples, and Trieste—there was the sound of music, but such music as might be expected from a tiny bird organ, whose handle Mrs Van Heldre was turning as she gazed wistfully up at a bullfinch, whose black cap was set on one side, and little beady eyes gazed down from the first one and then the other side of their owner's little black stumpy beak, which it every now and then used to ruffle the delicate red feathers of its breast or the soft grey blue of its back.

The notes that came from the little box-like instrument—a very baby of an organ—as Mrs Van Heldre turned, were feeble in the extreme, but there was a method in the machine which piped forth most irregularly and in the most feeble way the quaint old French air "Ma Normandie;" and as Madelaine heard it, her broad white forehead grew perplexed and a thrill of misery and discomfort ran through her.

"Ah, my dear, I'm so glad you've come back. Where's papa?"

"I have not seen him, mamma."

"Busy, I suppose. How he does work! But do look, dear, at this tiresome bird. He'll never learn to pipe."

"Not with patience, mamma? I think so."

"I don't, Maddy. It seems to take more patience than I've got. It's worse than trying to teach that parrot. It never would learn the words you wanted it to."

"Is it worth the trouble, mamma, dear?"

"No, my dear, I don't think it is; but I seemed to fancy that I should like to have a piping bullfinch. Every body has some fancy, dear; and I'm sure mine's better than Margaret Vine's for aristocratic connections. Ah! how cross that woman does make me feel."

"She is rather irritating," said Madelaine, holding the tip of a white finger between the bars of the cage.

"Irritating?" said the plump little woman flushing; "I call her maddening. The life she leads that poor patient man! dictating as she does, and worrying him about the French estates and the family name, while George Vine is so patient that—"

"He would succeed in teaching a bullfinch to pipe, mamma."

"Ah, now you're laughing at me, and thinking me weak; but it's better to have my weakness than hers. Only fancy: ever since she formed that mad, foolish attachment for that French scoundrel, who coaxed the whole of her money away from her and then threw her over, has George Vine taken her to his home and let her tyrannise over him. A silly woman! Your father always said the man was a scamp. And, by the way, that Mr Pradelle, I don't like him, my dear."

"Neither do I, mamma."

"That's right, my dear; I'm very glad to hear you say so; but surely Louie Vine is not going to be beguiled by him?"

"Oh, no."

"Ah, that's all very well; but Luke Vine came in as he went by, to say in his sneering fashion that Louie and Mr Pradelle were down on the shore, and that you were walking some distance behind with Harry."

"Mr Luke Vine seems to have plenty of time for watching his neighbours," said Madelaine, contemptuously.

"Yes; he is always noticing things; but don't blame him, dear. I'm sure he means well, and I can forgive him anything for that. Ah! here's your father."

"Ah! my dears," said Van Heldre cheerily. "Tired out."

"You must be," said Mrs Van Heldre, bustling about him to take his hat and gloves. "Here do come and sit down."

The merchant went into the drawing-room very readily, and submitted to several little pleasant attentions from wife and daughter, as he asked questions about the bullfinch, laughing slily the while at Madelaine.

Evening came on with Van Heldre seated in his easy chair, thoughtfully watching wife and daughter, both of whom had work in their laps; but Mrs Van Heldre's was all a pretence, for, after a few stitches, her head began to nod forward, then back against the cushion, and then, as if by magic, she was fast asleep.

Madelaine's needle, however, flew fast, and she went on working, with her father watching her attentively, till she raised her eyes, let her hands rest in her lap, and returned his gaze with a frank, calm look of love and trust that made him nod his head in a satisfied way.

"You want to say something to me, Maddy," he said in a low voice.

"Yes, papa."

"About your walk down on the beach?"

Madelaine nodded.

"You know I went."

"Yes; I saw you, and Luke Vine came and told me as well."

"It was very kind of him," said Madelaine, with a touch of sarcasm in her voice.

"Kind and unkind, my dear. You see he has no business—nothing to do but to think of other people. But he means well, my dear, and he likes you."

"I have often thought so."

"Yes; and you were right. He warned me that I was not to let your intimacy grow closer with his nephew."

"Indeed, papa!"

"Yes, my dear. He said that I was a—well, I will not tell you what, for not stopping it directly, for that Harry was rapidly drifting into a bad course—that it was a hopeless case."

"That is not the way to redeem him, father."

"No, my dear, it is not. But you were going to say something to me?"

"Yes," said Madelaine, hesitating. Then putting down her work she rose and went to her father's side, knelt down, and resting her arms upon his knees, looked straight up in his face.

"Well, Maddy?"

"I wanted to speak to you about Harry Vine."

There was a slight twitching about the merchant's brows, but his face was calm directly, and he said coolly—

"What about Harry Vine?"

Madelaine hesitated for a few moments, and then spoke out firmly and bravely.

"I have been thinking about his position, father, and of how sad it is for him to be wasting his days as he is down here."

"Very sad, Maddy. He is, as Luke Vine says, going wrong. Well?"

"I have been thinking, papa, that you might take him into your office and give him a chance of redeeming the past."

"Nice suggestion, my dear. What would old Crampton say?"

"Mr Crampton could only say that you had done a very kind act for the son of your old friend."

"Humph! Well?"

"You could easily arrange to take him, papa, and with your firm hand over him it would do an immense deal of good."

"Not to me."

There was a pause during which Van Heldre gazed into his child's unblenching eyes.

"So we are coming at facts," he said at last. "Harry asked you to interfere on his behalf?"

Madelaine shook her head and smiled.

"Is this your own idea?"

"Entirely."

"Then what was the meaning of the walk on the beach to-day?"

"Harry sought for it, and said that we had been playfellows from children, that he loved me very dearly, and he asked me to be his wife."

"The—"

Van Heldre checked himself.

"And what did you say?"

"That it was impossible."

"Then you do not care for him?" cried Van Heldre eagerly.

Madelaine was silent.

"Then you do not care for him?" said Van Heldre again.

"I'm afraid I care for him very much indeed, father," said Madelaine firmly; "and it grieves me so to see him drifting away that I determined to ask you to come to his help."

"Let me thoroughly understand you, my darling. You love George Vine's son—your old friend's brother?"

"Yes, father," said Madelaine, in a voice little above a whisper.

"And he has asked you to be his wife?"

"Yes."

"Tell me what answer you gave him?"

"In brief, that I would never marry a man so wanting in self-respect and independence as he has shown himself to be."

"Hah!"

It was a softly-uttered ejaculation, full of content.

"He said that our parents were rich, that there was no need for him to toil as he had done, but that if I consented it would give him an impetus to work."

"And you declined conditionally?"

"I declined absolutely, father."

"And yet you love him?"

"I'm afraid I love him very dearly, father."

"You are a strange girl, Madelaine."

"Yes, father."

"Do you know what it means for me to take this wilful young fellow into my office?"

"Much trouble and care."

"Yes. Then why should I at my time of life fill my brain with worry and care?"

"Because, as you have so often taught me, we cannot live for ourselves alone. Because he is the son of your very old friend."

"Yes," said Van Heldre softly.

"Because it might save him from a downward course now that there is, I believe, a crisis in his life."

"And because you love him, Maddy?"

She answered with a look.

"And if I were so insane, so quixotic, as to do all this, what guarantee have I that he would not gradually lead you to think differently — to consent to be his wife before he had redeemed his character?"

"The trust you have in me that I should not do anything you did not consider right."

"Hah!" ejaculated Van Heldre again. And there was another long silence.

"I feel that I must plead for him, father. It would be the turning-point of his life. You could influence him so much."

"I'm afraid not, my child. If he has not the manliness to do what is right for your sake, I'm afraid that anything I could do or say would not be of much avail."

"You underrate your power, father," said Madelaine, with a look full of pride in him.

"And if I did this I might have absolute confidence that matters should go no farther until he had completely changed?"

"You know you might."

"Hah!" sighed Van Heldre. "You will think this over, father?"

"There is no need, my dear."

"No need?"

"No, my child. I have for some days past been thinking over this very thing, just in the light in which you placed it."

"You have, father?"

"Yes, and I had a long talk with George Vine this afternoon respecting his son."

"Oh, father!"

"I told him I could see that the trouble was growing bigger and telling upon him, and proposed that I should take Harry here." Madelaine had started to her feet.

"Presuming that he does not refuse after his father has made my proposals known, Harry Vine comes here daily to work under Crampton's guidance." Madelaine's arms were round her father's neck.

"You have made me feel very happy and satisfied, my dear," said Van Heldre, pressing her to his breast; "and may heaven speed what is going to be a very arduous task. He will commence in the office next week."

Just then Mrs Van Heldre raised her head and looked round.

"Bless my heart!" she exclaimed. "I do believe I have nearly been to sleep."

Chapter Eight
Uncle Luke Speaks His Mind

"Hallo, Scotchman!"

"Hallo, Eng— I mean, French—What am I to call you Mr Luke Vine?"

"Englishman, of course."

Uncle Luke was seated, in a very shabby-looking grey aged Norfolk jacket made long, a garment which suited his tastes, from its being an easy comfortable article of attire. He had on an old Panama hat, a good deal stained, and a thick stick armed with a strong iron point useful for walking among the rocks; and upon this staff he rested as he sat outside his cottage door watching the sea and pondering as to the probability of a shoal of fish being off the point.

His home with its tiny scrap of rough walled-in garden, which grew nothing but sea holly and tamarisk, was desolate looking in the extreme, but the view therefrom of the half-natural pier sheltering the vessels in the harbour of the twin town, with its busy wharves and warehouses and residences, rising in terrace above terrace, and of the blue, ever-changing sea, was glorious.

He had had his breakfast and taken his seat out in the sunshine, when he became aware of the fact that Duncan Leslie was coming down from the mine buildings above, and he hailed him with a snarl and the above words.

"Glorious morning."

"Humph! Yes," said the old man, looking up at the handsome young mine-owner with his face all in lines, "but what's that got to do with you?"

"Everything. Do you suppose I don't like fine weather?"

"I thought you didn't care for anything but money grubbing."

"Then you were mistaken, because I do."

"Nonsense! You think of nothing but copper, spoiling the face of nature with the broken rubbish your men dig out of the bowels of the earth, poisoning the air with the fumes of those abominable furnaces. Look at that!"

The old man raised his stick and made a vicious dig with it in the direction of the mine.

"Look at what?"

"That shaft. Looks like some huge worm that your men disturbed down below, and sent it crawling along the hill slope till it could rear its abominable head in the air and look which way to go to be at rest."

"What an idea! It isn't pretty looking. I must say."

"Pretty looking! No. Why do you have it then?"

"It was there when I bought the mine, and it answers its purpose."

"Bah! What purpose? To make money?"

"Yes; to make money. Very useful thing, Mr Leslie."

"Rubbish! You're as bad as Van Heldre with his ships and his smelting works. Money! Money! Money! Always money, morning, noon and night. One constant hunt for the accursed stuff. Look at me!"

"I was looking at you, old fellow; and studying you."

"Humph! Waste of time, unless you follow my example."

"Then it will be waste of time, sir, for I certainly shall not follow your example."

"Why not, boy? Look at me. I have no troubles. I pay no rent. My wants are few. I am nearly independent of trades-people and tax men. I've no slatternly wife to worry me, no young children to be always tumbling down the rocks or catching the measles. I'm free of all these troubles and I'm a happy man."

"Well, then, your appearance belies you, sir, for you do not look it," said Leslie, laughing.

"Never you mind my appearance," said Uncle Luke sharply. "I am happy; at least, I should be, if you'd do away with that great smoky chimney and stop those rattling stamps."

"Then I'm afraid that I cannot oblige you, neighbour."

"Humph! Neighbour!"

"I fancy that an unbiassed person would blame you and not me."

"Of course he would."

"He'd say if a man chooses to turn himself into a sort of modern Diogenes—"

"Diogenes be hanged, sir! All a myth. I don't believe there ever was such a body. And look here, Leslie, I imitate no man—no myth. I prefer to live this way for my own satisfaction, and I shall."

"And welcome for me, old fellow; only don't scold me for living my way."

"Not going to. Here, stop! I want to talk to you. How's copper?"

"Up a good deal, but you don't want to know."

"Of course I don't. But look here. What do you think of my nephew?"

"Tall, good-looking young fellow."

"Humph! What's the good of that? You know all about him, of course?"

"I should prefer not to sit in judgment on the gentleman in question."

"So I suppose. Nice boy, though, isn't he?"

Leslie was silent.

"I say he's a nice boy; isn't he?" cried the old man, raising his voice.

"I heard what you said. He is your nephew."

"Worse luck! How is he getting on at Van Heldre's?"

"I have not the least idea, sir."

"More have I. They won't tell me. How about that friend of his? What do you think of him?"

"Really, Mr Vine," said Leslie laughing, "I do not set up as a judge of young men's character. It is nothing to me."

"Yes, it is. Do you suppose I'm blind? Do you suppose I can't tell which way the wind blows? If I were young, do you know what I should do?"

"Do away with the chimney shaft and the stamps," said Leslie, laughing.

"No; I should just get hold of that fellow some night, and walk him to where the coach starts."

Leslie's face looked warm.

"And then I should say, 'Jump up, and when you get to the station, book for London; and if ever you show your face in Hakemouth again I'll break your neck.'"

"You must excuse me, Mr Luke; I'm busy this morning," said Leslie; and he walked on and began to descend the steep path.

"Touched him on the tender place," said Uncle Luke, with a chuckle. "Humph! wonder whether Louie will come and see me to-day."

Duncan Leslie went on down the zig-zag cliff path leading from the Wheal Germains copper mine to the town. It was a picturesque way, with a fresh view at every turn west and east; and an advanced member of the town board had proposed and carried the suggestion of placing rough granite seats here and there in the best parts for resting those who climbed, and for giving others attractive places for sunning themselves and looking out to sea.

The plan was a great success, and these seats were largely patronised by the fishermen in the case of those nearest the shore, where they could follow out their favourite pastime to the full, and also by the towns-people, especially by the invalids and those young folk who had arrived at the billing and cooing stage of life, when there are only two people in the world—themselves.

About half way down Leslie passed an invalid, who had taken possession of a seat, and was gazing right away south, and dreaming of lands where the sun always shone—wondering whether the bright maiden Health could be found there.

Lower still Leslie was going on thoughtfully, pondering on Uncle Luke's hints, when the blood suddenly flushed into his cheeks, his heart began to beat rapidly, and he increased his pace. For there unmistakably were two ladies going down the zig-zag, and there were no two others in Hakemouth could be mistaken for them.

He hurried on to overtake them. Then he checked himself.

"Where had they been?"

His sinking heart suggested that they had been on their way to visit Uncle Luke, but that they had caught sight of him, and in consequence returned.

His brow grew gloomy, and he walked slowly on, when the blood flushed to his cheeks again, as if he had been surprised in some guilty act, for a sharp voice said—

"No, Mr Leslie; you would not be able to overtake them now."

He stopped short, and turned to the warm sheltered nook among the rocks where Aunt Margaret was seated; her grey lavender dress was carefully spread about her, her white hair turned back beneath a black velvet satin-lined hood, and a lace fichu pinned across her breast.

"You here, Miss Vine?" said Leslie, hiding his annoyance.

"Yes; and I thought I would save you a thankless effort. I know these paths so well, and they are very deceptive as to distance. You could not overtake the girls unless you ran."

"I was not going to try and overtake them, Miss Vine," said Leslie coldly.

"Indeed! I beg your pardon; I thought you were. But would you mind, Mr Leslie—it is a very trifling request, but I set store by these little relics of our early history—Miss *Marguerite* Vine, if you would be so kind?"

Leslie bowed. "Certainly, Miss Marguerite," he said quietly.

"Thank you," she said, detaining him. "It is very good of you. Of course you are surprised to see me up here?"

"Oh, no," said Leslie quietly. "It is a delightful place to sit and rest and read."

"Ye-es; but I cannot say that I care much for the rough walking of this part of the world, and my brother seems somehow to have taken quite a dislike to the idea of having a carriage?"

"Yes?"

"So I am obliged to walk when I do come out. There are certain duties one is forced to attend to. For instance, there is my poor brother up yonder. I feel bound to see him from time to time. You see him frequently, of course?"

"Every day, necessarily. We are so near."

"Poor fellow! Yes. Very eccentric and peculiar; but you need be under no apprehension, Mr Leslie. He is quite harmless, I am sure."

"Oh, quite harmless, Miss Marguerite. Merely original."

"It is very good of you to call it originality; but as friends, Mr Leslie, there is no harm in our alluding to his poor brain. Softening, a medical man told me."

"Hardening, I should say," thought Leslie.

"Very peculiar! very peculiar! Father and uncle both so different to my dear nephew. So you were going to overtake the girls?"

"No, Miss Marguerite; I had no such idea."

"Indeed! They walked with me as far as here; and then I said, 'My dears, it is impossible for me to go up to Uncle Luke to-day, so I will sit down and rest, and go back alone.' I believe the air will refresh me."

"I am sure it will. It is so fresh and sweet up here."

"Ye-es," said Aunt Marguerite. "Have you seen my nephew to-day? No? Poor boy! He is in very bad spirits. Ah! Mr Leslie, I shall be very glad to see him once more as a des Vignes should be. With him placed in the position that should be his, and that engagement carried out regarding my darling Louise's future, I could leave this world of sorrow without a sigh."

Leslie winced, but it was not perceptible to Aunt Marguerite, who, feeling dissatisfied with the result of her shot, fired again.

"Of course it would involve losing my darling: but at my time of life, Mr Leslie, one has learned that it is one's duty always to study self-sacrifice. The des Vignes were always a self-sacrificing family. When it was not for some one or other of their kindred it was for their king, and then for their faith. You know our old French motto, Mr Leslie?"

"I? No. I beg pardon."

"Really? I should have thought you could not fail to see that. It is almost the only trace of our former greatness that my misguided brother—"

"Were you alluding to Mr Luke Vine?"

"No, no, no, no! To my brother, George des Vignes. Surely, Mr Leslie, you must have noted our arms upon the dining-room windows."

"Oh, yes, of course, of course: and the motto, *Roy et Foy.*"

"Exactly," said Aunt Marguerite, smiling, "I thought it must have caught your eye."

Something else was catching Duncan Leslie's eye just then—the last flutter of the scarf Louise wore before it disappeared round the foot of the cliff.

"I shall bear it, I daresay, and with fortitude, Mr Leslie, for it will be a grand position that she will take. The de Lignys are a family almost as old as our own; and fate might arrange for me to visit them and make a long stay. She's a sweet girl, is she not, Mr Leslie?"

"Miss Vine? Yes: you must be very proud of her," said the young man, without moving a muscle.

"We are; we are indeed, Mr Leslie; but I am afraid I am detaining you."

"I will not call it detaining me, Miss Marguerite," said Leslie, mockingly assuming a courtly manner in accord with that of his tormentor. "The Scotch had so much intercourse with the French years ago that they gave us a little polish, and I hope we have some trace of the old politeness left."

He smiled and bowed before passing on, and Aunt Marguerite watched him till he disappeared down the zig-zag path, her own smile remaining so fixed that it seemed to be frozen on her lip, the more so that it was a cold, cruel-looking smile, verging on the malignant as she said softly—"That will be something for you to think about, Mr Duncan Leslie; and you shall find I am not a woman to be despised."

"It is curious," said the object of her thoughts, as he walked slowly down the cliff path. "Surely there was never a family before whose various members were so different in their ways. De Ligny, de Ligny? Who is de Ligny? Well," he added with a sigh, "I ought to thank Heaven that the name is not Pradelle."

Chapter Nine
In Office Hours

"Now, my dear Mr Crampton, believe me, I am only actuated by a desire to do good."

"That's exactly what actuates me, sir, when I make bold, after forty years' service with you and your father, to tell you that you have made a great mistake."

"All men make mistakes, Crampton," said Van Heldre, to his plump, grey, stern-looking head clerk.

"Yes, sir; but if they are then worth their salt they see where they have made a mistake, and try and correct it. We did not want him."

"As far as actual work to be done, no; but I will tell you plainly why I took on the young man. I wish to help my old friend in a peculiarly troubled period of his life."

"That's you all over, Mr Van Heldre," said the old clerk, pinching his very red nose, and then arranging his thin hair with a pen-holder; "but I can't feel that it's right. You see the young man don't take to his work. He comes and goes in a supercilious manner, and treats me as if I were his servant."

"Oh, that will soon pass off, Crampton."

"I hope so, Mr Van Heldre, sir, but his writing's as bad as a schoolboy's."

"That will improve."

"He's always late of a morning."

"I'll ask him to correct that."

"And he's always doing what I hate in a young man, seeing how short is life, sir, and how soon we're gone—he's always looking at the clock and yawning."

"Never mind, Crampton, he'll soon give up all that sort of thing. The young man is like an ill-trained tree. He has grown rather wild, but now he has been transplanted to an orderly office, to be under your constant supervision, he will gradually imbibe your habits and precision. It will be his making."

"Now, now, now," said the old clerk, shaking his head, "that's flattering, sir. My habits and precision. No, no, sir; I'm a very bad clerk, and I'm growing old as fast as I can."

"You are the best clerk in the west of England, Crampton, and you are only growing old at the customary rate. And now to oblige me, look over these little blemishes in the young man's character. There is a good deal of the spoiled boy in him, but I believe his heart's right; and for more reasons than one I want him to develop into a good man of business—such a one as we can make of him if we try."

"Don't say another word, Mr Van Heldre. You know me, and if I say as long as the young man is honest and straightforward I'll do my best for him, I suppose that's sufficient."

"More than sufficient, Crampton."

"But you know, sir, he ought to have made some little advance in a month."

"No, no, Crampton," said Van Heldre, smiling, "he has not grown used to the new suit yet: have patience, and he'll come right."

"That's enough, sir," said Crampton, climbing on to a high stool in front of a well-polished desk, "now for business. The *Saint Aubyn* has taken in all her cargo, and will sail to-morrow. We ought soon to have news of the *Madelaine*. By the way, I hope Miss Madelaine's quite well, sir. Haven't seen her for a day and a half."

"Quite well, Crampton."

"That's right, sir," said the old man, smiling and rubbing his hands. "Bless her! I've only one thing against her. Why wasn't she a boy?"

Van Heldre smiled at his old confidential man, who still rubbed his hands softly, and gazed over his silver-rimmed spectacles at a file of bills of lading hanging from the wall.

"What a boy she would have made, and what a man I could have made of him! Van Heldre and Son once more, as it ought to be. I'd have made just such a man of business of him as I made of you. Going, sir?"

"Yes, I'm going up to Tolzarn. By the way, send Mr Henry Vine up to me about twelve."

"Yes," said Crampton, beginning to write away very busily. "I suppose he'll come?"

"Of course, of course," said Van Heldre hastily, and leaving the office he went into the house just as Mrs Van Heldre had made her way into the hall to cover up her bullfinch's cage; and her hand was upon the bird organ when she heard her husband's step, when, colouring like a girl, she hurried up-stairs.

Van Heldre crossed the hall and entered the morning-room, where Madelaine was busy with her needle.

She looked at him in an inquiring way, to which he had become accustomed during the past month, and in accordance with an unwritten contract.

"No, my dear, not come yet."

Madelaine's countenance changed as she saw her father glance at his watch, and she involuntarily darted a quick look at the clock on the chimney-piece.

"I'm going up to the works," continued Van Heldre. "Back before one. Morning."

Madelaine resumed her work for a few minutes, and then rose to stand where, unseen, she could watch the road. She saw her father go by up the valley, but her attention was turned toward the sea, from which direction Harry Vine would have to come.

She stood watching for nearly a quarter of an hour before she heard a familiar step, and then the young man passed smoking the end of a cigar, which he threw away before turning in at the way which led to Van Heldre's offices.

Directly after, as Madelaine sat looking very thoughtful over her work, there was the quick patter of Mrs Van Heldre's feet.

"Madelaine, my dear," she said as she entered; "I thought you said that Mr Pradelle had gone away a fortnight ago."

"I did, mamma."

"Well, then, he has come back again."

"Back again?" said Madelaine, letting her work fall in her lap.

"Yes, I was at the up-stairs window just now, and I saw him pass as I was looking out for Harry Vine. He's very late this morning, and it does make papa so vexed."

It was late, for instead of being nine o'clock, the clock in the office was on the stroke of ten as Harry Vine hurriedly entered, and glanced at the yellowy-white faced dial.

"Morning, Mr Crampton. I say that clock's fast, isn't it?"

"Eh? fast?" said the old man grimly. "No, Mr Harry Vine; that's a steady old time-keeper, not a modern young man."

"Disagreeable old hunks," said Harry to himself, as he hung up his hat. "Bad headache this morning, Mr Crampton, thought I shouldn't be able to come."

"Seidlitz powder," said the old man, scratching away with his pen, and without looking up.

"Eh?"

"Dissolve the blue in a tumbler of warm water."

"Bother!" muttered Harry, frowning.

"The white in a wineglassful of cold. Pour one into the other—and— drink—while effervescing."

The intervals between some of the words were filled up by scratches of the pen.

"Headache, eh? Bad things, sir, bad things."

He removed himself from his stool and went to the safe in the inner office, where Van Heldre generally sat, and Harry raised his head from his desk and listened, as he heard the rattling of keys and the clang of a small iron door.

"Yes, bad things headaches, Mr Harry," said the old man returning. "Try early hours for 'em, and look here: Mr Van Heldre says—"

"Has he been in the office this morning?" cried Harry hastily.

"Yes, sir, he came in as soon as I'd come, nine to the minute, and he wants you to join him at the tin works about twelve."

"Wigging!" said guilty conscience.

"Do your head good, sir."

Old Crampton resumed his seat, and for an hour and three-quarters, during which period Harry had several times looked at the clock and yawned, there was a constant scratching of pens.

Then Harry Vine descended from his stool.

"I'd better go now?"

"Yes, sir, you'd better go now. And might have gone before for all the good you've done," grumbled the old man, as Harry passed the window. "Tut—tut—tut! What careless writing. He's spoiling my books, that he is."

The old man had hardly spent another half-hour over his work when there was a sharp tapping at the door, such as might be given by the knob on a stick.

"Come in."

The door was opened, and Pradelle entered and gave a sharp look round.

"Morning," he said in a cavalier way. "Tell Mr Vine I want to speak to him for a moment."

Old Crampton looked up from his writing, and fixed his eyes on the visitor's hat.

"Not at home," he said shortly.

"How long will he be?"

"Don't know."

"Where has he gone?"

"Tin works," said Crampton, resuming his writing.

"Confounded old bear!" muttered Pradelle as he went out, after frowning severely at the old clerk, who did not see it.

"Idle young puppy!" grumbled Crampton, dotting an I so fiercely that he drove his pen though the paper. "I'd have knocked his hat off if I had had my ruler handy. Now what does he want, I wonder?"

Van Heldre was busy at work with a shovel when Harry Vine reached the tin-smelting works, which the merchant had added to his other ventures. He was beside a heap of what rather resembled wet coarsely ground coffee.

"Ah, Harry," he said, "you may as well learn all these things. Be useful some day. Take hold of that shovel and turn that over. Tell me what you think of it."

A strong mind generally acts upon one that is weak, and it was so here.

Harry felt disposed, as he looked at his white hands, the shovel, and the heap, to thrust the said white hands in his pocket and walk away.

But he took the shovel and plunged it in the heap, lifted it full, and then with a look of disgust said: —

"What am I to do with it?"

"Shovel it away and get more out of the centre."

Harry obeyed, and looked up for fresh orders.

"Now take a couple of handfuls and examine them. Don't be afraid, man, it's honest dirt."

Van Heldre set the example, took a handful and poured it from left to right and back again.

"Now," he said, "take notice; that's badly washed."

"Not soap enough," said Harry, hiding his annoyance with an attempt at being facetious.

"Not exactly," said Van Heldre drily; "bad work. Now when that tin is passed through the furnace, there'll be twice as much slag and refuse as there ought to be. That will do. Leave the shovel, I want you to take account of those slabs of tin. Mark them, number them, and enter them in this book. It will take you an hour. Then bring the account down to me at the office."

"I can have a man to move the slabs?" said Harry.

"No, they are all busy. If I were doing it, I should work without a man."

"Hang it all! I'm about sick of this," said Harry, after he had been alone about half an hour, and feeling more disgusted moment by moment with his task. "How mad Aunt Marguerite would be if she could see me now!"

He looked round at the low dirty sheds on one side, at the row of furnaces on the other, two of which emitted a steady roar as the tin within gradually turned from a brown granulated powder to a golden fluid, whose stony scum was floating on the top.

"It's enough to make any man kick against his fate. Nice occupation for a gentleman, 'pon my word!"

A low whistle made him look up quickly, and his countenance brightened.

"Why, Vic," he cried; "I thought you were in town."

"How are you, my Trojan?" cried the visitor boisterously. "I was in town, but I've come back. I say, cheerful work this for Monsieur le Comte Henri des Vignes!"

"Don't chaff a fellow," said Harry angrily. "What brought you down?"

"Two things."

"Now, look here, Vic. Don't say any more about that. Perhaps after a time I may get her to think differently, but now—"

"I was not going to say anything about your sister, my dear boy. I can wait and bear anything. But I suppose I may say something about you?"

"About me?"

"Yes. I've got a splendid thing on. Safe to make money—heaps of it."

"Yes; but your schemes always want money first."

"Well, hang it all, lad! you can't expect a crop of potatoes without planting a few bits first. It wouldn't want much. Only about fifty pounds. A hundred would be better, but we could make fifty do."

Harry shook his head.

"Come, come; you haven't heard half yet. I've the genuine information. It would be worth a pile of money. It's our chance now—such a chance as may never occur again."

"No, no; don't tempt me, Vic," said Harry, after a long whimpered conversation.

"Tempt? I feel disposed to force you, lad. It makes me half wild to see you degraded to such work as this. Why, if we do as I propose you will be in a position to follow out your aunt's instructions, engage lawyers to push on your case, and while you obtain your rights, I shall be in a position to ask your sister's hand without the chance of a refusal. I tell you the thing's safe."

"No, no," said Harry, shaking his head; "it's too risky. We should lose and be worse off than ever."

"With a horse like that, and me with safe private information about him!"

"No," said Harry, "I won't. I'm going to keep steadily on here, and, as the governor calls it, plod."

"That you're not, if I know it," cried Pradelle indignantly. "I won't stand it. It's disgraceful. You shan't throw yourself away."

"But I've got no money, old fellow."

"Nonsense! Get some of the old man."

"No; I've done it too often. He won't stand it now."

"Well, of your aunt."

"She hasn't a penny but what my father lets her have."

"Your sister. Come, she would let you have some."

Harry shook his head.

"No, I'm not going to ask her. It's no good, Vic; I won't."

"Well," said Pradelle, apostrophising an ingot of tin as it lay at his feet glistening with iridescent hues, "if any one had told me, I wouldn't have believed it. Why, Harry, lad, you've only been a month at this mill-horse life, and you're quite changed. What have they been doing to you, man?"

"Breaking my spirit, I suppose, they'd call it," said the young man bitterly.

"Nonsense! yours isn't a spirit to be broken in to a beggarly trade. Think of what your aunt has said to you, as well as to me. Your estates, your title, the woman you are to marry. Why, Harry, lad, you don't think I'm going to sit still and see you break down without a word?"

Harry shook his head.

"Get out! I won't have it. You want waking up," said Pradelle in a low, earnest voice. "Think, lad, a few pounds placed as I could place 'em, and there's fortune for in both, without reckoning on what you could do in France. As your aunt say, there's money and a title waiting for you if you'll only stretch out your hand to take 'em. Come, rouse yourself. Harry Vine isn't the lad to settle down to this drudgery. Why, I thought it was one of the workmen when I came up."

"It's of no use," said Harry gloomily, as he seated himself on the ingots of tin. "A man must submit to his fate."

"Bah! a man's fate is what he makes it. Look here; fifty or a hundred borrowed for a few days, and then repaid."

"But suppose—"

"Suppose!" cried Pradelle mockingly; "a business man has no time to suppose, he strikes while the iron's hot. You're going to strike iron, not tin."

"How? Where's the money?"

"Where's the money?" said Pradelle mockingly. "You want fifty or a hundred for a few days, when you would return it fifty times over; and you say, where's the money?"

"Don't I tell you I have no one I could borrow from?" said Harry angrily.

"Yes, you have," said Pradelle, sinking his voice. "It's easy as easy. Only for a few days. A temporary loan. Look here."

He bent down, and whispered a few words in the young man's ear, words which turned him crimson, and then deadly pale.

"Pradelle!" he cried, in a hoarse whisper; "are you mad?"

"No. I was thinking of coming over to Auvergne to spend a month with my friend, the Count. By-and-by, dear lad—by-and-by."

"No, no; it is impossible," said Harry hoarsely, and he gave a hasty glance round.

"No," whispered Pradelle, "no; it is not impossible, but as simple as A B C."

"But," faltered Harry, who was trembling now.

"Hush! some one coming. No; you need not mind," said Pradelle with a sneer; "only two ladies walking up the road. Now, I wonder whom they've come to see."

"No, no," said Harry in a husky whisper, as his companion's last words seemed unheeded; "I couldn't do that."

"You could," said Pradelle, and then to himself: "and, if I know you, Harry Vine, you shall."

Chapter Ten
Harry Vine has a Want

Breakfast-time, with George Vine quietly partaking of his toast, and giving furtive glances at a *Beloe* in a small squat bottle. He was feeding his mind at the same time that he supplied the wants of his body. Now it was a bite of toast, leaving in the embrowned bread such a mark as was seen by the dervish when the man asked after the lost camel: for the student of molluscous sea life had lost a front tooth. Now it was a glance at the little gooseberry-shaped creature, clear as crystal, glistening in the clear water with iridescent hues, and trailing behind it a couple of filaments of an extreme delicacy and beauty that warranted the student's admiration.

Louise was seated opposite, performing matutinal experiments, so it seemed, with pots, cups, an urn, and various infusions and crystals.

Pradelle was reading the paper, and Harry was dividing his time between eating some fried ham and glancing at the clock, which was pointing in the direction of the hour when he should be at Van Heldre's.

"More tea, Louie; too sweet," said the head of the house, passing his cup, *via* Pradelle.

The cup was filled up and passed back, Louise failing to notice that Pradelle manoeuvred to touch her hand as he played his part in the transfer. Then the door opened, and Liza, the brown-faced, black-haired Cornish maid, entered, bearing a tray with an untouched cup of tea, a brown piece of ham on its plate, and a little covered dish of hot toast.

"Please, 'm, Miss Vine says she don't want no breakfast this morning."

The *Beloe* bottle dropped back into George Vine's pocket.

"Eh? My sister ill?" he said anxiously.

"No, sir; she seems quite well, but she was gashly cross with me, and said why didn't Miss Louie bring it up."

"Liza, I forbade you to use that foolish word—'gashly,'" said Louise, pouring out a fresh cup of tea, and changing it for the one cooling on the tray.

"Why don't you take up auntie's breakfast as you always do? You know she doesn't like it sent up."

Louise made no reply to her brother, but turned to Pradelle.

"You will excuse me for a few minutes, Mr Pradelle," she said as she rose.

"Excuse—you?" he replied with a peculiar smile; and, rising in turn he managed so badly as he hurried to the door to open it for Louise's passage with the tray, that he and Liza, bent on the same errand, came into collision.

"Thank you, Mr Pradelle," said Louise, quietly, as she passed out with the tray, and Liza gave him an indignant glance as she closed the door.

"Ha, ha! What a bungle!" cried Harry mockingly, as he helped himself to more ham.

George Vine was absorbed once more in the study of the *Beloe*.

"Never you mind, my lord the count," said Pradelle in an undertone; "I don't see that you get on so very well."

Harry winced.

"What are you going to do this morning?"

"Fish!"

"Humph! well to be you," said Harry, with a vicious bite at his bread, while his father was too much absorbed in his study even to hear. "You're going loafing about, and I've got to go and turn that grindstone."

"Which you can leave whenever you like," said Pradelle meaningly.

"Hold your tongue!" cried Harry roughly, as the door re-opened, and Louise, looking slightly flushed, again took her place at the table.

"Aunt poorly?" said Vine.

"Oh, no, papa; she is having her breakfast now."

"If you're too idle to take up auntie's breakfast, I'll take it," said Harry severely. "Don't send it up by that girl again."

"I shall always take it myself. Harry," said Louise quietly.

The breakfast was ended; George Vine went to his study to feed his sea-anemones on chopped whelk; Pradelle made an excuse about fishing lines, after reading plainly enough that his presence was unwelcome; and Harry stood with his hands in his pockets, looking on as his sister put away the tea-caddy.

"Will you not be late, Harry?"

"Perhaps," he said, ill-humouredly. "I shall be there as soon as old bottle nose, I daresay."

"How long is Mr Pradelle going to stay?"

"Long as I like."

There was a pause. Then Harry continued: "He's a friend of mine, a gentleman, and Aunt Marguerite likes him to stay."

"Yes," said Louise gravely. "Aunt Marguerite seems to like him."

"And so do you, only you're such a precious coquette."

Louise raised her eyebrows. This was news to her, but she said nothing.

"The more any one sees of Pradelle the more one likes him. Deal nicer fellow than that Scotch prig Leslie."

There was a slight flush on Louise Vine's face, but she did not speak, merely glanced at the clock.

"All right; I'm not going yet."

Then, changing his manner—

"Oh, Lou, you can't think what a life it is," he cried impetuously.

"Why, Harry, it ought to be a very pleasant one."

"What, with your nose over an account book, and every time you happen to look up, old Crampton staring at you as much as to say, 'Why don't you go on?'"

"Never mind, dear. Try and think that it is for your good."

"For my good!" he said with a mocking laugh.

"Yes, and to please father. Why, Harry, dear, is it not something to have a chance to redeem your character?"

"Redeem my grandmother! I've never lost it. Why, Lou, it's too bad. Here's father rich as a Jew, and Uncle Luke with no end of money."

"Has he, Harry?" said Louise thoughtfully. "Really I don't know."

"I'm sure he has—lots. A jolly old miser, and no one to leave it to; and I can't see then why I should be ground down to work like an errand boy."

"Don't make a sentimental grievance of it, dear, but go and do your duty like a man."

"If I do my duty like a man I shall go and try to recover the French estates which my father neglects."

"No, don't do that, dear; go and get my old school spelling-book and read the fable of the dog and the shadow."

"There you go, sneering again. You women can't understand a fellow. Here am I worried to death for money, and have to drudge as cld Van Heldre's clerk."

"Worried for money, Harry? What nonsense!"

"I am. You don't know. I say, Lou, dear."

"Now, Harry! you will be so late."

"I won't go at all if you don't listen to me. Look here; I want fifty pounds."

"What for?"

"Never mind. Will you lend it to me?"

"But what can you want with fifty pounds, Harry? You're not in debt?"

"You've got some saved up. Now, lend it to me, there's a good girl; I'll pay you again, honour bright."

"Harry, I've lent you money till I'm tired of lending, and you never do pay me back."

"But I will this time."

Louise shook her head.

"What, you don't believe me?"

"I believe you would pay me again if you had the money; but if I lent it you would spend it, and be as poor as ever in a month."

"Not this time, Lou. Lend it to me."

She shook her head.

"Then hang me if I don't go and ask Duncan Leslie."

"Harry! No; you would not degrade yourself to that."

"Will you lend it?"

"No."

"Then I will ask him. The poor fool will think it will please you, and lend it directly. I'll make it a hundred whilst I'm about it."

"Harry!"

"Too late now," he cried, and he hurried away.

"Oh!" ejaculated Louise, as she stood gazing after him with her cheeks burning. "No," she said, after a pause; "It was only a threat; he would not dare."

"Harry gone to his office?" said Vine, entering the room.

"Yes, dear."

"Mr Pradelle gone too?"

"Yes, dear; fishing, I think."

"Hum. Makes this house quite his home."

"Yes, papa! and do you think we are doing right?"

"Eh?" said Vine sharply, as he dragged his mind back from where it had gone under a tide-covered rock. "Oh, I see, about having that young man here. Well, Louie, it's like this: I don't want to draw the rein too tightly. Harry is at work now, and keeping to it. Van Heldre says his conduct is very fair. Harry likes Mr Pradelle, and they are old companions, so I feel disposed to wink at the intimacy, so long as our boy keeps to his business."

"Perhaps you are right, dear," said Louise.

"You don't like Mr Pradelle, my dear?"

"No, I do not."

"No fear of his robbing me of you, eh?"

"Oh, father!"

"That's right; that's right; and look here, as we're talking about that little thing which makes the world go round, please, understand this, and help me, my dear. There's to be no nonsense between Harry and Madelaine."

"Then you don't like Madelaine?"

"Eh? What? Not like her? Bless her! You've almost cause to be jealous, only you need not be, for I've room in my heart for both of you. I love her too well to let her be made uncomfortable by our family scape-grace. Dear me! I'm sure that it has."

"Have you lost anything, dear?"

"Yes, a glass stopper. Perhaps I left it in my room. Mustn't lose it; stoppers cost money."

"And here's some money of yours, father."

"Eh? Oh, that change."

"Twenty-five shillings."

"Put it on the chimney-piece, my dear; I'll take it presently. We will not be hard on Harry. Let him have his companion. We shall get him round by degrees. Ah, here comes some one to tempt you away."

In effect Madelaine was passing the window on her way to the front entrance; but Vine forgot all about his glass stopper for the moment, and threw open the glass door.

"Come in here, my dear," he said. "We were just talking about you."

"About me, Mr Vine? Whatever were you saying?"

"Slander of course, of course."

"My father desired to be kindly remembered, and I was to say, 'Very satisfactory so far.'"

"Very satisfactory so far?" said Vine, dreamily.

"He said you would know what it meant."

"To be sure—to be sure. Louie, my dear, I'm afraid your aunt is right. My brain is getting to be like that of a jelly fish."

He nodded laughingly and left the room.

"Did you meet Harry as you came?" said Louise, as soon as they were alone.

"Yes; but he kept on one side of the street, and I was on the other."

"Didn't he cross over to speak?"

"No; he couldn't see the Dutch fraülein—the Dutch doll."

"Oh, that's cruel, Maddy. I did not think my aunt's words could sting you."

"Well, sometimes I don't think they do, but at others they seem to rankle. But, look, isn't that Mr Pradelle coming?"

For answer Louise caught her friend's hand to hurry her out of the room before Pradelle entered.

Chapter Eleven
Aunt Marguerite studies a Comedy

That morning after breakfast Aunt Marguerite sat by her open window in her old-fashioned French *peignoir*.

She saw Pradelle go out, and she smiled and beamed as he turned to look up at her window, and raised his hat before proceeding down into the back lanes of the port, to inveigle an urchin into the task of obtaining for him a pot of ragworms for bait.

Soon after she saw her nephew go out, but he did not raise his head. On the contrary, he bent it down, and heaved up his shoulders like a wet sailor, as he went on to his office.

"Mon pauvre enfant!" she murmured, as she half-closed her eyes, and kissed the tips of the fingers. "Just wait a while, Henri, *mon enfant*, and all shall be well."

There was a lapse of time devoted to thought, and then Aunt Marguerite's eyes glistened with malice as she saw Madelaine approach.

"Pah!" she ejaculated softly. "This might be Amsterdam or the Boompjes. Wretched Dutch wench! How can George tolerate her presence here?"

Then Pradelle came back, but he did not look up this time, merely went to the door and entered, his eyes looking searchingly about as if in search of Louise.

Lastly, a couple of particularly unseamanlike men, dressed in shiny tarpaulin hats and pea-jackets, with earrings and very smooth pomatumy hair, came into sight. Each man carried a pack and a big stick, and as they drew near their eyes wandered over window and door in a particularly searching way.

They did not come to the front, but in a slouching, furtive way went past the front of the house, and round to the back, where the next minute there was a new tapping made by the knob of a stick on a door, and a moment later a buzzing murmur of voices arose.

Aunt Marguerite had nothing whatever to do, and the murmur interested her to the extent of making her rise, go across her room, and through a door at the back into her bed-chamber, where an open lattice window had a chair beneath, and the said window being just over the back entrance from whence the murmur came. Aunt Marguerite had nothing to do but go and sit down there unseen, and hear every word that was said.

"Yes," said the familiar voice of brown-faced, black-haired Liza; "they're beautiful, but I haven't got the money."

"That there red ribbon'd just soot you, my lass," said a deep voice, so fuzzy that it must have come from under a woollen jacket.

"Just look at that there hankychy, too," said another deep voice. "Did you ever see a better match?"

"Never," said the other deep voice emphatically.

"Yes, they're very lovely, but I ain't got the money. I let mother have all I had this week."

"Never mind the gashly money, my lass," said the first deep-voiced man huskily, "ain'tcher got nothing you can sell?"

Then arose a good deal of murmuring whisper, and Aunt Marguerite's lips became like a pale pink line drawn across the lower part of her face, and both her eyes were closely shut.

"Well, you wait," was the concluding sentence of the whispered trio, and then the door was heard to shut.

The click of a latch rose to where Aunt Marguerite sat, and then there was a trio once again—a whispered trio—ending with a little rustling, and the sound of heavy steps.

Then the door closed, and Liza, daughter of Poll Perrow, the fish-woman, who carried a heavy maund by the help of a strap across her forehead, hurried up to her bedroom, and threw herself upon her knees as she spread two or three yards of brilliant red ribbon on the bed, and tastefully placed beside the ribbon an orange silk kerchief, whose united colours made her dark eyes sparkle with delight.

The quick ringing of a bell put an end to the colour-worship, and Liza, with a hasty ejaculation, opened her box, thrust in her new treasures, dropped the lid, and locked it again before hurrying down to the dining-room, where she found her young mistress, her master, and Madelaine Van Heldre.

"There was some change on the chimney-piece, Liza," said Louise. "Did you see it?"

"No, miss."

"It is very strange. You are quite sure you did not take it, papa?"

"Quite, my dear."

"That will do, Liza."

The girl went out, looking scared.

"It is very strange," said Vine.

"Yes, dear; and it is a great trouble to me. This is the third time money has been missing lately. I don't like to suspect people, but one seems to be forced."

"But surely, Louie, dear, that poor girl would not take it."

"I have always tried to hope not, Maddy," said Louise sadly.

"You had better make a change."

"Send her away, father? How can I do that? How can I recommend her for another situation?"

"Ah! it's a puzzle—it's a puzzle," said Vine irritably. "One of the great difficulties of domestic service. I shall soon begin to think that your uncle Luke is right after all. He has no troubles, eh, Louise?"

She looked up in his face with a peculiar smile, but made no reply. Her father, however, seemed to read her look, and continued:

"Ah, well, I daresay you are right, my dear; we can't get away from trouble; and if we don't have one kind we have another. Get more than our share, though, in this house."

Louise smiled in his face, and the comical aspect of chagrin displayed resulted in a general laugh.

"Is one of the sea-anemones dead?"

"Yes, confound it! and it has poisoned the water, so that I'm afraid the rest will go."

"I think we can get over that trouble," said Louise, laughing. "It will be an excuse for a pleasant ramble with you."

"Yes," said Vine dryly, "but we shall not get over the trouble of the thief quite so well. I'm afraid these Perrows are a dishonest family. I'll speak to the girl."

"No, father, leave it to me."

"Very well, my child; but I think you ought to speak." The old man left the room, the bell was rung, and Liza summoned, when a scene of tears and protestations arose, resulting in a passionate declaration that Liza would tell her mother, that she would not stop in a house were she was going to be suspected, and that she had never taken anybody's money but her own.

"This is the third time that I have missed money, Liza, or I would not have spoken. If you took it, confess like a good girl, and we'll forgive you if you promise never to take anything of the kind again."

"I can't confess, miss, and won't confess," sobbed the girl. "Mother shall come and speak to you. I wouldn't do such a thing."

"Where did you get the money with which you bought the red ribbon and orange kerchief this morning, Liza?" said a voice at the door.

All started to see that Aunt Marguerite was there looking on, and apparently the recipient of all that had been said.

Liza stood with eyes dilated, and jaw dropped.

"Then you've been at my box," she suddenly exclaimed. "Ah, what a shame!"

"At your box, you wretched creature!" said Aunt Marguerite contemptuously. "Do you suppose I should go into your room?"

"You've been opening my box," said the girl again, more angrily; "and it's a shame."

"I saw her take them up to her room, Louise. My dear, she was buying them under my window, of some pedlar. You had better send her away."

Liza did not wait to be sent away from the room, but ran out sobbing, to hurry up-stairs to her bed-chamber, open her box, and see if the brilliant specimens of silken fabric were safe, and then cry over them till they were blotched with her tears.

"A bad family," said Aunt Marguerite. "I'm quite sure that girl stole my piece of fine lace, and gave it to that wretched woman your uncle Luke encourages."

"No, no, aunt, you lost that piece of lace one day when you were out."

"Nonsense, child! your memory is not good. Who is that with you? Oh, I see; Miss Van Heldre."

Aunt Marguerite, after suddenly becoming aware of the presence of Madelaine, made a most ceremonious curtsey, and then sailed out of the room.

"Louise must be forced to give up the companionship of that wretched Dutch girl," she said as she reached her own door, at which she paused to listen to Liza sobbing.

"I wonder what Miss Vine would have been like," thought Madelaine, "if she had married some good sensible man, and had a large family to well employ her mind?" Then she asked herself what kind of man she would have selected as possessing the necessary qualifications, and concluded that he should have been such a man as Duncan Leslie, and wondered whether he would marry her friend.

"Why, Madelaine," said Louise, breaking her chain of thought, "what are you thinking about?"

"Thinking about?" said the girl, starting, and colouring slightly. "Oh, I was thinking about Mr Leslie just then."

Chapter Twelve
Uncle Luke's Spare Cash

"Late again," said old Crampton, as Harry Vine entered the office.

"How I do hate the sight of that man's nose!" said the young man; and he stared hard, as if forced by some attraction.

The old clerk frowned, and felt annoyed. "I beg pardon," he said.

"Granted," said Harry, coolly. "I said I beg pardon, Mr Harry Vine."

"I heard you."

"But I thought you spoke."

"No," grumbled Harry. "I didn't speak."

"Then I will," said old Crampton merrily. "Good morning, Mr Harry Vine," and he rattled the big ruler by his desk.

"Eh? oh, yes, I see. Didn't say it as I came in. Good morning, Mr Crampton."

"Lesson for the proud young upstart in good behaviour," grumbled old Crampton.

"Mother him!" muttered Harry, as he took his place at his desk, opened a big account book Crampton placed before him, with some amounts to transfer from one that was smaller, and began writing.

But as he wrote, the figures seemed to join hands and dance before him; then his pen ceased to form others, and an imaginary picture painted itself on the delicately tinted blue paper with its red lines—a pleasant landscape in fair France with sunny hill-sides on which ranged in rows were carefully cultured vines. To the north and cast were softened bosky woods, and dominating all, one of those antique castellated châteaux with pepperbox towers and gilded vanes, such as he had seen in pictures or read of in some books.

"If I only had the money," thought Harry, as he entered a sum similar to that which Pradelle had named. "He knows all these things. He has good advice from friends, and if we won,—Hah!"

The château rose before his eyes again, bathed in sunshine. Then he pictured the terrace overlooking the vineyards—a grey old stone terrace, with many seats and sheltering trees, and along that terrace walked just such a maiden as Aunt Marguerite had described.

Scratch! Scratch! Scratch! Scratch! His pen and Crampton's pen; and he had no money, and Pradelle's project to borrow as he had suggested was absurd.

Ah, if he only had eighty-one pounds ten shillings and sixpence! the sum he now placed in neat figures in their appropriate columns.

Old Crampton tilted back his tall stool, swung himself round, and lowered himself to the ground. Then crossing the office, he went into Van Heldre's private room, and there was the rattle of a key, a creaking hinge, as an iron door was swung open; and directly after the old man returned.

Harry Vine could not see his hands, and he did not raise his eyes to watch the old clerk; but in the imagination which so readily pictured the château that was not in Spain, he seemed to see as he heard every movement of the fat white fingers, when a canvas bag was dumped down on the mahogany desk, the string untied, and a little heap of coins were poured out. Then followed the scratching of those coins upon the mahogany, as they were counted, ranged in little piles, and finally, after an entry had been checked, they were replaced in the bag, which the old man bore back into the safe in the private room.

"Fifty or a hundred pounds," said Harry to himself, as a curious sensation of heat came into his cheeks, to balance which there seemed to be a peculiarly cold thrill running up his spine, to the nape of his neck.

"Anybody at home?"

"Yes, sir; here we are hard at work."

Harry had looked up sharply to see Uncle Luke standing in the opening, a grim-looking grey figure in his old Norfolk jacket and straw hat, one hand resting on his heavy stick, the other carrying a battered fish-basket. The old man's face was in shadow, for the sunshine streamed in behind him; but there was plenty of light to display his grim, sardonic features, as, after a short nod to Crampton, he gazed from under his shaggy brows piercingly at his nephew.

"Well, quill-driver," he said sneeringly; "doing something useful at last?"

"Morning, uncle," said Harry shortly; and he muttered to himself, "I should like to throw the ledger at him."

"Hope he's a good boy, hey?"

"Oh, he's getting on, Mr Luke Vine—slowly," said Crampton unwillingly. "He'll do better by-and-by."

A sharp remark was on Harry's lips, but he checked it for a particular reason. Uncle Luke might have the money he wanted.

"Time he did," said the old man. "Look here, boy," he continued with galling, sneering tone in his voice. "Go and tell your master I want to see him."

Harry drew a long breath, and his teeth gritted together.

"I caught a splendid conger this morning," continued Uncle Luke, giving his basket a swing, "and I've brought your master half."

"My master!" muttered Harry.

"Like conger-pie, boy?"

"No," said Harry, shortly.

"More nice than wise," said Uncle Luke. "Always were. There, be quick. I want to see your master."

"To see my master," thought Harry, with a strange feeling of exasperation in his breast as he looked up at Crampton.

Crampton was looking up at him with eyes which said very clearly, "Well, why don't you go?"

"They'll make me an errand boy next," said the young man to himself, as after twisting his locket round and round like a firework, he swung himself down, "and want me to clean the knives and boots and shoes."

"Tell him I'm in a hurry," said Uncle Luke, as Harry reached the door which led into the private house along a passage built and covered with glass, by one side of what was originally a garden.

"Ah," said Uncle Luke, going closer to old Crampton's desk, and taking down from where it rested on two brass hooks the heavy ebony ruler. "Nice bit o' wood that."

"Yes, sir," said the old clerk, in the fidgety way of a workman who objects to have his tools touched.

"Pretty weighty," continued Uncle Luke, balancing it in his hand. "Give a man a pretty good topper that, eh?"

"Yes, Mr Luke Vine—I should like to give him one with it," thought Crampton.

"Do for a constable's staff, or to kill burglars, eh?"

"Capitally, sir."

"Hah! You don't get burglars here, though, do you?"

"No, sir; never had any yet."

"Good job, too," said Uncle Luke, putting the ruler back in its place, greatly to Crampton's relief. "Rather an awkward cub to lick into shape, my nephew, eh?"

"Rather, sir."

"Well, you must lick away, Crampton, not with that ruler though," he chuckled. "Time something was made of him—not a bad sort of boy; but spoiled."

"I shall do my best, Mr Luke Vine," said Crampton dryly; "but I must tell you candidly, sir, he's too much of the gentleman for us, and he feels it."

"Bah!"

"Not at all the sort of young man I should have selected for a clerk."

"Never mind; make the best of him."

"Mr Van Heldre is coming, sir," said Harry coldly, as he re-entered the office.

"Bah! I didn't tell you to bring him here. I want to go in there."

As Luke Vine spoke, he rose and moved to the door.

"Be a good boy," he said, turning with a peculiar smile at his nephew. "I daresay you'll get on."

"Oh!" muttered Harry, as he retook his place at his desk; "how I should like to tell you, Uncle Luke, just what I think."

The door closed behind the old man, who had nearly reached the end of the long passage, when he met Van Heldre.

"Ah, Luke Vine, I was just coming."

"Go back," said the visitor, making a stab at the merchant with his stick. "Brought you something. Where's Mrs Van Heldre?"

"In the breakfast-room. Come along."

Van Heldre clapped the old man on the shoulder, and led him into the room where Mrs Van Heldre was seated at work.

"Ah, Mr Luke Vine," she cried, "who'd have thought of seeing you?"

"Not you. How are you? Where's the girl?"

"Gone up to your brother's."

"Humph! to gad about and idle with Louie. I suppose. Here, I've brought you some fish. Caught it at daylight this morning. Ring for a dish."

"It's very kind and thoughtful of you, Luke Vine," said Mrs Van Heldre, with her pink face dimpling as she rang the bell, and then trotted to the door which she opened, and cried, "Bring in a large dish, Esther! I always like to save the servant's legs if I can," she continued as she returned to her seat, while Van Heldre stood with his hands in his pockets, waiting. He knew his visitor.

Just then a neat-looking maid-servant entered with a large blue dish, and stood holding it by the door, gazing at the quaint-looking old man, sitting with the basket between his legs, and his heavy stick resting across his knees.

"Put it down and go."

The girl placed the dish on the table hurriedly, and left the room.

"See if she has gone."

"No fear," said Van Heldre, obeying, to humour his visitor. "I don't think my servants listen at doors."

"Don't trust 'em, or anybody else," said Uncle Luke with a grim look, as he opened his basket wide. "Going to trust her?"

"Well, I'm sure, Mr Luke Vine!" cried Mrs Van Heldre, "I believe you learn up rude things to say."

"He can't help it," said Van Heldre laughing. "Yes," he continued, with a droll look at his wife, which took her frown away, "I think we'll trust her, Luke, my lad—as far as the fish is concerned."

"Eh! What?" said Uncle Luke, snatching his hands from his basket. "What do you mean?"

"That the dish is waiting for the bit of conger."

"Let it wait," said the old man snappishly. "You're too, clever Van—too clever. Look here; how are you getting on with that boy?"

"Oh, slowly. Rome was not built in a day."

"No," chuckled the old man, "no. Work away, and make him a useful member of society—like his aunt, eh Mrs Van."

"Useful!" cried Mrs Van. "Ah!"

Then old Luke chuckled and drew the fish from the basket.

"Fine one, ain't it?" he said.

"A beauty," cried Mrs Van Heldre ecstatically.

"Pshah!" ejaculated Uncle Luke. "Ma'am you don't care for it a bit; but there's more than I want, and it will help keep your servants."

"It would, Luke," said Van Heldre laughing as the fish was laid in the dish, "but they will not touch it. Well?"

"Eh? What do you mean by well?" snorted the old man with a suspicious look. "Out with it."

"Out with what?"

"What you have brought."

The two men gazed in each other's faces, the merchant looking half amused, the visitor annoyed; but his dry countenance softened into a smile and he turned to Mrs Van Heldre. "Artful!" he said dryly. "Don't you find him too cunning to get on with?"

"I should think not indeed," said Mrs Van Heldre indignantly.

"Might have known you'd say that," sneered Uncle Luke. "What a weak, foolish woman you are!"

"Yes, I am, thank goodness! I wish you'd have a little more of my foolishness in you, Mr Luke Vine. There, I beg your pardon. What have you got there, shrimps?"

"Yes," said Uncle Luke grimly, as he brought a brown paper parcel from the bottom of his basket, where it had lain under the wet piece of conger, whose stain was on the cover, "some nice crisp fresh shrimps. Here, Van—catch."

He threw the packet to his brother's old friend and comrade, by whom it was deftly caught, while Mrs Van Heldre looked on in a puzzled way.

"Put 'em in your safe till I find another investment for 'em. Came down by post this morning, and I don't like having 'em at home. Out fishing so much."

"How much is there?" said Van Heldre, opening the fishy brown paper, and taking therefrom sundry crisp new Bank of England notes.

"Five hundred and fifty," said Uncle Luke. "Count 'em over."

This was already being done, Van Heldre having moistened a finger, and begun handling the notes in regular bank-clerk style.

"All right; five fifty," he said.

"And he said they were shrimps," said Mrs Van Heldre.

"Eh? I did?" said Uncle Luke with a grim look and a twinkle of the eye. "Nonsense, it must have been you."

"Look here, Luke Vine," said Van Heldre; "is it any use to try and teach you at your time of life?"

"Not a bit; so don't try."

"But why expose yourself to all this trouble and risk? Why didn't your broker send you a cheque?"

"Because I wouldn't let him."

"Why not have a banking account, and do all your money transactions in an ordinary way?"

"Because I like to do things in my own way. I don't trust bankers, nor anybody else."

"Except my husband," said Mrs Van Heldre, beaming.

"Nonsense, ma'am, I don't trust him a bit. You do as I tell you, Van. Put those notes in your safe till I ask you for them. I had that bit of money in a company I doubted, so I sold out. I shall put it in something else soon."

"You're a queer fellow, Luke."

"Eh? I'm not the only one of my family, am I? What's to become of brother George when that young scape-grace has ruined him? What's to become of Louie, when we're all dead and buried, and out of all this worry and care? What's to become of my mad sister, who squandered her money on a French scamp, and made what she calls her heart bankrupt?"

"Nearly done questioning?" said Van Heldre, doubling the notes longwise.

"No, I haven't, and don't play with that money as if it was your wife's curl-papers." Van Heldre shrugged his shoulders, and placed the notes in his pocket.

"And as I was saying when your husband interrupted me so rudely, Mrs Van Heldre, what's to become of that boy by-and-by? Money's useful sometimes, though I don't want it myself."

"Ah! you needn't look at me, Mr Luke Vine. It's of no use for you to pretend to be a cynic with me."

"Never pretend anything, ma'am," said Uncle Luke rising; "and don't be rude. I did mean to come in and have some conger-pie to-night; now I won't."

"No, you didn't mean to do anything of the sort, Luke Vine," said Mrs Van Heldre tartly; "I know you better than that. If I've asked you to come and have a bit of dinner with us like a Christian once, I've asked you five hundred times, and one might just as well ask the hard rock."

"Just as well, ma'am; just as well. There, I'm going. Take care of that money, Van. I shall think out a decent investment one of these days."

"When you want it there it is," said Van Heldre quietly.

"Hope it will be. And now look here; I want to know a little more about the Count."

"The Count?" said Mrs Van Heldre.

"My nephew, ma'am. And I hope you feel highly honoured at having so distinguished a personage in your husband's service."

"What does he mean, dear?"

"Mean, ma'am? Why you know how his aunt has stuffed his head full of nonsense about French estates."

"Oh! that, and the old title," cried Mrs Van Heldre. "There, don't say any more about it, for if there is anything that worries me, it's all that talk about French descents."

"Why, hang it, ma'am, you don't think your husband is a Frenchman, and that my sister, who has made it all the study of her life, is wrong?"

"I don't know and I don't care whether my husband's a Dutchman or a double Dutchman by birth; all I know is he's a very good husband to me and a good father to his child; and I thank God, Mr Luke Vine, every night that things are just as they are; so that's all I've got to say."

"Tut—tut! tut—tut! This is all very dreadful, Van," said Uncle Luke, fastening his basket, and examining his old straw hat to see which was the best side to wear in front; "I can't stand any more of this. Here, do you want a bit of advice?"

"Yes, if it's good."

"Ah! I was forgetting about the Count. Keep the curb tight and keep him in use."

"I shall do both, Luke, for George's sake," said Van Heldre warmly.

"Good, lad!—I mean, more fool you!" said Uncle Luke, stumping out after ignoring extended hands and giving each a nod. "That's all."

He left the room, closing the door after him as loudly as he could without the shock being considered a bang; and directly after the front door was served in the same way, and they saw him pass the window.

"Odd fish, Luke," said Van Heldre.

"Odd! I sometimes think he's half mad."

"Nonsense, my dear; no more mad than Hamlet. Here he is again."

For the old man had come back, and was tapping the window-frame with his stick.

"What's the matter?" said Van Heldre, throwing open the window, when Uncle Luke thrust in the basket he carried and his stick, resting his arms on the window-sill.

"Don't keep that piece of conger in this hot room all the morning," he said pointing with his stick.

"Why, goodness me, Luke Vine, how can you talk like that?" cried Mrs Van Heldre indignantly.

"Easy enough, ma'am. Forgot my bit of advice," said Uncle Luke, speaking to his old friend, but talking at Mrs Van Heldre.

"What is it?"

"Send that girl of yours to a boarding school."

"Bless my heart, Luke Vine, what for?" cried the lady of the house. "Why, she finished two years ago."

"To keep her out of the way of George Vine's stupid boy, and because her mother's spoiling her. Morning."

Chapter Thirteen
To Reap the Wind

Late dinner was nearly over—at least late according to the ideas of the West-Country family, who sat down now directly Harry returned from his office work. Aunt Marguerite, after a week in her bedroom, had come down that day, the trouble with Liza exciting her; and that maiden had rather an unpleasant time as she waited at table, looking red-eyed and tearful, for Aunt Marguerite watched her with painful, basilisk-like stare all through the meal, the consequence being a series of mishaps and blunders, ending with the spilling of a glass dish of clotted cream.

With old-fashioned politeness, Aunt Marguerite tried to take Pradelle's attention from the accident.

"Are you going for a walk this evening, Mr Pradelle?"

"Yes," he said; "I daresay we shall smoke a cigar together after the labours of the day."

Aunt Marguerite sighed and looked pained.

"Tobacco! Yes, Mr Pradelle," she sighed; and she continued, in a low tone, "Do pray try to use your influence on poor Henri, to coax him from these bad pursuits."

Harry was talking cynically to his sister and Madelaine, who had been pressed by Vine to stay, a message having been sent down to the Van Heldres to that effect.

"The old story," he said to himself; and then, as he caught his sister's eye after she had gazed uneasily in the direction of her aunt; "yes, she's talking about me. Surely you don't mind that."

He, too, glanced now in Aunt Marguerite's direction, as Pradelle talked to her in a slow, impressive tone.

"Ah! no," said Aunt Marguerite, in a playful whisper, "nothing of the kind. A little boy and girl badinage in the past. Look for yourself, Mr Pradelle; there is no warmth there! My nephew cannot marry a Dutch doll."

"Lover's tiff, perhaps," said Pradelle.

"No, no," said Aunt Marguerite, shaking her head confidently. "Harry is a little wild and changeable, but he pays great heed to my words and advice. Still I want your help, Mr Pradelle. Human nature is weak. Harry must win back his French estates."

"Hear that, Louie?" said Harry, for Aunt Marguerite had slightly raised her voice.

"Yes, I heard," said Louise quietly.

"Aunt is sick of seeing her nephew engaged in a beggarly trade."

"For which Mr Henry Vine seems much too good," said Madelaine to herself, as she darted an indignant glance at the young man. "Oh, Harry, what a weak, foolish boy you are! I don't love you a bit. It was all a mistake."

"I hate business," continued Harry, as he encountered her eyes fixed upon him.

"Yes," said Louise coldly, as an angry feeling of annoyance shot through her on her friend's behalf. "Harry has no higher ambition than to lead a lap-dog kind of life in attendance upon Aunt Marguerite, and listening to her stories of middle-aged chivalry."

"Thank goodness?" said Harry, as they rose from the table. "No, no, aunt, I don't want any coffee. I should stifle if I stopped here much longer."

Aunt Marguerite frowned as the young man declined the invitation to come to her side.

"Only be called a lap-dog again. Here Vic, let's go and have a cigar down by the sea."

"Certainly," said Pradelle, smiling at all in turn.

"Yes, the room is warm," said the host, who had hardly spoken all through the dinner, being deep in thought upon one of his last discoveries.

Harry gave his sister a contemptuous look, which she returned with one half sorrowful, half pitying, from which he turned to glance at Madelaine, who was standing by her friend.

Aunt Marguerite smiled, for there was certainly the germ of an incurable rupture between these two, and she turned away her head to hide her triumph.

"She will never forgive him for speaking as he did about the beggarly trade." Then crossing with a graceful old-world carriage, she laid her hand on Madelaine's arm.

"Come into the drawing-room, my dear," she said, smiling, and to Madelaine it seemed that her bright, malicious-looking eyes were full of triumph. "You and I will have a good hard fight over genealogies, till you confess that I am right, and that your father and you have no claim to Huguenot descent."

"Oh, no, Miss Vine," said the girl, laughing, "my father must fight his own battle. As for me, I give up. Perhaps you are right, and I am only a Dutch girl after all."

"Oh, I wish we were back in London!" cried Harry as they strolled along towards the cliff walk.

"Ah, this is a dead-and-alive place, and no mistake," said Pradelle.

"Why don't you leave it then?" said Harry sulkily. "You are free."

"No, I am not. I don't like to see a friend going to the bad; and besides I have your aunt's commission to try and save you from sinking down into a miserable tradesman."

"Why don't you save me, then?"

"That's just like you. Look here, sink all cowardice, and go lip to the old boy like a Trojan. Plenty of money, hasn't he?"

"I suppose so. I don't know."

"He's sure to have."

"But he's such an old porcupine."

"Never mind. Suppose you do get a few pricks, what of that? Think of the future."

"But that venture must be all over now."

"What of that? You get the money and I can find a dozen ways of investing it. Look here, Harry, you profess to by my friend, and to have confidence in my judgment, and yet you won't trust me."

"I trusted you over several things, and see how I lost."

"Come, that's unkind. A man can't always win. There, never look back, look forward. Show some fight, and make one good plunge to get out of that miserable shop-boy sort of life."

"Come along then."

"You'll go up and ask him?"

"Yes, if you'll back me up."

"Back you up, lad? I should think I will. Lead on, I'll follow thee."

"We'll do it sensibly, then. If you speak before Uncle Luke in that theatrical way we shall come down faster then we go up."

"I'll talk to the old man like a young Solomon. And he shall say that never did youth choose more wisely for his friend than Harry Vine, otherwise Henri, Comte des Vignes."

"Look here," said Harry, peevishly—"'otherwise Comte des Vignes.' Why don't you say *alias* at once? Why, if the old man heard that, he'd want to know how long it was since you were in a police-court. Here, you'd better stay down here."

"All right, my dear fellow. Anything to help you on."

"No; I'd rather you came too."

There was a pause in a niche of the rocks, and then, after the scratching of a match, the young men went up the cliff path, smoking furiously, as they prepared themselves for the attack.

Chapter Fourteen
Diogenes in his Tub

Uncle Luke was in very good spirits. He had rid himself of his incubus, as he called the sum of money, and though he would not own it, he always felt better when he had had a little converse with his fellow-creatures. His lonely life was very miserable, and the more so that he insisted upon its being the highest form of happiness to exist in hermit fashion, as the old saints proved.

The desolate hut in its rocky niche looked miserable when he climbed up back on his return from Van Heldre's, so he stopped by the granite wall and smiled.

"Finest prospect in all Cornwall," he said, half aloud; "freshest air. Should like to blow up Leslie's works, though."

The door was locked, but it yielded to the heavy key which secured it against visitors, though they were very rare upon that rocky shelf.

He was the more surprised then, after his frugal mid-day meal, by a sharp rapping at the door, and on going he stared angrily at the two sturdy sailor-dressed pedlars, who were resting their packs on the low granite wall.

"Can we sell a bit o' bacco, or a pound o' tea, master?" said the man who had won over Liza to the purchase of his coloured silk.

"Bang!"

That was Uncle Luke's answer as the man spoke to him, and his fellow swept the interior of the cottage with one quick glance.

"Steal as soon as sell any day," grumbled Uncle Luke. "Tobacco and tea, indeed!"

Outside one of the men gave his companion a wink and a laugh, as he shouldered his pack, while the other chuckled and followed his example.

Meanwhile Uncle Luke had seated himself at his rough deal table, and written a long business letter to his lawyer in London.

This missive he read over twice, made an addition to the paragraph dealing most particularly with the mortgage on which he had been invited to lend, and then carefully folded the square post paper he used in old-fashioned letter shape, tucking one end into the other from objects of economy, so as to dispense with envelopes, but necessitating all the same the use of sealing-wax and a light.

However, it pleased him to think that he was saving, and he lit a very thin candle, took the stick of red wax from a drawer, a curious old-fashioned signet gold ring bearing the family crest, from a nail where it hung over the fireplace, and then sitting down as if to some very important piece of business, he burned his wax, laid on a liberal quantity, and then impressed the seal. This done, the ring was hung once more upon its nail, and the old man stood gazing at it and thinking. The next minute he took down the ring, and slipped it on one of his fingers, and worked it up and down, trying it on another finger, and then going back to the first.

"Used to fit too tightly," he said; "now one's fingers are little more than bone."

He held up the ring to the light, his white hand looking very thin and wasted, and the worn gold glistened and the old engraved blood-stone showed its design almost as clearly as when it was first cut.

"'Roy et Foy!'" muttered the old man, reading the motto beneath the crest. "Bit of vanity. Margaret asked where it was, last time I saw her. Let's see; I lost you twice, once when I wore you as I was fishing off the pier, and once on the black rock you slipped off my bony finger, and each time the sea washed you into a crack."

He smiled as he gazed at the ring, and there was a pleasant, handsome trace of what he had been as a young man in his refined features.

"Please the young dog—old family ring," he muttered. "Might sell it and make a pound. No, he may have it when I'm gone. Can't be so very long."

He hung the ring upon the nail once more, and spent the rest of the afternoon gazing out to sea, sometimes running over the past, but more often looking out for the glistening and flashing of the sea beneath where a flock of gulls were hovering over some shoal of fish.

It was quite evening when there was a staid, heavy step and the click of nailed boots, as the old fish-woman came toiling up the cliff path, her basket on her back, and the band which supported it across her brow.

"Any fish to sell, Master Vine?" she said in a sing-song tone. "I looked down the pier, but you weren't there."

"How could I be there when I'm up here, Poll Perrow?"

"Ah, to be sure; how could you?" said the old woman, trying to nod her head, but without performing the feat, on account of her basket. "Got any fish to sell?"

"No. Yes," said the old man.

"That's right. I want some to-night. Will you go and fetch it?"

"Yes. Stop there," said Uncle Luke sourly, as he saw a chance of making a few pence, and wondered whether he would get enough from his customer.

"Mind my sitting down inside, Master Luke Vine, sir? It's hot, and I'm tired; and it's a long way up here."

"Why do you come, then?"

"Wanted to say a few words to you about my gal when we've done our bit o' trade."

"Come in and sit down, then," said the old man gruffly. And his visitor slipped the leather band from her forehead, set her basket on the granite wall, and went into the kitchen-like room, wiping her brow as she seated herself in the old rush-bottomed chair.

"I'll fetch it here," said Uncle Luke, and he went round to the back, to return directly with the second half of the conger.

"There," said the old man eagerly, "how much for that?"

"Oh. I can't buy half a conger, Mr Luke Vine, sir; and I don't know as I'd have took it if it had been whole."

"Then be off, and don't come bothering me," grunted the old man snappishly.

"Don't be cross, master; you've no call to be. You never have no gashly troubles to worry you."

"No, nor don't mean to have. What's the matter now?"

"My gal!"

"Serve you right. No business to have married. You never saw me make such a fool of myself."

"No, master, never; but when you've got gals you must do your best for 'em."

"Humph! what's the matter?"

Poll Perrow looked slowly round the ill-furnished, untidy place.

"You want a woman here, Master Luke Vine, sir," she said at last.

"Don't talk nonsense!"

"It aren't nonsense, Master Luke Vine, and you know it. You want your bed made proper, and your washing done, and your place scrubbed. Now why don't you let my gal come up every morning to do these things?"

"Look here," said Uncle Luke, "what is it you mean?"

"She's got into a scrape at Mr Vine's, sir—something about some money being missing—and I suppose she'll have to come home, so I want to get her something to do."

"Oh, she isn't honest enough for my brother's house, but she's honest enough for mine."

"Oh, the gal's honest enough. It's all a mistake. But I can't afford to keep her at home, so, seeing as we'd had dealings together, I thought you'd oblige me and take her here."

"Seeing that we'd had dealings together!" grumbled Uncle Luke.

"Everything is so untidy like, sir," said the old fish-dealer, looking round. "Down at your brother's there's everything a gentleman could wish for, but as to your place—why, there; it's worse than mine."

"Look here, Poll Perrow," said the old eccentricity fiercely, "this is my place, and I do in it just as I like. I don't want your girl to come and tidy my place, and I don't want you to come and bother me, so be off. There's a letter; take it down and post it for me; and there's a penny for your trouble."

"Thank ye, master. Penny saved is a penny got; but Mr George Vine would have given me sixpence—I'm not sure he wouldn't have given me a shilling. Miss Louise would."

Uncle Luke was already pointing at the door, towards which the woman moved unwillingly.

"Let me come up to-morrow and ask you, Mr Luke, sir. Perhaps you'll be in a better temper then."

"Better temper!" he cried wrathfully. "I'm always in a better temper. Because I refuse to ruin myself by having your great, idle girl to eat me out of house and home. I'm not in a good temper, eh? There, be off! or I shall say something unpleasant."

"I'm a-going, sir. It's all because I wouldn't buy half a fish, as I should have had thrown on my hands, and been obliged to eat myself. Look here, sir," cried the woman, as she adjusted the strap of her basket, "if I buy the bit of fish will you take the poor gal then?"

"No!" cried Uncle Luke, slamming the door, as the woman stood with her basket once more upon her back.

"Humph!" exclaimed the old woman, as she thrust the penny in her pocket, and then hesitated as to where she should place the letter.

While she was considering, the little window was opened and Uncle Luke's head appeared.

"Mind you don't lose that letter."

"Never you fear about that," said the old woman; and as if from a bright inspiration she pitched it over her head into her basket, and then trudged away.

"She'll lose that letter as sure as fate," grunted Uncle Luke. "Well, there's nothing in it to mind. Now I suppose I can have a little peace, and—who's this?"

He leaned a little farther out of his window, so as to bring a curve of the cliff path well into view.

"My beautiful nephew and that parasite. Going up to Leslie, I suppose—to smoke. Waste and debauchery—smoking."

He shut the window sharply, and settled himself down with his back to it, determined not to see his nephew pass; but five minutes later there was a sharp rapping at the door.

"Uncle Luke! Uncle!"

The old man made no reply.

"Here, Uncle Luke. I know you're at home; the old woman said so."

"Hang that old woman!" grumbled Uncle Luke; and in response to a fresh call he rose, and opened his door with a snatch.

"Now, then, what is it? I'm just going to bed."

"Bed at this time of the day?" cried Harry cheerfully. "Why you couldn't go to sleep if you did go."

"Why not?" snapped the old man; "you can in the mornings—over the ledger."

Harry winced, but he turned off the malicious remark with a laugh.

"Uncle loves his joke, Pradelle," he said. "Come, uncle, I don't often visit you; ask us in."

"No, you don't often visit me, Harry," said the old man, looking at him searchingly; "and when you do come it's because you want something."

Harry winced again, for the old man's words cut deeply.

"Oh, nonsense, uncle! Pradelle and I were having a stroll, and we thought we'd drop in here and smoke a cigar with you."

"Very kind," said the old man, looking meaningly from one to the other. "Missed meeting the girls, or have they snubbed you and sent you about your business?"

"Have a cigar, uncle?" said Harry, holding out his case. "I tell you we came on purpose to see you."

"Humph!" said Uncle Luke, taking the handsome morocco cigar case, and turning it over and over with great interest. "How much did that cost?"

"Don't remember now; fifteen shillings I think."

"Ah," said Uncle Luke, pressing the snap and opening it. "One, two, three, four; how much do these cigars cost?"

"Only fourpence, uncle; can't afford better ones."

"And a cigar lasts—how long?"

"Oh, I make one last three-quarters of an hour, because I smoke very slowly. Try one."

"No, thankye; can't afford such luxuries, my boy," said the old man, shutting the case with a snap, and returning it. "That case and the cigars there cost nearly a pound. Your income must be rising fast."

Harry and Pradelle exchanged glances. The reception did not promise well for a loan.

"Cigar does you good sometimes."

"Harry," said the old man, laughing and pointing at case.

"What's the matter, uncle?" said Harry eagerly; "want one?"

"No, no. Why didn't you have it put on there?"

"What?"

"Crest and motto, and your title—Comte des Vignes. You might lose it, and then people would know where to take it."

"Don't chaff a fellow, uncle," said Harry, colouring. "Here, we may come and sit down, mayn't we?"

"Oh, certainly, if your friend will condescend to take a seat in my homely place."

"Only too happy, Mr Luke Vine."

"Are you now? Shouldn't have thought it," sneered the old man. "No wine to offer you, sir; no brandy and soda; that's the stuff young men drink now, isn't it?"

"Don't name it, my dear sir; don't name it," said Pradelle, with an attempt at heartiness that made the old man half close his eyes. "Harry and I only came up for a stroll. Besides we've just dined."

"Have you? That's a good job, because I've only a bit of conger in the house, and that isn't cooked. Come in and sit down, sir. You, Harry; you'll have to sit down on that old oak chest."

"Anywhere will do for me, uncle. May we smoke?"

"Oh, yes, as fast as you like; it's too slow a poison for you to die up here."

"Hope so," said Harry, whose mission and the climb had made him very warm.

"Now, then," said Uncle Luke, fixing his eyes on Pradelle—like gimlets, as that gentleman observed on the way back; "what is it?"

"Eh? I beg pardon; the business here is Harry's."

"Be fair, Vic," said Harry, shortly; "the business appertains to both."

"Does it really?" said Uncle Luke, with a mock display of interest.

"Yes, uncle," said the nephew, uneasily, as he sat twiddling the gold locket attached to his chain, and his voice sounded husky: "it relates to both."

"Really!" said Uncle Luke, with provoking solemnity, as he looked from one to the other. "Well, I was young myself once. Now, look here; can I make a shrewd guess at what you want?"

"I'll be bound to say you could, sir," said Pradelle, in despite of an angry look from Harry, who knew his uncle better, and foresaw a trap.

"Then I'll guess," said the old man, smiling pleasantly; "you want some money."

"Yes, uncle, you're right," said Harry, as cautiously as a fencer preparing for a thrust from an expert handler of the foils.

"Hah; I thought I was. Well, young men always were so. Want a little money to spend, eh?"

"Well, uncle, I—"

"Wait a minute, my boy," said the old man, seriously; "let me see. I don't want to disappoint you and your friend as you've come all this way. Your father wouldn't let you have any, I suppose?"

"Haven't asked him, sir."

"That's right, Harry," said the old man earnestly; "don't, my boy, don't. George always was close with his money. Well, I'll see what I can do How much do you want to spend—a shilling?"

"Hang it all, uncle!" cried Harry angrily, and nearly tearing off his locket, "don't talk to me as if I were a little boy. I want a hundred pounds."

"Yes, sir, a hundred pounds," said Pradelle.

"A hundred, eh? A hundred pounds. Do you, now?" said Uncle Luke, without seeming in the slightest degree surprised.

"The fact is, uncle, my friend Pradelle here is always hearing of openings for making a little money by speculations, and we have a chance now that would make large returns for our venture."

"Hum! hah!" ejaculated Uncle Luke, as he looked at Pradelle in a quiet, almost appealing way. "Let me see, Mr Pradelle. You are a man of property, are you not?"

"Well, sir, hardly that," said Pradelle nonchalantly, and he rose, placed his elbows on the rough chimney-piece, and leaned back with his legs crossed as he looked down at Uncle Luke. "My little bit of an estate brings me in a very small income."

"Estate here?"

"No, no; in France, near Marseilles."

"That's awkward; a long way off."

"Go on," said Pradelle with his eyes, as he glanced at Harry.

"No good. Making fun of us," said Harry's return look; and the old man's eyes glistened.

"Hundred pounds. Speculation, of course?"

"Hardly fair to call it speculation, it is so safe," said Pradelle, in face of a frown from his friend.

"Hum! A hundred pounds—a hundred pounds," said Uncle Luke thoughtfully. "It's a good deal of money."

"Oh, dear me, no, sir," said Pradelle. "In business matters a mere trifle."

"Ah! you see I'm not a business man. Why don't you lend it to my nephew, Mr Pradelle?"

"I—I'm—well—er—really, I—The fact is, sir, every shilling I have is locked up."

"Then I should advise you to lose the key, Mr Pradelle," chuckled the old man, "or you may be tempted to spend it."

"You're playing with us, uncle," cried Harry. "Look here, will you lend me a hundred? I promise you faithfully I'll pay it to you back."

"Oh! of course, of course, my dear boy."

"Then you'll lend it to me."

"Lend you a hundred? My dear boy, I haven't a hundred pounds to lend you. And see how happy I am without!"

"Well, then, fifty, uncle. I'll make that do."

"Come, I like that, Harry," cried the old man, fixing Pradelle with his eye, "There's something frank and generous about it. It's brave, too; isn't it, sir?"

"Yes, sir. Harry's as frank and good-hearted a lad as ever stepped."

"Thank you, Mr Pradelle. It's very good of you to say so."

"Come along, Vic," said Harry.

"Don't hurry, my dear boy. So you have an estate in France, have you, Mr Pradelle?"

"Yes, sir."

"Humph; so has Harry—at least he will have some day, I suppose. Yes, he is going to get it out of the usurper's hands—usurper is the word, isn't it, Harry?"

Harry gave a kick out with one leg.

"Yes, usurper is the word. He's going to get the estate some day, Mr Pradelle; and then he is going to be a count. Of course he will have to give up being Mr Van Heldre's clerk then."

"Look here, uncle," cried the young man hotly; "if you will not lend me the money, you needn't insult me before my friend."

"Insult you, my dear boy? Not I. What a peppery fellow you are! Now your aunt will tell you that this is your fine old French aristocratic blood effervescing; but it can't be good for you."

"Come along, Vic," said Harry.

"Oh, of course," said Pradelle. "I'm sorry, though. Fifty pounds isn't much, sir; perhaps you'll think it over."

"Eh? think it over. Of course I shall. Sorry I can't oblige you, gentlemen. Good-evening."

"Grinning at us all the time—a miserable old miser!" said Harry, as they began to walk back. "He'd have done it if you hadn't made such a mess of it, Vic, with your free-and-easy way."

"It's precious vexatious, Harry; but take care, or you'll sling that locket out to sea," said Pradelle, after they had been walking for about ten minutes. "You'll have to think about my proposal. You can't go on like this."

"No," said Harry fiercely; "I can't go on like this, and I'll have the money somehow."

"Bravo! That's spoken like a man who means business. Harry, if you keep to that tone, we shall make a huge fortune a-piece. How will you get the money?"

"I'll ask Duncan Leslie for it. He can't refuse me. I should like to see him say 'No.' He must and he shall."

"Then have a hundred, dear lad. Don't be content with fifty."

"I will not, you may depend upon that," cried Harry, "and—"

He stopped short, and turned white, then red, and took half-a-dozen strides forward towards where Madelaine Van Heldre was seated upon one of the stone resting-places in a niche in the cliff—the very one where Duncan Leslie had had his unpleasant conversation with Aunt Marguerite.

The presence of his sister's companion, in spite of their being slightly at odds, might have been considered pleasant to Harry Vine; and at any other time it would have been, but in this instance, she was bending slightly forward, and listening to Duncan Leslie, who was standing with his back to the young men.

Only a minute before, and Harry Vine had determined that with the power given by Leslie's evident attachment to his sister, he would make that gentleman open his cash-box, or write a cheque on the Penzance bank for a hundred pounds.

The scene before him altered Harry Vine's ideas, and sent the blood surging up to his brain.

He stepped right up to Madelaine, giving Leslie a furious glance as that gentleman turned, and without the slightest preface, exclaimed—

"Look here, Madelaine, it's time you were at home. Come along with me."

Madelaine flushed as she rose; and her lips parted as if to speak, but Leslie interposed.

"Excuse me, Miss Van Heldre, I do not think you need reply to such a remark as that."

"Who are you!" roared Harry, bursting into a fit of passion that was schoolboy-like in its heat and folly. "Say another word, sir, and I'll pitch you off the cliff into the sea."

"Here, steady, old fellow, steady!" whispered Pradelle; and he laid his hand on his companion's arm.

"You mind your own business, Vic; and as for you—"

He stopped, for he could say no more. Leslie had quite ignored his presence, turning his back and offering his arm to Madelaine.

"Shall I walk home with you, Miss Van Heldre?" he said.

For answer, and without so much as looking at Harry Vine, Madelaine took the offered arm, and Pradelle tightened his hold as the couple walked away.

The grasp was needless, for Harry's rage was evaporating fast, and giving place to a desolate sensation of despair.

"Look here," said Pradelle; "you've kicked that over. You can't ask him now."

"No," said Harry, gazing at the departing figures, and trying to call up something about the fair daughters of France; "no, I can't ask him now."

"Then look here, old fellow, I can't stand by and see you thrown over by everybody like this. You know what your prospects are on your own relative's showing, not mine; and you know what can be done if we have the money. You are not fit for this place, and I say you shall get out of it. Now then, you know how it can be done. Just a loan for a few weeks. Will you, or will you not?" Harry turned upon him a face that was ghastly pale. "But if," he whispered hoarsely, "if we should fail?"

"Fail? You shan't fail."

"One hundred," said Harry, hoarsely. "Well, I suppose so. We'll make that do. Now then, I'm not going to waste time. Is it yes or no?"

Harry Vine felt a peculiar humming in the head, his mouth was hot and dry, and his lips felt parched. He looked Pradelle in the face, as if pleading to be let off; but there was only a cunning, insistent smile to meet him there, and once more the question came in a sharp whisper, "Yes or no?"

"Yes," said Harry; and as soon as he had said that word, it was as if a black cloud had gathered about his life.

Chapter Fifteen
My Aunt's Bête Noire

Duncan Leslie was a sturdy, manly young fellow in his way, but he had arrived at a weak period. He thought over his position, and what life would become had he a wife at home he really loved; and in spite of various displays of reserve, and the sneers, hints, and lastly the plain declaration that Louise was to marry some French gentleman of good family and position, Duncan found himself declaring that his ideas were folly one hour, and the next he was vowing that he would not give up, but that he would win in spite of all the Frenchmen on the face of the earth.

"I must have a walk," he used to say. "If I stop poring over books now, I shall be quite thick-headed to-morrow. A man must study his health."

So Duncan Leslie studied his health, and started off that evening in a different direction to the Vines'; and then, in spite of himself, began to make a curve, one which grew smaller and smaller as he walked thoughtfully on.

"I don't see why I should not call," he said to himself. "There's no harm in that. Wish I had found some curious sea-anemone; I could go and ask the old man what it was—and have her sweet clear eyes reading me through and through. I should feel that I had lowered myself in her sight."

"No," he said, emphatically; "I'll be straightforward and manly over it if I can."

"Hang that old woman! She doesn't like me. There's a peculiarly malicious look in her eyes whenever we meet. Sneering fashion, something like her old brother, only he seems honest and she does not. I'd give something to know whether Louise cares for that French fellow. If she doesn't, why should she be condemned to a life of misery? Could I make her any happier?"

"I'll go home now."

"No, I—I will not; I'll call."

These questions had been scattered over Duncan Leslie's walk, and the making up of his mind displayed in the last words was three-quarters of an hour after the first.

"I'm no better than a weak boy," he said, as he strode along manfully now. "I make mountains of molehills. What can be more natural and neighbourly than for me to drop in, as I am going to do, for a chat with old Vine?"

There was still that peculiar feeling of consciousness, though, to trouble him, as he knocked, and was admitted by Liza, whose eyelids were nearly as red as the ribbon she had bought.

The next minute he was in the pleasant homely drawing-room, feeling a glow of love and pride, and ready to do battle with any de Ligny in France for the possession of the prize whose soft warm hand rested for a few moments in his.

"Ah, Miss Van Heldre," he said, as he shook hands with her in turn, and his face lit up and a feeling of satisfaction thrilled him, for there was something in matter-of-fact Madelaine that gave him confidence.

Aunt Marguerite's eyes twinkled with satisfaction, as she saw the cordial greeting, and built up a future of her own materials.

"Miss Marguerite," said the young man ceremoniously, as he touched the extended hand, manipulated so that he should only grasp the tips; and, as he saluted, Leslie could not help thinking philosophically upon the different sensations following the touch of a hand.

A growing chill was coming over the visit, and Leslie was beginning to feel as awkward as a sturdy well-grown young tree might, if suddenly transplanted from a warm corner to a situation facing an iceberg, when the old naturalist handed a chair for his visitor.

"Glad to see you, Leslie," he said; "sit down."

"You will take some tea, Mr Leslie?"

Hah! The moment before the young man had felt ready to beat an ignominious retreat, but as soon as the voice of Louise Vine rang in his ears with that simple homely question, he looked up manfully, declared that he would take some tea, and in spite of himself glanced at Aunt Marguerite's tightening lips, his eyes seeming to say, "Now, then, march out a brigade of de Lignys if you like."

"And sugar, Mr Leslie?"

"And sugar," he said, for he was ready to accept any sweets she would give.

Then he took the cup of tea, looked in the eyes that met his very frankly and pleasantly, and then his own rested upon a quaint-looking cornelian locket, which was evidently French.

There was nothing to an ordinary looker-on in that piece of jewellery, but somehow it troubled Duncan Leslie; and as he turned to speak to Aunt Marguerite, he felt that she had read his thoughts, and her lips had relaxed into a smile.

"Well, George, if you do not mind Mr Leslie hearing, I do not," said Aunt Marguerite. "I must reiterate that the poor boy is growing every day more despondent and unhappy."

"Nonsense, Margaret!"

"Ah, you may say nonsense, my good brother, but I understand his nature better that you. Yes, my dear," she continued, "such a trade as that carried on by Mr Van Heldre is not a suitable avocation for your son."

"Hah!" sighed Vine.

"Now, you are a tradesman, Mr Leslie—" continued Aunt Marguerite.

"Eh? I, a tradesman?" said Leslie, looking at her wonderingly. "Yes, of course; I suppose so; I trade in copper and tin."

"Yes, a tradesman, Mr Leslie; but you have your perceptions, you have seen, and you know my nephew. Now, answer me honestly, is Mr Van Heldre's business suitable to a young man with such an ancestry as Henri's?"

Louise watched him wonderingly, and her lips parted as she hung upon his words.

"Well, really, madam," he began.

"Ah," she said, "you shrink. His French ancestors would have scorned such a pursuit."

"Oh, no," said Leslie, "I do not shrink; and as to that, I think it would have been very stupid of his French ancestors. Trading in tin is a very ancient and honourable business. Let me see, it was the Phoenicians, was it not, who used to come to our ports for the metal in question. They were not above trading in tin and Tyrian dye."

Aunt Marguerite turned up her eyes.

"And a metal is a metal. For my part, it seems quite as good a pursuit to trade in tin as in silver or gold."

Aunt Marguerite gave the young man a pitying, contemptuous look, which made Louise bite her lip.

"Aunt, dear," she said hurriedly, "let me give you some more tea."

"I was not discussing tea, my dear, but your brother's future; and pray, my dear child," she continued, turning suddenly upon Madelaine with an irritating smile, "pray do not think I am disparaging your worthy father and his business affairs."

"Oh, no, Miss Vine."

"Miss *Marguerite* Vine, my child, if you will be so good. Oh, by the way, has your father heard any news of his ship?"

"Not yet, Miss Marguerite," said Madelaine quietly.

"Dear me, I am very sorry. It would be so serious a loss for him, Mr Leslie, if the ship did not come safe to port."

"Yes, of course," said Leslie; "but I should suppose, Miss Van Heldre, that your father is well insured."

"Yes," said Madelaine quietly.

"There, never mind about Van Heldre's ship," said Vine pleasantly. "Don't croak like a Cassandra, Margaret; and as to Harry, a year or two in a good solid business will not do him any harm, eh, Leslie?"

"I should say it would do him a world of good."

"My nephew is not to be judged in the same light as a young man who is to be brought up as a tradesman," said Aunt Marguerite, with dignify.

"Only a tradesman's son, my dear."

"The descendant of a long line of ennobled gentry, George; a fact you always will forget," said Aunt Marguerite, rising and leaving the room, giving Leslie, who opened the door, a *menuet de la cour* curtsey on the threshold, and then rustling across the hall.

Her brother took it all as a matter of course. Once that Marguerite had ceased speaking the matter dropped, to make way for something far more important in the naturalist's eyes—the contents of one of his glass aquaria; but Louise, to remove the cloud her aunt had left behind, hastily kept the ball rolling.

"Don't think any more about aunt's remarks, Madelaine. Harry is a good fellow, but he would be discontented anywhere sometimes."

"I do not think he would be discontented now," she replied, "if his aunt would leave him alone."

"It is very foolish of him to think of what she says."

"Of course it is irksome to him at first," continued Madelaine; "but my father is not exacting. It is the hours at the desk that trouble your brother most."

"I wish I could see him contented," sighed Louise. "I'd give anything to see him settle down."

A very simple wish, which went right to Duncan Leslie's heart, and set him thinking so deeply that for the rest of his visit he was silent, and almost constrained—a state which Madelaine noted as she rose.

"Must you go so soon, dear!" said Louise consciously, for a terrible thought crossed her mind, and sent the blood surging to her cheeks—Madelaine was scheming to leave her and the visitor alone.

"Yes; they will be expecting me back," said Madelaine smiling, as she grasped her friend's thoughts; and then to herself, "Oh, you stupid fellow!"

For Leslie rose at once.

"And I must be going too. Let's see, I am walking your way, Miss Van Heldre. May I see you home?"

"I—"

"Yes, do, Mr Leslie," said Louise quietly.

"Ah! I will," he said hastily. "I want a chat with your father, too."

Madelaine would have avoided the escort, but she could only have done this at the expense of making a fuss; so merely said "Very well;" and went off with Louise to put on her hat and mantle, leaving Leslie alone with his host, who was seated by the window with a watchmaker's glass in his eye, making use of the remaining light for the study of some wonderful marine form.

"She would give anything to see her brother settled down," said Leslie to himself, over and over again. "Well why not?"

Five minutes later he and Madelaine were going along the main street, with Louise watching them from behind her father's chair, and wondering why she did not feel so happy as she did half an hour before; and Aunt Marguerite gazing from her open window.

"Ah!" said the old lady; "that's better. Birds of a feather do flock together, after all."

But the flocking pair had no such thoughts as those with which they were given credit, for directly they were outside, Duncan Leslie set Madelaine's heart beating by his first words.

"Look here," he said, "I want to take you into my counsel, Miss Van Heldre, because you have so much sound common sense."

"Is that meant for a compliment, Mr Leslie?"

"No; I never pay compliments. Look here," he said bluntly, "you take an interest in Harry Vine."

Madelaine was silent.

"That means yes," said Leslie. "Now, to be perfectly plain with you, Miss Van Heldre, so do I; and I want to serve him if I can."

"Yes?" said Madelaine, growing more deeply interested.

"Yes, it is—as the sailors say. Now it's very plain that he is not contented where he is."

"I'm afraid not."

"What do you say to this—I will not be a sham—I want to serve him for reasons which I dare say you guess; reasons of which I am not in the least ashamed. Now what do you think of this? How would he be with me?"

Madelaine flushed with pleasure.

"I cannot say. Is this a sudden resolve?"

"Quite. I never thought of such a thing till I went there."

"Then take time to think it over. Mr Leslie."

"Good advice; but it is a thing that requires very little thought. I cannot say what arrangements I should make—that would require consideration, but I should not tie him to a desk. He would have the overlooking of a lot of men, and I should try to make him as happy as I could."

"Oh, Mr Leslie!" said Madelaine, rather excitedly.

"Pray do not think I am slighting your father, or looking down upon what he has done, which, speaking as a blunt man, is very self-sacrificing."

"As it would be on your part."

"On mine? Oh, no," said Leslie frankly. "When a man has such an *arrière pensée* as I have, there is no self-sacrifice. There, you see, I am perfectly plain."

"And I esteem you all the more for it."

The conversation extended, and in quite a long discussion everything was forgotten but the subject in hand, till Leslie said:—

"There, you had better sit down and rest for a few minutes. You are quite out of breath."

Madelaine looked startled, for she had been so intent upon their conversation that she had not heeded their going up the cliff walk.

"Sit down," said Leslie; and she obeyed. "Get your breath, and we'll walk back to your house together; but what do you think of it all?"

"I cannot help thinking that it would for many reasons be better."

"So do I," said Leslie, "in spite of the risk."

"Risk?"

"Yes. Suppose I get into an imbroglio with Master Harry? He's as peppery as can be. How then?"

"You will be firm and forbearing," said Madelaine gravely. "I have no fear."

"Well, I have. I know myself better than you know me," said Leslie, placing a foot on the seat and resting his arm on his knee, as he spoke thoughtfully. "I am a very hot-headed kind of Highlander by descent, and there's no knowing what might happen. Now one more question. Shall I open fire on your father to-night?"

"That requires more consideration," said Madelaine. "We will talk that over as we go back. Here is Harry," she said quickly, as that gentleman suddenly burst upon them; and the walk back to Van Heldre's was accomplished without the discussion.

"I'm afraid I've made a very great mistake, Miss Van Heldre," said Leslie, as they neared the house.

"Don't say that," she replied. "It was most unfortunate."

"But you will soon set that right?" he added, after a pause.

"I don't know," said Madelaine quietly. "You will come in?"

"No; not this evening. We had better both have a grand think before anything is said."

"Yes," said Madelaine; and they parted at the door—to think.

"Why, John," said Mrs Van Heldre, turning from the window to gaze in her husband's face, "did you see that?"

"Yes," said Van Heldre shortly; "quite plainly."

"But what does it mean?"

"Human nature."

"But I thought, dear—"

"So did I, and now I think quite differently."

"Well, really, I must speak to Madelaine; it is so—"

"Silence!" said Van Heldre sternly. "Madelaine is not a child now. Wait, wife, and she will speak to us."

Chapter Sixteen
In a West Coast Gale

"That project is knocked over as if it were a card house," said Duncan Leslie, as he reached home, and sat thinking of Louise and her brother.

He looked out to see that in a very short time the total aspect of the sea had changed. The sky had become overcast, and in the dim light the white horses of the Atlantic were displaying their manes.

"Very awkward run for the harbour to-night," he said as he returned to his seat. "Can't be pleasant to be a shipowner. I wonder whether Miss Marguerite Vine would consider that a more honourable way of making money?"

"Yes, a tradesman, I suppose. Well, why not? Better than being a descendant of some feudal gentleman whose sole idea of right was might."

"My word!" he exclaimed; "what a sudden gale to have sprung up. Heavy consumption of coal in the furnaces to-night. How this wind will make them roar."

He faced round to the window and sat listening as the wind shrieked, and howled, and beat at the panes, every now and then sending the raindrops pattering almost as loudly as hail. "Hope it will not blow down my chimney on the top yonder. Hah! I ought to be glad that I have no ship to trouble me on a night like this."

"No," he said firmly just as the wind had hurled itself with redoubled fury against the house; "no, she does not give me a second thought. But I take heart of grace, for I can feel that she has never had that gentle little heart troubled by such thoughts. The Frenchman has not won her, and he never shall if I can help it. It's a fair race for both of us, and only one can win."

"My word! What a night!"

He walked to the window and looked out at the sombre sky, and listened to the roar of the rumbling billows before closing his casement and ringing.

"Is all fastened?" he said to the servant. "You need not sit up. I don't believe a dog would be out to-night, let alone a human being."

He was wrong; for just as he spoke a dark figure encased in oilskins was sturdily making its way down the cliff path to the town. It was hard work and in places on the exposed cliff-side even dangerous, for the wind seemed to pounce upon the figure and try to tear it off; but after a few moments' pause the walk was continued, the town reached, and the wind-swept street traversed without a soul being passed.

The figure passed on by the wharves and warehouses, and sheltered now from the wind made good way till, some distance ahead, a door was opened, a broad patch of light shone out on the wet cobble stones, Crampton's voice said "Good night," and the figure drew back into a deep doorway, and waited.

The old clerk had been to the principal inn, where, once a week, he visited his club, and drank one glass of Hollands and water, and smoked one pipe, talking mostly to one friend, to whom if urged he would relate one old story.

This was his one dissipation; and afterwards he performed one regular duty which took him close up to the watching figure, which remained there almost breathless till Crampton had performed his regular duty and gone home.

It was ten minutes or a quarter of an hour before he passed that watching figure, which seemed to have sunk away in the darkness that grew more dense as the gale increased.

Morning at last, a slowly breaking dawn, and with it the various sea-going men slowly leaving their homes, to direct their steps in a long procession towards one point, where the high cliff face formed a shelter from the south-west wind, and the great billows which rolled heavily in beneath the leaden sky. These came on with the regularity of machinery, to charge the cliffs at which they leaped with a hiss and a roar, and a boom like thunder, followed by a peculiar rattling, grumbling sound, as if the peal of thunder had been broken up into heavy pieces which were rolling over each other back toward the sea.

They were not pieces of thunder but huge boulders, which had been rolled over and over for generations to batter the cliffs, and then fall back down an inclined plane.

Quite a crowd had gathered on the broad, glistening patch of rugged granite, soon as the day broke, and this crowd was ever augmenting, till quite a phalanx of oilskin coats and tarpaulin hats presented its face to the thundering sea, while men shouted to each other, and swept the lead-coloured horizon with heavy glasses, or the naked hand-shaded eye, in search of some vessel trying to make the harbour, or in distress.

"She bites this morning," said one old fisherman, shaking the spray from his dripping face, after looking round the corner of a mass of sheltering rock.

"Ay, mate, and it aren't in me to tell you how glad I am my boat's up the harbour with her nose fast to a buoy," said another.

"There'll be widders and orphans in some ports 'fore nightfall."

"And thank the Lord that won't be in Hakemouth."

"I dunno so much about that," growled a heavy-looking man, with a fringe of white hair round his face. "Every boat that sails out of this harbour aren't in port."

"That it is. Why, what's yer thinking about?"

"'Bout Van Heldre's brig, my lad."

"Ah," chorused half-a-dozen voices, "we didn't think o' she."

"Been doo days and days," said the white-fringed old fisherman; "and if she's out yonder, I say, Lord ha' mercy on 'em all, Amen."

"Not had such a storm this time o' year since the Cape mail were wrecked off the Long Chain."

"Ah, and that warn't so bad as this. Bound to say the brig has put into Mount's Bay."

"And not a nice place either with the wind this how. Well, my lads, I say, there's blessings and blessings, and we ought all to be werry thankful as we aren't ship-owners with wessels out yonder."

This was from the first man who had spoken; but his words were not received with much favour, and as in a lull of the wind one of the men had to use a glass, he growled out:

"Well, I dunno 'bout sending one's ship to sea in such a storm, but I don't see as it's such a very great blessing not to have one of your own, speshly if she happened to be a brig like Mast' Van Heldre's!"

"Hold your row," said a man beside him, as he drove his elbow into his ribs, and gave a side jerk of his head.

The man thus adjured turned sharply, and saw close to him a sturdy-looking figure clothed from head to foot in black mackintosh, which glistened as it dripped with the showery spray.

"Ugly day, my lads."

"Ay, ay, sir; much snugger in port than out yonder."

Boom! came a heavy blow from a wave, and the offing seemed to be obscured now by the drifting spray.

Van Heldre focussed a heavy binocular, and gazed out to sea long and carefully.

"Any one been up to the look-out?" he said, as he lowered his glass.

"Two on us tried it, sir," said one of the men, "but the wind's offle up yonder, and you can't see nothing."

"Going to try it, sir?" said another of the group.

Van Heldre nodded; and he was on his way to a roughly-formed flight of granite steps, which led up to the ruins of the old castle which had once defended the mouth of the harbour, when another mackintosh-clothed figure came up.

"Ah, Mr Leslie," said Van Heldre, looking at the new-comer searchingly.

"Good morning," was the reply, "or I should say bad morning. There'll be some mischief after this."

Van Heldre nodded, for conversation was painful, and passed on.

"Going up yonder?" shouted Leslie.

There was another nod, and under the circumstances, not pausing to ask permission, Leslie followed the old merchant, climbing the rough stone steps, and holding on tightly by the rail.

"Best look out, master," shouted one of the group. "Soon as you get atop roosh acrost and kneel down behind the old parry-putt."

It was a difficult climb and full of risk, for as they went higher they were more exposed, till as they reached the rough top which formed a platform, the wind seemed to rush at them as interlopers which it strove to sweep off and out to sea.

Van Heldre stood, glass in hand, holding on by a block of granite, his mackintosh tightly pressed to his figure in front, and filling out behind till it had a balloon-like aspect that seemed grotesque.

"I daresay I look as bad," Leslie muttered, as, taking the rough fisherman's advice, he bent down and crept under the shelter of the ancient parapet, a dwarf breast-work, with traces of the old crude bastions just visible, and here, to some extent, he was screened from the violence of the wind, and signed to Van Heldre to join him.

Leslie placed his hands to his mouth, and shouted through them.

"Hadn't you better come here, sir?"

For the position seemed terribly insecure. They were on the summit of the rocky headland, with the sides going on three sides sheer down to the shore, on two of which sides the sea kept hurling huge waves of water, which seemed to make the rock quiver to its foundations. One side of the platform was protected by the old breast-work; on the opposite the stones had crumbled away or fallen, and here there was a swift slope of about thirty feet to the cliff edge.

It was at the top of this slope that Van Heldre stood gazing out to sea.

Leslie, as he watched him, felt a curious premonition of danger, and gathered himself together involuntarily, ready for a spring.

The danger he anticipated was not long in making its demand upon him, for all at once there was a tremendous gust, as if an atmospheric wave had risen up to spring at the man standing on high as if daring the fury of the tempest; and in spite of Van Heldre's sturdy frame he completely lost his balance. He staggered for a moment, and, but for his presence of mind in throwing himself down, he would have been swept headlong down the swift slope to destruction.

As it was he managed to cling to the rocks, as the wind swept furiously over, and chocked his downward progress for the moment. This would have been of little avail, for, buffeted by the wind, he was gliding slowly down, and but for Leslie's quickly rendered aid, it would only have been a matter of moments before he had been hurled down upon the rocks below.

Even as he staggered, Leslie mastered the peculiar feeling of inertia which attacked him, and, creeping rapidly over the intervening space, made a dash at the fluttering overcoat, caught it, twisted it rapidly, and held on.

Then for a space neither moved, for it was as if the storm was raging with redoubled fury at the chance of its victim being snatched away.

The lull seemed as if it would never come; and when it did Leslie felt afraid to stir lest the fragile material by which he supported his companion should give way. In a few moments, however, he was himself, and shouting so as to make his voice plainly heard—for, close as he was, his words seemed to be swept away as uttered—he uttered a few short clear orders, which were not obeyed.

"Do you hear?" he cried again, "Mr Van Heldre—quick!"

Still there was no reply by voice or action, and it seemed as if the weight upon Leslie's wrists was growing heavier moment by moment. He yelled to him now, to act; and what seemed to be a terrible time elapsed before Van Heldre said hoarsely—

"One moment; better now. I felt paralysed."

There was mother terrible pause, during which the storm beat upon them, the waves thundered at the base of the rock, and even at that height there came a rain of spray which had run up the face of the rock and swept over to where they lay.

"Now, quick!" said Van Heldre, as he lay face downward, spread-eagled, as a sailor would term it, against the face of the sloping granite.

What followed seemed to be a struggling scramble, a tremendous effort, and then with the wind shrieking round them, Van Heldre reached the level, and crept slowly to the shelter of the parapet.

"Great heavens!" panted Leslie, as he lay there exhausted, and gazed wildly at his companion. "What an escape!"

There was no reply. Leslie thought that Van Heldre had fainted, for his eyes were nearly closed, and his face seemed to be drawn. Then he realised that his lips were moving slowly, as if in prayer.

"Hah!" the rescued man said at last, his words faintly heard in the tempest's din. "Thank God! For their sake—for their sake."

Then, holding out his hand, he pressed Leslie's in a firm strong grip.

"Leslie," he said, with his lips close to his companion's ear, "you have saved my life."

Neither spoke much after that, but they crouched there—in turn using the glass.

Once Van Heldre grasped his companion's arm and pointed out to sea.

"A ship?" cried Leslie.

"No. Come down now."

Waiting till the wind had dropped for the moment, they reached the rough flight of steps, and on returning to the level found that the crowd had greatly increased; and among them Leslie saw Harry Vine and his companion.

"Can't see un, sir, can you?" shouted one of the men.

Van Heldre shook his head.

"I thought you wouldn't, sir," shouted another. "Capt'n Muskerry's too good a sailor to try and make this port in such a storm."

"Ay," shouted another. "She's safe behind the harbour wall at Penzaunce."

"I pray she may be," said Van Heldre. "Come up to my place and have some breakfast, Leslie, but not a word, mind, about the slip. I'll tell that my way."

"Then I decline to come," said Leslie, and after a hearty grip of the hand they parted.

"I thought he meant Vine's girl," said Van Heldre, as he walked along the wharves street, "but there is no accounting for these things."

"I ought to explain to him how it was I came to be walking with Miss Van Heldre," said Leslie to himself. "Good morning."

He had suddenly found himself face to face with Harry, who walked by, arm in arm with Pradelle, frowning and without a word, when just as they passed a corner the wind came with a tremendous burst, and but for Leslie's hand Harry Vine must have gone over into the harbour.

It was but the business of a moment, and Harry seemed to shake off the hand which held him with a tremendous grip and passed on.

"Might have said thank you," said Leslie smiling. "I seem to be doing quite a business in saving people this morning, only they are of the wrong sex—there is no heroism. Hallo, Mr Luke Vine. Come down to look at the storm?"

"Couldn't I have seen it better up at home?" shouted the old man. "Ugh! what a wind. Thought I was going to be blown off the cliff. I see your chimney still stands, worse luck. Going home?"

"No, no. One feels so much unsettled at such a time."

"Don't go home then; stop with me."

Leslie looked at the quaint old man in rather an amused way, and then stopped with him to watch the tumbling billows off the point where his companion so often fished.

Chapter Seventeen
The News

The day wore on with the storm now lulling slightly, now increasing in violence, till it seemed as if the great rolling banks of green water must end by conquering in their attack, and sweeping away first the rough pier, and then the little twin towns on either side of the estuary. Nothing was visible seawards, but in a maritime place the attention of all is centred upon the expected, and in the full belief that sooner or later there would be a wreck, all masculine Hakemouth gathered in sheltered places to be on the watch.

Van Heldre and Leslie came into contact again that afternoon, and after a long look seaward, the merchant took the young man's arm.

"Come on to my place," he said quietly. "You'll come too, Luke Vine?"

"I? No, no," said the old fellow, shaking his head. "I want to stop and watch the sea go down."

His refusal was loud and demonstrative, but somehow there was a suggestion in it of a request to be asked again.

"Nonsense!" said Van Heldre. "You may as well come and take shelter for a while. You will not refuse, Leslie?"

"Thanks all the same, but I hope you will excuse me too," replied Leslie with his lips, but with an intense desire to go, for there was a possibility of Louise being at the house with Madelaine.

"I shall feel vexed if you refuse," said Van Heldre quietly. "Come along, Luke, and dine with us. I'm depressed and worried to-day; be a bit neighbourly if you can."

"Oh, I'll come," said the old man; "but it serves you right. Why can't you be content as I am, instead of venturing hundreds and hundreds of pounds in ships on the sea? Here, come along, Leslie, and let's eat and drink all we can to help him, the extravagant spendthrift."

Van Heldre smiled, and they went along to the house together.

"The boy in yonder at work?" said Uncle Luke, giving a wag of his head toward the office.

"Yes," said Van Heldre, and ushered his visitors in, the closed door seeming directly after to shut out the din and confusion of the wind-swept street.

"There, throw your mackintoshes on that chair," said Van Heldre; and hardly had Leslie got rid of his than Mrs Van Heldre was in the hall, her short plump arms were round Leslie's neck, and she kissed him heartily.

"God bless you!" she whispered with a sob; and before Leslie had well recovered from his surprise and confusion, Madelaine was holding one of his hands in both of hers, and looking tearfully in his face in a way which spoke volumes.

"Ah, it's nice to be young and good-looking, and well off," said Uncle Luke. "Nobody gives me such a welcome."

"How can you say that," said Madelaine, with a laugh. "Come, Uncle Luke, and we're very glad to see you."

As she spoke she put her hands on his shoulders, and kissed his wrinkled cheek.

"Hah! that's like old times, Maddy," said the grim-looking visitor, softening a little. "Why didn't you keep a nice plump little girl, same as you used to be?"

Madelaine gave him a smile and nod, but left the old man with her father, and followed her mother and Leslie into the dining-room.

"So that's to be it, is it, Van, eh?"

"I don't know," was the reply. "It's all very sudden and a surprise to me."

"Angled for it, haven't you?"

"Angled? No."

"She has then. My dear boy, son of my heart, the very man for my darling, eh?" chuckled Uncle Luke.

"Be quiet, you sham cynic," said Van Heldre dreamily. "Don't banter me, Luke, I'm sorely ill at case."

"About money, eh?" cried Uncle Luke eagerly.

"Money? No! I was thinking about those poor fellows out at sea."

"In your brig, eh? Ah, 'tis sad. But that money—quite safe, eh?"

"Oh, yes, safe enough."

"Oh, do come, papa dear," said Madelaine, reappearing at the door. "Dinner is waiting."

"Yes, yes, we're coming, my dear," said Van Heldre, laying his hand affectionately on Uncle Luke's shoulder, and they were soon after seated round the table, with the elder visitor showing at times quite another side of his character.

No allusion was made to the adventure of the morning, but Leslie felt in the gentle tenderness displayed towards him by mother and daughter that much had been said, and that he had won a very warm place in their regard. In fact, in word and look, Mrs Van Heldre seemed to be giving him a home in her motherly heart, which was rather embarrassing, and would have been more so, but for Madelaine's frank, pleasant way of meeting his gaze, every action seemed to be sisterly and affectionate, but nothing more.

So Leslie read them, but so did not the elders at the table.

By mutual consent no allusion was made to the missing brig, and it seemed to Leslie that the thoughts of mother and daughter were directed principally to one point, that of diverting Van Heldre from his troublesome thoughts. "Ah, I was hungry," said Uncle Luke, when the repast was about half over. "Very pleasant meal, only wanted one thing to make it perfect."

"Why, my dear Luke Vine, why didn't you speak? What is it? oh, pray say."

"Society," said Uncle Luke, after pausing for a moment to turn towards the window, a gust having giving it a tremendous shake. "I say if I find my place blown away, can you find me a dry shed or a dog kennel, or something, Leslie?"

"Don't talk such stuff, Luke Vine," cried Mrs Van Heldre. "Don't take any notice of him, Mr Leslie, he's a rich old miser and nothing else. Now Luke Vine, what do you mean?"

"Said what I meant, society. Why didn't you ask my sister to dinner? She'd have set us all right, eh, Madelaine?"

"Oh, I don't know," said Madelaine, smiling.

"But I do," cried her mother; "she'd have set us all by the ears with her nonsense. You are a strange pair."

"We are—we are. Nice sherry this, Van."

"Glad you like it," said Van Heldre, with his eyes turned towards the window, as if he expected news.

"How a woman can be so full of pride and so useless puzzles me."

"Mamma!" whispered Madelaine, with an imploring look.

"Let her talk, my dear," said Uncle Luke, "it doesn't hurt any one. Don't talk nonsense, Van's wife. What use could you make of her? She is like the thistle that grows up behind my place, a good-looking prickly plant, with a ball of down for a head. Let her be; you always get the worst of it. The more you excite her the more that head of hers sends out floating downy seeds to settle here and there, and do mischief. She has spoiled my nephew Harry, and nearly spoiled my niece."

"Don't you believe it, Mr Leslie," cried Madelaine, with a long earnest look in her eyes.

"Quite true. Miss Impudence," continued Uncle Luke. "Always was a war between me and the useless plants."

"Well, I can't sit here silent and listen to such heresy," cried Mrs Van Heldre, shaking her head. "Surely, Luke Vine, you don't call yourself a useful plant."

"Bless my soul, ma'am, then I suppose I'm a weed?"

"Not you," said Van Heldre, forcing a show of interest in the conversation.

"Yes, old fellow, I am," said Uncle Luke, holding his sherry up to the light, and sipping it as if he found real enjoyment therein. "I suppose I am only a weed, not a thistle, like Margaret up yonder, but a tough-rooted, stringy, matter-of-fact old nettle, who comes up quietly in his own corner and injures no one so long as people let him alone."

"No, no, no, no!" said Madelaine emphatically.

"Quite right. Miss Van Heldre," said Leslie.

"Hear, hear?" cried Van Heldre.

"Stir me up, then, and see," cried the old man grimly. "More than one person has found out before now how I can sting, and—hallo! what's wrong? You here?"

There had been a quick step in the long passage, and, without ceremony, the door was thrown open, Harry Vine entering, to stand in the gathering gloom hatless and excited.

He was about to speak, Van Heldre having sprung to his feet, when the young man's eyes alighted on Leslie and Madelaine seated side by side at the table, and the flash of anger which mounted to his brain drove everything else away.

"What is it?" cried Van Heldre hoarsely. "Do you hear?—speak?"

"There is a brig on the Conger Rock," said Harry quickly, as if roused to a recollection of that which he had come to say.

"Yes, sir," cried another voice, as old Crampton suddenly appeared. "And the man has just run up to the office with the news, for—"

"Well, man, speak out," said Van Heldre whose florid face was mottled with patches of ghastly white.

"They think it's ours."

"I felt it coming," groaned Van Heldre, as he rushed into the hall, Leslie following quickly.

As he hurriedly threw on his waterproof a hand caught his, and turning, it was to see Madelaine looking up imploringly in his eyes.

"My father, Mr Leslie. Keep him out of danger, pray!"

"Trust me. I'll do my best," said the young man quickly; and then he awoke to the fact that Harry Vine was beside him, white with anger, an anger which seemed to make him dumb.

The next minute the whole party were struggling down the street against the hurricane-like wind, to learn from a dozen voices, eager to tender the bad news, that the mist of spray had been so thick that in the early gloom of evening the vessel had approached quite unseen till she was close in, and directly after she had struck on the dangerous rock, in a wild attempt to reach the harbour, a task next to impossible in such a storm.

Chapter Eighteen
Harry Vine Shows His Bright Side

The wreck of a ship, on the threshold of the home where every occupant is known, is a scene of excitement beyond the reach of pen to adequately describe; and as the two young men reached the mouth of the harbour, following closely upon Van Heldre, their own petty animosity was forgotten in the face of the terrible disaster.

The night was coming fast, and a light had been hoisted in the rigging of the vessel, now hard on the dangerous rock—the long arc of a circle described by the dim star, showing plainly to those on shore the precarious position of the unfortunate crew.

The sides of the harbour were crowded, in spite of the tremendous storm of wind and spray; and, as Leslie followed the shipowner, he noted the horror and despair in many a spray-wet face.

As Van Heldre approached and was recognised, there was a cheer given by those who seemed to take it for granted that the owner would at once devise a way to save the vessel from her perilous position, and rescue the crew whose lives were dear to many gathered in agony around, to see, as it were, their dear ones die.

Steps had already been taken, however, and as the little party from Van Heldre's reached the harbour, it was to see the lifeboat launched, and a crew of sturdy fellows in their places ready to do battle with the waves.

It seemed to be a terrible task to row right out from the comparatively calm harbour, whose long rocky point acted as a breakwater, to where the great billows came rolling in, each looking as if it would engulf a score of such frail craft as that which, after a little of the hesitation of preparation, and amidst a tremendous burst of cheering, was rowed out into the middle of the estuary, and then straight away for the mouth.

But they were not all cheers which followed the boat. Close by where Leslie stood, with a choking sensation of emotion in his breast, a woman uttered a wild shriek as the boat went off, and her hands were outstretched towards one of the oilskin-cased men, who sat in his place tugging stolidly at his oar.

That one cry, heard above the roaring of the wind, the hiss of the spray, and the heavy thunder of the waves, acted like a signal to let loose the pent-up agony of a score of hearts; and wives, mothers, sisters, all joined in that one wild cry, "Come back!"

The answer was a hoarse "Give way!" from the coxswain; and the crew turned their eyes determinedly from the harbour wall and tugged at their oars.

The progress of the boat was followed as far as was possible by the crowd; and when they could go no farther, every sheltered spot was seized upon as a coign of vantage from which to watch the saving of the doomed crew.

Leslie was standing close to the harbour wall, sheltering his face with his hands as he watched the lifeboat fast nearing the mouth of the harbour, where the tug of war would commence, when he felt a hand laid upon his arm.

He turned sharply, to find Madelaine at his elbow, her hood drawn over her head and tightly secured beneath her chin.

He hardly saw her face, though, for close beside her stood another closely-hooded figure, whose face was streaming with the spray, while strand after strand of her dark hair had been torn from its place by the wind, and refused to be controlled.

"Miss Van Heldre! Miss Vine!"

"Yes. Where is my father?"

"Here; talking to this coastguardsman."

"And I thought we had lost him," murmured Madelaine.

"But is it wise of you two ladies?" said Leslie, as he grasped Louise's hand for a moment. "The storm is too terrible."

"We could not rest indoors," said Louise. "My father is down here, is he not?"

"I have not seen him. You want some better shelter."

"No, no; don't think of us," said Louise excitedly; "but if you can help in any way—"

"You know I will," said Leslie earnestly.

"Here, what are you two girls doing?" said a quick, angry voice. "Louie, I'm sure this is no place for you."

Harry spoke to his sister, but his eyes were fixed upon those of Leslie, who, however, declined his challenge, as it seemed, to quarrel, and glanced at the young man's companion.

At that moment the brothers Vine came up, and there was no farther excuse for Harry's fault-finding objections.

"Can't you young fellows do anything to help?" said Uncle Luke.

"I wish you would tell us what to do, Mr Vine," said Leslie coldly.

Just then Van Heldre turned to, and joined them.

"He is afraid the distance is too far," he said dreamily, as if in answer to a question.

"For the boat, Mr Van Heldre?" cried Louise.

"No, no; for the rocket apparatus. Ah! Vine," he continued, as he saw his old friend, "how helpless we are in such a storm!"

No more was said. It was no time for words. The members of the two families stood together in a group watching the progress of the boat, and even Aunt Marguerite's cold and sluggish blood was moved enough to draw her to the window, through whose spray and salt-blurred panes she could dimly see the tossing light of the brig.

It was indeed no time for words, and even the very breath was held, to be allowed to escape in a low hiss of exultation as the lifeboat was seen to rise suddenly and swiftly up a great bank of water, stand out upon its summit for a few moments, and then plunge down out of sight as the wave came on, deluged the point, and roared and tumbled over in the mouth of the harbour.

It was plain enough now, the lifeboat was beyond the protection of the point; and its progress was watched as it rose and fell, slowly growing more distant, and at times invisible for minutes together.

At such times the excitement seemed beyond bearing. The boat, all felt, must have been swamped, and those on board left tossing in the boiling sea. The catastrophe of the wreck of the brig seemed to be swallowed up now in one that was greater; and as Leslie glanced round once, it was to see Louise and Madelaine clinging together, wild-eyed and pale.

"There she is!" shouted a voice; and the lifeboat was seen to slowly rise again, as a hoarse cheer arose—the pent-up excitement of the moment.

It seemed an interminable length of time before the life-saving vessel reached the brig, and what followed during the next half-hour could only be guessed at. So dark had it become, that now only the tossing light on board the doomed merchantman could be seen, rising and falling slowly with rhythmical regularity, as if those on board were waving to those they loved a sad farewell.

Then at last a faint spark was seen for a few moments before it disappeared. Again it shone for a while and again disappeared.

"One of the lanthorns in the lifeboat."

"Coming back," said Van Heldre hoarsely.

"With the crew, sir?" cried Leslie.

"Hah!" exclaimed Van Heldre slowly; "that we must see."

Another long time of suspense and horror. A dozen times over that boat's light seemed to have gone for ever, but only to reappear; and at last, in the darkness it was seen, after a few minutes' tremendous tossing, to become steady.

The lifeboat was in the harbour once again, and a ringing burst of cheers, that seemed smothered directly after by the roar of the storm, greeted the crew as they rowed up to the landing-place, utterly exhausted, but bringing with them two half-dead members of the brig's crew.

"All we could get to stir," said the sturdy coxswain, "and we could not get aboard."

"How many are there?"

"Seven, sir—in main-top. Half-dead."

"You should have stayed and brought them off," cried Leslie frantically, for he did not realise the difficulties of the task the men had had to fulfil.

"Who goes next?" cried Van Heldre, as the half-drowned men were borne, under the direction of the doctor, to the nearest inn.

"No one can't go again, sir," said the old coxswain sternly. "It aren't to be done."

"A crew must go again," cried Van Heldre. "We cannot stand here and let them perish before our eyes. Here, my lads!" he roared. "Volunteers!"

"Mr Leslie! My father," whispered Madelaine; but the young mine-owner was already on his way to where Van Heldre stood.

"Do you hear?" roared the latter. "Do as you would be done by. Volunteers!"

Not a man stirred, the peril was too great.

"It's no good, master," said the old coxswain; "they're gone, poor lads, by now."

"No," cried Leslie excitedly; "the light is there still."

"Ay," said the coxswain, "a lamp'll burn some time longer than a man's life. Here, master, I'll go again, if you can get a crew."

"Volunteers!" shouted Van Heldre; but there was only a confused babble of voices, as women clung to their men, and held back these who would have yielded.

"Are you men!" roared Leslie excitedly: and Madelaine felt her arm grasped tightly.

"I say, are you men, to stand there and see those poor fellows perish before your eyes!"

"It's throwing lives away," cried a shrill woman's voice.

"Ay, go yoursen," shouted a man angrily.

"I'm going," roared Leslie. "Only a landsman. Now then, is there never a sailor who will come?"

There was a panting, spasmodic cry at Madelaine's ear, one which she echoed, as Harry Vine stepped up to Leslie's side.

"Here's another landsman," he cried excitedly. "Now, Pradelle, come on!"

There was no response from his companion, who drew back.

"No, no," panted Madelaine. "Louy—help me—they must not go."

Her words were drowned in a tremendous cheer, for Van Heldre, without a word, had stepped into the lifeboat, followed by the two young men.

Example is said to be better than precept. It was so here, for, with a rush, twenty of the sturdy Hakemouth fishers made for the boat, and the crew was not only made up, but a dozen men begged Van Heldre and the two young men to come out and let others take their places.

"No," said Leslie through his set teeth; "not if I never see shore again, Henry Vine."

"Is that brag to Hector over me, or British pluck?" said Harry.

"Don't know, my lad. Are you going ashore?"

"Let's wait and see," muttered Harry, as he tied on the life preserver handed to him.

"Harry, my boy!"

The young man looked up and saw his father on the harbour wall.

"Hallo! Father!" he said sadly.

"You are too young and weak. Let some strong man go."

"I can pull an oar as well as most of them, father," he shouted; and then to himself: "And if I don't get back—well—I suppose I'm not much good."

"Let him go," said Uncle Luke, as he held back his brother. "Hang the boy, he has stuff in him after all."

A busy scene of confusion for a few minutes, and then once more a cheer arose, as the lifeboat, well-manned, parted the waters of the harbour, and the lanthorns forward and astern shone with a dull glare as that first great wave was reached, up which the boat glided, and then plunged down and disappeared.

One long hour of intense agony, but not for those in the boat. The energy called forth, the tremendous struggle, the excitement to which every spirit was wrought, kept off agony or fear. It was like being in the supreme moments of a battle-charge, when in the wild whirl there is no room for dread, and a man's spirit carries him through to the end.

The agony was on shore, where women clung together no longer weeping, but straining their eyes seaward for the dancing lights which dimly crept up each billow, and then disappeared, as if never to appear again.

"Madelaine!"

"Louise!"

All that was said as the two girls clasped each other and watched the dim lanthorns far at sea. "Ah!"

Then a loud groan.

"I knowed it couldn't be long."

Then another deep murmur, whose strange intensity had made it dominate the shrieks, roars, and thunder of the storm.

The light, which had been slowly waving up and down in the rigging of the brig, had disappeared, and it told to all the sad tale—that the mast had gone, and with it those who had been clinging in the top.

But the two dim lanthorns in the lifeboat went on and on, the thunder of the surf on the wreck guiding them. As the crew toiled away, the landsmen sufficiently accustomed to the use of the oar could pretty well hold their own, till, in utter despair and hopelessness, after hovering hours about the place where the wreck should have been, the lifeboat's head was laid for the harbour-lights; and after a fierce battle to avoid being driven beyond, the gallant little crew reached the shelter given by the long low point, but several had almost to be lifted to the wharf.

A few jagged and torn timbers, and a couple of bodies cast up among the rocks, a couple of miles to the east, were all the traces of Van Heldre's handsome brig, which had gone to pieces in the darkness before the lifeboat, on its second journey, was half way there.

Chapter Nineteen
A Bad Night's Work

"Oh, yes, you're a very brave fellow, no doubt," said Pradelle. "Everybody says so. Perhaps if I could have handled an oar as well as you did I should have come too. But, look here, Harry Vine; all these fine words butter no parsnips. You are no better off than you were before, and you gave me your promise."

It was quite true: fine words buttered no parsnips. Aunt Marguerite had called him her gallant young hero; Louise had kissed him affectionately; his father had shaken hands very warmly; Uncle Luke had given him a nod, and Van Heldre had said a few kindly words, while there was always a smile for him among the fishermen who hung about the harbour. But that was all; he was still Van Heldre's clerk, and with a dislike to his position, which had become intensified since Madelaine had grown cold, and her intimacy with Leslie had seemed to increase. "Look here," said Pradelle; "it's time I was off."

"Why? What for?" said Harry, as they sat among the rocks.

"Because I feel as if I were being made a fool."

"Why, every one is as civil to you as can be. My father—"

"Oh, yes; the old man's right enough."

"My aunt."

"Yes, wish she wasn't so old, Harry, and had some money; I'd marry her."

"Don't be a fool."

"Not going to be; so I tell you I'm off."

"No, no, don't go. This place will be unbearable when you are gone."

"Can't help it, dear boy. I must do something to increase my income, and if you will not join in and make a fortune, why I must go and find some one who will."

"But I dare not, Vic."

"You gave me your word—the word of a gentleman. I ask you to borrow the money for a week or two, and then we would replace it, and nobody be a bit the wiser, while we shall be on the high-road to fortune and Fair France."

"I tell you I dare not."

"Then I shall do it myself."

"No, that you shall not."

"Then you shall."

"I daren't."

"Bah! what a milksop you are; you have nothing to care for here. Miss Van Heldre has pitched you over because you are now her father's clerk."

"Let that be, please."

"And taken up with Mr Bagpipes."

"Do you want to quarrel, Pradelle?"

"Not I, dear boy; I'm dumb."

He said no more on that subject, but he had said enough. That was the truth then. Madelaine had given him up on that account, and the sting rankled in Harry's breast.

"Money goes to the bank every day, you say?" said Pradelle.

"Yes. Crampton takes it!"

"But that sum of money in notes? How much is there of that?"

"Five hundred."

"Why don't that go to the bank?"

"I don't know. A deposit, I think; likely to be called for."

"May be; but that's our game, Harry. The other could not be managed without being missed; this, you see, is not in use."

"Pradelle, it's madness."

"Say Vic, dear boy."

"Well, Vic, I say it's madness."

"Nothing of the kind. It's making use of a little coin that you can get at easily. Why, hang it, old fellow, you talk as if I were asking you to steal the money."

"Hush! Don't talk like that."

"Well, you aggravate me so. Now, am I trying to serve you, or am I not?"

"To serve me, of course."

"Yes, and you behave like a child."

"I want to behave like an honourable man to my father's friend."

"Oh, if you are going to preach I'm off."

"I'm not going to preach."

"Then do act like a man. Here is your opportunity. You know what the old chap said about the tide in the affairs of men?"

Harry nodded.

"Well, your tide is at its height. You are going to seize your opportunity, and then you can do as you like. Why you might turn the tables on Miss Madelaine."

"If you don't want to quarrel, just leave her name alone," said Harry, with a bulldog-like growl.

"Oh, I'll never mention it again if you like. Now, then, once for all, is it business?"

Harry was silent for a few minutes, and then replied —

"Yes."

"Your hand on it."

Harry stretched out his hand unwillingly, and it was taken and held.

"I shall hold you to it now, my lad. Now, then, when is it to be?"

"Oh, first opportunity."

"No; it's going to be now—to-night—as soon as it's dark."

"Nonsense, it must be some day—when Crampton is not there."

"That means it will not be done at all, for Crampton never leaves; you told me so. Look here, Harry Vine, if you borrow the amount then, and it's missed, of course you are asked directly, and there you are. No, my lad, you'll have to go to-night."

"But it will be like housebreaking."

"Bah! You'll go quietly in by the back way, make your way along the passage to Van Heldre's room, take the keys down from the hook—"

"How did you know that the keys hung there?"

"Because, my dear little man, I have wormed it all out of you by degrees. To continue: you will go down the glass passage, open the office door, go to the safe, open that, get the two hundred—"

"Two hundred! You said fifty would do."

"Yes, but then I said a hundred, and now I think two will be better. Easier paid back. You can work more spiritedly with large sums than with small. You've got to do this, Harry Vine, so no nonsense."

Harry was silent.

"When you have the notes, you will lock all up as before, and then if they are missing before we return them, which is not likely, who can say that you have been there? Bah! don't be so squeamish. You've got to do that to-night. You have promised, and you shall. It is for your good, my lad."

"Yes, and yours," said Harry gloomily.

"Of course. Emancipation for us both."

Harry was silent, and soon after they rose and strolled back to the old house, where through the open window came the strains of music, and the voices of Madelaine and Louise harmonised in a duet.

"One less at Van Heldre's, lad. The old man will be having his evening pipe, and the doors open. Nothing could be better. Half-past nine, mind, while they are at tea. It will be quite dark then."

Harry was silent, and the two young men entered and sat down, their coming seeming to cast a damp on the little party, for the music was put aside and work taken up, Vine being busy with some notes of his day's observations of the actions of a newly found mollusc.

Tea was brought in at about a quarter-past nine, and Pradelle rose and went to the window.

"What a beautiful night, Harry," he said. "Coming for half an hour's stroll before bed?"

"Don't you want some tea?" said Harry, loudly.

"No. Do you?"

"No," said Harry shortly; and he rose and went out, followed by his friend.

"You mean this then," he said, as soon as they were out on the cliff.

"No; but you do. There is just time for it, so now go."

Harry hesitated for a few minutes, and then strode off down toward the town, Pradelle keeping step with him, till they reached the street where a lane branched off, going round by the back of Van Heldre's house, but on a higher level, a flight of steps leading down into the half garden, half yard, overlooked by the houses at the back, whose basements were level with Van Heldre's first floor.

The time selected by Pradelle for the carrying out of his scheme happened to be Crampton's club night, and, according to his weekly custom, he had gone to the old-fashioned inn where it was kept, passing a muffled-up figure as he went along, the said figure turning in at one of the low entrances leading to dock premises as the old clerk came out, so that he did not see the face.

It was a trifling matter, but it was not the first time Crampton had seen this figure loitering about at night, and it somehow impressed him so that he did not enjoy his one glass of spirits and water and his pipe. But the matter seemed to have slipped his memory for the time that he was transacting his club business, making entries and the like. Later on it came back with renewed force.

Harry and Pradelle parted in the dark lane with very few more words spoken, the understanding being that they should meet at home at half-past nine.

As soon as the former was alone he walked slowly on round the front of Van Heldre's house, and there, according to custom, sat the merchant smoking his nightly pipe, resting one arm upon the table, with the shaded lamp shining down on his bald forehead, and a thoughtful, dreamy look in his eyes. Mrs Van Heldre was seated opposite working and respecting her husband's thoughtful mood, for he was in low spirits respecting the wreck of his ship. Insurance made up the monetary loss, but nothing could restore the poor fellows who had gone down.

Harry stood on the opposite side watching thoughtfully.

"It would be very easy," he said to himself. "Just as we planned, I can slip round to the back, drop in the garden, go in, take the keys, get the money, lock up again, and go and hang up the keys. Yes; how easy for any one who knows, and how risky it seems for him to leave his place like that. But then it is people's want of knowledge which forms the safest lock."

"Yes," he said, after a pause, as he stood there in profound ignorance of the fact that the muffled-up figure which had taken Crampton's attention was in a low dark doorway, watching his every movement. "Yes, it would be very easy; and in spite of all your precious gloss, Master Victor Pradelle, I should feel the next moment that I had been a thief; and I'll drudge as a clerk till I'm ninety-nine before I'll do anything of the kind."

The Haute Noblesse | 153

He thrust his hands into his pockets and turned off down by the harbour side, and hardly had he reached the water when Pradelle walked slowly up to the front of the house, noted the positions of those within by taking his stand just beneath the arched doorway opposite, and so close to the watcher that they nearly touched.

The next moment Pradelle had passed on.

"I knew he hadn't the pluck," he muttered bitterly. "A contemptible hound! Well, he shall see."

Without a moment's hesitation, and as if he were quite at home about the place, Pradelle went round to the narrow back lane and stood by the gate leading down the steps into the yard. As he pressed the gate it gave way, and he could see that the doorway into the glazed passage was open, for the light in the hall shone through.

There was no difficulty at all; and after a moment's hesitation he stepped lightly down, ready with an excuse that he was seeking Harry, if he should meet any one; but the excuse was not needed. He walked softly and boldly into the passage, turned to his light, and entered the back room, which acted as Van Heldre's private office and study. The keys lay where he knew them to be—in a drawer, which he opened and took them out, and then walked straight along the glazed passage to the office. The door yielded to the key, and he entered. The inner office was locked, but that was opened by a second key, and the safe showed dimly by the reflected lights which shone through the barred window.

"How easy these things are!" said Pradelle to himself, as he unlocked the safe; "enough to tempt a man to be a burglar."

The iron door creaked faintly as he drew it open, and then began to feel about hastily, and with the perspiration streaming from his forehead. Books in plenty, but no notes.

With an exclamation of impatience, he drew out a little match-box, struck a light, and saw that there was an iron drawer low down. The flame went out, but he had seen enough, and stooping he dragged out the drawer, thrust in his hand, which came in contact with a leaden paper weight, beneath which, tied round with tape, was a bundle of notes.

"Hah!" he muttered with a half laugh, "I can't stop to count you. Yes, I must, or they'll miss 'em. Its tempting though. Humph! tied both—"

Thud!

One heavy blow on the back of Victor Pradelle's head which sent him staggering forward against the door of the safe; then he felt in a confused, half-stunned way that something had been snatched from his hand. A dead silence followed, during which his head swam, but he had sufficient sense left to totter across the outer office, and along the passage to the garden yard.

How he got outside into the little lane he could not afterwards remember, his next recollection being of sitting down on the steps by the water-side bathing his face.

Five minutes before Harry Vine had been in that very spot, from which he turned to go home.

"Let him say what he likes," muttered the young man, "I must have been mad to listen to him. Why—"

Harry Vine stopped short, for a thought had struck him like a flash.

How it was—why he should have such a suspicion he could not tell; but a terrible thought had seemed to burn into his brain. Then he felt paralysed as he shivered, and uttering an ejaculation full of rage and anger, he started off at a run toward Van Heldre's place.

"Nonsense!" he said to himself, and he checked his headlong speed. "What folly!"

He walked on past a group of seamen, who had just quitted a public-house, and was about to turn up the lane which led to his home, when the thought came once more.

"Curse him!" he said, half aloud, "I'd sooner kill him," and hurrying back, he made straight for the lane behind Van Heldre's.

The gate yielded, he stepped down quickly into the yard, walked to the open door, looked to the right toward the hall, and then to the left toward the office. A dim light shone down the passage, and his heart seemed to stand still. The office door was open, and without hesitation he turned down the passage panting with horror, as he felt that his suspicions were confirmed. He crossed the outer room, the inner door was shut, and entering, he paused for a moment.

"Vic?" he whispered harshly.

All was still.

Trembling now with agitation, he was rapidly crossing to the safe when he stepped on something which gave beneath his feet, and he nearly fell headlong.

Recovering himself, he stooped down to pick up the heavy ebony ruler used by old Crampton, and polished by rubs of his coat-tail till it shone.

Harry felt giddy now with excitement, but he went to the safe door, felt that it was swung open, and groaning to himself, "Too late, too late!" he bent his head; felt for the drawer.

Empty!

"You scoundrel!" he groaned; "but he shall give up every note, and—"

Once more he felt as if paralysed, for as he turned from the safe he knew that he was not alone in the office.

Caught in the act! Burglary—the open safe—the notes gone, who would believe in his innocence?

He could think of nothing else, as he heard Van Heldre's voice in the darkness—one fierce angry utterance—"Who's there?"

"He does not know me," flashed through Harry Vine's brain.

"You villain!" cried Van Heldre, springing at him.

It was the instinctive act of one smitten by terror, despair, shame, and the desire to escape—a mad act, but prompted by the terrible position. As Van Heldre sprang at him and grasped at his breast, Harry Vine struck with all his might, the heavy rule fell with a sickening crash upon the unguarded head, he felt a sudden tug, and with a groan his father's friend sank senseless on the floor.

For one moment Harry Vine stood bending over his victim; then uttering a hoarse sigh, he leaped over the body and fled.

Chapter Twenty
In the Black Shadow

Mrs Van Heldre let her work fall in her lap and gazed across at her husband.

"I suppose Harry Vine will walk home with Madelaine?" she said.

"Eh? Maddy? I'd forgotten her," said Van Heldre laying down his pipe. "No; I'll go up and fetch her myself."

"Do, dear, but don't stay."

"Not I," was the reply; and going out of the dining-room, where he always sat when he had his evening pipe, the merchant went into the study, where by the dim light he saw that his writing-table drawer was open.

"How's that?" he thought. "Did I—No."

He ran out into the passage, saw that his office door was open, and entered to receive the blow which laid him senseless before the safe.

Van Heldre did not lie there long.

Crampton came away from the old inn, stick in hand, conscious of having done a good evening's work over the business of the Fishermen's Benefit Club, the men having paid up with unusual regularity; but all the same, he did not feel satisfied. Those pedlar sailor men troubled him. They had been hanging about the town for some time, and though he knew nothing against them, he had, as a respectable householder, a confirmed dislike to all nomadic trading gentry. To him they were, whether Jew or Gentile, French or German, all gipsies, and belonging to a class who, to use his words, never took anything out of their reach.

He felt sure that the man he had seen in the darkness was one of these, and blaming himself now for not having taken further notice of the matter, he determined to call at his employer's on his way home to mention the fact.

"Better late than never," he said, and he stumped steadily down the main street as a man walks who is possessed of a firm determination to do his duty.

As he went on he peered down every one of the dark, narrow alleys which led to the water-side places, all reeking of tar and old cordage, and creosoted nets, and with more than a suspicion of the celebrated ancient and fishlike smell so often quoted.

"If I had my way," said Crampton, "I'd have a lamp at each end of those places. They're too dark—too dark."

But though he scanned each place carefully, he did not see any lurking figure, and he went on till he reached his employer's house, where, through the well-lit window, he could see Mrs Van Heldre looking plump, rosy, and smiling, as she busied herself in putting away her work.

Crampton stopped at the opposite side, took off his hat and scratched his head.

"Now if I go and tell him what I think, he'll call me a nervous old fool, and abuse me for frightening his wife."

He hesitated, and instead of going to the front door, feeling that perhaps, after all, he had taken an exaggerated view of things, he went on to the corner of the house and lane, with the intention of having a look round and then going on home.

He had just gone about half way, when there was a loud rap given by the gate leading down into Van Heldre's yard. Some one had thrown it violently back against the wooden step, and that somebody had sprung out and run down the lane in the opposite direction to that by which the old clerk had come.

"Hah!" he ejaculated, and hurrying on he hastily descended the steps, entered the passage, and trembling now in every limb, made his way into the office, where, with all the regular method of the man of business, he quickly took a box of matches from the chimney-piece, and turned on and lit one of the gas burners.

The soft light from the ground-glass globe showed nothing wrong as he glanced round.

Yes; something was missing—the heavy ebony ruler which always reposed on the two brass hooks like a weapon of war at the end of his desk. That was gone.

Crampton's brow knitted, and his hands shook so that he could hardly strike a second match, as he pushed open the door and entered the inner office where, forcing himself not to look round, he lit another gas jet before taking in the scene at a glance.

There lay Van Heldre, bleeding profusely from a terrible cut on the forehead, the safe was open, and in a very few minutes the old clerk knew that the packet of bank-notes was gone.

"But I've got all their numbers entered," he said to himself, as he went down on his knee by his master's side, and now, knowing the worst, growing moment by moment more calm and self-contained.

His first act was to take his voluminous white cravat from his neck, and bind it tightly round Van Heldre's temples to staunch the bleeding.

"I knew no good would come of it," he muttered. "I felt it from the first. Are you much hurt, sir?" he said aloud, with his lips close to the injured man's ear.

There was no reply; just a spasm and a twitching of the hands.

"What shall I do?" thought Crampton. "Give the alarm? No; only frighten those poor women into fits. Fetch the doctor."

He hurried out by the back way as quietly as he could, and caught the principal medical man just as he was going up to bed for a quiet night.

"Eh? Van Heldre?" he said. "Bless my soul! On directly. Back way?"

"Yes."

Crampton hurried out, displaying wonderful activity for so old a man, and took the police station on his way back.

The force in Hakemouth was represented by a sergeant and two men, the former residing at the cottage which bore the words "Police Station" over the door.

"Where is your husband?" said Crampton to a brisk-looking woman.

"On his rounds, sir."

"I want him at our office. Can I find him? Can you?"

"I know where he'll be in about ten minutes, sir," said the woman promptly, as if she were a doctor's helpmate.

"Very well," said Crampton. "Get him and send him on."

The divergence had taken so long that he had hardly reached the office and poured out some water from a table filter, to bathe the injured man's face, when he heard the doctor's step.

"Hah!" said the latter, after a brief examination, "we must get him to bed, Mr Crampton."

"Is he much hurt, sir?"

"Badly. There is a fracture of the skull. It must have been a terrible blow. Thieves, of course?"

"Or thief, sir," said the old clerk, with his lip quivering. "My dear master! what would his poor father have said?"

"Hush! Be firm, man," said the doctor, who was busy readjusting the bandage. "Does Mrs Van Heldre know?"

Crampton shook his head.

"I found him like this, sir, and came over to fetch you at once."

"But she must be told."

"John, John dear, are you there? I thought you had gone on to fetch Madelaine."

Crampton rose hastily to try and bar the way; but he was too late. Mrs Van Heldre was at the door, and had caught a glimpse of the prostrate man.

"Doctor Knatchbull! what is the matter—a fit?"

The trouble was culminating, for another voice was heard in the glass corridor.

"Papa! papa! here is Mr Vine. He walked home with me. I made him come in. Oh, what a shame to be at work so late!"

"Keep her—keep her back," gasped Mrs Van Heldre, and then with a piteous sob she sank down by Van Heldre's side.

"John, my husband! speak to me, oh, speak," she moaned as she raised his head to her lap.

"Ah, you want Brother Luke to you, John Van," cried Vine, as with Madelaine on his arm he came to the door of the inner room.

There was a moment's silence, and then Madelaine uttered a wild cry, and ran to her father's side.

"Good heavens! Crampton, what is it?" cried Vine excitedly,—"a fit?"

"No, sir, struck down by a villain—a thief—and that thief—"

Crampton stopped short in the midst of his excitement, for there was a heavy step now in the passage, and the sergeant of police and one of his men came in.

"Yes. I've had my eye on a couple of strangers lately," he said, as he took out a book and gave a sharp look round. "P'r'aps Mr Crampton, sir, you'll give me the information I want."

"Mr Crampton will give you no information at all," said the keen-looking doctor angrily. "The first thing is to save the man's life. Here, sergeant, and you, my man, help me to carry him up to his bed—or no—well, yes, he'll be better in his own room. Pray, ladies, pray stand aside."

"Yes, yes," cried Madelaine excitedly, as she rose. "Mother, dear, we must be calm and helpful."

"Yes; but—but—" moaned the poor woman.

"Yes, dearest," cried Madelaine, "afterwards. Dr Knatchbull wants our help."

"Good girl," said the doctor, nodding. "Get the scissors, some old linen, and basin, sponge and water, in the bedroom."

"Yes, doctor," said Madelaine, perfectly calm and self-contained now. "Mother, dear, I want your help."

She knelt down and pressed her lips for a moment to her father's cheek, and then placed her arm round her mother, and led her away.

An hour later, when everything possible had been done, and Mrs Van Heldre was seated by her husband's pillow, Vine being on the other side holding his friend's hand, Madelaine showed the doctor into the next room.

"Tell me," she said firmly. "I want to know the truth."

"My dear child," said the doctor, "You know all that I know. Some scoundrel must have been surprised by your father, and—"

"Doctor," said Madelaine quietly, and with her clear matter-of-fact eyes gazing into his, "I have been praying for strength to help my mother and my poor father in this terrible affliction. I feel as if the strength had been given to me, so speak now as if I were a woman whom you could trust. Tell me the whole truth."

The doctor gazed at her with a look full of admiration, and taking her hand, he said kindly:

"I was treating you as if you were a girl, but I will tell you the truth. I am going to telegraph to town for Mr Reston; there is a fracture and pressure on the brain."

"And great danger, doctor?"

"Yes," he said, after a pause, "and great danger. But, please God, my child, we will save his life. He is a fine, strong, healthy man. There; I can say no more."

"Thank you," said Madelaine calmly, and she quietly left the room.

"Any one might think that she did not feel it," said the doctor slowly; "but I know better than that. It's wonderful what a woman will suffer without making a sign. I cannot telegraph till eight o'clock, but I may as well write my message," he muttered, as he went down-stairs. "Humph! the news is spreading. Somebody come."

Chapter Twenty One
Harry Looks the Fact in the Face

Harry Vane checked his headlong pace as soon as he was out of the lane, and walked swiftly along by the harbour till he reached the sea. Here, in the shelter of a rock, he stooped down and lit a cigar, before throwing himself on a patch of shingle, and holding his temples with his hands, as he tried to quell the tumult in his brain and to think calmly.

But it was in vain. He felt half mad, and as if the best way out of his difficulty was to go and leap into the sea.

"Curse Pradelle!" he groaned. "I wish I had never seen him—coward, thief, cheat! Oh, what am I talking about? Why didn't I face it, and tell Van Heldre the honest truth? I was innocent. No, no; I was as bad as Pradelle, and he shall disgorge. Every penny shall go back. If he says no, come what may, I'll out with the whole truth."

"I couldn't help it," he groaned after a pause. "I'd give anything to have frankly told the truth."

He walked quickly home, and assuming a calmness he did not feel, entered the drawing-room, where Louise was seated reading.

"Your company gone?" he said roughly.

"Yes, dear. Papa has walked home with Madelaine."

Harry turned sharply round, for he mentally pictured in one agonising thought the scene at Van Heldre's home.

"Is anything the matter?" asked Louise.

"Matter? No. It's very dark outside, and the light makes one's eyes ache. Seen Pradelle?"

"No, dear," said Louise gravely. "I thought he went out with you."

"Yes, of course, but he likes to go wandering about the town. I wanted a quiet smoke by the water-side. I'm tired. I think I shall go to bed."

"Do, dear. I'll wait till papa comes."

"Good night."

"Good night, Harry dear," she said rising, and, putting her arms around his neck, she laid her cheek to his. "Good night, dear. Harry darling, don't worry about the work. Do it like a brave, true man; it will make father so happy."

There was a sudden catching sob in Harry Vine's throat, as like a flash, the memory of old happy boy and girl days came back. He caught his sister to his breast, and held her tightly there as he kissed her passionately again and again.

"My darling brother!" cried Louise as she tightened her grasp about his neck. "And you will try for all our sakes."

"Yes, yes," he said in a hoarse whisper.

"Never mind what poor aunt says. Be a man—a frank, honourable man, Harry. It is the order of the true *haute noblesse* after all. You will try?"

"Please God, yes, Lou—so hard—ah, so hard."

"That's like my dear brother once again," she cried, fondling him. "There, darling, I'm speaking to you like our mother would. Let me be your mother to you as well as sister. You will begin again?"

"Yes, yes, yes," he whispered hoarsely; "from this moment, Lou, I will."

"May I say more?" she said gently, as her hand played about his brow.

"Yes, anything, Lou; anything. I've been a fool, but that's all over now."

"Then about Mr Pradelle?"

"Curse Mr Pradelle," he cried passionately. "I wish I had never brought him here."

"Don't curse, dear," said Louise, with a sigh of relief. "Yes, there has been an ugly cloud over this house, but it is lifting fast, Harry dear, and we are all going to be very happy once again. Good night."

He could not speak; something seemed to choke him; but he strained her to his heart, and ran out of the room.

"Oh!" ejaculated Louise; and throwing herself into a chair, she burst into a passion of weeping; but her tears were those of joy, and a relief to her overburdened heart.

"Is it too late?" said Harry to himself, as a cold chilly hand seemed to grasp his heart. "No; I can keep my own secret, and I will turn over a new leaf now, and old Crampton shall rule it for me. What an idiot I have been!"

He shuddered as he recalled the scene in Van Heldre's office, and involuntarily held his hands close to the landing-lamp.

"Poor old fellow!" he said, as his hand involuntarily went towards his vest; "but he'll soon get over that. He couldn't have known me in the dark. I—My locket!"

He turned like ice as he gazed down to see that the gold locket he wore at his watch-chain had been torn off.

"No, no; I lost it when I threw myself down on the shingle," he muttered, as he fingered the broken link. "I could not have lost it there."

Just then he started, for there was a faint cough on his left.

"Then he has come back," he cried hastily; and going a few steps along the passage he tapped sharply, and entered Pradelle's room.

Chapter Twenty Two
The Punishment Begins

Pradelle was seated in a low chair with his head resting on his hand. He looked up curiously at Harry as the young man hastily closed and locked the door.

"You've come at last, then," said Pradelle sourly, as he winced from the pain he was in.

"Yes, I've come at last," replied Harry. "Now, Pradelle, no nonsense! There has been enough of this. Where is the money?"

"Where's what?"

"The money—those notes?"

"I don't know what you mean."

"Then I'll tell you plainly. I want five hundred pounds in Bank of England notes, stolen by you from Mr Van Heldre's safe."

Pradelle sank back in his chair.

"I like that," he said, with a low, sneering laugh.

"No nonsense. Give me those notes."

"You mean you want to give me the notes."

"I mean what I say," cried Harry, in a low, angry voice.

"Why, you went and got them, as we agreed."

"I did not go and get them as we agreed."

"Yes, you did, for I saw you."

"How dare you, you lying cur!" cried Harry, seizing him by the throat and holding him back against the chair. "Give me the notes."

"Don't! don't! You've hurt me enough once to-night. Look! my head's bleeding now."

Harry loosed his grasp, for the fact was patent.

"I—I hurt you?"

"Yes, with that ruler. What made you hit me like that? Take me for old Van Heldre?"

Harry's jaw dropped, and he stared wildly at his companion.

"I—I hit you!" he faltered, as he struggled with his memory and asked himself whether he had stricken Pradelle down and not the old merchant.

"Well, I've got a cut two inches long and my head all swollen up. What made you do it?"

"I—do it! Here, what do you mean?"

"Mean? Why, that you were so long getting the loan—"

"Say stealing the notes. It would be more like the truth," said Harry shortly.

"I won't. I say you were so long getting the loan that I came to see what you were about, and you flew at me and knocked me down with the big ruler. Took me for a watchman, I suppose."

"But when?—where?" cried Harry excitedly.

"Where? By the safe; inner office. What a fool you were!"

"Impossible!" thought Harry, as his confusion wore off. "Look here," he cried aloud, "this is a mean, contemptible lie. You have the money; give it me, I say."

"Supposing I had it," snarled Pradelle, "what for?"

"To restore it to its owner."

"Well, seeing that I haven't got the money I say you shall not give it back. If I had got it I'd say the same."

"You have got it. Come, no excuses."

"I tell you I haven't got a penny. You struck me down after you had taken it from the safe."

"It's a lie!" cried Harry fiercely. "I was not going to do the accursed work, and I did not strike you down."

"Then look here," cried Pradelle, pointing to his injured head.

"I know nothing about that. You have the money, and I'll have it before I leave this room."

"You'll be clever then," sneered Pradelle.

"Will you give it me?"

"No. How can I?"

"Don't make me wild, Pradelle, for I'm desperate enough without that. Give me those notes, or, by all that's holy, I'll go straight to the police and charge you with the theft."

"Do," said Pradelle, "if you dare."

The man's coolness staggered Harry for the moment.

"If I'd got the money do you think I should be fool enough to make all this fuss? What do you mean? What game are you playing? Come, honour among—I mean, be square with me. You've got the notes."

"Ah!" ejaculated Harry, with a look of disgust. "I tell you I have not."

"Harry! Harry!"

It was his sister's voice, and he heard her knocking sharply at his door.

"Look here, Pradelle, you've got those notes, and I tell you once more, you have to give them up or it's a case of police."

He had been moving towards the door, which he unfastened and threw open.

"I'm here, Louy," he said.

"Quick, dear! A message from papa. We are to go on to Mr Van Heldre's at once."

"Van Heldre's?" faltered Harry, whose legs seemed to give way beneath him.

"Yes, dear; a policeman brought the message."

"A policeman?"

"Something is wrong. No, no, don't turn like that. It is not father, but Mr Van Heldre, so the man said. I think it is a fall."

Harry Vine's breath came thick and short. What should he do? Fly at once? No; that meant being taken and brought ignominiously back.

"Don't hesitate, dear," said Louise; "Pray come quickly."

"Yes," said Harry huskily. "Of course, I'll come on. Will you—you go first?"

"Harry, what are you thinking, dear? Why do you look so shocked? Indeed I am not deceiving you."

"Deceiving me?"

"No, dear; I am sure it is not papa who is hurt. There come along, and see—for Madelaine's sake."

She said these last words very softly, almost in a whisper; but the only effect they had upon him was to make him shudder.

What should he do—face the danger or go? He must face it; he knew he must. It was his only hope, and already his sister was hurrying him to the door—his sister, perhaps unconsciously to hand him over to the police.

"No," he said to himself, with an attempt to be firm, "he could not have seen me; but was it after all Pradelle I struck down?"

A chill shot through him.

The locket torn from his watch-chain?

"Why, Harry dear, you seem quite upset."

"Upset—I—yes, it is so sudden. I am a bit—there, I'm all right now."

"Poor Madelaine! she must be in sad trouble."

Greater than the speaker realised.

She was in the dining-room with the elder Vine, and hung for a few moments on Louise's neck to sob forth her troubles when she entered. Then, without a word or look at Harry, she hurried up-stairs.

"Why did you not speak to her, Harry?" whispered Louise.

He made no reply, but sat listening to his father, his eyes dilated and throat dry.

"And—and do they suspect any one?" whispered the young man in a voice he did not know for his own.

"No; the police have been away since, and they think they have a clue—two pedlars who have been about the place lately."

"And Mr Van Heldre—is—is he badly hurt?"

"Very badly. It is doubtful whether he can recover."

The young man's breath came and went in a strange labouring way as he sat rigidly upon his seat, while his father went on telling him fact after fact that the son knew only too well.

"Poor Van Heldre! First the ship, then this terrible calamity. Crampton tells me that there was a sum of money deposited in the safe—five hundred pounds in notes, and all gone—every penny—all gone. Poor old Crampton! he almost worshipped Van Heldre. He is nearly wild with grief. One minute he scowled at me savagely; the next minute he was apologetic. It's a terrible business, children. I thought you had better both come on, for, of course, I could not leave now."

Just then Mrs Van Heldre came down, looking red-eyed and pale, to take Louise to her breast.

"Thank you, my dear, thank you," she sobbed; "it was like you to come. And you too, Harry Vine." She took and pressed the young man's hand which was dank and cold. Then, in a quick access of gratitude, she laid her hands upon his shoulders, and kissed him.

"Thank you, my dear," she said in a voice broken with sobs. "You seem always to have been like Maddy's brother. I might have known that you would come."

If ever man suffered agony, that man was Harry Vine as he listened to the poor simple-hearted woman's thanks. His punishment had commenced, and every time the door opened he gave a guilty start, and turned white as ash.

"Don't take it like that, Harry," said Louise tenderly. "There is always hope, dear."

She looked lovingly in his eyes, and pressed his hand, as their father went on talking in a low voice, and giving utterance to his thoughts.

"The scoundrels, as far as I can make out, Harry, my boy, seem to have got in by the back. The door was unfastened, and they must have known a good deal about the place—by watching I suppose, for they knew where to find the keys, and how to open the safe."

Harry's breath came in a spasmodic way, as he sat there chained, as it were, to his place.

"Five hundred pounds. A very heavy sum. I must not blame him, poor fellow, but I should have thought it a mistake to have so large a sum in the house."

At last the doctor descended looking very grave.

"Ah, Knatchbull," said Vine in an excited whisper as he rose and caught the doctor's hand; "how is he?"

The doctor shook his head.

"Has he recovered his senses?"

"No."

"Nor said a word about who his assailants were?"

"No, sir, nor is he likely to for some time to come."

Harry Vine sat with his eyes closed, not daring to look; and as the doctor's words came a terrible weight of dread seemed to be lifted from his brain.

"I may go up now, may I not?"

"No, sir, certainly not," said the doctor.

"But we are such old friends; we were boys together, Knatchbull."

"If you were twin-brothers, sir, I should say the same. Why, do you know, sir, I've forbidden Mrs Van Heldre to go into the room. She could not control her feelings, and absolute silence is indispensable."

"Then he is alone?"

"No, no; his daughter is with him. By George! Mr Vine, if I had been a married man instead of a surly old soured bachelor, I should be so proud and jealous of such a girl as Miss Van Heldre that I should have been ready to poison the first young fellow who dared to think about her."

"We are all very proud of Madelaine," said Vine slowly. "I love her as if she were my own child."

"Humph! your sister is not," said the doctor dryly.

"No, my sister is not," said the old man slowly.

"Then, now, Mr Vine, if you please, I am going to ask you people to go."

"Go?" said Vine, in angry remonstrance.

"Yes; you can do nothing. No change is likely to take place, perhaps for days, and with Miss Van Heldre for nurse and Crampton to act as my help if necessary, there will be plenty of assistance here. What I want most is quiet."

"Harry, take Louise home," said the old man quickly.

"And you will go with them, sir?"

"No," said Vine quietly. "If I lay in my room stricken down, John Van Heldre would not leave me, Knatchbull, and I am not going to leave him. Good night, my children. Go at once."

"But, Madelaine, father."

"I shall tell her when she comes down that you were driven away, but I shall send for you to relieve her as soon as I may."

Louise stifled a sob, and the old doctor took and patted her hand.

"You shall be sent for, my dear, as soon as you can be of use. You are helping me in going. There, good night."

A minute later, hanging heavily on her brother's arm, Louise Vine was walking slowly homeward through the silent night. Her heart was too full for words, and Harry uttered a low hoarse sigh from time to time, his lips never once parting to speak till they reached the house.

To the surprise of both, on entering they were confronted by Aunt Marguerite.

"What does all this mean?" she said angrily. "Why did every one go out without telling me a word?"

Louise gently explained to her what had befallen her father's friend.

"Oh," said Aunt Marguerite, with a slight shrug of the shoulders. "Well, it might have been worse. There, I am very tired. Take me up, child, to bed."

"Good night, Harry; you will go and lie down," whispered Louise. "Good night, dear."

She clung to him as if the trouble had drawn them closer, and then went into the hall to light a candle.

"Good night, Henri," said Aunt Marguerite, holding her cheek for the young man's mechanical kiss. "This is very sad, of course, but it seems to me like emancipation for you. If it is, I shall not look upon it as a calamity, but as a blessing for us all. Good night."

The door closed upon her, and Harry Vine sat alone in the dining-room with his hands clasped before him, gazing straight away into his future, and trying to see the road.

"If I had but thrown myself upon his mercy," he groaned; but he knew that it was impossible all through his regret.

What to do now? Where to go? Money? Yes; he had a little, thanks to his regular work as Van Heldre's clerk—his money that he had received, and he was about to use it to escape—where?

"God help me!" groaned the unhappy man at last; "what shall I do?"

He started up in horror for the door handle turned. Had they found out so soon? Was he to be arrested now?

"Harry—Harry!"

A quick husky whisper, but he could not speak.

"Harry, why don't you answer? What are you staring at?"

"What do you want?"

"Look here, old fellow; I've been waiting for you to come up—all these hours. What have you found out? Van Heldre was robbed to-night of five hundred pounds in notes, and you have that money."

"I haven't, I tell you again, not a shilling of it. Look here, what about the police? Have they put it in their hands?"

"The police are trying to trace the money and the man who struck Van Heldre down. Where is that money? It must be restored."

"Then you must restore it, for I swear I haven't a single note. Hang it, man, have I ever played you false?"

Harry was silent. His old companion's persistence staggered him.

"I tell you once more, I went to the office to see if you had got the loan, and was knocked down. Curse it all! is this true or is it not?"

He placed his head close to the light, and Harry shuddered.

"Don't believe me unless you like. I wish I had never come near the place."

"I wish so too," said Harry, coldly.

"There, don't talk like that, man. It has turned out a failure, unless you have got the coin—have you?"

"Have I?" said Harry with utter loathing in his voice, "No!"

"You can believe me or not, as you like, but I always was your friend, and always will be, come what may. Now, look here; we are safe to get the credit of this. If you didn't fell me, some one else did. Van Heldre, I suppose; and now some one must have knocked him down. Of course you'll say it wasn't you."

"No," said Harry coldly. "I shall not say it. I was by the safe, and he caught hold of me. In my horror I hit at him. I wish he had struck me dead instead."

"Don't talk like a fool. Now look here; the game's up and the world's wide. We can start at once, and get to Saint Dree's station in time to catch the up train; let's go, and start afresh somewhere. You and I are safe to get on. Come."

Harry made no reply.

"I've packed up my bag, and I'm ready. Get a few things together, and let's go at once."

"Go—with you?"

"Yes. Look sharp. Every minute now is worth an hour."

Go with Pradelle! the man who had been his evil genius ever since they had first met. A feeling of revulsion, such as he had never felt before, came over Harry Vine, and with a voice full of repressed rage he cried:—

"I'd sooner give myself up to the police."

"Don't be a fool. I tell you to come at once. It's now half-past two. Plenty of time."

"Then in heaven's name go!" said Harry; "and never let me see your face again."

"You'll talk differently to-morrow. Will you; once more?"

"No."

"Then I'm off. What do you mean to do?"

"Wait."

"Wait?"

"Yes. I shall not try to escape. If they suspect me, let them take me. I shall face it all."

"You'll soon alter your tune. Look here; I've been true to you; now you be true to me. Don't set the police on to me. No, you will not do that. You'll come after me; and mind this, you will always hear of me at the old lodgings. Great Ormond Street."

Harry stood gazing straight at him, believing, in spite of his doubts, that Pradelle had not taken the money.

The idea was strengthened.

"Look here; I've only three half-crowns. I can't go with that. How much have you?"

"Thirty shillings."

"Then come, and we'll share."

"No."

"Lend me half then. I'll manage with that."

For answer Harry thrust his hand into his pocket and took out all he had.

"What, all?" said Pradelle, as he took the money.

There was no reply.

"Once more. Will you come?"

Silence!

"Then I'm off."

Harry Vine stood gazing at vacancy; and once more tried to see his own path in the future, but all was dark.

One thing he did know, and that was that his path did not run side by side with Victor Pradelle's. His sister's words still rang in his ears; her kisses seemed yet to be clinging to his lips.

"No," he said at last, moodily; "I'll face what there is to come alone. No," he groaned, "I could not face it, I dare not."

He started guiltily and scared, for there was the sound of a door closing softly.

He listened, and there was a step, but it was not inside the house, it was on the shingle path; and as he darted to the old bay window, he could see a shadowy figure hurrying down the path.

"Gone!" he said in a low voice, "gone! Yes, I'll keep my word—if I can."

He opened the casement window, and stood there leaning against the heavy stone mullion, listening to the low soft beating of the waves far below. The cool air fanned his fevered cheek, and once more the power to think seemed to be coming back.

He had had no idea of the lapse of time, and a flash of broad sunlight came upon him like a shock, making him start away from the window, now lit up, with the old family shield and crest a blaze of brilliant colour.

"*Roy et Foy*," he read silently; and the words seemed to mock him.

Henri Comte des Vignes, the plotter in a robbery of the man who had been his benefactor, perhaps his murderer.

"Comte des Vignes!" he said, with a curious laugh. "Boy! vain, weak, empty-headed boy! What have I done—what have I done?"

"Harry!"

He started round with a cry to face his sister.

"Not been to bed?"

"No," he said wearily. "I could not sleep."

She laid her hands upon his shoulders and kissed him.

"Neither could I," she said, "for thinking of it all. Harry, if he should die!"

He looked down into the eyes gazing so questioningly into his, but his lips framed no answer.

He was listening to the echoing of his sister's words, which seemed to go on and on thrilling through the mazes of his brain, an infinitesimally keen and piercing sound at last, but still so plain and clear—

"*If he should die!*"

Chapter Twenty Three
Uncle Luke Grows Harder

"I would not stop over these, my dears," said Vine, as they sat at breakfast, which was hardly tasted, "but if I neglect them they will die."

He had a glass globe on the table, and from time to time he went on feeding with scraps of mussel the beautiful specimens of actinia; attached to a fragment of rock.

"We'll all go on directly and see if we can be of any use. I'm glad Knatchbull called as he went by."

"But what news!" said Louise sadly. "It seems so terrible. Only yesterday evening so well, and now—"

She finished her remark with a sob.

"It is very terrible," said her father; "but I hope we shall soon hear that the villains are caught."

Harry sat holding the handle of his tea-cup firmly, and gazing straight before him.

"You'll go up to the office, of course, my boy?" said Vine.

"Eh? Go up to the office?" cried Harry, starting.

"Yes, as if nothing had happened. Do all you can to assist Crampton."

"Yes, father."

"He was very quiet and reserved when I went in at seven; quite snappish, I might say. But he was too much occupied and troubled, I suppose, to be very courteous to such an old idler as I am. Ah!" he continued, as a figure passed the window, "here's Uncle Luke."

A cold chill had run through Harry at the mention of Crampton—a chill of horror lest he should suspect anything; and now, at the announcement of his uncle's approach, he felt a flush run up to his temples, and as if the room had suddenly become hot.

"Morning," said Uncle Luke, entering without ceremony, a rush basket in one hand, his strapped-together rod in the other.

"Breakfast? Late for breakfast, isn't it?"

"No, Luke, no; our usual time," said his brother mildly.

"You will sit down and have some, uncle?"

"No, Louy, no," he replied, nodding his head and looking a little less hard at her. "I've had some bread and skim milk, and I'm just off to catch my dinner. The idiot know?"

"My dear Luke!" said his brother mildly, as Uncle Luke made a gesture upward towards Aunt Marguerite's room; "why will you strive to increase the breach between you and our sister?"

"Well, she tells every one that I'm mad. Why shouldn't I call her an idiot? But nice goings on, these. Wonder you're all alive."

"Then you have heard?"

"Heard? Of course. If I hadn't I could have read it in your faces. Look here, sir," he cried, turning sharply on his nephew, "where were you last night?"

Harry clutched the table-cloth that hung into his lap.

"I? Last night?" he faltered.

"Yes; didn't I speak plainly? Where were you last night? Why weren't you down at Van Heldre's, behaving like a man, and fight for your master along with your henchman?"

"Uncle, dear, don't be so unreasonable," said Louise, leaning back and looking up in the old man's face—for he had thrown his basket and rod on a chair, and gone behind her to stand stroking her cheek—"Harry was at home with Mr Pradelle."

"Pradelle, eh?" said the old man sharply. "Not up?"

"Mr Pradelle has gone," said Louise.

"Gone, eh?" said Uncle Luke sharply.

"Yes," said his brother. "Mr Pradelle behaved very nicely. He left this note for me."

"Note, eh? Bank note—"

Harry winced and set his teeth.

"No, no, Luke. Nonsense!"

"Nonsense? I mean to pay for his board and lodging all the time he has been here."

"Absurd, Luke!" said his brother, taking up a liberal meal for a sea-anemone on the end of a thin glass rod. "He said that under the circumstances he felt that he should be an encumbrance to us, and therefore he had gone by the earliest train."

"Like the sneak he is, eh, Harry?"

The young man met his uncle's eyes for the moment, and then dropped his own.

"You'll kill those things with kindness, George. Any one would think you were fattening them for market. So Master Pradelle has gone, eh? Don't cry, Louy; perhaps we can coax him back."

He chuckled, and patted her cheek.

"Uncle, dear, don't talk like that. We are in such trouble."

"About Van Heldre, that boy's master. Yes, of course. Very sad for Mrs Van and little Madelaine. Leslie was down there as soon as one of the miners brought up the news, trying to comfort them."

Harry's teeth gritted slightly, but he relapsed into his former semi-cataleptic state, as if forced to listen, and unable to move.

"I like Leslie," said Vine sadly.

"So do I. At least, I don't dislike him so much as I do some folks. Now if he had been there, he'd have behaved better than you did, Master Harry."

"Uncle, dear, don't be so hard on poor Harry."

"Poor Harry! Good job he is poor. What's the good of being rich for thieves to break through and steal?"

"Ah! what indeed!" said his brother sadly.

"Look at Van Heldre, knocked on the head and going to die."

"Uncle!"

"Well, I dare say he will, and be at rest. Knocked on the head, and robbed of five hundred pounds. My money, every penny."

"Yours, Luke?" said his brother, pointing at him with the glass rod.

"Thanks, no, George; give it to the sea-anemone. I don't like raw winkle."

"But you said that money was yours?"

"Yes; a deposit; all in new crisp Bank of England notes, Harry. Taking care of it for me till I got a fresh investment."

"You surprise me, Luke."

"Always did. Surprised you more if Margaret had had five hundred pounds to invest, eh?"

"Then the loss will fall upon you, uncle," said Louise sympathetically, as she took the old man's hand.

"Yes, my dear. But better have the loss fall upon median Crampton's heavy ebony ruler, eh, Harry?"

The young man looked once more in the searching malicious eyes, and nodded.

"Bad job though, Louy. I'd left poor Harry that money in my will."

"Oh, uncle!" cried Louise, holding his hand to her cheek.

"Yes; but not a penny for you, pussy. There, it don't matter. I shan't miss the money. If I run short, George, you'll give me a crust, same as you do Margaret."

"My dear Luke, I've told you a hundred times, I should be glad if you would give up that—that—"

"Dog kennel?" sneered the old cynic.

"That hut on the cliff, and come and share my home."

"Yes, two hundred times. I'll swear," said Uncle Luke. "You always were weak, George. One idiot's enough for you to keep, and very little does for me. There's my larder," he continued, pointing toward the sea; "and as to Harry here, he won't miss the money. He's going to be the Count des Vignes, and take Aunt Marguerite over to Auvergne, to live in his grand château. Five hundred pounds is nothing to him."

The perspiration stood on Harry's brow, cold and damp, and he sat enduring all this torture. One moment he felt that his uncle suspected him, the next that it was impossible. At times a fierce sensation of rage bubbled up in his breast, and he felt as if he would have liked to strangle the keen-eyed old man; but directly after he felt that this was his punishment called down by his weakness and folly, and that he must bear it.

"Going, Harry?" said his father, as the young man rose.

"Yes; it is time I went on to the office."

"Good boy. Punctuality's the soul of business," said Uncle Luke. "Pity we have no corporation here. You might rise to be mayor. Here, I don't think I shall go fishing to-day. I'll stop, and go on with you two to see old Van. Louy, dear, go and tell your aunt I'm here. She might like to come down and have a snarl."

"Uncle, dear," said Louise, rising and kissing him, "you can't deceive me."

She went out after Harry.

"Not a pair, George," said Uncle Luke, grimly. "Louy's worth live hundred of the boy."

"He'd drive me mad, Lou, he'd drive me mad," cried Harry, tearing his hand from his sister's grasp, and hurrying away; but only to run back repentant and kiss her fondly before hurrying away.

Chapter Twenty Four
The Trifle that Tells Tales

As Harry Vine left his father's house, and hurried down the slope he gazed wildly out to sea. There were no thoughts of old Huguenot estates, or ancient titles, but France lay yonder over that glistening sea, and as he watched a cinnamon-sailed lugger gliding rapidly south and east, he longed to be aboard.

Why should he not do as Pradelle had done, escape from the dangers which surrounded and hemmed him in? It was the easiest way out of his difficulties.

There were several reasons.

To go would stamp him with the crime, and so invite pursuit. To do this was to disgrace father and sister, and perhaps be taken and dragged back.

When he reached the harbour, instead of turning down to the left, by the estuary, he made his way at once on to the shore, and after a little hesitation, picked out the spot where on the previous night he had thrown himself down, half mad with the course he had been called upon to take.

The engraved gold locket with which his nervous fingers had so often played would be lying somewhere among the stones, perhaps caught and wedged in a crevice. It was so easy when lying prone to catch such an ornament and snap it off without knowing. He looked carefully over the heap of stones, and then around in every direction; but the locket was not there.

"It must be somewhere about," he said angrily, as if he willed that it should; but there was no sign of the glittering piece of well-polished gold, and a suspicion that had for a long time being growing increased rapidly in force, till he could bear it no longer, and once more something seemed to urge him to fly.

He had clung so to that hope, shutting his eyes to the truth, and going down to the beach to search for the locket. Even when he had not found it, he said that perhaps some child had picked it up; but there was the truth now refusing to be smothered longer, and he walked on hastily to reach Van Heldre's office, so as to search for the locket there. For it was the truth he had fell that sudden snatch, that tug when the old merchant dashed at him, and then fell. The locket was torn off then. He might not be too late. In the hurry and confusion it might not have been seen.

The ordinary door of entrance to the offices was closed, and at the house the blinds were half drawn-down. He felt that he could not go to the front door. So after a little hesitation, he went round into the back lane, and with a strange sensation of dread, passed through the gateway and down the steps into the neatly kept garden yard.

Everything was very still; and Harry Vine, with an attempt to look as if entirely bent upon his ordinary task, went up to the door, entered the glass corridor, as he had entered it the night before, and by a tremendous effort of will walked quickly into the outer office.

The inner door was open, and after a hasty glance round, he was in the act of crossing to it when he found himself face to face with the old clerk. For some moments neither spoke—the old man gazing straight at Harry with a peculiar, stony glare, and the latter, so thrown off his balance, that no words would come.

"Good morning," he said at last.

The old man continued to stare as if looking him through and through.

"What do you want?" he said at last.

"Want? It is past nine o'clock, and—"

"Go back. The office is closed."

"Go back?" said Harry, troubled by the old man's manner more than by the announcement; for it seemed natural that the office should be closed.

"Yes, young man; you can go back."

"But—"

"I said, go back, sir—go back! The office is closed," said the old man fiercely; and there was something menacing in the manner of his approach, as he backed his junior to the closed door, and unlocked it and pointed to the street.

"Mr Crampton—" began Harry.

The old man looked at him as if he could have struck him down, waved him aside, and closed and locked the door.

Harry stood a few moments thinking. What could he do to gain an entrance there, and have a quiet search of the place? The only plan open seemed to be to wait until Crampton had gone away.

He had just come to this conclusion, after walking a short distance along the street and returning, when a fresh shock awaited him. Van Heldre's front door was open, and Duncan Leslie came out, walking quickly towards him, but not noticing whom he approached till they were face to face.

"Ah, Mr Vine," he said, holding out his hand; "I had some thought of coming up to you."

"What for?"

"What for? Surely at a time like this there ought not to be a gap between friends. I am afraid you misunderstood me the other night. I am very sorry. There is my hand."

But trembling with that other anxiety, Harry Vine had still the old sling of jealousy festering in his breast. Leslie had just come from Van Heldre's; perhaps he had been talking with Madelaine even there; and, ignoring the proffer, Harry bowed coldly and was passing on, but Leslie laid his hand upon his arm.

"If I have been more in the wrong than I think, pray tell me," said Leslie. "Come, Vine, you and I ought not to be ill friends."

For a moment the desire was upon him to grasp the extended hand. It was a time when he was ready to cling to anyone for help and support, and the look in his eyes changed.

"Ah, that's better!" said Leslie frankly. "I want to talk to you."

Why not go with him? Why not tell Leslie all, and ask his help and advice? He needed both sorely. It was but a moment's fancy, which he cast aside as mad. What would Leslie say to such a one as he? And how could he take the hand of a man who was taking the place which should be his?

Leslie stood still in the narrow seaport street for a few moments, looking after Harry, who had turned off suddenly and walked away.

Chapter Twenty Five
On the Rack

How was he to pass that day? At home in a state of agony, starting at every word, trembling at every knock which came to the door? He felt that he could not do that, and that he must be engaged in some way to crush down the thoughts which were fermenting in his brain.

Certain now that he had lost the locket in the slight struggle in the office, he literally determined to leave no stone unturned, and walked once more down to the beach, where he went on searching, till glancing up he saw Poll Perrow, the old fish-woman, resting her arm on the rail at the edge of the cliff, looking down at him, and apparently watching him.

That was sufficient to turn him from his quest, and he went off hastily, and without intent, to find himself upon the long, narrow, pier-like point which acted as a breakwater to the harbour.

He went on and on, till he reached the end, where with the sea on three sides, and the waves washing at his feet, he sat down on one of the masses of rock as his uncle so often took up his position to fish, and watched the swirling current that ran so swiftly by the end of the point.

"How easy it would be," he thought, "to step down off the end of the rock into the sea, and be carried right away."

"And disgrace them by acting like a coward," he said half aloud; and leaping up he walked swiftly back to the cliff, and then went up the path that led to home.

At the door he met Louise and his father.

"Back again, Harry?" said the latter, wonderingly.

"Yes; the place is shut up. No business to-day," he said hastily.

"Did you see Madelaine?" asked Louise, anxiously.

He shook his head.

"Or poor Mrs Van Heldre?" said his father.

"No; I thought it would worry them."

"But you asked how Van Heldre was?"

"No," said Harry, confusedly. "I—it seemed a pity to disturb them."

"Come back and make amends," said Vine rather sternly. "They must not think we desert them in their trouble."

"But both you and Louise have been on this morning."

"Yes, and would have stayed if it would have helped them," said Vine. "Come."

Harry hung back for a moment, and then, in the hope that he might be able to slip away from them, and search the office in Crampton's absence, he went on by their side.

To the surprise of all, as they reached the house the door was opened by Crampton, who stood scowling in the doorway, and barred the way.

"How is he now, Crampton?" said Vine, as Harry's heart began to palpitate with the fear that all this was intended for him.

"Dying," said the old man, shortly.

"No, no, not so bad as that," cried Louise and her father in a breath. "Doctor Knatchbull said—"

"What doctors always say, Miss Louise, that while there's life there's hope. 'Tisn't true. There's often life and no hope, and it's so here."

"Crampton, you are taking too black a view of the matter," said Vine, quickly. "It's very good of you to be so much moved as his old and faithful servant, but let's all, as a duty, look on the best side of things."

"There is no best side," said Crampton, bitterly. "The whole world's corrupt. Well; what do you people want to say?"

"To say? We have come to be of help if we can. Come, Louise, my dear."

He took a step forward, but the old man stood fast.

"You know all there is to know," said the old clerk sourly, as he looked half angrily at Vine, and then, totally ignoring Harry, he turned his eyes on Louise, when the hard look softened a little. "Send in by-and-by if you want to hear, or I'll send to you—if he dies."

"Dies!" cried Vine, with a start of horror. "No, no; he is not so bad as that."

"As bad as a man can be to live."

"You forget yourself, Crampton," said Vine, with dignity. "You forget yourself. But there, I can look over it all now. I know what you must feel. Go and tell Mrs Van Heldre or Miss Madelaine that we are here."

The old man hesitated for a few moments, and then drew back to allow Louise and her father to pass; but as Harry stepped forward hastily to follow, the old man interposed, and fiercely raised his hand.

"No," he said. "I'm master now. Go back! Go back!"

Harry shrank from him as Crampton stood pointing down the street, and then strove hard to master the abject sensation of dread which made him feel that all the old man said was true. He was master now, and with an angry gesture he turned and walked swiftly away, to turn as he reached the end of the street and see Crampton watching him from the door-step, and with his hand still raised.

"Am I such an abject coward that I am frightened of that old man?" he muttered, as he recalled how only a few hours back he used to treat him with a flippant condescending contempt. "Yes, he's master now, and means to show it. Why did I not go in boldly?"

He knew why, and writhed in his impotence and dread. The task of keeping a bold face on the matter was harder than he thought. He wandered about the town in an objectless way hour after hour, and then went home. His father and sister had not returned, but Aunt Marguerite was down, ready to rise in her artificial manner and extend her hand.

"Ah, Henri, my child," she said; "how pale and careworn you look! Where are they all?"

"Van Heldre's," said Harry shortly.

"Ah, poor man! Very bad, I hear. Yes, it's very sad, but I do not see why his accident should so reverse our regular lives at home. Henri, dear, you must break with Mr Van Heldre after this."

"I have broken with him, aunt," cried the young man fiercely.

"Ah! that's right; that is spoken like one of our race should speak. Good boy. And, Henri, my darling, of course there will be no more silly flirtings with you sister's friend. Remember what I have told you of the fair daughters of France, and let the fraülein marry that man Leslie."

"Aunt, you'll drive me mad," exclaimed Harry, grinding his teeth; and without another word he dashed out of the house. His first thought was to go up the cliff path on to the wild granite plain and moors which overlooked the town, but he could not stir in that direction. There was the hunting dread of that locket being found, and he went on down again into the town, and looked about the shore for hours.

The afternoon was growing old, and his mind was becoming better able to bear the brunt of all that was to come.

He raised his eyes, and was on the point of going back home to see if his father and sister had returned, when he caught sight of old Crampton coming out of the post-office, after which the old man walked on in the direction of his home.

The opportunity at last! The office would be unguarded; and, walking swiftly in the direction of Van Heldre's, he turned round into the back lane, and, strung up to act firmly and determinedly, he pressed the back gate.

It was fast.

Desperate and determined now, he went round to the principal office door, but it was locked. Harry drew a long breath, and walked straight to the front door and rang. The maid who opened drew back to let him pass.

"My father—sister here?"

"In the drawing-room; in with my mistress."

"No, no," said Harry hastily, as the maid moved towards the door; "never mind me; I'll go in soon."

The woman left him in the hall, and he waited till he heard the kitchen-door close, when he walked swiftly and softly to the glass window, and hurried into the office.

The inner office door was open, and he darted in, to hastily look all round, under table, chairs, beneath the bookshelves, among the newspapers that lay in places in a heap; but there was no sign of the missing trinket, and an icy feeling of dread began to grow upon him.

The waste-paper basket!

It was half full, and the locket might easily have dropped in there, but a hasty examination was without avail.

The fireplace!

He looked there, in the ready-laid fire, beneath the grate, in the fender; he even raised it, but without avail.

"It must be here somewhere," he muttered fiercely; and he looked round again, and in amongst the papers on the table.

Still without avail.

"It is in the waste-paper basket," he said, with a feeling of conviction upon him, as, trembling in every limb, he went to the other side of the table where it stood.

"What's that?"

A faint sound. Was it Crampton returning?

He stood listening, his brow glistening with the cold perspiration; and as he remained breathless and intent, he seemed to see again the office as it was on the previous night, almost totally dark, the safe opened, and the shadowy figure of Van Heldre dashing at him.

Was it fancy, or was the place really dark? A curious mist was before his eyes, but all was silent; and he went down on his knees, turned to a waste-paper basket upside down—the torn letters, envelopes, and circulars forming a heap on the well-worn Turkey carpet; but no piece of metal fell out with a low pat.

"It is here; it is here; it shall be here," he panted; and then he sprang to his feet shivering with shame and dread, face to face with Madelaine Van Heldre, who, pale with emotion, heavy-eyed with weeping, but erect and stern, flashed upon him a look full of anger and contempt.

"Ah, Madelaine!" he stammered, "have you seen a half-written letter— must be here somewhere—left on my desk?"

"Henri des Vignes—the soul of honour!" she said bitterly. "Have you fallen so low as this?"

"I—I don't understand you."

"You coward! And you can lie to me—the woman you professed to love!"

"Madelaine, for pity's sake."

"Let me tell you what you are looking for."

"I—looking for?"

"Yes; you are looking for something for fear it should fall into the hands of the police."

"I don't know what you mean."

"Oh! is it possible that a man can be so base? Let me tell you, then. You are looking for the locket snapped from your chain when my poor father was stricken down."

"Madelaine! what are you saying?"

"Stricken down by the wretch whom, in my pity and love, I had asked him to receive into his house, that he might redeem his character, and prove to the world that he had only been weak."

"You—you did this!" he gasped.

"I did this; and found that in his love for his old friend my father had already determined to be a second father to his son."

"Oh!"

"And for what? To bring him where he might play the part of serpent on the hearth, and sting him to the quick."

"Madelaine, for God's sake, mercy!"

She could have none then.

"To give shelter, ah! and, some day, the hand of the weak, trusting girl who loved him, and said, 'Give him time, father, and he will change'—to give him some day her hand and love, and welcome him as a son."

"Madelaine!" he cried, throwing himself on his knees, to clasp the hem of her dress and literally grovel at her feet.

"To the man who could stoop to be a vile contemptible thief!"

"No, no, no!" cried Harry, springing to his feet; "not that—not that."

"And rob him."

"No; anything but that. I swear I did not do that."

"And when detected in the act did not scruple to play the would-be murderer."

"Madelaine, have pity!"

"And cruelly struck him down."

"Madelaine. All you say is not true."

"Not true? Go up to where he lies hovering between life and death, and see your work. Coward! Villain! Oh, that I should e'er have been so weak as to think that I loved such a wretch as you!"

He drew himself up.

"It is not true," he said. "I did not commit that theft; and it was in my agony and shame at being found before the safe that I struck him down."

"You confess you were there—that you were a partner in the crime?"

"Yes, I was there," said Harry slowly; "and I sinned. Well, I am ready. Take your revenge. I am in your hands. You have the evidence of my crime. Denounce me, and let me go out of your sight for ever."

"And my father's old friend—my second father? And Louise, my more than sister. What of them?"

He quailed before her as she stood, her eyes flashing, a hectic flush on either cheek; and he felt he had never known Madelaine Van Heldre till then.

"Oh!" he groaned as he covered his face with his hands, "I am guilty. Let me suffer," he said slowly. "They will soon forget, for I shall be as one who is dead."

"No," she said; "I cannot speak. If he who is hovering between life and death could advise, he would say, 'Be silent; let his conscience be his judge.' I say the same. Go. The locket is not there."

"The police?" he cried in a questioning tone.

"No," she said, "the secret was mine. I found it tightly clasped in my poor father's hand."

"Then the secret is safe."

"Safe?" she said scornfully. "Safe? Yes, it is my secret. You asked for mercy. I give it you, for the sake of all who are dear to me; and because, if he lives, my poor father would not prosecute the son of his old friend. There is your locket. Take it, and I pray heaven we may never meet again. Crampton!"

"Yes, Miss Maddy, Crampton—old Crampton, who held you in his arms when you were one hour old."

"What are you doing here?"

"Watching my master's interests—watching over you."

"Then you have heard?"

"Every word, my child."

"You cursed spy!" cried Harry fiercely, as he seized the old man by the throat.

"You've done enough, Master Harry Vine, enough to transport you, sir; and if he dies to send you to your death."

"Crampton!" shrieked Madelaine, as Harry drew back trembling.

"Be merciful, like you, my dear? No, I cannot."

"Then you'll go and tell—"

"What I've heard now, my dear? No; there is no need."

"What do you mean?"

"To watch over you, whether my poor master lives or dies. I know you! You'd forgive him if he asked."

"Never! But Crampton, it is our secret. He must go—to repent. Dear Crampton," she cried, throwing her arms about his neck, "you must be merciful too!"

"Too late, my dear," said the old man sternly; "too late."

He placed his arm round her and drew her to his breast, as if to defend her from Harry.

"When I went home that night," he continued in a slow, solemn voice, "I felt that something was not right, and I came on here—in time to see—"

"Oh!" cried Madelaine.

"In time to see that shivering, guilty wretch flee from where he had struck my poor master down; and if I had been a young man and strong I could have killed him for his crime."

"You saw him?"

"Yes, my dear. No need for the locket to bear witness. I had my duty to do, and it is done."

"Done?"

"Yes; to punish him for his crime."

"Crampton, what have you said? Harry! before it is too late!"

"It is too late, my child. See here." He held out a scrap of reddish paper. "From the London police. I could not trust those bunglers here."

Madelaine snatched the paper from his hand and read it.

"Oh!" she moaned, and the paper dropped from her hand.

Harry snatched it from the floor, read it, let it fall, and reeled against the table, whose edge he grasped.

Madelaine struggled and freed herself from the old man's detaining arm.

"Harry!" she panted—"it would be my father's wish—escape! There may yet be time."

He leaned back against the table, gazing at her wildly, as if he did not grasp her words. Then he started as if stung by a sudden lash as old Crampton said: "I have done my duty. It is too late."

Chapter Twenty Six
Leslie Makes a Declaration

"Where is Harry?" said George Vine that same evening, as he sat in his study, surrounded by his living specimens of natural history, and with the paper before him that he had vainly tried to fill.

"He must be waiting about down in the town—for news," said Louise, looking up from her work.

"He ought to have been here to dinner, my dear," said the naturalist querulously; "it would have been some comfort. Tut—tut—tut! I cannot collect my thoughts; everything seems to slip from me."

"Then why not leave it, dear, for the present? This terrible trouble as unhinged you."

She had risen and gone to the back of his chair, to pass her arm lovingly about his neck, and he leaned back, dropping his pen to take her hand and play with it, pressing it to his lips from time to time.

"I suppose I had better," he said sadly; "but I am dreadfully behindhand—four letters from the Society unanswered. I wish they did not expect so much from me, my darling."

"I do not," said Louise, smiling. "Why should you wish to be less learned than you are?"

"Had we not better go on again to Van Heldre's now?"

"I think I would leave it till quite the last thing."

"Ye-es," said Vine, hesitating, "perhaps so; but I don't like it, my child. Van Heldre has always been to me like a brother, and it seems so strange and hard to be almost driven from his side. Doctor's like a tyrant, and as for Crampton—there, wait till the poor fellow is well again, and if we together do not give Master Crampton a severe setting down, my name is not what it is."

"You must forgive it, dear; he is so anxious about his master."

"Yes, yes, of course," said Vine pettishly; "but the man is so insolently overbearing. Really, my dear, if he has been in the habit of behaving to Harry as he has conducted himself towards us, I do not wonder at the poor boy's intense dislike to the office routine."

"It is not fair to judge him now," said Louise.

"No, my dear, I suppose not; but it is very painful, when I feel as if you and I have quite a right in that poor fellow's bedroom, to be literally expelled, Madelaine siding with the doctor, and poor Mrs Van Heldre really utterly broken down."

"We should only make matters more painful by interfering. Let us go and ask how Mr Van Heldre is about ten, and I will get Madelaine to let me sit up with her and help."

"No," said Vine, rising and pacing the room, "I shall not sit down quietly. I feel that it is my duty to insist upon being there. I shall go up at once."

"Wait till I put on my things, dear."

"No; I shall only go for an hour now, and I will come back and fetch you later on."

"But, papa, dear!"

"There, there, there! don't be alarmed, I shall not get out of temper with Crampton now. That will keep."

"Then you will go—now?"

"Yes," he said decidedly; "I cannot sit here."

"But you hardly tasted your dinner. Let me get you some tea first."

"My dear child, I can touch nothing; and pray don't oppose me. I am in such a state of nervous irritation that if you do I am sure I shall say something unkind, and then I shall be more upset than I am now."

"I am not afraid," said Louise, hanging on his shoulder for a few moments, and then kissing his wrinkled, careworn brow.

"Thank you, my darling, thank you. You will not mind being left? Harry ought to be here."

"Oh, no, dear; but you will come back soon and tell me all. Harry will be here before then."

"Of course, my dear, of course."

"And you will give my dear love to Madelaine," Louise cried, as her father moved away from the door.

He nodded, and with bended head went off down the path, while, after watching till he had disappeared, Louise stood gazing out to sea, as the evening began to close in, and a soft, melancholy breeze came whispering among the trees.

She could not tell why it was, but everything seemed to wear a different aspect, and a profound sense of dejection came upon her, which brought the tears to her eyes.

Where could Harry be? It was hours since she had seen him, and as she felt how much she required help and counsel at that time, her thoughts strayed to Duncan Leslie, and she looked across an intervening depression to the steep cliff path, which led up past Uncle Luke's den to the Mine House, where a faint light twinkled, and away beyond, like a giant finger pointing upward, the great chimney shaft towered.

She stood gazing at that faint light for some minutes, with her eyes growing dim, and the troubled feelings which had often assailed her in secret increasing till, with checks burning and an angry ejaculation, she turned into the house, where she fetched her work from the study, and was soon after seated by the window trying to sew. At the end of a few minutes she rose and rang for the lamp, which was brought in by the cook.

"Where's Liza?" said Louise.

"Gone down into the town, ma'am," said the cook, looking at her uneasily.

"What for? She did not ask leave."

"She said she would not be long, ma'am," said the woman evasively.

"Tell her to bring in the tea the moment my father returns. Let everything be ready."

"Yes, ma'am."

The woman hurried out, and Louise sat gazing at the door, thinking that the woman's manner was strange.

"I am upset," she said with a sigh, "and that makes things seem different."

She had been dreaming over her work for a few minutes when she started, for she heard voices talking loudly. She sat up in her chair with her senses on the strain, trembling lest there should be bad news from the Van Heldre's. She was nor kept long in suspense, for there was a quick step in the hall, a sharp rap at the door, and Liza entered, scarlet with excitement and exertion, her shawl over one arm, her hat hanging by its strings from the other.

"Liza!"

"Yes, miss, it's me. Can I speak to you a minute?"

"Have you brought news from Mr Van Heldre's?"

"Which I have, miss, and I haven't."

"How is he?" cried Louise, paying no heed to Liza's paradoxical declaration.

"No better, and no worse, miss; but it wasn't about that. I leaves you this day month, miss; and as much sooner as you can suit yourself."

"Very well, Liza. That will do."

"No, miss!" cried the girl excitedly, "it won't do. 'Cusing people o' being thiefs when it was nothing but a bit of a bundle o' old rags and things I saved, as might ha' been burnt, and they bought 'em of me, and I bought the ribbons o' them."

"I do not wish to hear anymore about that transaction, Liza; but I am glad to hear you can explain it away. You should have been frank at first."

"So ought other people, miss, if you'll excuse me; and not go taking away a poor servant's character by alluding to money left on no chimley-pieces as I never took."

"Liza!"

"Yes, miss; I know, and thinking o' sending for the police."

"I had too much feeling for you, Eliza, and for your future character. I did not even send you away."

"I should think not indeed, miss. Mother and me's as honest as the day; and if you want police send for 'em for them as has been picking and stealing."

"My good girl, what do you mean?"

"Oh, you don't know, o' course, miss; but you very soon will. And him with his fine airs, and his boots never shiny enough. He'll find out the difference now; and as to me staying in a home like this where one of us is a thief, I've got my character to look after, and—"

There was a sharp knock and ring, and from force of habit, Liza turned.

"In a month, miss, if you please; and now you're going to hear what come an hour ago, and is all over the town by now."

Louise caught at the table to steady herself, and her lips parted to question the girl, but she had hurried out of the room. The door was opened, a deep male voice was heard, and directly after Duncan Leslie hurried in.

"It is no time for ceremony," he gasped, breathlessly. "Where is your father?"

"At—Mr Van Heldre's," panted Louise as she turned to him with extended hands. "Mr Leslie, pray—pray tell me—what is wrong?"

"Tell you?" he cried, catching her almost in his arms, and holding her firmly; and his voice sounded deep, hoarse and full of commiseration. "How am I to dare to tell you, Louise?"

"Mr Leslie!"

She half struggled from him, but he retained her hands. "Tell me," he cried; "what shall I say? Am I to speak out?"

"Yes, quick! You torture me."

"Torture you, whom I would die to save from pain!" She trembled and flushed, and turned pale by turns.

"I must tell you," he said; "there is no time to spare. I have—try and bear it, my child, like the true, brave heart you are. Your brother—"

"Yes; quick! what do you mean?" Leslie stood looking at her for a few moments, his mind dragged two ways, and shrinking from giving his news as he gazed into her dilated eyes.

"Why do you not speak?" she said passionately. "Do you not see the pain you give me?"

"I must speak," he groaned. "Where is your brother? There is a horrible rumour in the town. Mr Crampton—"

"Crampton!"

"Accuses your brother of having robbed and struck down Mr Van Heldre."

"It is a lie!" she cried fiercely, as she snatched away her hands, gazing at him with flashing eyes and burning cheeks. "My brother a thief—almost a murderer! Oh!"

"It cannot be true," said Leslie; "but—"

"Weak and reckless and foolish; but—oh, why have you come up to say these things?"

"Because I love you!" he cried passionately; and he caught her hands in his, and held them tightly. "Because I knew that the horrible charge must soon reach your ears, and that it would be better that it should come from me—when you were in trouble—when you wanted help."

"It is not true—it is not true!" cried Louise, excitedly.

"Where is he? Let me see him. I may be able to advise and help. Louise, dear Louise, let this terrible time of trial be that which brings us together. Let me prove to you how I love you by being your counsellor, your aid in this time of need."

She heard his words, uttered with an earnestness which told their truth; but their effect was merely to arouse her indignation. How dared he take advantage of her agony and weakness at a time like this, and insult her with professions! It was an outrage.

"Don't shrink from me," he whispered. "I will say no more now. Forgive my clumsy blundering out of the words I have for months been longing to speak. Only let me feel that you understand me—that I may love; and then you will turn to me for help in this time of trouble."

For answer she pointed to the door.

"It is false," she cried; "my brother a common thief!"

"It must be false," he echoed, against his own belief; "but the charge has been made, and he must be warned in time."

"Warned in time?" she cried. "And you who profess to be our friend stood by and heard this charge made, and did not strike down the villain who made it."

"Miss Vine—Louise, you are hasty. The shock I know is terrible, but we must be prepared to meet it. He must not be taken unawares."

"My brother can meet such a charge as a gentleman should. It is not the first time that so foul an attack has been made against an innocent man."

"You are too hard upon me," he pleaded. "How could I, loving you as I do—"

"Loving!" she cried, scornfully.

"What have I done?" he groaned. "I ran up here directly to try and be of service. In my excitement, I spoke words that I should have kept back for a time, but they would have vent, and—No, I am not ashamed of what I have said," he cried, drawing himself up. "Louise Vine, I love you, and I must help you and your brother in this terrible strait."

"Then go back to the town, and tell all who have dared to say my brother committed this crime that what they say is false, and that his father, his sister will prove his innocence. Go!"

"Yes, go," said a shrill, hard voice. "Louise, go to your room and let me speak to this man."

"Aunt, you have heard?"

"Yes, from the servants. And I heard his last insulting words. Go to your room, child."

She threw open the room, and, accustomed to obey from her childhood, Louise moved slowly towards the hall; but as she turned slightly to dart a last indignant look at the man who had set her heart beating wildly as he at the same time roused her indignation, she saw such a look of agony that her courage failed, a strange sense of pity stole through her, and she stepped back and took her aunt's arm.

"Hush, aunt dear," she said, "there is no need to say more. Mr Leslie has made a great mistake in bringing up that cruel report, and he will go now and contradict it for my brother's sake."

"And apologise for his insult," cried Aunt Marguerite fiercely. "Child, I bade you go to your room."

"Yes, aunt. I am going."

"I must speak to this man alone."

"Aunt, dear—"

"Pray go, Miss Vine," said Leslie, approaching and taking her hand.

She yielded, and he led her to the door.

"Nothing your aunt can say will change my feelings towards you. When you are calm you will forgive me. Believe me, I will do everything to clear your brother from this charge."

She looked at him wildly, and still hesitated to obey her aunt's words. Finally, she gave way, Leslie held the door open till she was on the stairs, and then closed it, his manner completely changing as he turned and faced Aunt Marguerite, who stood with her head thrown back, and an indignant look of anger in her keen eyes.

"So, sir," she exclaimed, "you, in your common ignorance of everything connected with the social life of such a family as ours, dare to come up as a tale-bearer—as one of our servants did a few minutes back—and tell this pitiful story about my nephew."

"I grieved greatly, Miss Vine," said Leslie in quiet business-like tones.

"You grieved!" she cried. "A theft! Do you know that a des Vignes would prefer death to dishonour?"

"No, madam; but I am very glad to hear it, for that being the case Harry Vine must be innocent."

"Innocent!" she cried scornfully. "My nephew Henri! As if it could be for a moment in doubt!"

"I shall strive hard to help Mr Vine, your brother, to clear him from this disgrace."

"Disgrace, sir? It is no disgrace. If the *canaille* cast mud at one of noble lineage, does it disgrace him? No. The disgrace is where some plebeian—some trading person—is mad enough to advance his pretensions, and dares to address a lady as I heard you address my niece. Let me see, sir, did I not once give you to understand that Miss Louise des Vignes would in all probability be soon married to a gentleman of Auvergne—a gentleman whose lineage is as noble as her own?"

"I did understand something of the kind, madam; but until I see Miss Louise Vine another's wife, I shall boldly advance my pretensions, hoping to the last."

"Even supposing that her brother has committed some *faux pas*?"

"That would be the greater inducement to me to stand by her in her time of need."

"Most gratifying, I am sure, Mr Leslie, and highly creditable to one of your nationality," said Aunt Marguerite sneeringly, as she raised her glass to her eye, and gazed at him in an amused way. "Now may I ask you to leave me? My brother and my nephew are from home, and I cannot entertain you as I am sure you would wish. Good-evening, Mr Leslie—good-evening."

She bowed him out with a sneering smile upon her thin lips, and Leslie hurried back towards the town.

"What shall I do?" he muttered. "Oh, that sneering old woman, how she does raise one's gall? Poor Louise! she did look more gentle toward the last; and I don't believe in the Frenchman of great lineage. If there is one, let's do battle as they did of old, if he likes. What a fool I was to speak as I did just when she was so full of trouble! I must have been mad—a declaration of love, and an announcement that the poor girl's brother was in trouble. The young idiot! The scoundrel! How I should like to have his drilling for the next five years! What shall I do? I must help him. It's true enough, I'm afraid; and he must have the best legal help. If I had only someone to consult with. Van Heldre would have been the man."

There was a pause as the young man thought deeply of what steps he ought to take next.

"Yes, with all his sham cynicism and silly whims, the old man is shrewd, and can help when he likes. Uncle Luke?"

Chapter Twenty Seven
A Brother's Appeal

Louise Vine stood trembling in her own room, listening till she heard the door close, and Duncan Leslie's step on the gravel. Her agitation was terrible, and in place of being clear-headed and ready to act in this emergency, she felt as if her brain was in a turmoil of contending emotions. Indignation on her brother's behalf, anger against Leslie for his announcement, and another form of anger which she could not define struggled with a desire to go to her brother's help, and at last she placed her hands to her head and pressed them there.

"What shall I do?" she panted.

"Louise, Louise, my child!"

It was Aunt Marguerite's voice, and there was a sharp tapping on the panel of the door after the handle had been turned.

"Louise, my child, unlock this door."

She made no reply, but stood with her hands clasped together, listening to the sharp voice and the quick tapping repeated on the panel. Both ceased after a few minutes, and Aunt Marguerite's door was heard to close loudly.

"I could not talk to her now," muttered the girl. "She makes me so angry. She was so insulting to Mr Leslie. But he deserved it," she said aloud, with her cheeks burning once more, and her eyes flashing, as she drew herself up. "My brother—a common thief—the man who injured Mr Van Heldre! It is not true."

She started violently and began to tremble, for there was a sharp pattering on her window panes, as if someone had thrown a few small shots. Would Duncan Leslie dare to summon her like that? The pattering was repeated, and she went cautiously to the window, to make out in the gloom a figure that certainly was not that of Leslie.

She opened the casement with nervous anxiety now.

"Asleep?" cried a hasty voice. "There, stand aside—I'm coming up."

There was a rustling noise—a sharp crack or two, a hand was thrown over the window-sill, and, panting with exertion, Harry clambered in.

"Harry!" cried Louise in alarm, for his acts, his furtive way of coming to the house, and his manifest agitation did not suggest innocence.

"Hush! Don't talk aloud. Where's the governor?"

"Father is at Mr Van Heldre's."

Harry drew a quick spasmodic breath.

"And Aunt Marguerite?"

"In her room. But, Harry!"

"Be quiet. Don't talk. Let me get my breath."

Louise stood before him with her hands clasped, and a flow of agonising thoughts seemed to sweep her reason away. All was confusion, but above the flood there was one thing to which she clung—Harry was innocent. In spite of everything in the way of appearance, he was innocent; nothing should turn her from that.

"Well," he said suddenly, "haven't you anything to say?"

There was a savage vindictive tone in his voice which startled her more than his previous threatening way.

"Yes; where have you been? Why do you come back like this?"

"Where have I been? Up on the cliffs, wandering about among the rocks, and hiding till it grew dark and I could come home. And why did I come home like this? You know. Of course you have heard."

"Mr Leslie came, and—"

"Mr Leslie!" cried Harry with a mocking laugh. "Save us from our friends."

Louise's sympathy swung round on the instant to the side of the attacked; and, hardly knowing what she said—

"Mr Leslie came to bear some terrible news, and to offer to help you."

"To help me!" cried Harry with the eagerness of him who catches at straws. "And you—what did you say?"

"I said the information was false—a miserable invention. And I repeat it. Harry, it is not true?"

He made no reply for a few moments while, sobbing and terrified, Louise clung to him.

"Harry," she said excitedly, "why do you not speak?"

"Don't talk to me," he said hoarsely, "I'm thinking."

"But, Harry, I laugh at Aunt Marguerite's follies about descent and our degradation; but it is your duty to make a stand for our father's sake. Who has dared to accuse you of all this?"

"Don't talk to me," he said in an angry whisper, as he ran to the window and listened, crossing the room directly after to try the door.

Louise gazed at him in a horrified way, and her heart sank down, down, as her brother's acts suggested the possibility of his guilt. Then, like a flash of light, a thought irradiated her darkening soul, and she caught her brother's arm.

"I know!" she cried.

"You—you know?"

"Yes, I see it all now; and why this charge has been made. It was Mr Pradelle."

"Pradelle!"

"And that is why he left so suddenly. Harry, my poor brother!"

"Let Pradelle be," he said huskily. "I'm not going to hide behind another man."

"Oh! But, Harry!"

"Look here," he said uneasily; "I want your help, and you do nothing but talk."

"I will be silent; but tell me it is not true."

"Do you want me to make matters worse by telling some paltry lie?" he said. "Yes; it is true."

"Harry!"

"No; not all true. I did not steal that money."

"Ah!" ejaculated Louise; and she reeled to her bed, and would have fallen but for the post she grasped.

"I've no time to explain, but you must know. Yes; I did knock old Van Heldre down."

"Harry!" she groaned.

"And Crampton saw me come away; he has sent for the London police; and, unless I can get off, I shall be taken and tried."

Louise literally tottered towards him.

"No, no," he said angrily. "You are going to talk and preach. You don't want to see me disgracing you all by being cast in gaol?"

Disgracing them! Louise's first thought was of Duncan Leslie, and a pang of agony shot through her. How could she ever look him in the face again? A chill that seemed to paralyse shot through her. The hope that she had nursed was cast out, and her brother's words seemed to open out a future so desolate and blank that she turned upon him angrily.

"Harry!" she cried, "this is not—cannot be true." He paid no heed to her words, but stood biting his nails, evidently thinking, and at last he turned upon her like one at bay, as she said, after a painful pause: "You do not answer. Am I to believe all this? No, I cannot—will not believe it. Harry. It can't—it can't be true."

"Yes," he said, as if waking from a dream. "One of the lads would take me over in his lugger. Saint Malo: that would do. Louy, what money have you?"

"Then it is true?" she said.

"True? Yes; it's true enough."

"Then you—oh, Harry, for pity's sake—Harry!"

She burst into a wild fit of sobbing.

"That's right," he cried savagely. "I came to you for help and you go into hysterics. There, unlock that door, and get me something to eat, and while I'm enjoying myself, you can send Liza for the police."

"Harry!"

"Then why don't you act like a sensible girl? Listen: nobody must know that I have been here; not even the governor. I'm going to steal down to the harbour by-and-by; and I shall get Joe Lennen or Dick Paul to take me over to France. If I stay here I shall be arrested, and disgrace you all. There never was such an unlucky fellow as I am. Here, once more, what money have you?"

"Very little, Harry," she said; "about three sovereigns."

"Has aunt any? No; she must not know that I'm here. Louy, you must let me have your watch."

"Yes, Harry," she said, as she stood before him cold, and striving hard to master her emotion as a mute feeling of despair attacked her.

"And you'll help me, won't you?"

"Yes, Harry," she said, in the same cold mechanical way.

"Let me have your chain and rings, and any other trinket that will fetch money. Must have something to live upon till this trouble has blown over. You see I am penniless, I am not a thief. I shall soon get right again, and you shall have all these things a dozen times over." She suppressed a sigh. "Be quick then—there's a good girl. I've no time to waste."

Louise moved across the room to the drawers and took from the top a small rosewood box, which she placed upon the table. Then taking her watch from her waist, she was in the act of unfastening the chain, when there was the sound of a closing door below, and her father's voice, sounding loud and excited, as it called her by name.

Chapter Twenty Eight
In Defence of his Young

"Louise! Where is Louise?" The step on the stairs sounded like that of a younger man; and as the door was tried, Harry had reached the window, from whence he was about to climb, when he fancied he saw some one below, and he hastily closed the casement, and drew back trembling. "Louise! open this door."

"No, no," whispered Harry. "He must not know I am here."

"Not know?"

"Am I to break this door?" was thundered from the other side.

Harry glanced once more at the window. It was fancy. No one was below now that he could see; and he was in the act of unfastening it when there was a crash, the door flew open, and his father strode into the room. It did not seem to be the same man, and Harry shrank from the fierce, erect, angry figure which approached.

"As I might have guessed. You coward! So you would strip your sister of what money and jewels she has, and then escape!" Harry stood before him silent and with his head averted. "You did not counsel this flight, Louise?"

"No, father," she said, in a low voice full of pain; and she looked from one to the other, as if mentally stunned, and unable to realise the force of all that was taking place.

"I thought not. You abject, miserable wretch!"

Harry started, and gazed half in fear, half in wonder, at the stern, commanding figure before him.

"It—it was to save you all from disgrace."

Vine burst into a discordant laugh.

"From disgrace—to save us from disgrace? And is this part of your childish aunt's teaching?"

"Father! Pray!" whispered Louise, rousing herself and clinging to his arm.

"Silence, my child!" he cried. "I am not angry with you. I blame myself. Weak and indulgent. Tolerating that foolish woman's whims, that her old age might pass peacefully away, I have allowed all her follies to go on; but I did not believe these seeds could strike so deep a root. To save us from disgrace! So this is being the aristocratic gentleman of French descent! The man who would prefer death to dishonour—the man who scorns to sully his hands by embarking in some honest trade! And I, wrapped in my pursuits, riding my weak hobby, have let things go on till they have ended thus!"

"But, father, think! Be merciful."

"Think? I dare not, girl. Merciful? No. He is no longer my son. We must bear the disgrace as best we can; hide our shame elsewhere. You and I, father and sister of a miserable convict, who in the pursuit of money and title could stoop to rob."

"No, no, father; not rob."

"Scoundrel! don't speak or I may forget myself, and strike you down as you struck down your benefactor, the man who stretched out his hand to save you from the ruin that dogged your heels."

"It was a miserable accident, father. I did not steal."

"Bah! Lies come easily to such as you; but I have no words to waste, there is no time for that."

"No, father; quick before it is too late," whispered Louise. "Let him go; let him escape to France—to repent, father. He is your son."

"No. I disown him. And you counsel this—you, girl?"

"Yes, father, you will spare him," sobbed Louise; "he is my brother."

"He has broken those ties; neither son nor brother to us, my child. He has blasted your future by branding you as a convict's sister, and embittered the few years left to me, so that I would gladly end them now."

"Father!"

"Hush, my child! I am rightly punished for my weakness. I hoped that he would change. I was not blind, only patient, for I said that these follies would soon pass, and now I am awakened to this. My son in the hands of the police!" he laughed in a wild, discordant tone. "Monsieur le Comte des Vignes, I must have been mad."

"Go on!" said Harry, fiercely. "Trample me down. There, let me pass. Better in the hands of the police than here."

"No, no?" cried Louise excitedly. "Father, he must escape. It is one great horror, do not make it worse by letting him go there."

"Worse, girl? there is no worse!" cried Vine, sternly. "I thank my God that we are living in a land where stern, good laws are pre-eminent, and where justice rules with unswerving hand. You know not what you say."

"Yes, father—dearest father, help him to go and repent the evil he has done."

"Go and repent? Yes, that is the only hope; but it shall be as the honest repentant man, ready to acknowledge and bear the punishment of his crime."

"Father!"

"Yes; look at him—look at the base, cowering wretch, ready to go and hide his face in any shelter to escape the fate he has earned! Look at his guilty conscience, branding him even now! And you say, let him go!"

"Yes, father. What could I say?"

"Nothing!" cried Harry, turning round, as the trampled worm turns beneath the boot that crushes it into the earth. "It is true; I struck poor old Van Heldre down; but whatever I may have thought before, I did not go to steal that money. I did not steal it. And now what do you want me to do?"

"Go; act as a man who claims such descent as ours should do, in the country which opened to him its arms, and whose laws he has transgressed. The police are here from London. Go and give yourself up; suffer your punishment as one who would atone, and years hence in the future, when you are freed, come to me and ask my pardon—kneeling humbly by my grave."

"Father!"

"No more. The way is open now. Go at once, before you are dragged through the streets handcuffed like some common felon. To save us from disgrace, you say—that is the only way."

He stood erect, with his eyes flashing, his brows, and nostrils quivering, pointing to the door, while with his left arm he supported Louise, whose face gazed wildly into his, no mean representative of that *Haute Noblesse* which had sought refuge here when persecution drove them from their land.

"Father! Harry!" cried Louise, but only the latter spoke.

"Yes," he said, drawing himself up. "You are right, I'll go."

He strode quickly toward the door; but before he reached it, Liza threw it back.

"Miss Louise," she cried, "the police!"

With hasty strides the old man rushed to the door and thrust it to.

"Oh!" he gasped, and then after a pause, there was one low, hoarse appeal to heaven for aid, "My God!"

The adjuration spoke volumes, and for a few moments the old man stood there as if in a catalyptic state. Then a change came over him, his pale face flushed, the veins in his forehead stood out and throbbed, and he dashed to his son.

"Quick, Harry! France!"

As he spoke, Harry broke from him, and dashed to the window, threw it open, and was about to spring out, but he drew back. There was no fancy this time; two policemen could be dimly-seen below.

"Too late, father," he said calmly.

"No, my boy! this way, hush!"

He snatched open the door, and a quick-looking, well-knit man stood framed in the entry.

"Ah!" he said sharply, as he fixed Harry with his eye, "Mr Harry Vine, I arrest you on a warrant. Robbery and attempt to murder."

"No," roared the father frantically; and he flung himself upon the officer. "Run, Harry, run!"

Louise stood clinging to the ironwork of her bedstead, sick with horror, as a terrible struggle ensued. It only lasted a few moments; and as she saw her father and the detective officer wrestling together, her brother clenched his fists, set his teeth, and dashed at them.

"No, no; run!" roared the father in a voice she did not know; and in obedience, Harry dashed through the doorway and was gone.

"You're mad, old man!" cried the detective, tearing himself free, drawing back, and then rushing towards the door.

But with a wonderful display of activity and vigour, the old naturalist sprang at him once more, and with clenched fist struck him so fierce a blow full on the cheek, that the man swerved sidewise, and would have fallen but for the wall.

"When I come back!" he roared savagely, as he recovered himself, and, springing through the door, he bounded down the stairs after Harry Vine, father and sister staggering to the landing just as the door across the hall swung to with a heavy bang, and the sound of feet rapidly beating the shingle rose loudly on the silence of the night.

Chapter Twenty Nine
On His Behalf

"What have I done? what have I done?" groaned Vine. "I might have forgiven him and let him escape, and then—Louise, Louise, my child, come with me. We must find him and help."

Louise hurried back into her room to get hat and scarf, and returned to the landing to find her father and Aunt Margaret face to face.

"It is a judgment upon you, George—a judgment!" cried the old lady excitedly. "Yes; you dragged the poor boy down to that wretched life, and in his madness and misery he made one bold stroke for freedom."

"Louise, my child, quick!" cried Vine. "I cannot answer her now. Quick! get me away, or I shall say words to her that I shall repent as long as I live."

"I say it is a judgment!" cried Aunt Margaret. "Poor boy! if you had taken my advice—"

The door closed. They were out in the clear, starry night, hurrying down the path toward the town, but Aunt Margaret's words were ringing in Vine's ears. A judgment.

Why? What had he done?

"Have I been to blame? Is she right? Have I been to blame?" he muttered, as they hurried down, the words being the secret communings of his heart, but they were loud enough for Louise to hear, and as she clung to his arm she whispered emphatically—

"No, father, no!"

"No? Louise, what are you saying?"

"That you have not been to blame. My dear, patient, indulgent father."

"Indulgent?" he said hoarsely. "Yes; indulgent. I have been indulgent, and yet heaven knows how I have striven to make ours a happy home for all."

"And you have, father," sobbed Louise, "till Harry proved so wilful and went astray."

"Yes; went astray. But he must go, my child; he must not be taken. I have a little money with me, and will send him more. I want to do that which is just and right, but I could not bear to see him taken off to gaol."

Louise uttered a low moan as they hurried on down the path.

"Where will he hide? where will he hide?" whispered Vine excitedly. "He could not escape by the road, the railway station is certain to be watched, and there is the telegraph."

"Stop!" said Louise, holding one hand to her head, as in the terrible confusion of conflicting thoughts she tried to recall something her brother had said.

"Yes, I recollect now," she said. "He told me he meant to escape across to France, and that he would ask one of the fishermen to sail with him to Saint Malo."

"Hah! yes. Then he will escape. Whom did he say?"

"I cannot recollect the name, and yet it is familiar."

"Try, my child, try."

"I am trying hard, father," said Louise sadly, "but I cannot recollect."

"Oh!" groaned her father, as they hurried on down the path, "for pity's sake, try, my child, try."

"Yes, I remember," she cried at last—"Paul."

"Dick Paul—the man who sailed with us to the rocks near Scilly?"

"Yes, yes!"

"Hah! then if he has escaped so far he will be there."

"Do you know which is his cottage?"

"Yes, I know. Quick, girl, quick!"

They almost ran down the rest of the way, each looking excitedly about in the expectation of there being a hue and cry, and of seeing the fugitive rush by, hunted by a senseless crowd, eager to see him caught.

But all was perfectly still, the great stars shone down on the sleepy place, the lights burned in windows here and there, and as they reached a turn where the harbour lay before them the light at the mouth shone out like a lurid, fiery eye, staining the calm water with a patch of light, which seemed weird and strange amidst the spangled gleams reflected from the stars. Hardly a sound, till a swing door was opened a short distance in front, and there floated out in harmony one of the West-Country ditties the fishermen loved to sing. The door swung to, and the part-song became a murmur.

Vine gripped his daughter's hand with spasmodic violence, but she did not wince. There was a pain, an agony in her breast which neutralised all other, as she hurried on by her father's side, thinking now of her erring brother, now of Duncan Leslie. That dream, that growing love which she had tremblingly avowed to herself she felt for the frank, manly young mine-owner, was over, was crushed out, with all its bright-hued hopes of happiness; but he had said he loved her, and offered his aid. Why was he not there now to help, when her brother was in such peril? Why was he not there?

The answer came like a dull blow. She had reviled him, insulted him, and driven him away. Then her heart replied: He loves me, he will forgive my hasty words, and will save my brother if I humble myself and ask.

She started back to the reality from what seemed a dream, as her father hurried on along by a row of ill-built, rugged cottages on the cliff.

"It is in one of these," he said huskily, "but I cannot recall which."

As he hesitated one of the doors was opened, and a great, burly merman appeared, pipe in mouth.

"Dick Paul's," he said, in answer to a question, "first door furder on. Fine night, master."

"Yes, yes; thank you, thank you," cried Vine hastily.

"But he aren't at home."

"What?"

"Him and four more went out at sundown to shoot their nets."

Vine uttered a low groan.

"Good night!" said the man, and he moved off.

"Stop!" cried Vine, and the man's heavy boots ceased to clatter on the rugged pebbles with which the way was paved.

"Call me, Master Vine!"

"Yes. You know me?"

"Know you? Ay, and the young lady too. Liza Perrow's Uncle Bob. Didn't I take you 'long the coast one day?"

"Yes, yes, of course," said Vine hastily. "Look here, my man; you have a boat."

"Third share master, just going out now. My mates are waiting yonder."

"In the harbour?"

"Ay. That's their lantern."

"Look here, Perrow," said Vine excitedly, as he held the man tightly by the arm, "you are going fishing?"

"Going to have a try, master."

"And you will perhaps earn a pound a-piece."

"If we are lucky. P'r'aps naught."

"Perrow," whispered the old man, with his lips close to the man's face, "will you do me a service—a great service?"

"Sarvice, sir?—Ay, sure I will."

"Then look here. Your boat would sail across to France?"

"To France?" said the great bluff fellow, with a chuckle. "Why didn't some of our mates sail to Spain in a lugger a foot shorter than ours, and not so noo a boot! France, ay, or Spain either."

"Then look here; take a passenger over for me to-night; and I'll give you fifty pounds."

"Fifty pounds, Master Vine?"

"Yes. Be ready; take him safely over, and bring me back word from him that he's safe, and I'll pay you a hundred."

"Will you shake hands on that, master?"

"Will you do it?"

"Do it for you, Master Vine? Why, sir, bless you, we'd ha' done it for five. But if you tempt poor men wi' a big lump o' money like that—Do it? I should think we will."

"But your partners?" said Louise excitedly.

"Never you mind about them, miss. I'm cap'n of our boat. Where's our passenger? Lor', miss, don't do that."

The man started, for Louise had caught his rough hand and kissed it.

"I'll soon bring him to you," said the old man, with his voice trembling; "but look here, my man—you must ask no questions, you will not be put off, you will not refuse at the last moment?"

"Look here, Master Vine, sir," said the man stolidly, "I aren't a fool. Hundred pound's a lot o' money, and of course it's to smuggle some one away on the quiet. Well, so be it."

"Hah!" ejaculated Vine.

"It's to 'blige you as I've knowd for a kind-hearted gent these ever so many years, though there was that bit o' trouble 'bout my brother's lass, as I don't believe took that there money."

"No, no, she was innocent," cried Louise.

"Thanks for that, miss, and—say, has young Master Harry been up to some game?"

There was no reply.

"Never mind. Don't you speak without you like, Master Vine, sir. Yonder's our boot, and I'll go down to her, and she shall lie off just outside, and I'll wait in our little punt down by the harbour steps. Will that do?"

"Yes; and you will trust me to pay you a hundred pounds?"

"Trust *you*?"

The man uttered a low chuckle.

"How long will he be, master?"

"I don't know. Wait till he comes."

"Master Harry?" whispered the man.

"Yes."

"All right, sir. You trust me. I'll trust you. Night, miss. I'll wait there if it's a week."

"Hah!" ejaculated Vine, as the man's heavy step went on before them. "There is a way of escape for him. I am a father, and what I ought to do by my friend pales before that. Now to find him, my child, to find him. He *must* escape."

Louise clung to his arm, and they stood there on the cliff path listening, and each mentally asking the question, what to do?

"If I could only get the faintest clue of his movements," muttered Vine. "Louise, my child, can you not suggest something?"

She did not answer, for a terrible dread was upon her now. Her brother might have been taken; and if so, there was no need to hesitate as to the way to go.

As if the same thoughts had impressed him, Vine suddenly exclaimed:

"No, no, they would not have taken him. The man was a stranger, and Harry would be too quick."

For the next hour they hurried here and there, passing Van Heldre's house, where a dim light in the window showed where the injured man lay. There was a vague kind of feeling that sooner or later they would meet Harry, but the minutes glided slowly by, and all was still.

Out beyond the harbour-light the faint gleam of a lantern could be seen, showing that Bob Perrow had kept faith with them, and that the lugger was swinging in the rapid current, fast to one of the many buoys used by the fishermen in fine weather. But there was no sign or sound apparent; and with their hearts, sinking beneath the impression that Harry had been taken, and yet not daring to go and ask, father and daughter still wandered to and fro along the various streets of the little town.

"Can he have taken boat and gone?" whispered Vine at last.

"No," said Louise, "there would not have been time, and we should have seen the lights had a boat gone out."

"George!"

Two figures suddenly appeared out of the darkness, and stopped before them.

"Luke? You here?"

"Yes; have you seen him?"

"No; but is—is he—"

"No, Mr Vine," said Leslie quickly. "I have been up to the station twice."

"Sir!"

"For heaven's sake don't speak to me like that, Mr Vine," cried Leslie. "I know everything, and I am working for him as I would for my own brother."

"Yes, it's all right, George," said Uncle Luke, with his voice softening a little. "Leslie's a good fellow. Look here; we must get the young dog away. Leslie has chartered a fast boat, and she lies in the head of the harbour ready."

"Ah!"

It was an involuntary ejaculation from Louise.

"We'll have him taken across the Channel if we can find him. Where can he be hidden?"

"We have been twice on to your house, Mr Vine," said Leslie, who kept right away from Louise, and out of delicacy seemed to ignore her presence, but spoke so that she could hear every word. "I have three of my miners on the look-out—men I can trust, and law or no law, we must save him from arrest."

"Heaven bless you, Mr Leslie. Forgive—"

"Hush, sir. There is no time for words. The men from London with our own police are searching in every direction. He got right away, and he is hiding somewhere, for he certainly would not take to the hills or the road, and it would be madness to try the rail."

"Yes," said Uncle Luke. "He's safe to make for the sea, and so get over yonder. There's a boat lying off though, and I'm afraid that's keeping him back. The police have that outside to stop him."

"No; that is a boat I have chartered, Luke, waiting to save my poor boy."

"Then before many hours are gone he'll be down by the harbour, that's my impression," said Uncle Luke. "Confound you, George, why did you ever have a boy?"

George Vine drew a long breath and remained silent.

"If you will allow me, gentlemen," said Leslie, "I think we ought not to stay here like this. The poor fellow will not know what precautions his friends have taken, and some one ought to be on the look-out to give him warning whenever he comes down to the harbour."

"Yes; that's true."

"Then if I may advise, I should suggest, sir, that you patrol this side to and fro, where you must see him if he comes down to make for the west point; I'll cross over and watch the east pier, and if Mr Luke Vine here will stop about the head of the harbour, we shall have three chances of seeing him instead of one."

Louise pressed her hand to her throbbing heart, as she listened to these words, and in spite of her agony of spirits, noted how Leslie avoided speaking to her, devoting himself solely to the task of helping her brother; and as she felt this, and saw that in future they could be nothing more than the most distant friends, a suffocating feeling of misery seemed to come over her, and she longed to hurry away, and sob to relieve her overcharged breast.

"Leslie's right," said Uncle Luke, in a decisive way. "Let's separate at once. And look here, whoever sees him is to act, give him some money, and get him off at once. He must go. The trouble's bad enough now, it would be worse if he were taken, and it's the last thing Van Heldre would do, hand him to the police. Leslie!"

He held up his hand, but the steps he heard were only those of some fishermen going home from the river.

"Now, then, let's act; and for goodness' sake, let's get the young idiot away, for I warn you all, if that boy's taken there'll be far worse trouble than you know of now."

"Uncle Luke!" cried Louise piteously.

"Can't help it, my dear. There will, for I shall end a respectable life by killing old Crampton and being hung. Come along, Leslie."

The little party separated without a word, and Louise and her father stood listening till the steps of their late companions died away.

Chapter Thirty
In the Queen's Name

As they stood together at the lower end of the rocky point listening and waiting, it seemed to Louise Vine as if she were about to be an actor in some terrible scene.

Vine muttered a few words now and then, but they were inaudible to his child, who clung to his arm as he walked untiringly to and fro, watching the harbour and the way back into the town, while when he paused it was to fix his eyes upon the dimly-seen lantern of the lugger lying out beyond the point. The portion of their walk nearest the town was well kept and roughly paved with great slabs of granite, in which were here and there great rings for mooring purposes, while at some distance apart were projecting masses roughly hewn into posts. But as the distance from the town increased and the harbour widened, the jutting point was almost as if it had been formed by nature, and the footing was difficult, even dangerous at times.

But in his excitement Vine did not heed this, going on and on regardless of the difficulties, and Louise unmurmuringly walked or at times climbed along, till they were right out at the extreme point where, some feet below them, the water rushed and gurgled in and out of the crevices with terrible gasping noises, such as might be made by hungry sea-monsters thronging round to seize them if either of them should make a slip.

Here Vine paused again and again to watch the lantern in the lugger, and listen for the rattle of oars in the rowlocks, the oars of the boat conveying his son to the men who would at once hoist the sails and bear him away to a place of safety. But the dim light of the horn lantern rose and fell, there was no rattle of oars, not even the murmur of a voice; nothing but the sucking, gasping noises at their feet, as the tide swirled by like the race of waters from some huge mill.

Louise clung more tightly to her father's arm, as he stood again and again where she had often from a rock behind watched her uncle deftly throwing out his line to capture some silvery-sided bass or a mackerel, glowing with all the glories of the sea at sunrise.

"If he should slip," she said to herself, as she tightened her grasp of her father's thin arm, "if he should slip!" and she shuddered as she gazed down into the deep, black rushing water, where the star reflections were all broken up and sparkled deep down as if the current were charged with gold dust, swirling and eddying by. Then she started as her father spoke aloud to himself.

"No, no, no!" he murmured. Then sharply, "Come, let us get back."

Louise crept along by him in silence, her heart giving one violent leap, as Vine slipped once on the spray-wet rocks, but recovered himself and went on without a word. Again and again, she suffered that terrible catching of the breath, as her father slipped, caught his foot in some inequality, or would, but for her guidance, have stumbled over some projecting rock post and been thrown into the harbour. For as he walked on, his eyes were constantly searching the dark surface as he listened intently for some token of the escaping man.

But all was still as they neared the town, still with the silence of death. No one could have told that there were watchers by the ferry, where a rough boat was used for crossing from side to side of the harbour; that two boats were waiting, and that Duncan Leslie was patrolling the short arm of granite masonry that ran down to the tower-like building were the harbour lantern burned.

"Hist!" whispered Louise, for there was a step some little distance away, but it ceased, and as she looked in its direction, the cliffs seemed to tower up behind the town till a black, jagged ridge cut the starry sky.

"Let's go back," said her father, huskily. "I fancied I heard a boat stealing along the harbour; we cannot see the lugger light from here."

"George!" came from out of the darkness ahead.

"Yes, Luke!" was whispered back sharply, and the old man came up.

"Seen anything of him?"

"No. Have you?"

"Not a sign. I sent one of the fishermen up to the police to see what he could find out, and—"

"Uncle!" panted out Louise, as she left her father to cling to the old man.

"Poor little lassie! poor little lassie!" he said tenderly, as he took her and patted her head. "No news, and that's good news. They haven't got him, but they're all out on the watch; the man from London and our dunderheads.

All on the watch, and I fancy they're on the look-out close here somewhere, and that's what keeps him back."

Louise uttered a low moan.

"Ah, it's bad for you, my dear," said Uncle Luke, whose manner seemed quite changed. "You come with me, and let me take you home. We don't want mother trouble on our hands."

"No, no," she said firmly, "I cannot leave him."

"But you will be ill, child."

"I cannot leave him, uncle," she said again; and going back to her father, she locked her fingers about his arm.

"Hi! hoi! look out!" came from a distance; and it was answered directly by a voice not a hundred yards away.

A thrill of excitement shot through the little group as they heard now the tramp of feet.

"I knew it," whispered Uncle Luke. "He's making for the harbour now."

"Ah!" gasped Vine, as he almost dragged Louise over the rugged stones.

"Stop where you are," said Uncle Luke, excitedly; and he placed something to his lips and gave a low shrill whistle.

It was answered instantly from the other side of the harbour.

"Leslie's on the look-out. Yes, and the men with the boat," he whispered, excitedly, as another low whistle was heard.

Then there was a few moment's silence as if people were listening, followed by steps once more, and a quick voice exclaimed from out of the darkness:

"Seen him?"

Neither of the group answered, and a man stepped up to them and flashed the light of a lantern quickly over them before closing it again.

"That's you, is it?" he said. "I'll have a word with you by-and-by; but look here, I call upon you two men in the Queen's name to help me to take him. If you help him to get away, it's felony, so you may take the consequences. You haven't got to do with your local police now."

The man turned away and walked swiftly back toward the town, the darkness seeming to swallow him up. He paused for a few moments at the edge of the harbour, to throw the light of his lantern across the water.

"The London man," said Uncle Luke, unconcernedly. "Well, God save the Queen, but I'm sure she don't want us to help to capture our poor boy."

Chapter Thirty One
"Oh! Absalom, My Son, My Son"

Harry Vine had but one thought as he dashed out of his father's house, and that was to escape—far away to some other country where neither he nor his crime were known—to some place where, with the slate of his past life wiped clean, he might begin anew, and endeavour to show to his father, to his sister, perhaps to Madelaine Van Heldre, that he was not all bad. How he would try, he told himself. Only let him get aboard one of the fishing luggers, and after confiding in some one or other of his old friends, the bluff fishermen who had often given him a sail or a day's fishing, beg of him to take him across to Jersey or Saint Malo; anywhere, so as to avoid the terrible exposure of the law—anywhere to be free.

"I'd sooner die than be taken," he said to himself as he sped on downward at a rapid rate.

The way to the harbour seemed clear, and, though the officer was pursuing him, Harry had the advantage of the darkness, and the local knowledge of the intricate ways of the little town, so that he felt no fear of being able to reach the harbour and some boat. He was reckoning without his host. His host, or would-be host, was the detective sergeant who had gone about his business in a business-like manner, so that when Harry Vine was congratulating himself upon the ease with which he was able to escape, one of the local policeman started from his post right in the fugitive's way, nearly succeeding in catching him by the arm, an attention Harry avoided by doubling down one of the little alleys of the place. Over and over again he tried to steal down to the harbour, but so sure as he left his hiding place in one of the dark lanes or among the fishermen's stores he heard steps before him, and with the feeling that the whole town had now risen up against him, and that the first person he encountered would seize and hold him until the arrival of the police, he crept back, bathed with cold perspiration, to wait what seemed to be an interminable time before he ventured again.

His last hiding place was a wooden shed not far from the water-side—a place of old ropes and sails, and with a loft stored full of carefully dried nets, put away till the shoals of fish for which they were needed visited the shore. Here in profound ignorance of what had been done on his behalf, he threw himself down on a heap of tarred canvas to try and devise some certain means of escape. He had a vague intention of getting the fishermen to help him; but after thinking of several, he could not decide which of the sturdy fellows would stand by such a culprit as he. And as he lay there the bitter regrets for the past began to attack him.

"Louise—sister," he muttered to himself. "I must have been mad. And I lie here groaning like the coward I am," he said fiercely, as, thrusting back all thoughts of the past with the intention of beginning afresh, he stole out once more into the dark night, meaning to get to the harbour, and, failing a better means, to take some small sailing-boat, and to trust to his own skill to get safely across.

The place was far more quiet now; and, avoiding the larger lanes, he threaded his way through passage after passage among the net-stores and boat-houses till he reached the main street, along which he was walking noiselessly when a heavy regular pace ahead checked him, and, turning shortly round, he made for the first narrow back lane, reached it, and turned trembling as he recognised that it was the familiar path leading by the back of Van Heldre's, the way he knew so well.

Hurrying on, he had nearly reached the bottom, when he became aware of the fact that there was a policeman waiting. He turned sharply back, after nearly walking into the arms of one of his enemies, and was nearly at the top once more, when he found that the man whom he had tried to avoid was there too waiting.

"I'm caught," he said bitterly, as he paused midway. "Shall I dash for liberty? No," he said bitterly; "better give up."

He raised his hand to guide himself silently along, when he shivered, for it touched a gate which yielded, and as the steps advanced from front and rear, he stepped down. Fate in her irony had decided that, to avoid arrest, he should take refuge in the premises of the man he had injured. The steps came nearer, and trembling with horror the fugitive glanced upward to see that two windows were illumined, and there was light enough to show that the door leading into the corridor was open. He shrank from it, and was then driven to enter and stand inside, listening, for the steps stopped outside, the door yielded, and a voice said:

"Couldn't have been him. He wouldn't have gone there."

The gate swung gently to, and the fugitive began to breathe more freely, for after a low whispered conversation, it was evident that the watchers were about to separate, when there was a loud cough which Harry knew only too well; and to his horror he saw faintly in at the end of the passage his figure more plain by a light in the hall, the short stooping figure of Crampton coming towards him. To have stepped out into the yard would have been into the light, where the old man must have seen him; and, obeying his first instinct, Harry crouched down, and as Crampton advanced, backed slowly along the corridor till farther progress was stayed by the outer door of the office. Harry sank down in the corner, a dark shapeless heap to any one who had approached, and with heart throbbing, he waited.

"He is coming into the office," he thought.

But as the old man reached the opening into the yard he paused. There was a faint rustling, then a flash and a match flared out illuminating the old clerk's stern countenance, and it seemed as the tiny splint burned that discovery must take place now. But Crampton was intent upon the business which had brought him there. He had stolen out from his self-appointed task of watching over the house to have his nightly pipe, and for fully an hour, Harry Vine crouched in the corner by the office door, seeing over and over again the horrors of the past, and trembling as he waited for the fresh discovery, while old Crampton softly paced the little yard, smoking pipe after pipe.

That hour seemed as if it would never end, and at last in despair Harry was about to rise, when he heard Madelaine's voice, gently calling to the old man.

"Hah!" he said softly; "a bad habit, Miss Madelaine, but it seems to soothe me now."

Would he fasten the door and gate, and complete the horror of Harry's position by making him a prisoner? The young man crouched there trembling, for Crampton recrossed the yard, and there was the sound of two bolts being shot. Then he regained the glass door, and was about to close that.

"No," said Madelaine softly; "the night is so hot. Leave that open, Mr Crampton."

"Yes, my dear; yes, my dear," sighed the old man. "I shall be in the little room, and no one is likely to come here now."

Gone at last, and trembling so in his wild excitement that he could hardly stir, Harry Vine literally crept along the corridor, rose up and ran across the yard with the horrible sensation that the old clerk's hand was about to descend upon his shoulder. The two bolts were shot back with a loud snap, the gate was flung open; and, reckless now, he dashed out and down the narrow lane.

"He could bear no more," he said. "The harbour and a boat." He now ran rapidly, determined to end the terrible suspense, and for the first few moments, he felt that his task would be easy; then he heard a warning shout, and in his dread took refuge in the first alley leading down to the harbour.

Steps passed, and he emerged at the lower end, gained the main street by returning through another of the alleys by which, after the fashion of Yarmouth, the little town was scored.

"Five minutes will take me there now," he panted; and, forcing himself to walk, he was hurrying on when a shout told him that his enemies were well upon the alert. With the horrible sense of being hunted, he dashed on, blindly now, reckless as to which way he went, so long as he reached the water-side. As he ran, he was about to strike down to the left where the landing steps lay; and had he reached them there was a boat and men waiting, but the London detective had discovered that and was on the alert.

Harry almost ran into his arms, but with a cry of rage he doubled back and ran for the shore, where he might set pursuit at defiance by hiding in the rocks below the cliff. But another man sprang up in his way, and in his despair he ran off to his left again, right along the great pier, towards the point.

"We've got him now," shouted a voice behind as Harry rushed out, just conscious of a shriek as he brushed by a group of figures, hardly seen in the darkness. He heard, too, some confused words in which "boat" and "escape" seemed to be mingled. But in his excitement he could only think of those behind, as there came the patter of his pursuers' feet on the rough stones.

There was a shrill whistle from the other side of the harbour, followed by a hail, and the splash of oars in the darkness, while a low "ahoy!" came from off the point.

"Yes," muttered the officer between his teeth, "you're a nice party down here, but I've got my man."

What followed was the work of moments. Harry ran on till the rugged nature of the point compelled him to walk, then step cautiously from rock to rock. The harbour was on one side, the tide rushing in on the other; before him the end of the point, with its deep water and eddying currents, which no swimmer could stem, and behind him the London officer with the local police close up.

There was a boat, too, in the harbour, and the fugitive had heard the whistle, and cries. He saw the light of the lugger out ahead, and to him, in his mad horror of capture, they meant enemies—enemies on every hand.

And so he reached the extreme point, where, peering wildly about, like some hunted creature seeking a way of escape, he turned at bay.

"There, sir, the game's up," cried the officer. "You've made a good fight of it, so now give in."

"Keep back!" roared Harry hoarsely. And he stooped and felt about for a loose piece of rock where every scrap had been washed away.

"Will you give in?" cried the officer.

"Keep back!" cried Harry again, in a tone so fierce that for a moment the officer paused.

There was another whistle from across the harbour, a shout and a hail out of the darkness, but nothing save the dim lantern light could be seen.

"Now then, you two," said the officer decidedly, "back me up."

There was a faint click as he drew something from his pocket, and without hesitation stepped boldly over the few feet which separated him from Harry Vine.

Panting, half wild, hearing the whistles, the cries, and still dividing nothing but that there were enemies on every hand, the young man uttered a hoarse cry as the detective caught at his breast. With one well-aimed blow he struck out, sent the man staggering back, and then, as those who hail watched and waited came panting up, he turned quickly, stepped to the very edge, raised his hands and plunged into the rushing tide.

"Harry! my son!" rang out on the darkness of the night.

But there was no answer. The black water seemed to flash with myriad points of light and then ran, hissing and rushing in a contending current, out to sea.

Chapter Thirty Two
"The Lord Gave, and..."

"Boat ahoy! Whoever you are—this way—boat!"

"Ahoy!" came back from three-quarters—from two different points in the harbour, and from out to sea.

Then came another whistle from far back on the other side of the harbour, and in a shrill voice from between his hands Uncle Luke yelled:

"Leslie, another boat, man, for the love of heaven!"

"Here! you there, sir! the nearest boat—quick, pull!" roared the detective in stentorian tones. "Have you no light?"

"Ay, ay," came back; and a lantern that had been hidden under a tarpaulin coat shone out, dimly showing the boat's whereabouts.

"That's right; pull, my lads, off here. Man overboard off the rocks. This way."

An order was given in the boat, and her course was altered.

"No, no," cried the officer; "this way, my lads, this way."

"We know what we're about," came back.

"Yes, yes; they know," said Uncle Luke, hoarsely. "Let them be; the current sets the way they've taken. He's right out there by now."

The old man's arm was dimly-seen pointing seawards, but the detective was not convinced.

"It's a trick to throw me on the wrong scent," he said excitedly. "Here, you,"—to one of the local police—"why don't you speak?"

"Mr Luke Vine's right, sir; he knows the set o' the tide. The poor lad's swept right out yonder long ago, and Lord ha' mercy upon him, poor chap. They'll never pick him up."

"Can you see him?" roared the officer, using his hands as a speaking trumpet.

There was no reply; but the lantern could be seen rising and falling now, as the little craft began to reach the swell at the harbour bar.

Then there was a hail out of the harbour, as the second boat came along, and five minutes after the rapid beat of oars told of the coming of another boat.

"Ahoy, lad! this way," rose from the boat with the lantern.

"Whose boat's that?" said the detective, quickly.

"Dunno," replied the nearest policeman.

"They'll pick him up, and he'll escape after all. Confound it! Here, hoi! you in that boat. In the Queen's name, stop and take me aboard."

"They won't pick him up," said the nearest policeman solemnly. "You don't know this coast."

There was a low groan from a figure crouching upon its knees, and supporting a woman's head, happily insensible to what was passing around.

"George, lad," whispered Uncle Luke, "for the poor girl's sake, let's get her home. George! don't you hear me. George! It is I—Luke."

There was no reply, and the excitement increased as a swift boat now neared the end of the point.

"Where is he? Is he swimming for the boat?" cried a voice, hardly recognisable in its hoarse excitement for that of Duncan Leslie.

"He jumped off, Mr Leslie, sir," shouted one of the policemen.

"Row, my lads. Pull!" shouted Leslie; "right out."

"No, no," roared the detective; "take me aboard. In the Queen's name, stop!"

"Pull," cried Leslie to the men; and then turning to the detective, "while we stopped to take you the man would drown, and you couldn't get aboard at this time of the tide."

"He's quite right," said the policeman who had last spoken. "It's risky at any time; it would be madness now."

The detective stamped, as in a weird, strange way the voice kept coming from out of the darkness, where two dim stars could be seen, as the lanterns were visible from time to time; and now Leslie's voice followed the others, as he shouted:

"This way, Vine, this way. Hail, man! Why don't you hail?"

"Is this part of the trick to get him away?" whispered the detective to one of his men.

The man made no reply, and his silence was more pregnant than any words he could have spoken.

"But they'll pick him up," he whispered, now impressed by the other's manner.

"Look out yonder," said the policeman, a native of the place; "is it likely they'll find him there?"

"Hah!" ejaculated the detective.

"And there's no such current anywhere for miles along the coast as runs off here."

"Hah!" ejaculated the man again, as he stood now watching the lights, one of which kept growing more distant, while the hails somehow seemed to be more faint and wild, and at last to resemble the despairing cries of drowning men.

"Listen," whispered the detective in an awe-stricken tone, as he strove to pierce the darkness out to sea.

"It was Master Leslie, that," said the second policeman; "I know his hail."

Just then there was a wild hysterical fit of sobbing, and George Vine rose slowly from his knees, and staggered towards the group.

"Luke!" he cried, in a half-stunned, helpless way, "Luke you know— Where are you? Luke!"

"Here, George," said Uncle Luke sadly, for he had knelt down in the place his brother had occupied the moment before.

"You know the currents. Will they—Will he—"

He faltered and paused, waiting his brother's reply, and the three officers of the law shuddered, as, after a few minutes' silence, broken only by a groan from the kneeling man, George Vine cried in a piteous voice that sounded wild and thrilling in the solemn darkness of the night:

"God help me! Oh, my son, my son!"

"Quick, mind! Good heavens, sir! Another step and—"

The detective had caught the stricken father as he tottered and would have fallen headlong into the tide, while, as he and another of the men helped him back to where Louise still lay, he was insensible to what passed around.

But still the dim lights could be seen growing more and more distant, and each hail sounded more faint, as the occupants of the boats called to each other, and then to him they sought, while, after each shout, it seemed to those who stood straining their eyes at the end of the pier, that there was an answering cry away to their left; but it was only the faint echo repeating the call from the face of the stupendous cliffs behind the town.

"Why don't they come back here and search?" cried the officer angrily.

"What for?" said a voice at his elbow; and he turned to see dimly the shrunken, haggard face of Uncle Luke.

"What for?" retorted the officer. "He may have swum in the other direction."

"So might the world have rolled in the other direction and the sunrise to-morrow in the west," said the old man angrily. "No swimmer could stem that current."

"But why have they gone so far?"

"They have gone where the current took them," said Uncle Luke, coldly. "Want the help of your men to get these poor creatures home."

The detective made no reply, but stood gazing out to sea and listening intently. Then turning to his men—

"One of you keep watch here in case they try to land with him. You come with me."

The two policemen followed his instructions, one taking his place at the extreme end of the point, the other following just as voices were heard, and a group of fishermen, who had been awakened to the fact that there was something wrong, came down the rocky breakwater.

"Here, some of you, I want a boat—a swift boat, and four men to pull. Ah, you!"

This to a couple of the coastguard who had put in an appearance, and after a few hurried words one party went toward the head of the breakwater, while another, full of sympathy for the Vines, went on to the end of the point.

There was plenty of willing help, but George Vine had now recovered from his swoon, and rose up to refuse all offers of assistance.

"No, Luke," he said more firmly now; "I must stay."

"But our child, Louise?"

"She must stay with me."

Louise had risen to her feet, as he spoke, and clung to his arm in mute acquiescence; and once more they stood watching the star-spangled sea.

Ten minutes later a well-manned boat passed out of the harbour, with the detective officer in her bows and a couple of the strongest lights they could obtain.

Just as this boat came abreast of the point the rowing ceased, and a brilliant glare suddenly flashed out as the officer held aloft a blue signal light; and while the boat was forced slowly along he carefully scanned the rocks, in the expectation of seeing his quarry clinging somewhere to their face.

The vivid light illumined the group upon the point, and the water flashed and sparkled as it ran eddying by, while from time to time a gleaming drop of golden fire dropped with a sharp hissing explosion into the water, and a silvery grey cloud of smoke gathered overhead.

The officer stayed till the blue light had burned out, and then tossing the wooden handle into the water, he gave his orders to the men to row on out toward the other boats.

The transition from brilliant light to utter darkness was startling as it was sudden; and as the watchers followed the dim looking lanterns, they saw that about a mile out they had paused.

George Vine uttered a gasping sigh, and his child clung to him as if both realised the meaning of that halt. But they were wrong, for when the men in the detective's boat had ceased rowing, it was because they were close abreast of the lugger, whose crew had hailed them.

"Got him?"

"No. Is he aboard your boat?"

Without waiting for an answer, the detective and his men boarded the lugger, and, to the disgust of her crew, searched from end to end.

"Lucky for you, my lads, that he is not here," said the officer.

"Unlucky for him he aren't," said one of the men. "If he had been we shouldn't have had you aboard to-night."

"What do you mean?"

"Only that we should have been miles away by now."

"Do you think either of the other boats have picked him up?"

"Go and ask 'em," said another of the men sulkily.

"No, sir," said one of the coastguard, "they haven't picked him up."

"Back!" said the detective shortly; and, as soon as they were in the boat, he gave orders for them to row towards the faint light they could see right away east. They were not long in coming abreast, for the boat was returning.

"Got him?" was shouted.

"No."

"Then why did you make the signal?"

The detective officer was a clever man, but it had not occurred to him that the blue light he had obtained from the coastguard station and burned would act as a recall. But so it was, and before long the second boat was reached, and that which contained Duncan Leslie came up, the latter littering an angry expostulation at being brought back from his search.

"It's no good, Mr Leslie, sir," said the fisherman who had made the bargain with Vine.

"No good?" cried Leslie angrily. "You mean you're tired, and have not the manhood to continue the search."

"No, sir, I don't," said the man quietly. "I mean I know this coast as well as most men. I'll go on searching everywhere you like; but I don't think the poor lad can be alive."

"Ay, ay, that's right, mate," growled two others of his fellows.

"He was a great swimmer," continued the man sadly; "but it's my belief he never come up again."

"Why do you say that?" cried the detective from his boat, as the four hung clustered together, a singular-looking meeting out there on the dark sea by lantern light.

"Why do I say that? Why 'cause he never hailed any on us who knew him, and was ready to take him aboard. Don't matter how good a swimmer a man is, he'd be glad of a hand out on a dark night, and with the tide running so gashly strong."

"You may be right," said Leslie, "but I can't go back like this. Now, my lads, who's for going on?"

"All on us," said the fisherman who had first spoken, and the boats separated to continue their hopeless task.

All at once there was a faint streak out in the east, a streak of dull grey, and a strange wild, faint cry came off the sea.

"There!" cried the detective; "pull, my lads, pull! he is swimming still. No, no, more towards the right."

"Swimming?—all this time, and in his clothes!" said one of the coastguard quietly. "That was only a gull."

The detective struck his fist into his open left hand, and stood gazing round over the glistening water, as the stars paled, the light in the east increased till the surface of the sea seemed steely grey, and by degrees it grew so light that near the harbour a black speck could be seen, toward which the officer pointed.

"Buoy," said the nearest rower laconically, and the officer swept the surface again. Then there was a faint shade of orange nearly in the zenith, a flock of gulls flew past, and here and there there were flecks and splashes of the pale silvery water, which ere long showed the reflection of the orange sky, and grew golden. The rocks that lay at the foot of the huge wall of cliff were fringed with foam, and wherever there was a break in the shore and some tiny river gurgled down, a wreathing cloud of mist hung in the hollow.

Moment by moment the various objects grew more distinct; black masses of rock fringed with green or brown sea-wrack, about which the tide eddied and played, now hiding, now revealing for some crested wave to pounce upon as a sea-monster might upon its prey. The dark slaty rocks displayed their wreaths of ivy, and the masses of granite stood up piled in courses of huge cubes, as if by titanic hands, grey with parched moss, dull and dead looking; and then all at once, as the sun slowly rose above the sea, glorious in God's light, sparkling as if set with myriads of gems, the grey became gold, and all around there was a scene of beauty such as no painter could do more than suggest. Everything was glorified by the rising sun; sea, sky, the distant houses, and shipping, all gleamed as if of burnished gold—all was of supreme beauty in the birth of that new day. No, not at all: here and there slowly using their oars as they scanned sea and rock, sat a crew of haggard men, while back on the golden point clustered a crowd watching their efforts, and hanging back with natural kindly delicacy from the group of three at the extreme edge of the granite point—two pale-faced, grey, wild-eyed men, and the girl who sat crouching on a fragment of rock, her hair loose, her hands clasped round her knees, and a look of agonised sorrow in the piteous drawn face, ever directed towards the east.

"They're all coming back," said some one close at hand.

The man was right; slowly one by one the boats crept over the glorious sea towards the harbour, Duncan Leslie's last.

"Nothing?" said Uncle Luke in a low whisper as the coastguard boat was backed toward the point, and the detective sprang ashore.

"Nothing, sir. Poor foolish, misguided lad! Might have been my boy, sir, I've only done my duty; but this is a dark night's work I shall never forget. I feel as if I were answerable for his death."

Ten minutes later Duncan Leslie landed in the same way, and laid his hand upon Uncle Luke's arm.

"I was obliged to come back," he said; "my men are fagged out."

"No signs of him!"

Leslie shook his head and spoke in a whisper.

"I'll be off again as soon as I can get a fresh crew, and search till I do find him. For Heaven's sake, sir, do take them home!"

It was a kindly whisper, but Louise heard every word, and shuddered as she turned, and hid her face in her father's breast. For she knew what it meant; it was to spare her the agonising sight, when the sea, according to its wont, threw something up yonder among the rugged stones, where, to use the fishermen's words, the current bit hardest on the shore. She fought hard to keep back the wild cry that struggled in her breast; but it was in vain, and many a rough fellow turned aside as he heard the poor girl's piteous wail out there in the sunshine of that glorious morn.

"Harry! brother! what shall I do?"

George Vine's lips parted as he bent down over his child. "The Lord gave, and—"

His voice failed, but his lips completed poor old stricken Job's words, and there was a pause. Then he seemed to draw himself up, and held out his hand for a moment to Duncan Leslie.

"Luke!" he said then calmly and gravely. "Your arm too. Let us go home."

The little crowd parted left and right, and every hat was doffed in the midst of a great silence, as the two old men walked slowly up the rough pier, supporting the stricken girl.

Duncan Leslie followed, and as they passed on through the narrow lane of humble, sympathising people of the port, these turned in and slowly followed, two and two, bare-headed, as if it were a funeral procession.

Just then, high above the top of the grand cliff, a lark soared up, sprinkling the air as from a censer of sound, with his silvery notes joyous, loud, and thrilling; and one patriarchal fisherman, who had seen many a scene of sorrow in his time, whispered to the mate walking at his side—

"Ay, lad, and so it is; midst of life we are in death."

"Ah," sighed his companion; "but on such a morn as this!"

Chapter Thirty Three
At the Granite House

The Vines had hardly reached their home when quietly and in a furtive way boat after boat put off down the harbour, from the little punt belonging to some lugger, right up to the heavy fishing-craft, rowed by some six or eight men. There was no communication one with the other; no general order had been given, but, with one consent, all were bent upon the same mission, and hour after hour, every mass of weedy rock, chasm, hollow, and zorn was scanned, where it was known that the current was likely to throw up that which it had engulfed; but, though every inch of shore was searched, the task proved to be without avail, and the brothers, seated together in the quaint, old-fashioned dining-room, waiting to be summoned for the reception of their dead, sat waiting, and without receiving the call.

Louise had refused to leave them, and had clung to her father, asking to be allowed to stay; but no sooner was the consent obtained than it proved to be useless, for the poor girl was completely prostrated by the excitement and horror of the past night, and had to be helped up to her couch.

And there the brothers sat in silence, George Vine calm, stern, and with every nerve on the strain; Uncle Luke watching him furtively without attempting to speak.

When any words had passed between the brothers, the old cynic's voice sounded less harsh, and its tones were sympathetic, as he strove to be consolatory to the suffering man. They had been seated some time together in silence, when Uncle Luke rose, and laid his hand upon his brother's shoulder.

"I don't know what to say to you, George," he whispered softly. "For all these years past I've been, what you know, a childless, selfish man; but I feel for you, my lad—I feel for you, and I'd bear half your agony, if I could."

George Vine turned upon him with a piteous smile, and took the hand resting on his shoulder.

"You need not speak, Luke," he said sadly. "Do you think we have lived all these years without my understanding my brother, and knowing what he is at heart?"

Luke shook his head, gripped the hand which held his firmly, but could not speak.

"I am going to bear it like a man, please God; but it is hard, Luke, hard; and but for poor Louise's sake I could wish that my journey was done."

"No, no. No, no, George," said the brother huskily. "There is, lad, much to do here yet—for you, my boy—for Louise—that poor, half-crazy woman up-stairs, and Uncle Luke, who is not much better, so they say. No, my boy, you must fight—you must bear, and bear it bravely, as you will, as soon as this first shock is over, and there's always hope—always hope. The poor boy may have escaped."

"Ay, to where? Luke, brother, for heaven's sake let me be in peace. I cannot bear to speak now. I feel as if the strain is too great for my poor brain."

Luke pressed his hand, and walked slowly to the window, from whence he could gaze down at the boats going and coming into the harbour; and he shuddered as he thought what any one of them might bring.

"Better it should, and at once," he said to himself. "He'll know no rest until that is past."

He turned and looked in wonder at the door, which opened then, and Aunt Marguerite, dressed in one of her stiffest brocades, pale, but with her eyes stern and fierce, entered the room, to sweep slowly across, till she was opposite to George Vine, when she crossed her arms over her breast, and began to beat her shoulder with her large ivory fan, the thin leaves making a peculiar pattering noise against her whalebone stiffened bodice.

"Don't talk to him, Margaret," said Uncle Luke, coming forward. "He is not fit. Say what you have to say another time."

"Silence! you poor weak imbecile!" she cried, as her eyes flashed at him. "What do you do here at a time like this? Now," she continued, darting a vindictive look at her broken-hearted brother, "what have you to say?"

"To say, Margaret?" he replied piteously. "God help me, what can I say?"

"Nothing, miserable that you are. The judgment has come upon you at last. Have I not striven to save that poor murdered boy from you—to raise him from the slough into which you plunged him in your wretched degradation? Time after time I have raised my voice, but it has been unheard. I have been treated as your wretched dependant, who could not even say her soul was her own, and with my heart bleeding, I have seen—"

"Margaret, you were always crazy," cried Uncle Luke fiercely; "are you raving mad?"

"Yes," she cried. "Worm, pitiful crawling worm. You are my brother by birth, but what have I seen of you but your wretched selfish life—of you who sold your birthright to sink into the degraded creature you are, so degraded that you side with this man against me, now that he is worthily punished for his crime against his son."

"I cannot listen to this," cried Uncle Luke furiously. "Let her speak," said George Vine sadly; "she thinks she is right."

"And so do you," cried Aunt Marguerite. "If you had kept the poor boy a gentleman all this would not have happened. See to what extent you have driven the poor, brave-hearted, noble boy, the only true des Vignes. You, degenerate creature that you are, maddened him by the life you forced him to lead, till in sheer recklessness he took this money, struck down the tyrant to whom you made him slave, and at last caused him to be hunted down till, with the daring of a des Vignes, he turned, and died like one of his chivalrous ancestors, his face to his foes, his—"

"Bah!" cried Uncle Luke, with a fierce snarl, "his chivalrous ancestors!"

"Luke!"

"I tell you, George, I'm sick of the miserable cant. Died like a hero! Woman, it was your miserable teaching made him the discontented wretch he was."

"For pity's sake, Luke."

"I must speak, now," cried the old man furiously; "it's time she knew the truth: but for you who, in return for the shelter of your brother's roof, filled the boy's head with your vain folly, he would have been a respectable member of society, an honest Englishman, instead of a would-be murderer and thief."

"It is false!" cried Aunt Marguerite.

"It is true!" thundered the old man, in spite of his brother's imploring looks; "true, and you know it's true. Died like a hero, with his face to the foe! He died, if he be dead, like a coward, afraid to face the officer of the law he had outraged—a disgrace to the name of Vine."

Aunt Marguerite stood gazing at him, as if trying to stay him with the lightning of her eyes, but his burst of passion was at an end, and he did not even realise that her vindictive looks had faded out, and that she had grown ghastly as a sheet, and tottered half palsied from the room.

For, horrified by the agony he read in his brother's face, Luke Vine had seized his hands, and was gazing imploringly at him.

"Forgive me, George," he whispered. "I knew not what I said."

"Let me be alone—for a while," faltered his brother. "I am weak. I cannot bear it now."

But the strain was not yet at an end, for at that moment there was a tap at the door, and Liza entered, looking red-eyed and strange; and a sob escaped her as she saw her master's face.

"A gentleman to see you, sir. He must see you at once," she stammered.

"If you please, Mr Vine," said a short, stern voice, and, without further ceremony, the detective officer entered the room.

George Vine rose painfully, and tried to cross to where the man stood inside the door, looking sharply from one to the other.

"No," he said, inaudibly, as his eyes seemed to grasp everything; "they're honest. Don't know where he is."

George Vine did not cross to the officer; his strength seemed to fail him.

"You have come," he said slowly, as he tried to master a piteous sigh. "Luke, you will come with me?"

"Yes, lad, I'll come," said Uncle Luke. Then turning towards the officer, he whispered, "Where did you find the poor lad?"

"You are labouring under a mistake, sir," said the man. "We have not found him—yet. My people are searching still, and half the fishermen are out in their boats, but they say it is not likely that they will find him till after a tide or two when he will be cast ashore."

The words sounded hard and brutal, and Luke gave the speaker a furious look as he saw his brother wince.

"Why have you come here, then?" said Uncle Luke, harshly. "Do you think he has not suffered enough?"

The officer made no reply, but stood, note-book in hand, thinking. Then sharply:

"A person named Pradelle has been staying here."

"Yes," said Uncle Luke, with a snap of his teeth; "and if you had taken him instead of hunting down our poor boy you would have done some good."

"All in good time, sir. I expect he was at the bottom of it all. Have you any information you can give me as to where he is likely to have gone?"

"Where do all scoundrels and thieves go to hide? London, I suppose."

"I expected that," said the officer, talking to Uncle Luke, but watching George Vine's drawn, grief-stricken face the while. "I daresay we shall be able to put a finger upon him before long. He does not seem to have a very good record, and yet you gentlemen appear to have given him a welcome here."

George Vine made a deprecating movement with his hands, the detective watching him keenly the while, and evidently hesitating over something he had to say.

"And now, sir," said Uncle Luke, "you'll excuse me if I ask you to go. This is not a time for cross-examination."

"Eh? perhaps not," said the officer sharply, as he gave the old man a resentful glance. Then to himself, "Well—it's duty. He had no business to. I've no time for fine feelings."

"At another time," continued Uncle Luke, "if you will come to me, I daresay I can give you whatever information you require."

"Oh, you may rest easy about that, sir," said the officer, half laughingly, "don't you be afraid. But I want a few words now with this other gentleman."

"And I say no; you shall not torture him now," cried Uncle Luke, angrily. "He has suffered enough."

"Don't you interfere, sir, till you are called upon," said the officer roughly. "Now, Mr George Vine, if you please."

"I will not have it," cried Uncle Luke; "it is an outrage."

"Let him speak, brother," said George Vine, with calm dignity; "now sir, go on."

"I will, sir. It's a painful duty, but it is a duty. Now, sir, I came here with a properly signed warrant for the arrest of Henry Vine, for robbery and attempted murder."

"Ah!" sighed Vine, with his brow wrinkling.

"The young man would have resigned himself quietly, but you incited him to resist the law and escape." "It is quite true. I have sinned, sir," said Vine, in a low pained voice, "and I am ready to answer for what I have done."

"But that is not all," continued the officer. "Not content with aiding my prisoner to escape, you attacked me, sir, and twice over you struck me in the execution of my duty."

"Is this true, George?" cried Uncle Luke, excitedly.

"Yes," said his brother, calmly bending to this new storm; "yes, it is quite true."

"Well, sir, what have you to say?"

"Nothing."

"You know, I suppose, that it is the duty of every citizen to help the officers of the law?"

"Yes."

"And yet you not only fought against me; but struck me heavily. I have the marks."

"Yes; I own to it all."

"And you know that it is a very serious offence?"

"Yes," said the wretched man; and he sank into the nearest chair, looking straight before him into vacancy.

"Well, sir," said the officer sharply, "I'm glad you know the consequences." Then turning sharply on Uncle Luke, who stood biting his lips in an excited manner, "Perhaps you'll come into the next room with me, sir. I should like a few words with you."

Uncle Luke scowled at him, as he led the way into the drawing-room, and shut the door angrily.

"Now, sir," he began fiercely, "let me—"

"Hold hard, old gentleman!" said the officer; "don't be so excitable. I want a few words, and then, for goodness' sake, give me a glass of wine and a biscuit. I've touched nothing since I came here last night."

"Ah!" ejaculated Uncle Luke, furiously; but the man went on.

"Of course it's a serious thing striking an officer; let alone the pain, there's the degradation, for people know of it. I'm sore at losing my prisoner, and if he had not held me I should have had the young fellow safe, and that horrible accident wouldn't have happened."

"And now what are you going to do?" snarled Uncle Luke, "drag him off to gaol?"

"Going to act like a man, sir. Think I'm such a brute? Poor old fellow, I felt quite cut, hard as I am, and I'd have asked him to shake hands over it, only he couldn't have taken it kindly from me. You seem a man of the world, sir. He's one of those dreamy sort of naturalist fellows. Tell him from me I'd have given anything sooner than all this should have happened. It was my duty to see him about his resistance to the law. But, poor old fellow, he was doing his natural duty in defence of his boy, just as I felt that I was doing mine."

Uncle Luke did not speak but stood holding out his hand. The officer gripped it eagerly, and they two stood gazing in each other's faces for a few moments.

"Thank you," said Uncle Luke gently; and after a time the officer rose to go.

"Yes, sir," he said, at parting, "I shall stay down here till the poor boy is found. Some one in town will be on the look-out for our friend Pradelle, for, unless I'm very much mistaken, he's the monkey who handled the cat's paws. Good morning."

Uncle Luke stood at the door watching the officer till he was out of sight, and then returned to the old dining-room, to find his brother still gazing into vacancy, just as he had been left.

"News, Luke?" he said, as he looked eagerly. "No, you need not speak. Perhaps it is better so. Better death than this terrible dishonour."

Chapter Thirty Four
George Vine Asks for Help

"She shall go. I always knew she was a thief," said Aunt Marguerite, as she stood by her open window, listening to a whispered communication going on. "Wait till Louise can act like a woman, and see to her housekeeping again, and that girl shall go."

She listened again, and could hear a rough woman's voice urging something, while the more familiar voice of Liza was raised again and again in a whispered protest.

Then followed more talking, and at last there was a pause, followed by a hasty whisper, and the heavy step of old Poll Perrow, with her basket on her back, supported by the strap across her brow. Aunt Marguerite had been to her niece's door again and again, and tried it to find it fastened; and she could get no response to her taps and calls. She seemed to feel no sorrow only rage against all by whom she was surrounded; and, isolated as it were, she spent the afternoon going to and fro between her own room and one which gave her a good view of the harbour mouth with boats going and returning; for the search for the body of Harry Vine was kept up without cessation, the fishermen lending themselves willingly to the task, and submitting, but with an ill grace, to the presence of the police.

Aunt Marguerite, however, in spite of her vindictive feeling, suffered intense grief; and her sorrow seemed to deepen the lines in her handsome old face.

"They've murdered him, they've murdered him?" she kept on muttering as she watched the passing boats. "No one understood him but me."

She drew back sharply from the window, for just then a closely-veiled figure came hurriedly into view, her goal being evidently the old granite house.

Aunt Marguerite's eyes sparkled with vindictive malice.

"Yes," she said, half aloud; "and you too, madam—you had your share in the poor boy's death. Oh! how I do hate your wretched Dutch race."

She crossed to the door, and opened it slightly, to stand listening, to hear voices a few minutes later, and then steps on the stairs, which stopped, after a good deal of whispering, at her niece's door, after which there was a low tapping, and Liza's voice arose:

"Miss Louise! Miss Louise!"

"Yes, knock again. She will not answer. One of them has some pride left."

"Miss Louise, Miss Louise, you're wanted, please."

There was no reply to the repeated knocks. There was a smile of satisfaction on Aunt Marguerite's face as she drew herself up, and opened her fan as if at some presentation, or about to dismiss an intruder; but her countenance changed directly, and, forgetting her dignity, she craned forward, for all at once a pleading voice arose.

"Louise, Louise, for pity's sake let me in."

There was a short pause, and then the sharp sound of the shooting back of a bolt and the creaking of a door. Then it was closed again, and as the listener threw her own open there came the faint sound of a passionate cry and a low sobbing.

Aunt Marguerite stepped out into the passage, her head erect, and her stiff silk training noisily behind her, to go to her own room, but the way was barred by the presence of Liza, who was down on the floor crouched in a heap, sobbing passionately, with her apron up to her eyes.

"Get up!" said Aunt Marguerite imperiously, as she struck at the girl's hand with her fan.

Liza leaped to her feet, looked aghast at the figure before her, and fled, while Aunt Marguerite strode into her room, and loudly closed the door. As she passed her niece's chamber, Louise was clasped tightly in Madelaine's arms, and it was long before the two girls were seated, hand in hand, gazing wonderingly at the inroads made so soon by grief.

"It is so horrible—all so horrible," whispered Madelaine at last, for the silence was for long unbroken, save by an occasional sob.

Louise looked at her wildly, and then burst into a passion of tears.

"Maddy!" she cried at last, "is it all true?"

They could say no more, but sat gathering comfort from the sympathetic grasp of each other's hands.

At last, in a dull heavy way, the words came, each sounding as if the speaker were in despair, but willing to suffer so that her companion might be spared, and by degrees Louise learned that Van Heldre still lay in the same insensible state, the awaking from which Madelaine shrank from with horror, lest it should mean the return for a brief time of sense before the great final change.

"I could not come to you," said Louise, after a long silence, as she gazed wistfully in her friend's face, "and thought we should never meet again as friends."

"You should have known me better," replied Madelaine. "It is very terrible, such a—such a—oh Louy, dearest, there must have been some mistake. Harry—Harry could not have been so base."

Louise was silent for a time. At last she spoke.

"There must be times," she said gently, "when even the best of us are not answerable for our actions. He must have been mad. It was when, too—he had—promised—he had told me—that in the future—oh," she cried, shuddering, as she covered her face with her hands, "it can't be true—it cannot be true."

Again there was a long silence in the room, whose drawn-down blind turned the light of a sickly yellow hue. But the window was open, and from time to time the soft sea breeze wafted the blind inward, and a bright ray of sunny light streamed in like hope across the two bent forms.

"I must not stay long," said Madelaine. "I shiver whenever I am away, lest—"

"No, no," cried Louise, passionately, as she strained her friend to her breast, "we will not despond yet. All this comes across our lives like a dense black cloud, and there must be a great change in the future. Your father will recover."

"I pray that he may," said Madelaine.

"And I will not believe that Harry is—dead."

"I pray that he may be alive, Louy, to come some time in the future to ask forgiveness of my father. For I did love him, Louy; at first as a sister might the brother with whom she had played from childhood, and of late in sorrow and anguish, as the woman whom he had always said he loved. I fought with it, oh, so hard, but the love was there, and even when I was most hard and cold—"

"And he believed you cared for Mr Leslie."

The words slipped from Louise Vine's lips like an escaped thought, and the moment they were spoken, she shrank away with her pale cheeks crimsoning, and she gazed guiltily at her companion.

"It was a foolish fancy on his part," said Madelaine gravely. "I cannot blame myself for anything I ever said or did to your brother. If I had been wrong, my lapse would have come upon me now like the lash of a whip; but in the long hours of my watches by my poor father's bed, I have gone over it again and again, and I cannot feel that I have been wrong."

Louise drew her more closely to her breast.

"Maddy," she whispered, "years will have to pass, and we must separate. The pleasant old days must end, but some day, when all these horrors have been softened by time, we may call each other sister again, and in the long dark interval you will not forget."

"Forget!" said Madelaine, with a smile full of sadness. "You know that we shall always be unchanged."

"Going—so soon?" exclaimed Louise, for her friend had risen.

"He is lying yonder," said Madelaine. "I must go back. I could not stay away long from you though without a word."

They stood for a few moments clasped in each other's arms, and then in a slow, sad way, went hand in hand towards the door. As she opened it for her friend to pass through, Louise shrank back from the burst of sunshine that flooded the passage, and placed her hand across her eyes. It was a momentary act, and then she drew a long breath and followed her friend, as if her example had given the needed strength, and acted as an impetus to raise her from the lethargic state into which she had fallen.

In this spirit she went down with her to the door, when, as their steps sounded on the hall floor, the dining-room door was thrown open quickly, and Vine stood in the darkened opening, gazing wildly at the veiled figure of Madelaine.

"Van Heldre?" he said, in an excited whisper; "not—not—" He could not finish his speech, but stood with his hand pressed to his throat.

"My father's state is still unchanged," said Madelaine gently.

"Then there may yet be hope, there may yet be hope," said Vine hoarsely as he shrank once more into the darkened room.

"Mr Vine," said Madelaine piteously, as she stood with extended hands asking sympathy in her grievous trouble.

"My child!" he cried, as he caught her to his breast, and she clung there sobbing bitterly. Then he softly disengaged her hands from his neck. "No, no," he said dreamily, "I am guilty too; I must never take you to my heart again."

"What have I done?" sobbed Madelaine, as she clung to him still.

"You?" he said fondly. "Ah! it was once my dream that you would be more and more my child. Little Madelaine!"

He drew her to his breast again, kissed her with spasmodic eagerness, and then held out a hand to Louise, who flew to his breast as with an angry, malicious look, Aunt Marguerite advanced to the end of the landing and looked down at the sobbing group.

"Good-bye!" whispered the stricken man hoarsely, "good-bye, my child. I am weak and helpless. I hardly know what I say; but you must come here no more. Good-bye."

He turned from them hastily, and glided back into the darkened room, where Louise followed him, as Madelaine went slowly down toward the town.

Vine was seated before the empty grate, his head resting on his hand, as Louise went to his side, and he started as if from a dream when she touched his shoulder.

"You, my child?" he said, sinking back. "Ah, stay with me—pray with me. It is so hard to bear alone."

Chapter Thirty Five
The Old Watchdog

The silence as if of death reigned for days and days at Van Heldre's house, which, unasked, old Crampton had made his residence. In a quiet furtive way he had taken possession of the inner office, to which he had brought from his own house a sofa-cushion and pillow, carrying them there one dark night unseen, and at times, no doubt, he must have lain down and slept; but to all there it was a mystery when he did take his rest.

If Mrs Van Heldre called him to partake of a meal he came. If he was forgotten he ate one of a store of captain's biscuits which he kept in his desk along with his very strong tobacco, which flavoured the said biscuits in a way that, being a regular smoker, he did not notice, while at ten o'clock he regularly went out into the yard to have his pipe. He was always ready to sit up and watch, but, to his great annoyance, he had few opportunities, the task being shared between Madelaine and her mother.

As to the business of the office, that went on as usual as far as the regular routine was concerned, everything fresh being put back till the principal resumed his place at his desk. Bills of lading, the smelting-house accounts bank deposits, and the rest, all were attended to, just as if Van Heldre had been there instead of lying above between life and death. From time to time Mrs Van Heldre came down to him to beg that he would ask for everything he wanted.

"I cannot help neglecting you, Mr Crampton," she said with her hands playing about the buttons of her dress.

"Never you mind about me, ma'am," he said, admonishing her with a pen-holder. "I'm all right, and waiting to take my turn."

"Yes, yes, you're very good, Mr Crampton, and you will see that everything goes on right, so that when he comes down he may find that we have not neglected any single thing."

Crampton frowned, but his face grew smooth again as he looked at the little anxious countenance before him.

"Don't you be afraid, ma'am. If Mr Van Heldre came down to-day everything is ready for him—everything."

"Yes, of course, Mr Crampton. I might have known it. But I can't help feeling anxious and worried about things."

"Naturally, ma'am, naturally; and I've been trying to take all worry away from you about the business. Everything is quite right. Ah!" he said as the little woman hurried away from the office, "if Miss Maddy would only talk to me like that. But she won't forgive me, and I suppose she never will." He made an entry and screwed up his lips, as he dipped a pen in red ink and ruled a couple of lines, using the ebony ruler which had laid his master low. "Poor girl! I never understood these things; but they say love makes people blind and contrary, and so it is that she seems to hate me, a man who wouldn't rob her father of a penny, and in her quiet hiding sort of way worships the man who robbed him of five hundred pounds, and nearly killed him as well. Ah! it's a curious world."

"I've—I've brought you a glass of wine and a few biscuits, Mr Crampton," said Mrs Van Heldre, entering, and speaking in her pleasant prattling way. Then she set down a tray, and hurried out before he could utter his thanks.

"Good little woman," said Crampton. "Some people would have brought a glass of wine and not the decanter. Well, yes, ma'am, I will have a glass of wine, for I feel beat out."

He poured out a glass of good old sherry, held it up to the light, and closed one eye.

"Your health, Mr Van Heldre," he said solemnly. "Best thing I can wish you. Yours, Mrs Van Heldre, and may you never be a widow. Miss Madelaine, your health, my dear, and may your eyes be opened. I'm not such a bad man as you think."

He drank the glass of wine, and then made a grimace.

"Sweet biscuits," he said, "only fit for children. Hah, well! Eh? What's the matter?"

He had heard a cry, and hurrying across the office, he locked the door, and ran down the glass corridor to the house.

"Worse, ma'am, worse?" he cried, as Mrs Van Heldre came running down the stairs and into the dining-room, where she plumped herself on the floor, and held her hands to her lips to keep back the hysterical sobs which struggled for vent.

"Shall I run for the doctor, ma'am?"

"No, no!" cried Mrs Van Heldre, in a stifled voice, with her mouth still covered. "Better."

"Better?"

She nodded violently.

"Then it was very cruel of you, ma'am," said the old man, plaintively. "I thought—I thought—"

Crampton said no more, but he walked to the window with his face buried in his great yellow silk handkerchief, blowing his nose with a continuity and force which became at last so unbearable that Mrs Van Heldre went out into the hall.

She went back soon into the dining-room where Crampton was waiting anxiously.

"He looked at me when I was in the room with my darling child, Mr Crampton, and his lips parted, and he spoke to me, and I was obliged to come away, for fear I should do him harm."

"Come away, ma'am! and at a time like that!" said Crampton, angrily.

Mrs Van Heldre drew herself up with dignity.

"My child signed to me to go," she said quietly; and then with her eyes brimming over with tears, "Do you think I would not have given the world to stay?"

At that moment Madelaine came quickly and softly into the room.

"He is sleeping," she whispered excitedly; "he looked at me and smiled, and then his eyes closed and he seemed to go into a calm sleep, not that terrible stupor, but sleep. Mother, come and see—it must be sleep."

Old Crampton was left alone to begin pacing the room excitedly for a few minutes, when Madelaine came down once more.

"Pray go for Dr Knatchbull!" she cried piteously. "But isn't he—"

"We do not know—we are afraid to hope—pray, pray go."

"She hasn't spoken so gently since that night," muttered Crampton, as he hurried down the street. "Poor girl! it is very hard; and this may be only the change before—No, I won't think that," cried the old clerk, and he broke into a run.

Chapter Thirty Six
Crampton Reports Progress

"Yes," said Dr Knatchbull, confidently; "he will get over it now. Can't say," he said, rubbing his hands in his satisfaction, "whether it's the doctor's physic or the patient's physique, but one of them has worked wonders. What do you say, Miss Van Heldre?"

"That we can never be sufficiently grateful to you."

"Never," cried Mrs Van Heldre, wringing his hand. "Bah!" exclaimed the doctor, "that's what you people say now that you have got to the turn; but by-and-by when I send in my bill—and I mean to make this a pretty stiff one, Mrs Van Heldre—you will all be as grumpy as possible, and think it a terrible overcharge."

"Well, really, Dr Knatchbull," began Mrs Van Heldre, ruffling up like an aggravated hen, "I am quite sure my dear husband will pay any—"

"Mamma, mamma, dear!" cried Madelaine, smiling through her tears; "can you not see that Dr Knatchbull is laughing at us?"

"No, my dear," said the little lady angrily; "but if he is, I must say that it is too serious a matter for a joke."

"So it is, my dear madam," said the doctor, taking her hand, "far too serious; but I felt in such high spirits to find that we have won the fight, that I was ready to talk any nonsense. All the same though, with some people it's as true as true."

"Yes, but we are not some people," said Mrs Van Heldre. "But now tell us what we are to do."

"Nothing, my dear madam, but let him have rest and peace."

"But he has been asking for Mr Crampton this morning, and that means business."

"Well, let him see him to-morrow, if he asks. If he is not allowed, he will fidget, and that will do him more harm than seeing him, only I would not let him dwell on the attack. Divert his attention all you can, and keep from him all you possibly can about the Vines."

John Van Heldre did not ask for his confidential clerk for two days more, the greater part of which time he spent in sleep; but in the intervals he talked in a low voice to his wife or Madelaine, not even alluding once, to their great surprise, to the cause of his illness.

"He must know it, mamma," said Madelaine, sadly; "and he is silent, so as to spare me."

At last the demand for Crampton was made, and the old clerk heard it looking eager and pleased.

"At last ma'am," said Crampton, rubbing his hands.

"You'll go up very quietly, Mr Crampton," said Mrs Van Heldre. "If you would not mind."

She pointed to a pair of slippers she had laid ready. The old clerk looked grim, muttered something about the points of his toes, and ended by untying his shoes, and putting on the slippers.

Madelaine was quite right, for no sooner had Van Heldre motioned the clerk to a chair by the bed's head, learned that all was right in his office, and assured the old man that he was mending fast, than he opened upon him regarding the attack that night.

"Was that money taken?" he said, quickly.

"Is it right for you to begin talking about that so soon?" replied Crampton.

"Unless you want me to go backwards, yes," said his employer, sharply. "There, answer my questions. I have nothing the matter now; only weak, and I cannot ask any one else."

"I'm your servant, Mr Van Heldre," said Crampton, stiffly. "Go on, sir."

"That money, then?"

"Gone, sir, every note. Five hundred pounds."

"Dead loss," said Van Heldre; "but it must be repaid."

"Humph! pretty opinion you seem to have of me, sir, as a confidential clerk."

"What do you mean, Crampton?"

"Mean, sir? Why, that I did my duty, and stopped every note at the Bank of England, of course."

"You did that, Crampton?"

"Yes, sir; and those notes are of no use to anybody."

"Capital. Hah! that's better. Five hundred just coming on the other misfortune worried me. Why, Crampton, that's a white paper plaster for my sore head."

"Glad you're satisfied, sir."

"More than satisfied. Now tell me: have the police any notion who committed the robbery?" Crampton nodded. "Do you know?"

Crampton looked at his employer curiously, and nodded again.

"Have they taken any one?"

"No, sir," said the old man sadly.

"Hah! That's bad. Who was it?"

"Well, sir, you know of course."

"I? No!"

"You don't know, sir?"

"I have no idea, Crampton. I heard a noise, and went in and surprised the scoundrel, but it was quite dark, and as I tried to seize him I was struck down."

"And you mean to assure me, sir, that you don't know who it was?"

"I have not the most remote idea."

"Well then, sir, I must tell you it was him who had been robbing you ever since the first day he came to us."

"Robbing me?"

"Well, not exactly of money in hard cash, but of your time, which is just the same. Time's money. Always an hour late."

Van Heldre turned upon him fiercely. "Crampton, can you let your prejudice go so far as to suspect that young man?"

"Yes, sir. I can... Suspect? No, I am sure. I doubted him from the first."

"It is monstrous. You were unjust to him from the first."

"I, sir?"

"Yes. But then how can a man who has never had a child be just to the weaknesses of the young?"

"I can be just, sir, and I have been. You don't know the supercilious way in which that boy treated me from the day he entered our office. Always late, and as soon as he was settled down to his work, in must come that scoundrel with the French name to ask for him, and get him away. Why, Mr Van Heldre, sir, if I hadn't been a law-abiding subject of her most gracious Majesty Queen Victoria, I'd have knocked that man down."

"Pish!" said Van Heldre impatiently, as he lay back frowning, and looking very thoughtful. "I am sorry that you should have entertained such a suspicion about the son of my old friend."

"Ah!" sighed Crampton. "Poor Mr Vine! It's heart-breaking work, sir. It is, indeed."

"Heart-breaking!" said Van Heldre. "It is atrocious. There, I will not speak angrily, Crampton."

"No, sir. You must not; and now I'm going, sir. You've talked twice as much as is good for you."

"Sit down," said Van Heldre sternly.

Crampton, who had moved towards the door, slowly resumed his place.

"I am not too weak to talk about this terrible accusation. I am not going to say much now, only to ask you to throw aside all this prejudice and to look upon the mishap as an unfortunate occurrence. Come, Crampton, be a little broader. Don't be so ready to suspect the first person you dislike, and then to keep obstinately to your opinion."

"Better not talk any more," said Crampton, shortly.

"I must talk," said Van Heldre, more sternly. "Mind this, Crampton, you are wrong."

The care, want of rest, and anxiety had produced a state of acidity in the old clerk's organisation which had made him exceptionally irritable.

"Wrong, eh?" he said sharply.

"Yes; and I must call upon you to be careful to keep these fancies to yourself."

"Fancies, sir?"

"Yes, fancies, man. I would not on any consideration have Mr Vine know that such a suspicion had existed in my office, and —"

He paused for a few moments, and then held out his hand to the old clerk, who took it, and felt his own gripped warmly.

"Come, Crampton," continued Van Heldre, smiling; "after all these years together, I trust we are something more than master and man. You have always proved yourself a friend in the way in which you have looked after my interests."

"I've always tried to do my duty, Mr Van Heldre."

"And you always have done your duty—more than duty. Now just go quietly down, and ask Henry Vine to step up-stairs with you. I must have this put straight at once. Crampton, you and my old friend's son must make a fresh start."

Crampton's fresh countenance grew dingy-looking, and Van Heldre felt his hand twitch.

"Come, I tell you that your suspicions are absurd, and I must have you two work well together. The young man only wants a little humouring to make him all that we could wish. Go and fetch him up."

"He—he is not here this morning, sir," gasped Crampton, at last.

"Not here?"

"No, sir," said the old man hastily; and he passed the hand at liberty across his face.

"I am sorry. I should have liked to settle this, now it is on my mind."

Crampton looked wildly towards the door, in the hope that the coming of wife or daughter would bring about a diversion.

"Of course," said Van Heldre suddenly, "you have not shown the young man that you have had this idea in your head?"

Crampton was silent, and as Van Heldre looked at him he saw the great beads of perspiration were standing upon his face.

"Why, good heavens, Crampton," he cried, "you have not breathed a word of all this to a soul?"

The old clerk looked at him wildly.

"Ah! you are keeping something back," said Van Heldre.

"Hush, sir, hush!" cried the old clerk in alarm; "for goodness sake don't be excited. Think of how weak you are."

"Then answer," said Van Heldre, in a low whisper. "Tell me what you have done."

"I—I did everything for the best, sir."

"Henry Vine! You did not accuse him of this terrible affair?"

Crampton's face grew gradually hard and stern. His tremulous state passed off, and he turned as if at bay.

"Crampton! Good heavens, man! What have you done."

"I had to think of you, sir, lying here. Of Mrs Van Heldre, sir, and of Miss Madelaine."

"Yes, yes; but speak, man. What have you done?"

"My duty, sir."

"And accused him of this—this crime?"

Crampton was silent.

"Are you mad? Oh, man, man, you must have been mad."

Crampton drew a long breath.

"Do my wife and daughter know?"

"Yes, sir," said Crampton slowly.

"And—and they have spoken as I speak? They told you it was prejudice."

Crampton drew a long breath once more.

"Don't, pray don't say any more, sir—not now," he said at last pleadingly.

"They—surely they don't—there, quick! Ring that bell."

"Mr Van Heldre, sir. Pray—pray don't take it like that; I on'y did my duty by you all."

"Duty! In a fit of madness to make such a charge as this and prejudice others!" cried Van Heldre angrily. "Ring that bell, man. I cannot rest till this is set right."

"Think, sir, how I was situated," pleaded the old clerk. "You were robbed; I saw you lying, as I thought, dying, and I saw the scoundrel who had done all this escape. What could I do but call in the police?"

"The police! Then it is known by every one in the place?"

Crampton looked pityingly down at the anguished countenance before him.

"And Henry Vine? He refuted your charge? Speak, man, or you will drive me mad."

"Henry Vine did not deny the charge, sir. He was manly enough for that."

"Crampton, is this all true?"

"It was my duty, sir."

"He does not deny it? Oh! it seems monstrous. But you said the police; you gave information. Crampton—his father—his sister—my poor child!"

"Is saved from a villain, Mr Van Heldre?" cried the old clerk fiercely. "Better she should have died than have married such a man as he."

"And I—I lying here helpless as a child," said the sick man feebly. "But this must all be stopped. Crampton, you should not have done all this. Now go at once, fetch George Vine here, and—Henry—the young man. Where is he?"

"Gone, sir, to answer for his crime," said the old man solemnly. "Henry Vine is dead."

Chapter Thirty Seven
A Title of Honour

Duncan Leslie sought patiently and well, but he was as unsuccessful as the rest, and after searching from a boat and being pulled close in along the shore, he rose at daybreak one morning, and crossing the harbour, went up along the cliff away to the east, and wherever he could find a place possible for a descent, he lowered himself from among the rocks, and searched there.

The work was toilsome, but it was an outlet for his pent-up energy, and he went on and on, reaching places where the boat could not land him; but even here he found that he had been forestalled, for hunting along among the broken rocks, he could see a figure stepping cautiously from crag to crag, where the waves washed in, and the slimy sea-wrack made the task perilous, the more so that it was the figure of a woman whom he recognised as the old fish-dealer by the maund hanging on her back from the band across her forehead.

As he toiled after her she looked round, and waited till he came up, and addressed him in a singing tone.

"Not found him, have you, sir?"

Leslie shook his head, and continued his search, seeing the old woman on two alternate days still peering about among the rocks, like many more, for the young master, and more stubborn in her search than any of the rest.

By slow degrees the search was given up. It had been kept up long after what would have been customary under the circumstances, some of the searchers working from sheer respect for the Vines, others toiling on in the hope of reward.

But there was no result, and the last of the boats, that containing Duncan Leslie, returned to the harbour, after days of seeking to and fro along the coast.

"I felt it were no good all along, Mr Leslie, sir," said the old fisherman who had been chartered for the escape. "Sea's a mystery, sir, and when she gets hold of a body she hides it where mortal man can't find it, and keeps it till she's tired, and then she throws it ashore. I've watched it well these thirty years, and one gets to know by degrees."

Leslie bowed his head dejectedly.

"Course I wasn't going to say so before, sir, because it's a man's dooty like to go on seeking for what's lost; but, mark my words, sir, one o' these days that poor fellow will be throwed up pretty close to where he jumped in. You mark my words, he will, and Poll Perrow will be the first to see."

Leslie thought but little of the man's words then; in fact he hardly heard them, for in those hours his mind was full of Louise's sufferings, and the terrible misfortune which had come upon the homes of those two families so linked together, and now so torn apart. Unsuccessful in his search, he was now terribly exercised in mind as to what he should do to help or show some sympathy for the poor girl who, in the sorrow which had befallen her home, seemed nearer and dearer to him than ever.

It was a hard problem to solve. He wished to show his willingness to help, but he felt that his presence at the Vines' could only be looked upon now as an intrusion, and must inflict pain.

On the other hand, he was in dread lest he should be considered indifferent, and in this state of perplexity he betook himself to Uncle Luke.

"Nonsense, my good fellow," said the old man, quickly; "what more could you have done?"

"I don't know," he said desolately. "Tell me; I want to help—to serve you all if I can, and yet I seem to do nothing."

"There is nothing that we can do," said the old man solemnly. "Time must be the only cure for their trouble. Look at me, Duncan Leslie; I came to live up here with the fewest of necessities—alone, without wife or child, to be away from trouble, and you see I have failed. I cannot even help myself, so how can you expect to help them? There, leave it all to time."

"And your brother, how is he?"

Leslie felt that he had been speaking for the sake of saying something, and he bit his lip, as the old man gave him a peculiar look.

"How is a man likely to be who has lost a son as he has lost his?"

Leslie was silent.

"And now you would ask after my niece, young man, but you feel as if you dare not."

Leslie gave him an imploring look.

"Broken-hearted as her poor father, Leslie, seeing nothing in the future but one black cloud of misery. There, let's go out and sit in the sunshine and think."

Leslie followed the old man without a word. He longed to ask his advice about that future, and to question him about the friend in France, for in spite of himself he could not help feeling a thrill of satisfaction at the thought that for a certainty there must be an end to that engagement. No scion of a great house could enter into an alliance with the sister of a man whose career had ended as had ended Harry Vine's.

But he could not lay bare his heart to that cynical old man, who read him as easily as the proverbial book, and on whose lip there was always lurking the germ of a sneering smile.

He accompanied him then to his favourite seat among the rocks, just in front of his cottage, and they sat in silence for a time, Leslie hardly caring to start a topic lest it should evoke a sneer.

"Let's go down into the town," said Uncle Luke, jumping up suddenly.

Leslie rose without a word, and looked wonderingly at the old man, who, with his eyes shaded by his hands, was gazing along the rugged coast towards where, looking like dolls, a couple of fishermen were standing by something lying on a pebbly patch of sand.

Leslie looked at Uncle Luke, but the old man avoided his gaze, as if unwilling to lay bare his thoughts, and together they walked pretty quickly down the steep slope.

"Yes," said Uncle Luke; "the doctor says he will pull him through."

"Mr Van Heldre?"

"Yes. Why don't you go and see him?"

"I have sent to ask again and again, but I felt that any call on my part in the midst of such trouble would be out of place."

"Walk faster," said the old man excitedly, "if you can. No. Let me go on alone. Look at them—running. Look!"

Leslie had already noted the fact, and out of respect for the old man he stopped short at once, with the result that Uncle Luke stopped too.

"Why don't you come on?" he cried. "Good heavens, man, what can I do alone? There, there, Leslie, it's of no use, I can play the cynic no longer. Man is not independent of his fellows I never felt more in need of help than I do now."

Leslie took the old man's arm, and could feel that he was trembling, as they hurried on down towards the harbour, which they would have to cross by the ferry before they could reach the little crowd gathering round the first two men on the patch of sand.

"Keep a good heart, sir," said Leslie, gently. "It may not be after all."

"Yes, it is—it is," groaned Uncle Luke. "I've hung on so to the belief that being a clever swimmer he had managed to get away; but I might have known better, Leslie, I might have known better."

"Let's wait first and be sure, sir."

"There is no need. I don't think I cared for the boy, Leslie; there were times when he made me mad with him for his puppyism; but he was my brother's son, and I always hoped that after a few years he would change and become another man."

"Well, sir, let's cling to that hope yet."

"No, no," said the old man gloomily. "There is the end. He was no thief, Leslie. Believe that of him. It was his wretched scoundrel of a friend, and if Harry struck down poor Van Heldre, it was in his horror of being taken. He was no thief."

As they reached the lowest turn of the cliff path, the old man gripped Leslie's arm with spasmodic violence and stopped short, for the far side of the harbour lay before them, and they could see clearly all that was going on amid the rocks behind.

"We should be too late," he said huskily. "Your eyes are younger than mine. That's the police sergeant yonder in that boat, isn't it?"

"Yes."

Uncle Luke stood motionless, watching, and they could see that a boat rowed out from the harbour had gone on, and put in just opposite to the patch of the sand where that remote something had been cast up by the sea. To have carried it would have meant the use of a boat at the little ferry, and it was evident that the sergeant had decided to bring the sad flotsam and jetsam round to the harbour steps.

Leslie felt the old man's arm tremble, and his efforts to be firm, as they stood and watched the boat put off again, after a few minutes' delay. Then the little crowd which had collected came slowly back over the rugged shore, till they reached the eastern arm of the harbour just as the boat was coming in, and a piece of sail spread in the stern sheets told but too plainly the nature of her load.

"Mr Luke Vine," said Leslie.

"Yes," cried the old man, starting and speaking in a harsh way, as if suddenly brought back to the present.

"Will you let me make a suggestion?"

The old man only stared hard at him.

"Let me spare you this painful scene. It may not be as you think, and if it is not, it will be a shock; but if—there, let me go, and if it prove to be according to your fears, let me send you word by a trusty messenger, and you can then go up to your brother's house and break the terrible news as gently as you can."

Uncle Luke shook his head and began to descend the slope, timing his speed so as to reach the harbour steps at the same time as the boat.

There was a crowd waiting, but the people parted respectfully to allow the boat-man and his companion to pass, and the next minute Uncle Luke was questioning the sergeant with his eyes.

The man stepped ashore, and gave an order or two which sent a constable off at a trot, and another policeman took his post at the head of the steps, to keep the way down to the boat.

"Am I to speak plainly, sir?" said the detective in a low voice.

"Yes; let me know the worst."

"I'm afraid it is, sir. We have made no examination yet."

He did not finish all he had to say aloud, but whispered in the old man's ear. Uncle Luke made an effort to be firm, but he shuddered and turned to Leslie.

"Up to the King's Arms," he said huskily; and taking Leslie's arm, the old man walked slowly towards the water-side inn; but they had not gone half way before they encountered George Vine coming hastily down.

Uncle Luke's whole manner changed.

"Where are you going?" he cried, half angrily.

His brother merely pointed to the boat.

"How did you know? Who told you?" he said harshly.

"No one," was the calm reply. "Luke, do you suppose I could rest without watching for what I knew must come?"

His piteous, reproachful voice went to the heart of his hearers.

"Tell me," he continued earnestly, "Mr Leslie, the truth."

"There is nothing to tell, sir," said Leslie gravely, "so far it is only surmise. Come with us and wait."

Their suspense was not of long duration. In a very short time they were summoned from where they were waiting to another room, where Dr Knatchbull came forward with a face so full of the gravity of the situation, that any hope which flickered in Duncan Leslie's breast died out on the instant; and he heard George Vine utter a low moan, as, arm in arm, the two brothers advanced for the identification, and then Luke led his brother away.

Leslie followed to lend his aid, but Uncle Luke signed to him to go back.

He stood watching them till they disappeared up the narrow path leading to the old granite house, and a sense of misery such as he had never before felt swelled in the young man's breast, for, as he watched the bent forms of the two brothers, he saw in imagination what must follow, and his brow grew heavy, as he seemed to see Louise sobbing on her father's neck, heart-broken at her loss.

"And yet I could not help clinging to the hope that he had swum ashore," muttered Leslie, as he walked back to the inn, where he found Dr Knatchbull in conversation with the officer.

"I wish I had never seen Cornwall, sir," said the latter warmly, "poor lad! poor lad!"

"Then there is no doubt whatever?" said Leslie hurriedly.

"Identification after all these days in the water is impossible," said the doctor; "I mean personal identification."

"Then it may not be after all," said Leslie excitedly.

The detective shrugged his shoulders, and took a packet from a little black bag. This he opened carefully, and placed before Leslie a morocco pocket-book and a card-case, both stamped with a gold coronet and the motto *Roy et Foy*, while, when the card-case was drawn open and its water-soaked contents were taken out, the cards separated easily, and there, plainly enough, was the inscription, the result of Aunt Marguerite's inciting—

"Henri Comte des Vignes."

Chapter Thirty Eight
Poll Perrow goes a-Begging

Dark days of clouds with gloomy days of rain, such as washes the fertile soil from the tops of the granite hills, leaving all bare and desolate, with nothing to break the savage desolation of the Cornish prospect but a few projecting blocks, and here and there a grim-looking, desolate engine-house standing up like a rough mausoleum erected to the memory of so much dead coin.

There were several of these in the neighbourhood of Hakemouth, records of mining adventures where blasting and piercing had gone on for years in search of that rich vein of copper or tin, which experts said existed so many feet below grass, but which always proved to be a few feet lower than was ever reached, and instead of the working leading to the resurrection of capital, it only became its grave.

The rain fell, and on the third day the wind beat, and much soil was washed down into the verdant ferny gullies, and out to sea. The waves beat and eddied and churned up the viscous sea-wrack till the foam was fixed, and sent flying in balls and flakes up the rocks and over the fields, where it lay like dirty snow.

In and out of the caverns the sea rushed and bellowed and roared, driving the air in before it, till the earth seemed to quiver, and the confined air escaped with a report like that of some explosion. Then the gale passed over, the stars came out, and in the morning, save that the sea looked muddy instead of crystal clear and pure, all was sunshine and joy.

During the storm there had been an inquest, and with rain pouring down till there were inches of water in the grave, the body of the unfortunate man was laid to rest.

Duncan Leslie had been busy for a couple of hours in a restless, excited way, till, happening to look down from up by his engine-house, he caught sight of a grey-looking figure seated upon a stone by the cliff path. Giving a few orders, he hurried along the track.

Uncle Luke saw him coming, out of the corner of one eye, but he did not move, only sat with his hands resting upon his stick gazing out at the fishing-boats, which seemed to be revelling in the calm and sunshine, and gliding out to sea.

"Good morning."

"Bah! nothing of the kind," said Uncle Luke, viciously. "There isn't such a thing."

"No?" said Leslie, smiling sadly.

"Nothing of the kind. Life's all a mistake. The world's a round ball of brambles with a trouble on every thorn. Young Harry has the best of it, after all. Get wet?"

"Yesterday, at the funeral? Yes, very."

"Hah! Saw you were there. Horrible day. Well, good job it's all over."

Leslie was silent, and stood watching the old man.

"Something upset you?" he said at last.

"Upset me? Do you think it's possible for me to go to my brother's without being upset?"

"No, no. It has been a terrible business for you all."

"Wasn't talking about that," snapped out Uncle Luke. "That's dead and buried and forgotten."

"No, sir; not forgotten."

"I said, 'and forgotten.'"

Leslie bowed.

"Confound that woman!" continued Uncle Luke, after a pause. "Talk about Huguenot martyrs, sir; my brother George and that girl have lived a life of martyrdom putting up with her."

"She is old and eccentric."

"She has no business to be old and eccentric. Nobody has, sir; unless— unless he shut himself up all alone as I do myself. I never worry any one; I only ask to be let alone. There, you needn't sneer."

"I did not sneer, sir."

"No, you didn't, Leslie. I beg pardon. You're a good fellow, Leslie. True gentleman. No man could have done more for us. But, only to think of that woman attacking poor George and me as soon as we got back from the funeral. Abused him for degrading his son, and driving him to his terrible death. It was horrible, sir. Said she would never forgive him, and drove Louise sobbing out of the room."

Duncan Leslie winced, and Uncle Luke gave him a stern look.

"Ah, fool—fool—fool!" he exclaimed. "Can't you keep out of those trammels? Louise? Yes, a nice girl—now; but she'll grow up exactly like her aunt. We're a half-mad family, Leslie. Keep away from us."

"Mr Luke Vine—"

"No, no. You need not say anything. Be content as you are, young man. Women are little better than monkeys, only better looking. Look at my sister. Told George last night that he was living under false pretences, because he signed his name Vine. Bah! she's an idiot. Half mad."

He turned sharply round from gazing out to sea, and looked keenly in Leslie's face.

"Very well," he said quickly. "I don't care if you think I am."

"Really, Mr Luke Vine, I—"

"Don't trouble yourself to say it. You thought I wasn't much better than my sister. I could see you did. Very well; perhaps I am not, but I don't go dancing my lunacy in everybody's face. Ah, it's a queer world, Leslie."

"No, sir; it is the people who are queer."

"Humph! That's not bad for you, Leslie. Yes; you are about right. It is the people who are queer. I'm a queer one, so my folks think, because I sent my plate to the bank, had my furniture in a big town house sold, and came to live down here. My sister says, to disgrace them all. There, I'm better now. Want to speak to me?"

"N-no, nothing very particular, Mr Vine."

Uncle Luke tightened his lips, and stared fiercely out to sea.

"Even he can't tell the truth," he said. "Stupid fellow! Just as if I couldn't read him through and through."

The meeting was assuming an unpleasant form when there was a diversion, Poll Perrow coming slowly up, basket on back, examining each face keenly with her sharp, dark eyes.

"Morning, Master Leslie," she said in her sing-song tone. "Nice morning, my son. Morning, Master Luke Vine, sir. Got any fish for me to-day?"

Leslie nodded impatiently; Uncle Luke did not turn his head.

"I said to myself," continued the old woman, "Master Luke Vine saw that shoal of bass off the point this morning, and he'll be sure to have a heavy basket for me of what he don't want. Dessay I can sell you one, Mr Leslie, sir."

"Can't you see when two gentlemen are talking?" said Uncle Luke, snappishly. "Go away."

"Ay, that I will, Master Luke, only let's have the fish first."

"I told you I haven't been fishing."

"Nay, not a word, Master Luke. Now, did he, Master Leslie? No fish, and I've tramped all the way up here for nothing."

"Shouldn't have come, then."

"It's very hard on a poor woman," sighed Poll, sinking on a stone, and resting her hands on her knees, her basket creaking loudly. "All this way up and no fish."

"No; be off."

"Iss, Master Luke, I'll go; but you've always been a kind friend to me, and I'm going to ask you a favour, sir. I'm a lone woman, and at times I feel gashly ill, and I thought if you'd got a drop of wine or sperrits—"

"To encourage you in drinking."

"Now listen to him, what hard things he can say, Master Leslie, when I'm asking for a little in a bottle to keep in the cupboard for medicine."

"Go and beg at my brother's," snarled Uncle Luke.

"How can I, sir, with them in such trouble? Give me a drop, sir; 'bout a pint in the bottom of a bottle."

"Hear her, Leslie? That's modest. What would her ideas be of a fair quantity? There, you can go, Poll Perrow. You'll get no spirits or wine from me."

"Not much, sir, only a little."

"A little? Ask some of your smuggling friends that you go to meet out beyond the East Town."

The woman's jaw dropped, and Leslie saw that a peculiar blank look of wonder came over her countenance.

"Go to meet—East Town?"

"Yes, you're always stealing out there now before daybreak. I've watched you."

"Now think of that, Master Leslie," said the woman with a forced laugh. "I go with my basket to get a few of the big mussels yonder for bait, and he talks to me like that. There see," she continued, swinging round her basket and taking out a handful of the shell-fish, "that's the sort, sir. Let me leave you a few, Master Luke Vine."

"I don't believe you, Poll. It would not be the first time you were in a smuggling game. Remember that month in prison?"

"Don't be hard on a poor woman," said Poll. "It was only for hiding a few kegs of brandy for a poor man."

"Yes, and you're doing it again. I shall just say a word to the coastguard, and tell them to have an eye on some of the caves yonder."

"No, no; don't, Master Luke, sir," cried the woman, rising excitedly, and making the shells in her basket rattle. "You wouldn't be so hard as to get me in trouble."

"There, Leslie," he said with a merry laugh; "am I right? Nice, honest creature this! Cheating the revenue. If it was not for such women as this, the fishermen wouldn't smuggle."

"But it doesn't do any one a bit of harm, Master Luke, sir. You won't speak to the coastguard."

"Indeed, but I will," cried Uncle Luke; "and have you punished. If you had been honest your daughter wouldn't have been charged with stealing down at my brother's."

"And a false charge too," cried the woman, ruffling up angrily. Then changing her manner, "Now, Master Luke, you wouldn't be so hard. Don't say a word to the coastguard."

"Not speak to them? Why time after time I've seen you going off after some game."

"And more shame for you to watch. I didn't spy on you when you were down the town of a night, and I used to run against you in the dark lanes by the harbour."

Uncle Luke started up with his stick in his hand, and a curious grey look in his face.

"Saw—saw me!" he cried fiercely. "Why, you—but there, I will not get out of temper with such a woman. Do you hear? Go, and never come here again."

"Very well, Master Luke, sir, I'm going now," said the woman, as she adjusted the strap across her forehead; "but you won't be so hard as to speak to the coastguard. Don't sir, please."

The woman spoke in a low, appealing way; and after trying in vain to catch Luke Vine's eye, she went slowly up the hill.

"Bad lot—a bad family," muttered Uncle Luke uneasily, as he glanced sharply up at Leslie from time to time.

"Good thing to rid the place of the hag. Begging at my brother's place for food and things every time I've been there. Yes. Good morning, Leslie, good morning."

He nodded shortly and went into the cottage, cutting short all further attempts at being communicative.

Leslie walked steadily back up the hill to his works, and had not been at his office five minutes before Poll Perrow's basket was creaking outside.

"I know you won't be so gashly hard on a poor woman, Master Leslie," she said. "It aren't true about me getting brandy, sir. Let me have a drop in the bottom of a bottle, sir. You'll never miss it, and you don't know what good you'll do a poor soul as wants it bad."

"Look here," said Leslie, "I'll give you some on one condition; that you do not come here again to beg."

"Not if I can help it, sir; but a well-off gentleman like you will never miss a drop. A pint will be plenty, sir, in as small a bottle as you can."

Leslie could not help laughing at the woman's impudence, but he said nothing, only went into the house and returned with a pint bottle filled with the potent spirit.

"And bless you for it, Master Leslie!" cried Poll Perrow, with her eyes sparkling. "Now, sir, only one little thing more."

"No," said Leslie, sternly. "I have given you what you asked; now go."

"I only want you to put in a word for me to Master Luke, sir. Don't let him speak to the coastguard."

"Don't be alarmed; the old man is too good-hearted to do anything of the kind. But I should advise you to give up all such practices. There, good-day."

"Good-day, and bless you, my son!" cried Poll eagerly. "I shan't forget this."

"I was foolish to give it to her," said Leslie to himself, as he watched the woman's slowly retiring figure; and then he turned his eyes in the direction of the Vines', as it stood peaceful and bright-looking on its shelf by the cliff, across the intervening valley.

"Might venture to-night. Surely they would not think it intrusive? Yes; I will."

Duncan Leslie felt better after coming to this determination, and went busily about his work at the mine.

Poll Perrow went straight down into the little town and then up the path at the back, trudging steadily along and at a very good pace, till she saw about fifty yards in front a figure going in the same direction.

"Miss Madlin!" she said to herself. "I'd know her walk anywhere. And all in black, too. Ah!"

Poll Perrow stopped short with her mouth open.

"How horrid!" she ejaculated. "It killed him then, after all. Poor Master Van Heldre! Poor Master Harry Vine!"

She rubbed a tear away with her rough brown hand. Then starting up, she made the mussels in her basket rattle.

"What nonsense!" she said. "Why Master Crampton told me last night, and down the street, that Master Van Heldre was much better, and he couldn't ha' died and Miss Madlin gone in mourning since last night. They couldn't ha' got the gownd made."

By this time Madelaine had reached the Vines' gate and gone in.

"Phew!"

Poll Perrow gave vent to a low whistle, something like the cry of a gull.

"Why, I know!" she muttered. "Miss Madlin's gone into mourning all along o' Master Harry. Then my Liza's a great goose. She was fond of him after all. Why I only to think!"

She turned off down a narrow path, so as to get round to the back door, where she was met by Liza, looking very red and angry.

"Now, what have you come for again? I saw you coming as I let Miss Madlin in, and it's too bad."

"Oh, Liza, Liza?" said the fish-woman, "what a wicked girl you are to talk to your poor mother like that?"

"I don't care whether it's wicked or whether it aren't wicked, but I just tell you this: if you come begging again, you may just go back, for you'll get nothing here. It's disgraceful; you taking to that."

"No, no, not begging, my dear," said Poll, staring at her daughter's red-brown face, as if lost in admiration. "Lor', Liza, what a hansum gal you do grow!"

"Now, do adone, mother, and don't talk like that."

"I can't help it, Liza. I wonder half the fisher lads in port aren't half mad after you."

"Now, mother, be quiet; you'll have Miss Margreet hear!"

"Nay, she'll be down-stairs with the company, won't she? Yes, Liza, you do grow more and more hansum every day."

"Then you oughtn't to tell me so, mother. It'll only make me prouder than I am. Now, what do you want again? This is four times you've been here this week."

"Is it, my dear? Well, you see, I've got some of them big mussels as you're so fond on, and I brought you a few to cook for your supper."

"It's very good of you. Well, there; give them to me, and do please go."

"Yes, my dear, there you are. That's right. Haven't got a bit o' cold meat, and a bit o' bread you could give me, have you, Liza?"

"No, I haven't, mother; and you ought to be ashamed to ask."

"So I am, my dear, almost. But you have got some, or half a chicken and some ham."

"Chicken! Oh, the idea!"

"Yes. There's a good girl; and if there's a bit o' cold pudden, or anything else, let's have it too. Put it all together in a cloth."

"Now, mother, I won't. It's stealing, and I should feel as if I'd stole it."

"Oh, what a gal you are, Liza! Why, didn't I wash, and iron, and bring home that last napkin, looking white as snow?"

"Yes, but—"

"And so I will this."

"But you won't bring back the cold chicken and ham," retorted Liza.

"Why, how could I, my dear? You know they won't keep."

"Well, once for all, mother, I won't, and there's an end of it."

"You'll break my heart, Liza, 'fore you've done," whimpered the fish-woman. "Think o' the days and days as I've carried you 'bout in this very basket, when I've been out gathering mussels or selling fish."

"Now, don't talk stuff, mother. You weared out half-a-dozen baskets since then."

"P'r'aps I have, Liza, but I haven't weared out the feeling that you're my gal, as lives here on the fat o' the land, and hot puddens every day, and refuses to give your poor mother a bit o' broken wittle to save her from starving. Oh!"

"Mother, don't?" cried Liza, stamping her foot. "If you cry like that they'll hear you in the parlour."

"Then give me a bit o' something to eat, and let me go."

"I won't, and that's flat, mother."

"Then I shall sit down on the front door-step, and I'll wait till Miss Louy comes; and she'll make you give me something. No, I won't; I'll stop till cook comes. Where is she?"

"A cleaning herself."

"Then I shall wait."

"Oh, dear! oh, dear!" cried Liza, stamping about, and speaking in a tearful whisper. "I do wish I never hadn't had no mother, that I do."

"There's a ungrateful gal," said the fish-woman; "and you growed up so beautiful, and me so proud on you."

"Well, will you promise to go away, mother, and never come and ask no more if I give you something this time?"

"To be sure I will, my dear, of course. There, be quick, before any one comes, and do it up neat in a napkin, there's a good gal, and I'll bring you a lobster next time I come."

"There, now, and you promised you wouldn't come no more."

"Ah, well, I won't then, my dear."

"Then I'll get you a bit this time; but mind, never no more."

"No, never no more, my beauty. Only be quick."

Liza disappeared, and Poll Perrow took off her basket and sat down on the edge, rubbing her knees and laughing heartily to herself, but smoothing her countenance again directly, as she heard her daughter's step.

"There, mother," whispered Liza, "and I feel just as if there was the police after me, same as they was after Master Harry. This is the last time, mind."

"Yes, my beauty, the last time. What is there?"

"No, no, don't open it," cried the girl, laying her hand sharply upon the parcel she had given to her mother. "There's half a pork pie, and a piece of seed cake, and a bit o' chicken."

"Any bread?"

"Yes, lots. Now hide it in your basket, and go."

"To be sure I will, Liza." And the white napkin and its contents were soon hidden under a piece of fishing-net. "There, good-bye, my dear. You'll be glad you've helped your poor old mother, that you will, and—Good mornin', Miss Margreet."

"Put that basket down," said the old lady sharply, as she stood gazing imperiously at the detected pair.

"Put the basket down, miss?"

"Yes, directly. I am glad I came down and caught you in the act. Shameful! Disgraceful! Liza, take out that parcel of food stolen from my brother."

"No, no, Miss Margreet, only broken wittles, as would be thrown away."

Liza stooped down, sobbing, and pulled the bundle out of the basket.

"I always said you'd be the ruin of me, mother," she sobbed.

"No, no, my dear," cried the woman; "Miss Margreet won't be hard on us. Let me have it, miss, do please."

"Go away!" cried Aunt Marguerite fiercely.

"Pray, pray do, miss," cried the woman imploringly.

"Go away, I say!" cried Aunt Marguerite, "and if you set foot on these premises again, you shall leave with the police. Go."

Poor Liza stood inside the door, sobbing, with the bundle of good things neatly pinned up in her hand, while Aunt Marguerite stood pointing imperiously with her closed fan, as if it were a sceptre, till Poll Perrow, with her basket swung once more upon her back, disappeared out of the gate.

"Now, madam," said Aunt Marguerite, "the moment that young person in the drawing-room has gone, you shall receive your dismissal, and in disgrace."

Chapter Thirty Nine
A Meeting in Pain

George Vine sat in his easy chair in front of the fireplace, gazing at the cut paper ornaments and willow shavings, and seeing in them the career of his son, and the dismal scene in the churchyard, with the rain falling and making little pearls on the black coffin cloth.

He had not spoken for hours, but from time to time, as Louise laid her hand upon his arm, he had slowly taken and pressed it between his own before raising it with a sigh to his lips.

"Don't speak to me, my darling," he had pleaded to her when he first took his place there that morning. "I want to think."

She had respected his prayer, and in her endeavours to take her thoughts from the horrors which oppressed her she had stolen into her father's study, as an idea struck her, but only to come away sadly. Her visit had been too late; the cherished collection of marine objects were one and all dead.

Her father looked up as she returned. He had not seemed to notice her, but he knew where she had been, and as he gave her a questioning look Liza entered the room.

"Miss Van Heldre, miss."

Vine caught his child's hand, as if too weak for the encounter; but, as the closely-veiled figure in black crossed the room quickly, and both realised the meaning of those mourning garments, Louise burst into a wild fit of sobbing, and turned away for a moment, but only to be clasped in Madelaine's arms.

There was an earnest, loving embrace, and then Madelaine turned to Vine, laying her hands upon his breast, and kissing him as a child would its parent.

"So much better," she said, in answer to the wistful, inquiring look directed at her. "I have come to fetch you both."

"To fetch us?" faltered Vine with a horrified look.

"My father begs you will come to him. I am his ambassador. You will not refuse?"

"I cannot meet him," said Vine in a faint voice full of despair; "and," he added to himself, "I could not bear it."

"He would come to you, but he is weak and suffering," said Madelaine as she laid her hand upon the stricken man's arm. "Tell him 'I beg he will come to me,' he said," she whispered. "You will not refuse, Mr Vine?"

"No, I will not refuse. Louise, dear?"

"Yes, father, I will go with you," she said slowly; and in a few minutes she returned, ready for the walk, and crossed to where her father sat holding Madelaine's hand.

As she entered he rose and met her.

"Louise, my child, must we go?" he said feebly. "I feel as if it where almost more than I can bear. Must we go?"

"Yes," she replied gravely; "we must go."

Vine bowed his head.

"Come, my child," he said, turning to Madelaine, and he was half way to the door when Aunt Marguerite entered.

"Going out?" she said, shrinking from the sombre figure in black.

"Yes, aunt."

"You must attend first to what I have to say, Louise. Miss Van Heldre can, I daresay, wait."

Madelaine bent her head and drew back.

"I have business with Mr Van Heldre, Marguerite," said Vine more sternly than he had ever spoken to her before. "You must wait till our return."

Aunt Marguerite's eyes flashed an indignant look at Madelaine, as the cause of this rebuff, and she drew back with a stiff curtsey and walked slowly before them out of the room.

George Vine gazed wildly round him as he walked slowly down the steep way toward the town. It seemed terrible to him that in such a time of suffering and mourning, sea, sky, and earth should be painted in such lovely colours. The heavy rain of the previous days seemed to have given a brilliancy to leaf and flower that before was wanting; and as, from time to time, he glanced wildly at the rocky point, the scene of the tragedy of his life, the waves were curling over, and breaking in iridescent foam upon the rocks, to roll back in silvery cataracts to the sea.

He turned away his eyes with a shudder, fighting hard to keep his thoughts from the horrors of that night; but he was doomed to have them emphasised, for, just before reaching the foot of the steep way, the little party came suddenly upon the great burly fisherman, who had undertaken to sail across to Saint Malo with the fugitive that night.

"Mornin', master," he said.

Vine turned ghastly pale, and his brain reeled; but he soon recovered himself.

"Louise, Madelaine, my children, go on, and I will follow."

Louise looked at him appealingly; but he was perfectly firm, and she went on with her friend.

"I fear, in the midst of my trouble, Perrow, that I had forgotten my engagement with you."

"Like enough, master, no wonder. There was no hurry."

"Yes, but there is," said Vine slowly. "Will you come to my house to-night or to-morrow morning? and I'll give you my cheque to take to the bank."

"For how much?" said the man eagerly.

"One hundred pounds; the amount I promised you."

"Ay, but that was for taking the poor boy across. No, Master Vine, we've been talking it over, the five on us, and there's the boat, and one night's fishing gone as might have been a good one or it mightn't been nothing; so we're going to ask you to pay us a pound a-piece."

"But—"

"Good-day, Master Vine, busy now. I'll come on in a day or two."

The man turned away abruptly, and, with his brow heavily wrinkled, as he felt moved by the man's generosity, Vine walked slowly on, and overtook Louise and Madelaine.

Mrs Van Heldre was waiting in the hall as the little party entered, and she hurried forward with extended hands, and her lips parted to speak, but no words would came. She could only press her old friend's hand before leading him up to where Van Heldre lay, his face ghastly pale beneath his bandaged head.

As they entered he held out his hand to Vine, who stood gazing at him without an attempt to accept the friendly grip.

"Louise, my child," said Van Heldre, turning to her; and she stepped quickly across to take the extended hand. "Now leave us," he said quietly; and, in obedience to his wish, the rest quitted the room.

"You did not take my hand, George Vine," said Van Heldre, as soon as they were alone.

"How can I, after the wrong you have received at mine?"

"Hah! that is why I sent for you," said Van Heldre. "I have lain here insensible and ignorant of what was done, else those proceedings would never have been taken. You have much to forgive me, Vine."

"You have much to forgive me," said the latter slowly.

"Then take my hand, and let us forgive, if there is any call for such a proceeding on either side. Vine, old friend, how you must have suffered, and I not there to say one kindly word!"

"Van Heldre," said Vine slowly, as, holding his friend's hand, he slowly seated himself by the bed's head, "did you ever know what it was to pray for death?"

"Thank Heaven, no," replied Van Heldre with a slight shudder, for there was something weird and strange about his old friend's manner. "Since I have regained my senses I have prayed to live. There seems so much to be done at times like this. But, Vine, old friend, what can I say to you? For pity's sake don't look at me like that!"

"Look at you—like that?" said Vine slowly.

"Yes; your eyes seem so full of reproach. I tell you, my dear old fellow, that I would rather have died than that poor boy should have been prosecuted for my sake."

"I know everything," said Vine slowly. "I do not reproach you, John. I reproach myself, and at times it seems more than I can bear."

"Louise," said Van Heldre softly.

"Louise? Ah, Louise!" said Vine eagerly. "Without her I must have died."

The two old friends sat, hand clasped in hand, in perfect silence for quite an hour before there was a gentle tap at the door, and Madelaine entered.

"He is so weak yet, Mr Vine," she said, taking and separating their hands.

"Madelaine—my child!"

"Mr Vine may come again in the evening for a little while," said Madelaine, smiling, as she bent down, and kissed her father's brow.

"So stern and tyrannical," protested Van Heldre.

"Only to make you well, father," replied Madelaine smiling; and she led their old friend from the room.

"He spoke as if he wanted my forgiveness," said Vine as he walked slowly back, noting as they went the kindly deference paid to them by those they met.

"Mr Van Heldre, father?" said Louise gently.

"Did I speak aloud, my child?"

"Yes, dear."

"Ah, these thoughts are too keen, and will not be crushed down. Yes, child, yes. My forgiveness, when it is I who should plead, for all the honours of the past, plead for his forgiveness, Louise. He must have suffered terribly to be brought down to this."

Louise looked wistfully in her father's face, whose sunken cheeks and hollow eyes told of mental suffering greater far than that which their friend had been called upon to bear.

"Will time heal all this agony and pain?" she asked herself; and it was with a sigh of relief that she reached the gate, and her father went straight to his chair, to sit down and stare straight before him at the unlit grate, as if seeing in the burning glow scene after scene of the past, till he started excitedly, for there was a ring at the gate bell.

Louise rose to lay her hand upon his shoulder.

"Only some visitors, or a letter," she said tenderly.

"I thought—I thought it might be news," he said wearily. "But no, no, no. There can be no news now."

"Mr Leslie, miss," said Liza from the door.

"To see me, Liza? Say that—"

"No, sir. In the drawing-room, sir. 'Tis to see Miss Louise, if she will give him an interview, he said."

Louise looked wildly at her father.

"Must I see him, father?" she said, with her face now ghastly pale.

He did not answer for some moments, and then slowly said the one word:—

"Yes."

She bent down and kissed him, and then summoning up all her courage, slowly left the room.

Chapter Forty
Duncan Leslie Speaks Out

Duncan Leslie was standing at a table on which was a photograph of Louise, as she entered the room silently; and as, after a long contemplation of the counterfeit, he drew a long breath, and looked up to see the object of his thoughts standing just inside the doorway, too much agitated to give notice of her presence, he coloured like a boy caught in some act of which he was ashamed.

"Miss Vine," he cried, advancing quickly with extended hands.

Louise did not speak, but slowly raised one hand for him to take, and suffered him to lead her to a chair.

He remained standing before her as she looked up at him in a wild, frightened manner, as if imploring him not to speak, and for a few moments silence reigned.

"You will forgive me," said Leslie, at last, "if my visit is ill-timed, for I am a busy man, ill-versed in the etiquette of such matters. I was in a dilemma. I wished to try and show my sympathy, and I was afraid to stay away for fear of seeming neglectful."

"Mr Leslie need have been under no apprehension," said Louise slowly, and speaking as if sorrow had exhausted itself, and there was nothing left but resignation. "My father and I have thought very deeply, and can never be sufficiently grateful for all that has been done."

"You have suffered so," he said in a low voice, "that I am going to beg of you not to refer to the past. Of course, I know," he added quickly, "how easy it is to speak platitudes—how hard to express what one feels at a time like this."

"Mr Leslie need not speak," said Louise quietly. "He has shown his sympathy in a way that no words can express."

Leslie gazed down at the piteous, sorrow-stricken face before him; and, as if wrenching himself away, he walked to the window, and stood gazing out for a few moments while Louise sat watching him, and fighting hard with her emotions. She felt weakened by all that had gone by, and as if, had he extended his arms to her, she could have flown to him, nestled in his breast, and begged him to help her in this terrible strait. And yet all the time her sorrow had strengthened, as well as enfeebled, for she was able to master her weakness and follow out the course she had planned.

Leslie returned to her side.

"I must speak," he said hoarsely. "It is not cruelty at a time like this; it is the desire to help, to console, to be near you in distress, Miss Vine— Louise—you—forgive me for saying it—you must have known that for months past I have loved you."

She looked up at him wistfully, and there was a look of such pain and sorrow in her eyes that he paused, and took the hand which she resigned to him without shrinking, but only to send a thrill of pain through him, for the act was not that of one accepting the offer of his love.

"Yes," she said after a painful pause, "I did think that you must care for me."

"As I do," he whispered earnestly, "and is this my excuse for speaking now? No; don't shrink from me. I only ask you to think of me as one whose sole thought is of you, and of how he may help and serve you."

"You have helped us in every way," she said sadly.

"I have tried so hard," he said huskily; "but everything has seemed little compared to what I wished; and now—it is all I ask: you will let this formal barrier between us be cast away, so that in everything I may be your help and counsellor. Louise, it is no time to talk of love," he cried earnestly, "and my wooing is that of a rough, blunt man; and—don't shrink from me—only tell me that some day, when all this pain and suffering has been softened by time, I may ask you to listen to me; and now that I may go away feeling you believe in my love and sympathy. You will tell me this?"

She softly drew away her hand, giving him a look so full of pity and sorrow that a feeling akin to despair made his heart swell within his breast. He had read of those who resigned the world with all its hopes and pleasures from a feeling that their time was short here, and of death bed farewells, and there was so much of this in Louise's manner that he became stricken and chilled.

It was only by a tremendous effort over self that he was able to summon up the strength to speak; and, in place of the halting, hesitating words of a few minutes before, he now spoke out earnestly and well.

"Forgive me," he said; and she trembled as she shrank away to cover her eyes with her hand. "It was folly on my part to speak to you at such a time, but my love is stronger than worldly forms, and though I grieve to have given you pain, I cannot feel sorry that I have spoken the simple, honest truth. You are too sweet and true to deal lightly with a man's frank, earnest love. Forgive me—say good-bye. I am going away patiently—to wait."

His manner changed as he took her disengaged hand and kissed it tenderly and respectfully.

"I will not ask to see your father to-day. He is, I know, suffering and ill; but tell him from me he has only to send a messenger to bring me here at once. I want to help him in every way. Good-bye."

"Stop!"

He was half way to the door when that one word arrested him, and with a sense of delicious joy flooding his breast, he turned quickly to listen to the words which would give him a life's happiness. The flash of joy died out as quickly as that of lightning, and in the same way seemed to have the hope that had arisen scathed and dead. For here was no mistaking that look, nor the tone of the voice which spoke what seemed to him the death warrant of his love.

"I could not speak," she said in a strange low voice full of the pain she suffered. "I tried to check you, but the words would not come. What you ask is impossible; I could not promise. It would be cruel to you—unjust, and it would raise hopes that could never be fulfilled."

"No, no. Don't say that," he cried appealingly. "I have been premature. I should have waited patiently."

"It would have been the same. Mr Leslie, you should not have asked this. You should not have exposed yourself to the pain of a refusal, me to the agony of being forced to speak."

"I grant much of what you say," he pleaded. "Forgive me."

"Do not misunderstand me," she continued, after a brave effort to master her emotion. "After what has passed it would be impossible. I have but one duty now: that of devoting myself to my father."

"You feel this," he pleaded; "and you are speaking sincerely; but wait. Pray say no more—now. There: let me say good-bye."

"No," she said sternly; "you shall not leave me under a misapprehension. It has been a struggle that has been almost too great; but I have won the strength to speak. No; Mr Leslie, it is impossible."

"No, Mr Leslie, it is impossible!" The words were like a thin, sharp echo of those spoken by Louise, and they both started and turned, to see that Aunt Marguerite had entered the room, and had not only heard her niece's refusal of Leslie, but gathered the full import of the sentence.

She stood drawn up half way between them and the door, looking very handsome and impressive in her deep mourning; but there was the suggestion of a faint sneering smile upon her lip, and her eyes were half-closed, as with hands crossed over her breast, she seemed to point over her shoulder with her closed black fan.

"Aunt!" exclaimed Louise. "How could—"

Her strength was spent. She could say no more. Her senses seemed to reel, and with the impression upon her that if she stayed she would swoon away, she hurried from the room, leaving Leslie and the old woman face to face.

He drew a long breath, set his teeth, and meeting Aunt Marguerite's angry look firmly, he bowed, and was about to quit the house.

"No, not yet," she said. "I'm no eavesdropper, Mr Leslie; but I felt bound to watch over that poor motherless girl. It was right that I should, for in spite of all my hints, I may say my plain speaking regarding my child's future, you have taken advantage of her helplessness to press forward your suit."

"Miss Vine."

"Miss Marguerite Vine, if you please, Mr Leslie," said the lady with a ceremonious bow.

"Miss Marguerite Vine then," cried Leslie angrily, "I cannot discuss this matter with you: I look to Mr Vine."

"My brother is weak and ill. I am the head of this family, sir, and I have before now told you my intentions respecting my niece."

"Yes, madam, but you are not her father."

"I am her father's sister, and if my memory serves me rightly, I told you that Monsieur de Ligny—"

"Who is Monsieur de Ligny?" said Vine entering the room slowly.

"Mr Vine, I must appeal to you," cried Leslie.

"No. It would be indecorous. I have told Mr Leslie, who has been persecuting Louise with his addresses, that it is an outrage at such a time; and that if our child marries there is a gentleman of good French lineage to be studied. That his wishes are built upon the sand, for Monsieur de Ligny—"

"Monsieur de Ligny?"

"A friend of mine," said Aunt Marguerite quickly.

"Mr Vine," said Leslie hotly, "I cannot stay here to discuss this matter with Miss Vine."

"Miss Marguerite Vine," said the old lady with an aggravating smile.

Leslie gave an impatient stamp with one foot, essayed to speak, and choking with disappointment and anger, failed, and hurried out of the house.

"Such insufferable insolence! And at a time like this," cried Aunt Marguerite, contemptuously, as her brother with a curiously absorbed look upon his face began to pace the room.

"He has sent the poor girl sobbing to her room."

"Louise has not engaged herself to this man, Marguerite?"

"Engaged herself. Pah! You should have been here. Am I to sit still and witness another wreck in our unhappy family through your weakness and imbecility? Mr Leslie has had his answer, however. He will not come again."

She swept out of the room, leaving her brother gazing vacantly before him.

"She seems almost to have forgotten poor Harry. I thought she would have taken it more to heart. But Monsieur de Ligny—Monsieur de Ligny? I cannot think. Another time I shall remember all, I daresay. Ah, my darling," he cried eagerly, as Louise re-entered the room. "You heard what Mr Leslie said?"

"Yes, father."

"And refused him?"

"Yes."

Her father took her hand, and stood trying to collect his thoughts, which, as the result of the agony from which he had suffered, seemed now to be beyond control.

"Yes," he said at last, "it was right. You could not accept Mr Leslie now. But your aunt said—"

He looked at her vacantly with his hand to his head.

"What did your aunt say about your being engaged?"

"Pray, pray, do not speak to me about it, dear," said Louise, piteously. "I cannot bear it. Father, I wish to be with you—to help and comfort, and to find help and comfort in your arms."

"Yes," he said, folding her to his breast; "and you are suffering and it is not the first time that our people have been called upon to suffer, my child. But your aunt—"

"Pray dearest, not now—not now," whispered Louise, laying her brow against his cheek.

"I will say no more," he said tenderly. "Yes, to be my help and comfort in all this trouble and distress. You are right, it is no time for thinking of such things as that."

Chapter Forty One
Aunt Marguerite Makes Plans

"I could not—I could not. A wife should accept her husband, proud of him, proud of herself, the gift she gives him with her love; and I should have been his disgrace. Impossible! How could I have ever looked him bravely in the face? I should have felt that he must recall the past, and repented when it was too late."

So mused Louise Vine as she sat trying to work that same evening after a wearisome meal, at which Aunt Marguerite had taken her place to rouse them from their despondent state. So she expressed it, and the result had been painful in the extreme.

Aunt Marguerite's remedy was change, and she proposed that they should all go for a tour to the south of France.

"Don't shake your head, George," she said. "You are not a common person. The lower classes—the uneducated of course—go on nursing their troubles, but it is a duty with people of our position to suffer and be strong. So put the trouble behind us, and show a brave face to the world. You hear this, Louise?"

"Yes, aunt," said Louise, sadly.

"Then pray listen to it as if you took some interest in what I said, and meant to profit by it, child."

Louise murmured something suggestive of a promise to profit by her aunt's wisdom, and the old lady turned to her brother.

"Yes, George, I have planned it all out. We will go to the south of France, to the seaside if you wish, and while Louise and I try and find a little relaxation, you can dabble and net strange things out of the water-pools. Girl; be careful."

This to poor Liza, whose ears seemed to be red-hot, and her cheeks alternately flushed and pale, as she brought in and took out the dinner, waiting, at other times being dispensed with fortunately. For Liza's wits were wool-gathering, according to Aunt Marguerite's theory, and in her agitation respecting the manner in which she had been surprised, when yielding to her mother's importunities, she was constantly watching the faces or her master and Louise, and calculating the chances for and against ignominious dismissal. One minute she told herself they knew all. The next minute her heart gave a thump of satisfaction, for Louise's sad eyes had looked so kindly in hers, that Liza told herself her young mistress either did not know or was going to forgive her.

Directly after Liza dropped the cover of a vegetable dish in her agitation right on Aunt Marguerite's black silk crape-trimmed dress, for her master had told her to bring him bread, and in a tone of voice which thrilled through her as he looked her in the face with, according to her idea, his eyes seeming to say, "This is some of the bread you tried to steal."

Liza escaped from the room as soon as possible, and was relieving her pent-up feelings at the back door when she heard her name whispered.

"Who's there? what is it?" she said.

"It's only me, Liza, my dear. Has she told—"

"Oh, mother! You shouldn't," sobbed Liza. "You won't be happy till you've got me put in prison."

"Nonsense, my dear, they won't do that. Never you fear. Now look here. What became of that parcel you made up?"

"I don't know; I've been half wild ever since, and I don't know how it's going to end."

"Then I'll tell you," cried the old fish-woman. "You've got to get me that parcel, or else to make me up another."

"I won't; there?" cried Liza angrily.

"How dare you say won't to your mother, miss!" said the old woman angrily. "Now look here; I'm going a bit farther on, and then I'm coming back, and I shall expect to find the napkin done up all ready. If it isn't you'll see."

Liza stood with her mouth open, listening to her mother's retiring footsteps; and then with a fresh burst of tears waiting to be wiped away, she ran in to answer the bell, and clear away, shivering the while, as she saw that Aunt Marguerite's eyes were fixed upon her, watching every movement, and seeming to threaten to reveal what had been discovered earlier in the day.

Aunt Marguerite said nothing, however, then, for her thoughts were taken up with her project of living away for a time. She had been talking away pretty rapidly, first to one and then to the other, but rarely eliciting a reply; but at last she turned sharply upon her brother.

"How soon shall we be going, George?"

"Going? Where?" he replied dreamily.

"On the Continent for our change."

"We shall not go on the Continent, Marguerite," he said gravely. "I shall not think of leaving here."

Aunt Marguerite rose from the table, and gazed at her brother, as if not sure that she had heard aright. Then she turned to her niece, to gaze at her with questioning eyes, but to gain no information there, for Louise gazed down at the work she had taken from a stand.

"Did you understand what your father said?" she asked sharply.

"Yes, aunt."

"And pray what did he say?"

"That he would not go on the Continent."

"What?"

"That he would not leave home with this terrible weight upon his mind."

Aunt Marguerite sat bolt upright in her chair for a few moments without speaking, and the look she gave her brother was of the most withering nature.

"Am I to understand," she said at last, "that you prefer to stay here and visit and nurse your Dutch friend?"

Her brother looked at her, but there was no trace of anger in his glance.

Aunt Marguerite lowered her eyes, and then turned them in a supercilious way upon Louise.

"May I count upon your companionship," she said, "if I decide to go through Auvergne and stay there for a few days, on my way to Hyères."

"If you go, aunt?" said Louise wonderingly.

"There is a certain estate in the neighbourhood of Mont d'Or," she continued; "I wish to see in what condition it is kept. These things seem to devolve now on me who am forced to take the lead as representative of our neglected family."

"For Heaven's sake, Marguerite!" cried Vine impetuously. "No—no, no," he muttered, checking himself hastily. "Better not—better not."

"I beg pardon, brother," she said, raising her glass.

"Nothing—nothing," he replied.

"Well, Louise, child, I am waiting," she continued, turning her eyes in a half pitying, condescending way upon her niece. "Well? May I count upon you?"

"Aunt dear—"

"It will do you good. You look too pale. This place crushes you down, and narrows your intellect, my child. A little French society would work a vast change in you."

"Aunt, dear," said Louise, rising and crossing to her to lay her hands upon the old lady's shoulder, "don't talk about such things now. Let me come up to your room, and read to you a little while."

Aunt Marguerite smiled.

"My dear Louise, why do you talk to me like this? Do you take me for a child?"

George Vine heaved a deep sigh, and turned in his chair.

"Do you think I have lived all these years in the world and do not know what is best for such a girl as you?"

"But indeed, aunt, I am not ill. I do not require a change."

"Ah, poor young obstinacy! I must take you well in hand, child, and see if I cannot teach you to comport yourself more in accordance with your position in life. I shall have time now, especially during our little journey. When would it be convenient for you to be ready?"

"Aunt dear! It is impossible; we could not go."

"Impossible? Then I must speak. You will be ready in three days from now. I feel that I require change, and we will go."

"Margaret!" cried Vine, who during the past few minutes had been writhing in his seat, "how can you be so absurd!"

"Poor George!" she said, with a sigh, as she rose from her chair. "I wish I could persuade him to go. Mind, Louise, my child, in three days from now. We shall go straight to Paris, perhaps for a month. You need not trouble about dress. A few necessaries. All that you will require we can get in Paris. Come in before you go to bed, I may have a few more words to say."

She sailed slowly across the room, waving her fan gently, as if it were a wing which helped her progress, as she preserved her graceful carriage. Then the door closed behind her, and Louise half ran to her father's side.

"Shall I go up with her?" she whispered anxiously.

Her father shook his head.

"But did you not notice how strange she seemed?"

"No more strange, my dear, than she has often been before, after something has agitated her greatly. In her way she was very fond of poor Harry."

"Yes, father, I know; but I never saw her so agitated as this."

"She will calm down, as she has calmed down before."

"But this idea of going abroad?"

"She will forget it by to-morrow. I was wrong to speak as I did. It only sets her thinking more seriously. Poor Margaret! We must be very patient and forbearing with her. Her life was turned out of its regular course by a terrible disappointment. I try always to remember this when she is more eccentric—more trying than usual."

Louise shrank a little more round to the back of her father's chair, as he drew her hand over his shoulder, and she laid her cheek upon his head as, with fixed eyes, she gazed straight before her into futurity, and a spasm of pain shot through her at her father's words, "a terrible disappointment," "eccentric." Had Aunt Marguerite ever suffered as she suffered now? and did such mental agony result in changing the whole course of a girl's young life?

The tears stood in her eyes and dimmed them; but in spite of the blurring of her vision, she seemed to see herself gradually changing and growing old and eccentric too. For was not she also wasting with a terrible disappointment—a blow that must be as agonising as any Aunt Marguerite could have felt?

The outlook seemed so blank and terrible that a strange feeling of excitement came over her, waking dream succeeding waking dream, each more painful than the last; but she was brought back to the present by her father's voice.

"Why, my darling," he said, "your hand is quite cold, and you tremble. Come, come, come, you ought to know Aunt Margaret by now. There, it is time I started for Van Heldre's. I faithfully promised to go back this evening. Perhaps Luke will be there."

"Yes, father," she said, making an effort to be calm, "it is time you went down. Give my dear love to Madelaine."

"Eh? Give your love? why, you are coming too."

"No, no," she said hastily; "I—I am not well this evening."

"No, you are not well," he said tenderly. "Your hands are icy, and—yes, I expected so, your forehead burns. Why, my darling, you must not be ill."

"Oh no, dear. I am not going to be ill, I shall be quite well to-morrow."

"Then come with me. The change will do you good."

"No; not to-night, father. I would rather stay."

"But Madelaine is in sad trouble, too, my child, and she will be greatly disappointed, if you do not come."

"Tell her I felt too unwell, dear," said Louise imploringly, for her father's persistence seemed to trouble her more and more; and he looked at her wonderingly, she seemed so agitated.

"But I don't like to leave you like this, my child."

"Yes, yes; please go, dear. I shall be so much better alone. There, it is growing late. You will not stop very long."

"No; an hour or two. I must be guided by circumstances. If that man is there—I cannot help it—I shall stay a very short time."

"That man, father?"

"Yes," said Vine, with a shudder. "Crampton. He makes me shiver whenever we meet."

His face grew agonised as he spoke; and he rose hastily and kissed Louise.

"You will not alter your mind and come?" he said tenderly.

"No, no, father; pray do not press me. I cannot go to-night."

"Strange!" said George Vine thoughtfully. "Strange that she should want to stay."

He had crossed the little rock garden, and closed the gate to stand looking back at the old granite house, dwelling sadly upon his children, and mingling thoughts of the determined refusal of Louise to come, with projects which he had had *in petto* for the benefit of his son.

He shuddered and turned to go along the level platform cut in the great slope before beginning the rapid descent.

Chapter Forty Two
A Startling Visitation

"Fine night, master, but gashly dark," said a gruff voice, as Vine was nearly at the bottom of the slope.

"Ah, Perrow! Yes, very dark," said Vine quietly. "Not out with your boat to-night?"

"No, Master Vine, not to-night. Sea brimes. Why, if we cast a net to-night every mash would look as if it was a-fire. Best at home night like this. Going down town?"

"Yes, Perrow."

"Ah, you'll be going to see Master Van Heldre. You don't know, sir, how glad my mates are as he's better. Good night, sir. You'll ketch up to Master Leslie if you look sharp. He come up as far as here and went back."

"Thank you. Good night," said Vine, and he walked on, but slackened his pace, for he felt that he could not meet Leslie then. The poor fellow would be suffering from his rebuff, and Vine shrank from listening to any appeal.

But he was fated to meet Leslie all the same, for at a turn of the steep path he encountered the young mine-owner coming towards him, and he appeared startled on finding who it was.

"Going out, Mr Vine?" he stammered. "I was coming up to the house, but—er—never mind; I can call some other time."

"I would turn back with you, only I promised to go down to Mr Van Heldre's to-night."

"Ah, yes, to Van Heldre's," said Leslie confusedly. "I'll walk with you if you will not mind."

"I shall be glad of your company," said Vine quietly; and they continued down to the town, Leslie very thoughtful, and Vine disinclined to converse.

"No, I am not going in, Mr Vine. Will you let me come and say a few words to you to-morrow?"

"Yes," replied Vine gently.

He had meant to speak firmly and decisively, but a feeling of pity and sympathy for the young man, whose heart he seemed to read, changed his tone. It had been in his heart, too, to say, "It will be better if you do not come," but he found it impossible, and they parted.

Leslie hesitated as soon as he was alone. What should he do? Go home? Home was a horrible desert to him now; and in his present frame of mind, the best thing he could do was to go right off for a long walk. By fatiguing the body he would make the brain ask for rest, instead of keeping up that whirl of anxious thought.

He felt that he must act. That was the only way to find oblivion and repose from the incessant thought which troubled him. He started off with the intention of wearying his muscles, so as to lie down that night and win the sleep to which he was often now a stranger.

His first intent was to go right up by the cliff path, by Uncle Luke's, and over the hill by his own place, but if he went that way there was the possibility of finding Uncle Luke leaning over the wall, gazing out at the starlit sea, and probably he would stop and question him.

That night his one thought was of being alone, and he took the opposite direction, went down to the ferry, hunted out the man from the inn hard by, and had himself rowed across the harbour, so as to walk along the cliff eastwards, and then strike in north and round by the head of the estuary, where he could recross by the old stone bridge, and reach home—a walk of a dozen miles.

At the end of a couple of miles along the rugged pathway, where in places the greatest care was needed to avoid going over some precipitous spot to the shore below, Leslie stopped short to listen to the hollow moaning sound of the waves, and he seated himself close to the cliff edge, in a dark nook, which formed one of the sheltered lookouts used by the coastguard in bad weather.

The sea glittered as if the surface were of polished jet, strewn with diamonds, and, impressed by the similarity of the scene to that of the night on which the search had been carried on after Harry Vine, Leslie's thoughts went back to the various scenes which repeated themselves before his mental gaze from the beginning to that terrible finale when the remains lay stark and disfigured in the inn shed, and the saturated cards proclaimed who the dead man was.

"Poor girl!" he said half aloud, "and with all that trouble fresh upon her, and the feeling that she and her family are disgraced for ever, I go to her to press forward my selfish, egotistical love. God forgive me! What weak creatures we men are."

He sat thinking, taking off his hat for the cool, moist sea air to fan his feverish temples, when the solemn silence of the starry night seemed to bring to him rest and repose such as he had not enjoyed since the hour when Aunt Marguerite planted that sharp, poisoned barb in his breast.

"It is not that," he said to himself, with a sigh full of satisfaction. "She never felt the full force of love yet for any man, but if ever her gentle young nature turned towards any one, it was towards me. And, knowing this, I, in my impatience and want of consideration, contrived my own downfall. No, not my downfall; there is hope yet, and a few words rightly spoken will remove the past."

The feverish sensation was passing away swiftly. The calm serenity of the night beneath the glorious dome of stars was bringing with it restfulness, and hope rose strongly, as, far away in the east, he saw a glittering point of light rise above the sea slowly higher and higher, a veritable star of hope to him.

"What's that?" he said to himself, as heard above the boom of the waves which struck below and then filled some hollow and fell back with an angry hiss, he fancied he heard a sob.

There was no mistake; a woman was talking in a low, moaning way, and then there came another sob.

He rose quickly.

"Is anything the matter?" he said sharply.

"Ah! Why, how you frightened me! Is that you, Master Leslie?"

"Yes. Who is it? Poll Perrow?"

"Yes, Master Leslie, it's me."

"Why, what are you doing here?" said Leslie, as cynical old Uncle Luke's hints about the smuggling flashed across his mind.

"Nothing to do with smuggling," she said, as if divining his thoughts.

"Indeed, old lady! Well, it looks very suspicious."

"No, it don't, sir. D'you think if I wanted to carry any landed goods I should take 'em along the coastguard path?"

"A man would not," said Leslie, "but I should say it's just what a cunning old woman's brain would suggest, as being the surest way to throw the revenue men off the scent."

"Dessay you're right, Master Leslie, but you may search me if you like. I've got nothing to-night."

"I'm not going to search you, old lady. I'll leave that to the revenue men. But what's the matter?"

"Matter, Master Leslie?"

"Yes; I heard you sobbing. Are you in trouble?"

"Of course I am, sir. Aren't I a lone widow?"

"So you have been these fifteen years."

"Fourteen and three-quarters, sir."

"Ah, well, I was near enough. But what is it, old lady? Want a little money?"

"No, no, no, Master Leslie, sir; and that's very kind of you, sir; and if I don't bring you up half-a-dozen of the finest mack'rel that come in these next days, my name aren't Perrow."

"Thank you. There, I don't want to be inquisitive, but it seems strange for a woman like you to be crying away here on the cliff two miles from home on a dark night."

"And it seems strange for a young gen'leman like you to be up here all alone and three miles from home. You was watching me, Master Leslie."

"You'll take my word, Poll Perrow," said Leslie quietly. "I did not know you were here."

"Yes, I'll believe you, Master Leslie, sir. But you was watching someone else?"

"No, I came for a walk, my good woman, that's all."

"Then I won't stop you, sir. Good night, sir."

"Good night," said Leslie; and feeling more content, he took out his cigar case, and after selecting one by feeling he went back into the coastguard's station and struck a match.

He looked along the cliff path as the match flashed, and caught sight faintly of the old woman.

"Watching me anyhow," he said to himself, as he lit his cigar. "Now, what can that old girl be doing here? She's fifty-five if she's a day, but if she is not courting and had a quarrel with her youthful lover, I'm what that old lady says that Van Heldre is—a Dutchman."

He turned back along the path feeling comparatively light-hearted and restful. The long, dark, weary walk to tire himself was forgotten, and he went slowly back along the coastguard path, turning a little from time to time to gaze over his left shoulder at the brilliant planet which rose higher and higher over the glistening sea.

"Hope!" he said half aloud. "What a glorious word that is, and what a weary world this would be if there were none! Yes, I will hope."

He walked slowly on, wondering whether Poll Perrow was watching and following him. Then he forgot all about her, for his thoughts were fixed upon the granite house across the estuary, and the sweet sad face of Louise half in shadow, half lit by the soft glow of the shaded lamp.

"Mr Vine will be back by now," he said. "I might call in and ask how Van Heldre is to-night. It would he sociable, and I should see her, and let my manner show my sorrow for having grieved her and given her pain; and, is it possible to let her see that I am full of patient, abiding hope, that some day she will speak differently to the way in which she spoke to-day? Yes, a woman would read all that, and I will be patient and guarded now."

It was astonishing how eager Duncan Leslie felt now to see what news George Vine had brought from Van Heldre's; and with the beautiful absurdity of young men in his position, he never allowed himself to think that when he crossed the ferry he would be within a stone's throw of the merchant's house, and that all he need do was to knock and ask old Crampton or Mrs Van Heldre for the latest bulletin, which would be gladly given.

It was so much easier to go on by the house, make for the path which led up the steep slope, and go right to the home on the shelf of the cliff, and ask there.

Meanwhile, Louise Vine had seated herself by the dining-room table, with the light of the shaded lamp falling athwart her glossy hair, and half throwing up her sweet pale face, just as Leslie had pictured it far away upon the cliff. Now and then her needle glittered, but only at rare intervals, for she was deep in thought.

At times her eyes closed, and as she sat there bending forward, it seemed as if she slept; but her lips moved, and a piteous sigh escaped her overladen breast.

The night seemed hot and oppressive, and she rose after a time and unhasped the casement window, beneath the old painted glass coat-of-arms; and, as she approached it, dimly-seen by the light cast from behind her, she shuddered, for it struck her there was a black stain across the painting, and a shadowy dark mark obliterated the proud words of the old family motto.

As she threw back the easement she stood leaning her head against the window, gazing out into the starlit space, and listening to the faint whisper of the coming tide.

While she listened it seemed to her that the faint boom and rush of the water obliterated every other sound, as she tried in vain to detect her father's step slowly ascending the steep path.

"Too soon—too soon," she said softly, and she returned to her seat to try and continue her work, but the attempt was vain. The light fell upon her motionless hands holding a piece of some black material, the thread was invisible, and only at times a keen thin gleam of light betrayed the whereabouts of the needle. Her sad eyes were fixed on the dark opening of the window, through which she could see a scarcely defined patch of starry sky, while the soft night air gave her a feeling of rest, such as had come to the man who had told her that he loved.

"Never more," she sighed at last; "that is all passed. A foolish dream."

Making an effort over herself, she resumed her work, drawing the needle through quickly for a few moments, and trying hard to dismiss Duncan Leslie from her thoughts. As she worked, she pictured her father seated by Van Heldre's side; and a feeling of thankfulness came over her as she thought of the warm friendship between her elders, and of how firm and staunch Van Heldre seemed to be. Then she thought of the home troubles with her Aunt Marguerite, and her father's patient forbearance under circumstances which were a heavy trial to his patience.

"Poor Aunt Marguerite!" she sighed, as her hands dropped with her work, and she sat gazing across the table straight out at the starry heavens. "How she loved poor Harry in her way; and yet how soon he seems to have passed out of her mind!"

She sighed as the past came back with her brothers wilfulness and folly; but, throwing these weaknesses into the shade, there were all his frank, good qualities, his tenderness to her before the troubles seemed to wrench them apart; the happy hours they had passed with Madelaine as boy and girls together; all happy days—gone for ever, but which seemed to stand out now as parts of Harry's life which were to be remembered to the exclusion of all that was terrible and black.

"My brother!" she breathed, as she gazed straight out seaward, and a faint smile passed her lips; "he loved me, and I could always win him over to my side."

The thought seemed frozen in her brain, her half-closed eyes opened widely, the pupils dilated, and her lips parted more and more, as she sat there fixed to her seat, the chilly drops gathering on her white brow, and a thrill of horror coursing through her veins. For as she looked she seemed to have conjured up the countenance of her brother, to gaze in there by the open casement—the face as she had seen it last—when he escaped from her bedroom, but not flushed and excited; it was now pale, the eyes hollow, and his hair clinging unkempt about his brow.

Was she awake, or was this some evolution of her imagination, or were those old stories true that at certain times the forms of those we loved did return to visit the scenes where they had passed their lives? This then was such a vision of the form of the brother whom she loved; and she gazed wildly, with her eyes starting, excited, more than fearing, in the strange exaltation which she felt.

Then she sank back in her chair with the chill of dread now emphasised, as she gazed fixedly at the ghastly face, for she saw the lips part as if to speak, and she uttered a low, gasping sound, for from the open window came in a quick hoarse whisper—"Louy, why don't you speak? Are you alone?"

Chapter Forty Three
For Liberty and Life

Naturalists and students of animal life tell us that the hunted deer sheds tears in its agony and fear, and that the hare is ignorant of what is before it, for its eyes are strained back in its dread as it watches the stride of the pursuing hounds.

The reverse of the latter was the case with Harry Vine, who in his horror and shame could only see forward right into the future. For there before him was himself—handcuffed, in gaol, before the magistrates, taking his trial, sentenced, and then he, the scion of a good family, inflated by the false hopes placed before him by his aunt, dressed in the broad-arrow convict's suit, drudging on in his debased and weary life—the shame, the disgrace of those who loved him, and whom, in those brief moments of agony, he knew he dearly loved.

"Better death!"

He muttered these words between his teeth, as in a mad fit of cowardice and despair, he turned suddenly at the end of the rock pier and plunged headlong into the eddying tide.

Whatever the will may wish at such a time, instinct always seems to make a frantic effort to combat this mad will, and the struggle for life begins.

It was so here, for the sudden plunge into the cold dark water produced its instantaneous effect. The nerves and muscles grew tense, and after being borne for some distance straight out to sea, Harry Vine rose to the surface, and in obedience to the natural instinct of a good swimmer, struck out and tried to regain the pier.

But as he turned he hesitated. There were the police waiting for him when he landed, and his people were on the shore waiting to see him disgraced—for he was, of course, in utter ignorance of the efforts that had been made to enable him to escape. And even as he hesitated he knew that such a proceeding was impossible. Had he been tenfold the swimmer he could not have reached that point, for the current, after coming from the west and striking full against the rocks, was bearing him seaward at a tremendous rate. The voices that had been in a clamour of excitement and the shouts and orders were growing distant; the lights that were flashing over the water seemed minute by minute more faint, and as, almost without effort, he floated on, he wondered at the feeling of calm, matter-of-fact reasoning which the cold plunge seemed to have aroused.

Always a clever swimmer from the days when the sturdy fisherman Perrow had tied a stout hake-line about his waist, and bid him leap into the sea from the lugger's side, and taught him to feel confidence in the water, he had never felt so much at home as now. He was clothed, but the strong current bore him along, and the slightest movement of his limbs kept him with his nostrils clear of the golden-spangled water.

What should he do?

He looked seaward, and there, right off the harbour mouth, was a lantern. He could not make out the shape of the boat; but his guilty conscience suggested that it was one placed there by the police for his capture; shoreward he could see other moving lights, and he knew as well as if he were there that they were boat lanterns, and that people were putting off in pursuit.

It did not seem to occur to him that they would be essaying to save him; he had committed an offence against the law, and in his then frame of mind he could only admit one thought in connection with them into his brain, and that was that any boat's crew which pushed off would have but one idea—to make every effort to capture him, and so he swam, letting the swift tide carry him where it would.

Shouts arose, sounding faint and strange as they came from where the lanterns gleamed faintly; and there was an answering hail from the light off the harbour—the light toward which he was being borne.

"They'll see me," he thought, and he made a few vigorous strokes to turn aside, but gave up directly, as he felt it possible that he might be carried by in the darkness.

To his horror, he found that he would be taken so close, that he could easily swim to and touch the boat. For one moment fear swayed him of another kind, and he felt that he must give up.

"Better be taken aboard to prison than drown," he muttered; and he swam toward the boat.

"Better be drowned then taken off to prison," he said the next moment; and then, "why should I drown?"

His confidence returned as he was borne nearer and nearer to the lugger riding here to its buoy; and he could hear the voices of the men on board talking eagerly as they gazed shoreward.

"Keep a bright look-out," said a rough voice; and Harry ceased swimming after turning over on his back, and let the current bear him swiftly and silently along.

The spangled water seemed hardly disturbed by his presence as he neared the light, then saw it eclipsed by the boat's hull, just as he felt that he must be seen. Then he was past the boat, and in a few seconds the light reappeared from the other side, shining full upon his white face, but the men were looking in the other direction and he was not seen.

Once more the horror of drowning came upon him, and he turned on his face to swim back. It was only a momentary sensation, and as he swam and felt his power in the water he closed the lips firmly that had parted to hail, and swam on.

The shouts came and were answered from time to time, he could hear the regular rattle and beat of an oar, and then the blue light flashed out brilliantly, and as he raised himself at each long steady stroke he could see quite a crowd of figures had gathered on the pier, and he was startled to see how far he was from the shore. And all this time there upon his left was the bright red harbour-light, glaring at him like an eye, which seemed to be watching him and waiting to see him drown. At times it looked to be so lifelike that it appeared to blink at him, and as he swam on he ceased to gaze at the dull yellow light of the moving lanterns, and kept on watching that redder eye-like lamp.

The blue light blazed for a time like a brilliant star and then died out; the shouts of the men in the boat floated to him, and the lights of the town grew farther away as he still swam steadily on with a sea of stars above him, and another concave of stars apparently below; on his right the open sea, and on his left, where the dull land was, arose a jagged black line against the starry sky showing the surface of the cliff.

"What shall I do?" he said to himself, as he looked back at light after light moving slowly on the water, but all far behind him, for he was, as he well knew, in one of the swiftest currents running due east of the quay, and for a distance from that point due south. It was a hard question to answer. He might swim on for an hour—he felt as if he could swim for two—and what then?

He could not tell, but all the time the tide was bearing him beyond the reach of pursuit so fast that the hails grew more faint, and every minute now the roar of the surf grew plainer.

Should he swim ashore—land—and escape?

Where to? "Hah!"

He uttered a faint cry, for just then his hand touched something cold and slimy, and for the moment he felt paralysed, as he recalled how often a shark had come in with the tide. For the object he had touched seemed to glide by him, and what felt like a slimy moving fin swept over his hand. He struck out now with all his strength, blindly, and moved solely by one impulse—that of escaping from a death so hideous—a chill of horror ran through him, and for the moment he felt half paralysed. The sensation was agonising, and the strokes he gave were quick, spasmodic, and of the kind given by a drowning man; but as he swam on and the moments passed without his being seized, the waning courage began to return strongly once more, he recovered his nerve, and ceasing his frantic efforts swam slowly on.

The efforts he had made had exhausted him, however, and he turned over on his back to rest, and lie paddling gently, gazing straight up at the glorious stars which burned so brilliantly overhead. The change was restful, and conscious that the current swept him still swiftly along, he turned once more and began to swim.

That fit of excitement, probably from touching some old weed-grown piece of timber, must have lasted longer than he thought, for he had toiled on heedless of which direction he took, and this direction had been shoreward, the current had done the rest; and now that he swam it was into one of the back tidal eddies, and the regular dull roar and rush and the darkness ahead taught him that he was only a few hundred yards from the cliffs. He rose up as he swam and looked sharply from side to side, to see a faint lambent light where the phosphorescent waves broke, and before him the black jagged line which seemed to terminate the golden-spangled heavens, where the stars dipped down behind the shore.

He hesitated for a few moments—not for long. It was madness to strike out again into the swift current, when in a short time he could land or, if not, reach one of the detached masses of rock, and rest there till the tide went down. But what to do then? Those who searched for him would be certain to hunt along the shore, and to land and strike inland was, in his drenched condition, to invite capture.

He shuddered at the thought, and awaking now to the fact that he was rapidly growing exhausted, he swam on into the black band that seemed to stretch beneath the cliffs.

He was weaker than he realised, and, familiar as he was with this part of the coast, it now in the darkness assumed a weird, horrifying aspect; the sounds grew, in his strangely excited state, appalling, and there were moments when he felt as if the end had come. For as he swam on it was every now and then into some moving mass of anchored wrack, whose slimy fronds wrapped round and clung to his limbs, hampering his movements and calling forth a desperate struggle before he could get clear.

Then, as he reached the broken water, in spite of the lambent glare he struck himself severely again and again upon some piece of jagged rock, once so heavily that he uttered a moan of pain, and floated helplessly and half unnerved, listening to the hissing rush and hollow gasping of the waves as they plunged in and out among the cavities and hollows of the rocks. A hundred yards out the sea was perfectly smooth, but here in shore, as the tidal swell encountered the cliffs, the tide raced in and out through the chaos of fallen blocks like some shoal of mad creatures checked in their career and frightened in their frantic efforts to escape.

Then every now and then came a low hollow moan like a faint and distant explosion, followed by the rattling of stones, and a strange whispering, more than enough to appal the stoutest swimmer cast there in the darkness of the night.

Three times over was the fugitive thrown across a mass of slimy rock, to which, losing heart now, he frantically clung, but only to be swept off again, confused, blinded by the spray and with the water thundering in his ears. Once his feet touched bottom, and he essayed to stand for a moment to try and wade across, but he only stepped directly into a deep chasm, plunging over his head, to rise beating the waves wildly, half strangled, and in the strange numbed feeling of confusion which came over him, his efforts grew more feeble, his strokes more aimless, and as once more he went under and rose with the clinging weeds about his neck, the fight seemed to be over, and he threw back his head gasping for breath.

Rush! A wave curled right over, swept him from among the clammy weed, and the next moment his head was driven against a mass of rock.

What followed seemed to take place in a feverish dream. He had some recollection afterwards of trying to clamber up the rough limpet-bossed rock, and of sinking down with the water plunging about his eyes and leaping at intervals right up his chest, but some time elapsed before he thoroughly realised his position, and dazed and half helpless climbed higher up to lie where the rock was dry, listening with a shudder to the strange sounds of the hurrying tide, and gazing up from time to time at the watching stars.

Chapter Forty Four
A Place of Refuge

If ever miserable wretch prayed for the light of returning day that wretch was Harry Vine. It seemed hours of agony during which the water hissed and surged all round him, as if in search of the victim who has escaped before the faint light in the east began to give promise of the morn.

Two or three times over he had noted a lantern far out toward the distant harbour, but to all appearances the search had ceased for the night, and he was too cold and mentally stunned to heed that now.

He had some idea of where he must be—some three miles from the little harbour, but he could not be sure, and the curve outward of the land hid the distant light.

Once or twice he must have slept and dreamed in a fevered way, for he started into wakefulness with a cry of horror, to sit chilled and helpless for the rest of the night, trying to think out his future, but in a confused, dreamy way that left him where he had started at the first.

As the day broke he knew exactly where he was, recollecting the rock as one to which he had before now rowed with one of the fishermen, the deep chasms at its base being a favourite resort of conger. Hard by were the two zorns to which they had made the excursion that day, and searched for specimens for his father's hobby—that day when he had overbalanced himself and fallen in.

Those zorns! either of those caves would form a hiding place.

"That is certain to be seen," he said bitterly, and with the feeling upon him that even then some glass might be directed toward the isolated rock on which he sat, a hundred yards from the cliff, in a part where the shore was never bared even at the lowest tides, he began to lower himself into the deep water to swim ashore and climb up the face of the cliff in search of some hiding place.

He was bitterly cold and longing for the sunshine, so that he might gain a little warmth for his chilled limbs, and under the circumstances it seemed in his half-dried condition painful in the extreme to plunge into the water again.

Half in he held on by the side of the barnacle-covered rock, and scanned the face of the cliff, nearly perpendicular facing there, and seeming to offer poor foothold unless he were daring in the extreme.

He was too weak and weary to attempt it, and he turned his eyes to the right with no better success.

"Better give up," he said bitterly. "I couldn't do it now."

As he gazed to his left the rock, however, seemed more practicable. There was a chasm there, up which it would certainly be possible to climb, and, feeling more hopeful, he was about to make the attempt, when a flush of excitement ran though him. There in full view, not fifty yards to the left, was the zig-zag water-way up which they had sent the boat that day toward the narrow hole at the foot of the cliff, the little entrance to the cavern into which he had swum, and there sat for his own amusement, startling the occupants of the boat.

"The very place!" he thought. "No one would find me there."

His heart began to throb, and a warm glow seemed to run through his chilled limbs as carefully picking his time, he swam amongst the waving seaweed to the narrow channel, and then in and out, as he had gone on that bright sunny day which seemed to him now as if it was far away in the past, when he was a careless, thoughtless boy, before he had become a wretched, hunted man.

The sun, little by little, rose above the sea and flooded the face of the rocks; the black water became amethystine and golden, and the mysterious gasping and moaning sounds of the current were once more the playful splashings of the waves as they leaped up the empurpled rocks and fell in glittering cascades. It was morning, glorious morning once again, and the black, frowning cliffs of the terrible night were now hope-inspiring in their hanging wreaths of clustering ivy and golden stars.

The swell bore him on, and he rode easily to the mouth of the cave, a low rift now that was nearly hidden when a wave ran up, and when it retired not more than a yard high. And as he recalled the day when he swam in his hopes rose higher, for even if careful search were made it was not likely that any one would venture into such a place as that. Then, as he held on by a piece of rock at the mouth, he hesitated, for strange whispering sounds and solemn gurgling came out as he peered in. Where he clung, with his shoulders above the water, all was now bright sunshine; beneath that rough arch all was weird and dark, and it was not until he had felt how possible it was that he might be seen that he gave a frightened glance in the direction of the harbour, and then, drawing a long breath, waited for the coming of a wave, lowering himself down at the right moment, and allowing the water to bear him in.

He must have glided in, riding, as it were, on that wave some twenty or thirty yards, when, after a hissing, splashing, and hollow echoing noise, as a heavy breath of pent-up air, like the expiration of some creature struck upon his face, he felt that he was being drawn back.

The rugged sides of the place, after his hands had glided over the clinging sea-anemones for a few moments, gave him a firm hold, and as the wave passed out he found bottom beneath his feet, and waded on in the darkness with a faint shadow thrown by the light at the mouth before him.

The place opened out right and left, and as his eyes grew more used to the gloom he found himself in a rugged chamber rising many feet above his head, and continuing in a narrow rift right on into the darkness. Where he stood the water was about three feet deep, and his feet rested on soft sand, while, as he continually groped along sidewise, he found the water shallowed. Then another wave rushed in, darkening the place slightly, and it seemed to pass him, and to go on and on into the depths of the narrow rift onward, and return. The tide he knew was falling, so that some hours must elapse before there was any danger of his being shut in and deprived of air, while there was the possibility of the cavern being secure in that respect, and remaining always sufficiently open for him to breathe. But there were other dangers. There might be enough air, but too much water, and at the next tide he might be shut in and drowned. Then there was starvation staring him in the face. But on the other side there was a balance to counteract all this; he had found sanctuary, and as long as he liked to make this place his refuge he felt that he would be safe.

The waves came and went, always pursuing their way along a rift-like channel inward, while he cautiously groped his way along to the left into the darkness, with the water shallowing, and his hands as he went on, bent nearly double, splashing in the water or feeling the rough, rocky wall, which at times he could not reach, on account of the masses projecting at the foot.

The place was evidently fairly spacious, and minute by minute, as more of the outer sunshine penetrated, and his eyes grew accustomed to the place, it became filled with a dim greenish light, just sufficient to show him the dripping roof about ten feet above him, while all below was black.

All at once, as he waded in with the water now to his knees, his hands touched something wet, cold, and yielding, and he started back in horror, with the splashing noise he made echoing strangely from the roof.

For the moment his imagination conjured up the form of some hideous sea-monster, which must make the zorn its home, but once more sense and experience of the coast told him that the creature he had touched must be a seal, and that the animal, probably more frightened than he was himself, had escaped now out into the open water.

A couple of yards farther and he was on dry sand, while, on feeling about, he found that the side of the cave had been reached, and that he could climb up over piled-up rocks heaped with sand till he could touch the roof.

For some few minutes, as he stood there with the water streaming from him, he could not make out whether the heaped-up sand which filled in the rifts among the rocks was thoroughly dry or only lately left by the tide, but at last, feeling convinced that no water, save such as might have dripped from the roof, could have touched it, he carefully explored it with his hands till he found a suitable place, where he could sit down and rest.

He was so near the roof that the sandy spot he selected seemed to be more suitable for reclining than sitting, and, lying down, chilled to the very marrow, he tried to think, but could only get his thoughts to dwell upon the rushing in of the waves as he watched them coming along what seemed to be a broad beam of light, and go on and on past where he lay right into a dimly-seen rift to his left.

He was cold, hungry, and wretched. A feeling of utter hopelessness and despair seemed to rob him of the power to act and think. His wet clothes clung to him, and it was not till he had lain there some time that the thought occurred to him to try and wring out some of the water. This he at last did, and then lay down to think once more.

He had not so much difficulty in making out the shape of the place now, but it presented few differences from the many rifts in the rocks which he had examined when boating. There were dimly-seen shell-fish on the sides, scarce specimens such as would at one time have gladdened his father's heart, just visible by the opening, which grew brighter and brighter as the tide went down, and the entrance broadened till a new dread assailed him, and that was that the place would be so easy of access that he would be sought for and found.

The bitter, chilled sensation seemed to abate somewhat now, but he was tortured by hunger and thirst. Every louder lap or splash of the waves made him start and try to make out the shadow of a coming boat, but these frights passed off, leaving him trying still to think of the future and what he should do.

How beautiful the water seemed! That glistening band where the light fell, and cut on either side by a band of inky blackness, while the light was thrown from the water in curious reflections on the glistening rock, which seemed to be covered with a frosted metal of a dazzling golden green.

He could think of that, and of the amethystine water which ran on through what was evidently a deep channel, into the far depths of the cave, along which, in imagination, he followed it on and on right into the very bowels of the earth, a long, strange journey of curve and zig-zag, with the water ever rushing and gurgling on, and the noise growing fainter and fainter till it was just a whisper, then the merest breath, and then utter darkness and utter silence.

The excitement and exhaustion of the past night were playing their part now, and Harry Vine lay utterly unconscious of everything around.

Chapter Forty Five
The Horror in the Zorn

"Yes! What is it? Aunt Marguerite ill?"

Harry Vine started up, listening.

"Did any one call?"

There was no reply, and he sat there listening, still with the impression strong upon him that he had heard someone knock at his bedroom door and call him by name.

Then a curious sense of confusion came over him as he tried to make out what it meant. His head was hot, but his hands were cold, and he felt that he ought to know something which constantly eluded his mental grasp.

Land—rock—water running, gurgling, and splashing, and utter darkness. Where was he? What did it all mean?

For along time the past was a blank. Then, as he sat with his hands pressed to his head, staring wildly before him, it all came back like a flash— his trouble, the escape, the long swim, and his taking refuge in this cave.

Then he must have slept all day, and it was now night, or else the tide had risen above the mouth of the entrance and the water was slowly rising to strangle him, and Heaven have mercy upon him, there was no escape!

He began to creep down slowly toward the water, determined to swim with the next retiring wave, and try to reach the shore. Even if he drowned in the effort, it would be better than sitting there in that horrible cave, waiting for a certain death.

But he found that comparatively he had to descend some distance before he could feel the water, and as he touched it with his extended hand, he fancied that he could detect a gleam of light.

For a long time he could not convince himself that it was not fancy, but at last he was sure that there was a faint reflection as from a star whose light struck obliquely in. Then the month of the cave was open still and he could swim out if he wished. But did he wish?

He felt about, and in a short time could distinguish by the sense of touch now high the tide had risen, and that it had not been within a couple of feet of where he had lain, where the sand was quite warm still. He too was dry, and therefore it must be night, and he had been plunged in a state of stupor for many hours. Suddenly a thought struck him.

He had a match-box in his pocket, a little tight-fitting, silver match-box, which held a few cigar lights. That match-box was inside his cigar case, and both fitted so lightly that the water might have been kept out. A light, if only for a few moments, would convince him of his position, and then there were his cigars. He was ravenously hungry now, and if he smoked that would perhaps dull the sensation.

He drew out his cigar case and opened it, and took out a cigar. This was dry comparatively; and as with trembling fingers he felt the little silver case, he wondered whether it closed tightly enough to keep out the water.

He took out a match. It felt dry, and the box was quite warm, but when he gave the match one rub on the sand-faced end, he obtained nothing but a faint line of light. He tried again and again, but in vain; and hesitated about testing another match till some hours had passed.

He could not resist the temptation, and taking another of the frail waxen tapers, he struck it sharply, and to his great delight it emitted a sharp, crackling sound. Another stroke and it flashed out, and there beamed steadily a tiny clear flame which lit up the place, revealing that it was just such a zorn as his touch and imagination had painted, while the water was about a couple of feet below where he knelt on the sand, and—

The young man uttered a wild cry of horror, the nearly extinct match fell from his fingers, and burned out sputtering on the wet sands at his feet.

His first effort was to crawl right away as high up as possible, and there, shuddering and confused, he sat, or, rather, crouched, gazing down beyond where the match had fallen.

At times he could see a tiny, wandering point of light in the water, which gradually faded out, and after this seemed to reappear farther away, but otherwise all was black and horrible once more. More than once he was tempted to walk down into the water and swim out, but in his half-delirious, fevered state he shrank from doing this, and waited there in the darkness, suffering agonies till, after what seemed to be an interminable time, there was a faint, pearly light in the place which gradually grew and grew till it became opalescent, then growing, and he knew that the sun had risen over the sea.

Half frantic with horror, a sudden resolve came upon him. There was so strong a light now in the cavern that he could dimly see the object which had caused him so much dread, an object which he had touched when he first waded in, and imagined to be a seal.

Trembling with excitement, he crept down to the water's edge, waded in to his knees, and in haste, forcing himself now to act, he drew from where it lay entangled among the rocks, the body of a drowned man, the remains of one of the brave fellows who had been lost at the wreck of Van Heldre's vessel. The body was but slightly wedged in just as it had been floated in by a higher tide than usual, and left on the far side of some piece of rock when the water fell, but had not since risen high enough to float it out.

The horrifying object yielded easily enough as he drew it away along the surface, and he was about to wade and swim with it to the mouth, when he stopped short, for a sudden thought occurred to him.

It was a horrible thought, but in his excitement he did not think of that, for in the dim light he could see enough to show him that it was the body of a young man of about his own physique, still clothed and wearing a rough pea-jacket.

Disguise—a means of evading justice—the opportunity for commencing anew and existing till his crime had been forgotten, and then some day making himself known to those who thought him dead.

"They think me dead now," he muttered excitedly. "They must. They shall."

Without pausing for further thought, and without feeling now the loathsome nature of the task, he quickly stripped the pea-jacket and rough vest from the dead form, and trembling with excitement now in place of fear, tore off his own upper garments, pausing for a few moments to take out pocket-book and case and cigars, but only to empty out the latter, thrust the book and case back, and at the end of a few minutes he was standing in shirt and trousers, the rough jacket and vest lying on the sands, and the form of the drowned sailor tightly buttoned in the dry garments just put on.

Harry stood trembling for a few minutes, shrinking from achieving his task. Then with the full knowledge that the body if borne out of the cave would be swept here and there by the current, perhaps for days, and finally cast ashore not many miles away, he softly waded into the water, drew the waif of the sea along after him, right away to the mouth of the cave, where he cautiously peered out, and made well sure that no fishermen were in sight before swimming with his ghastly burden along the zig-zag channel, out beyond the rocks, where after a final thrust, he saw the current bear it slowly away before he returned shuddering into the cave, and then landed on the dry sand to crawl up and crouch there.

"They think me dead," he said in a husky whisper, "let them find that, and be sure."

He was silent for a time, and then as the thoughts of the past flooded his soul, he burst into a wild fit of sobbing.

"Home—sister—Madelaine," he moaned, "gone, gone for ever! Better that I had died; better that I was dead?"

But the horror was no longer there, and in a short time he roused up from his prostrate condition half wild and faint with hunger.

After a few minutes' search he found a couple of his cigars lying where he had thrown them on the sand, and lighting one, he tried to dull the agony of famine by smoking hard.

The effect was little, and he rose from where he was seated and began to feel about the shelves of the rock for limpets, a few of which he scraped from their conical shells and ate with disgust; but they did something towards alleviating his hunger, and seemed to drive away the strange half-delirious feeling which came over him from time to time, making him look wildly round, and wonder whether this was all some dreadful dream.

About mid-day he heard voices and the beating of oars, when, wading towards the opening, he stood listening, and was not long in convincing himself that the party was in search of him, while a word or two that he heard spoken made him think that the party must have picked up the body of the drowned sailor.

The voices and the sound of the oars died away, and in the midst of the deep silence he crept nearer and peered out, to be aware that a couple of boats were passing about a quarter of a mile out, while from their hailing some one, it seemed that a third boat, invisible to the fugitive, was coming along nearer in.

He crept back into the semi-darkness and listened with his ear close to the water, till, after a time, as he began to conclude that this last boat must have gone back, and he wondered again and again whether the drifting body had been found, he heard voices once more, every word coming now with marvellous clearness.

"No, sir, only a bit of a crevice."

"Does it go far in?"

"Far in, Mr Leslie, sir? Oh, no. Should waste time by going up there. You can see right up to the mouth, and there's nothing."

"But the current sets in there."

"Yes, sir, and comes out round that big rock yonder. Deal more likely place for him to ha' been washed up farther on."

"Leslie, and in search of me," said Harry to himself as the boat passed by. "Yes; they do believe I'm dead."

That day dragged wearily on with the occupant of the cave, tossed by indecision from side to side till the shadow began to deepen, when, unable to bear his sufferings longer, he crept out of the opening with the full intent of climbing the cliff, and throwing himself on the mercy of one of the cottagers, if he could find no other means of getting food.

The tide was low, and he was standing hesitating as to which way to go, when he turned cold with horror, for all at once he became aware of the fact that not fifty yards away there was a figure stooping down with a hand resting on the rock, peering into an opening as if in search of of him.

His first instinct was to dart back into the cavern, but in the dread that the slightest movement or sound would attract attention, he remained fixed to the spot, while the figure waded knee deep to another place, and seemed to be searching there, for an arm was plunged deeply into the water, a rope raised, and after a good deal of hauling, a dripping basket was drawn out and a door opened at the side, and flapping its tail loudly, a good-sized lobster was brought out and deposited in the basket the figure bore upon her back.

"Mother Perrow!" exclaimed Harry beneath his breath, and then an excited mental debate took place. "Dare he trust her, or would she betray him?"

Fear was mastering famine, when Poll Perrow, after rebaiting her lobster pot, was about to throw it back into deep water, but dropped it with a splash, and stood staring hard at the shivering man.

"Master Harry!" she exclaimed, and, basket on back, she came through water and over rock toward him with wonderful agility for a woman of her age. "Why, my dear lad," she cried in a voice full of sympathy, "is it you?"

"Yes, Poll," he said tremulously, "it is I."

"And here have I been trying to find you among the rocks while I looked at my crab pots. For I said to myself, 'If Master Harry's washed up anywhere along the coast, there's nobody more like to find him than me.' And you're not dead after all."

"No, Poll Perrow," he said agitatedly, "I'm not dead."

"Come on back home," she cried. "I am glad I found you. Master Vine and Miss Louise, oh, they will be glad!"

"Hush, woman!" he gasped, "not a word. No one must know you have seen me."

"Lor', and I forget all about that," she said in a whisper. "More I mustn't. There's the police and Master Leslie, and everybody been out in boats trying to find you washed up, you know."

"And now you've found me, and will go and get the reward," he said bitterly.

"I don't know nothing about no reward," said the woman staring hard at him. "Why, where's your jacket and weskut? Aren't you cold?"

"Cold? I'm starving," he cried. "You look it. Here, what shall I do? Go and get you something to eat?"

"Yes—no!" he cried bitterly. "You'll go and tell the police."

"Well, I am ashamed o' you, Master Harry, that I am."

"But it was all a misfortune, Poll Perrow, an accident. I am not guilty. I'm not indeed."

"I warn't talking about that," said the woman surlily, "but 'bout you saying I should tell the police. It's likely, aren't it?"

"Then you will not tell—you will not betray me?"

"Yah! are it likely, Master Harry? Did I tell the pleece 'bout Mark Nackley when he was in trouble over the smuggling and hid away?"

"But I am innocent; I am indeed."

"All right, my lad, all right, Master Harry. If you says so, that's 'nough for me. Here, I'll go and tell Master Vine I've found you."

"No, no; he thinks I'm dead."

"Well, everybody does; and I said it was a pity such a nice, handsome young lad should be drowned like that. I told my Liza so."

"My father must not know."

"Miss Louy then?"

"No, no. You must keep it a secret from everybody, unless you want to see me put in prison."

"Now is that likely, my lad? Here, I've got it. I'll go and tell Master Luke Vine."

"Worst of all. No; not a word to a soul."

"All right, Master Harry; I can keep my mouth shut when I try. But what are you going to do?"

"I don't know yet. I'm hiding yonder."

"What! in the little seal zorn?"

"Yes. Don't betray me, woman, pray!"

"Betray you, Master Harry? You know I won't."

"You will not tell a soul?"

"You tell me not to tell nobody, and I won't say a word even to my Liza. But they're seeking for you everywhere—dead. Oh! My dear lad, shake hands. I am glad you warn't drowned."

The warm grasp of the rough woman's coarse hand and the genuine sympathy in her eyes were too much for Harry Vine. Weak from mental trouble—more weak from hunger—manhood, self-respect, everything passed from him as he sank upon one of the hard pieces of weedy rock; and as the woman bent over him and laid her hands upon his shoulder, he flung his arms about her, let his head sink upon her breast, and cried like a child.

"Why, my poor, poor boy!" she said tenderly, with her hard wooden stay busk creaking in front, and her maund basket creaking behind, "don't— don't cry like that, or—or—or—there, I knew I should," she sobbed, as her tears came fast, and her voice sounded broken and hoarse.

"There, what an old fool I am! Now, look here; you want to hide for a bit, just as if it was brandy or a bit o' lace."

"Yes, Poll; yes."

"Then wait till it's dark, and then come on to my cottage."

"No, no," he groaned; "I dare not."

"And you that cold and hungry?"

"I've tasted nothing but the limpets since that night."

"Limpets!" she cried, with a tone of contempt in her voice, "why they ain't even good for bait. And there are no mussels here. Look here, my dear lad, I've got a lobster. No, no; it's raw. Look here; you go back to where you hide, and I'll go and get you something to eat, and be back as soon as I can."

"You will?" he said pitifully.

"Course I will."

"And you'll keep my secret?"

"Now don't you say that again, my lad, because it aggravates me. There, you go back and wait, and if I don't come again this side of ten o'clock Poll Perrow's dead!"

She bent down, kissed his cold forehead, and hurried back among the rocks, splashing and climbing, till he saw her begin to ascend the narrow rift in the cliff; and in a few minutes the square basket, which looked like some strange crustacean of monstrous size creeping out of the sea and up the rocks, disappeared in the gathering gloom; and Harry Vine, half-delirious from hunger, crept slowly back into the cave, half wondering whether it was not all a dream.

Chapter Forty Six
The Friend of Adversity

It was a dream from which he was aroused three hours later—a wild dream of a banquet served in barbaric splendour, but whose viands seemed to be snatched from his grasp each time he tried to satisfy the pangs which seemed to gnaw him within. He had fallen into a deep sleep, in which he had remained conscious of his hunger, though in perfect ignorance of what had taken place around.

His first thought was of capture, for his head was clear now, and he saw a rough hand as he gazed up wildly at a dim horn lantern.

The dread was but momentary, for a rough voice full of sympathy said:—

"There, that's right. Sit up, my dear, and keep the blankets round you. They're only wet at one corner. I did that bringing them in. There, drink that!"

He snatched at the bottle held to him, and drank with avidity till it was drawn away.

"That'll put some life into you, my dear; it's milk, and brandy too. Now eat that. It's only bread and hake, but it was all I could manage now. To-morrow I'll bring you something better, or I'll know the reason why."

Grilled fish still warm, and pleasant home-made bread. It was a feast to the starving man; and he sat there with a couple of blankets sending warmth into his chilled limbs, while the old fish-woman sat and talked after she had placed the lantern upon the sand.

"Let them go on thinking so," said Harry at last. "Better that I should be dead to every one I know."

"Now, Master Harry, don't you talk like that. You don't know what may happen next. You're talking in the dark now. When you wake up in the sunshine to-morrow morning you'll think quite different to this."

"No," he said, "I must go right away; but I shall stay in hiding here for a few days first. Will you bring me a little food from time to times unknown to any one?"

"Why of course I will, dear lad. But why don't you put on your pea-jacket and weskit. They is dry now."

Harry shuddered as he glanced at the rough garments the woman was turning over.

"Throw them here on the dry sand," he said hastily. "I don't want them now."

"There you are then, dear lad," said the old woman, spreading out the drowned man's clothes; "p'r'aps they are a bit damp yet. And now I must go. There's what's left in the bottle, and there's a fried mack'rel and the rest of the loaf. That'll keep you from starving, and to-morrow night I'll see if I can't bring you something better."

"And you'll be true to me?"

"Don't you be afraid of that," said the old woman quietly, as Harry clasped her arm.

"Why, you are quite wet," he said.

"Wet! Well, if you'll tell me how to get in there with the tide pretty high and not be wet I should like to know it. Why, I had hard work to keep the basket out of the water, and one corner did go in."

"And you'll have to wade out," said Harry thoughtfully.

"Well, what of that? How many times have I done the same to get alongside of a lugger after fish? Drop o' salt water won't hurt me, Master Harry; I'm too well tanned for that."

"I seem to cause trouble and pain to all I know," he said mournfully.

"What's a drop o' water?" said the old woman with a laugh. "Here, you keep that lantern up in the corner, so as nobody sees the light. There's another candle there, and a box o' matches: and now I'm going. Good-bye, dear lad."

"Good-bye," he said; with a shudder; "I trust you, mind."

"Trust me! Why, of course you do. Good night."

"One moment," said Harry. "What is the time?"

"Lor', how particular people are about the time when they've got naught to do. Getting on for twelve, I should say. There, good night. Don't you come and get wet, too."

She stepped boldly into the water, and waded on with the depth increasing till it was to her shoulders, and then Harry Vine watched her till she disappeared, and the yellow light of the lantern shone on the softly heaving surface, glittering with bubbles, which broke and flashed. Then, by degrees, the rushing sound made by the water died out, and the lit-up place seemed more terrible than the darkness of the nights before.

The time glided on; now it was day, now it was night; but day or night, that time seemed to Harry Vine one long and terrible punishment. He heard the voices of searchers in boats and along the cliffs overhead, and sat trembling with dread lest he should be discovered: and with but one thought pressing ever—that as soon as Poll Perrow could tell him that the heat of the search was over, he must escape to France, not in search of the family estates, but to live in hiding, an exile, till he could purge his crime.

After a while he got over the terrible repugnance, and put on the rough pea-jacket and vest which had lain upon a dry piece of the rock, for the place was chilly, and in his inert state he was glad of the warmth; while as the days slowly crept by, his sole change was the coming of the old fish-woman with her basket punctually, almost to the moment, night by night.

He asked her no questions as to where she obtained the provender she brought for him, but took everything mechanically, and in a listless fashion, never even wondering how she could find him in delicacies as well as in freshly-cooked fish and home-made bread. Wine and brandy he had, too, as much as he wished; and when there was none for him, it was Poll Perrow who bemoaned the absence, not he.

"Poor boy!" she said to herself, "he wants it all badly enough, and he shall have what he wants somehow, and if my Liza don't be a bit more lib'ral, I'll go and help myself. It won't be stealing."

Several times over she had so much difficulty in obtaining supplies that she determined to try Madelaine and the Van Heldres; but her success was not great.

"If he'd only let me tell 'em," she said, "it would be as easy as easy." But at the first hint of taking any one into their confidence, Harry broke out so fiercely in opposition that the old woman said no more.

"No," he said; "I'm dead—they believe I'm dead. Let them think so still. Some day I may go to them and tell them the truth, but now let them think I'm dead."

"Which they do now," said the old woman.

"What do you mean?"

She hesitated to tell him what had taken place, but he pressed her fiercely, and at last he sat trembling with horror, and with great drops bedewing his brow as she told him of the finding of the body and what had followed.

It was only what he had planned and looked for, but the fruition seemed too horrible to bear, and at last a piteous groan escaped from his breast.

That night, after the old woman had gone, the food she had obtained from his old home remained untouched, and he lay there upon the sand listening to the sighing wind and the moaning and working of the waves, picturing the whole scene vividly—the finding of the body, the inquest, and the funeral.

"Yes," he groaned again and again, "I am dead. I pray God that I may escape now, forgotten and alone, to begin a new life."

He pressed his clasped hands to his rugged brow, and thought over his wasted opportunities, the rejected happiness of his past youth, and there were moments when he was ready to curse the weak old woman who had encouraged him in the chimerical notions of wealth and title. But all that passed off.

"I ought to have known better," he said bitterly. "Poor weak old piece of vanity! Poor Louise! My sweet, true sister! Father!" he groaned, "my indulgent, patient father! Poor old honest, manly Van Heldre! Madelaine! my lost love!" And then, rising to his knees for the first time since his taking refuge in the cave, he bowed himself down in body and spirit in a genuine heartfelt prayer of repentance, and for the forgiveness of his sin.

One long, long communing in the gloom of that solemn place with his God. The hours glided on, and he still prayed, not in mere words, but in thought, in deep agony of spirit, for help and guidance in the future, and that he might live, and years hence return to those who had loved him and loved his memory, another man.

The soft, pearly light of the dawn was stealing in through the narrow opening, and the faint querulous cry of the gull fell upon his ear, and seemed to arouse him to the knowledge that it was once more day—a day he spent in thinking out what he should do.

Time glided slowly on, and a hundred plans had been conceived and rejected. Poll Perrow came and went, never once complaining of the difficulties she experienced in supplying him and herself, and daily did her best to supply him with everything but money. That was beyond her.

And that was the real necessary now. He must have money to enable him to reach London, and then France. So long a time had elapsed, and there had been so terrible a finale to the episode, that he knew he might endeavour to escape unchallenged; and at last, after a long hesitancy and shrinking, and after feeling that there was only one to whom he could go and confide in, and who would furnish him with help, he finally made up his mind.

It was a long process, a constant fight of many hours of a spirit weakened by suffering, till it was swayed by every coward dread which arose. He tried to start a dozen times, but the heavier beat of a wave, the fall of a stone from the cliff, the splash made by a fish, was sufficient to send him shivering back; but at last he strung himself lip to the effort, feeling that if he delayed longer he would grow worse, and that night poor old Poll Perrow reached the hiding place after endless difficulties, to sit down broken-hearted and ready to sob wildly, as she felt that she must have been watched, and that in spite of all her care and secrecy her "poor boy" had been taken away.

Chapter Forty Seven
Brother—Lover

Trembling, her eyes dilated with horror, Louise Vine stood watching the dimly-seen pleading face for some moments before her lips could form words, and her reason tell her that it was rank folly and superstition to stand trembling there.

"Harry!" she whispered, "alone? yes."

"Hah!" he ejaculated, and thrusting in his hands he climbed into the room.

Louise gazed wildly at the rough-looking figure in sea-stained old pea-jacket and damaged cap, hair unkempt, and a hollow look in eye and cheek that, joined with the ghastly colourless skin, was quite enough to foster the idea that this was one risen from the grave.

"Don't be scared," he said harshly, "I'm not dead after all."

"Harry! my darling brother."

That was all in words, but with a low, moaning cry Louise had thrown her soft arms about his neck and covered his damp cold face with her kisses, while the tears streamed down her cheeks.

"Then there is some one left to—My darling sis!"

He began in a half-cynical way, but the genuine embrace was contagious, and clasping her to his breast, he had to fight hard to keep back his own tears and sobs as he returned her kisses.

Then the fugitive's dread of the law and of discovery reasserted itself, and pushing her back, he said quickly:—

"Where is father?"

"At Mr Van Heldre's. Let me—"

"Hush! answer my questions. Where is Aunt Marguerite?"

"Gone to bed, dear."

"And the servants?"

"In the kitchen. They will not come without I ring. But Harry—brother—we thought you dead—we thought you dead."

"Hush! Louy, for heaven's sake! You'll ruin me," he whispered as she burst into a fit of uncontrollable sobbing, so violent at times that he grew alarmed.

"We thought you dead—we thought you dead."

It was all she could say as she clung to him, and looking wildly from door to window and back.

"Louy!" he whispered at last passionately, "I must escape. Be quiet or you will be heard."

By a tremendous effort she mastered her emotion, and tightening her grasp upon him, she set her teeth hard, compressed her lips, and stood with contracted brow gazing in his eyes.

"Now!" he said, "can you listen?"

She nodded her head, and her wild eyes seemed so questioning, that he said quickly—

"I can't tell you much. You know I can swim well."

She nodded silently.

"Well, I rose after my dive and let the current carry me away till I swam ashore three miles away, and I've been in hiding in one of the zorns."

"Oh, my brother?" she answered.

"Waiting till it was safe to come out."

"But Harry!" she paused; "we—my father—we all believed you dead. How could you be so—"

She stopped.

"Cruel?" he said firmly. "Wouldn't it have been more cruel to be dragged off to prison and disgrace you more?"

"But—"

"Hush! I tell you I have been in hiding. They think me dead?"

"Yes; they found you—"

"Hush, I tell you. I have no time to explain. Let them go on thinking me dead."

"But Harry?" she cried; "my poor broken-hearted father—Madelaine."

"Hold your tongue!" he said in a broken voice, "unless you want to drive me mad."

He paused, for his face was working; but at last with a stamp he controlled his emotion.

"Look here," he said hoarsely. "I had no one to come to but you. Will you help me?"

"Harry?" she whispered reproachfully, as she clung to him more firmly.

"Hah! that's better," he said. "Now don't talk, only listen. But are you sure that we shall not be overheard?"

"Quite, dear, we are alone."

"Then listen. I have thought all this out. I've been a blackguard; I did knock old Van Heldre down."

Louise moaned.

"But once more I tell you I'm not a thief. I did not rob him, and I did not go to rob him. I swear it."

"I believe you, Harry," she whispered.

"Well, I'll tell you what I'm going to do."

She nodded again, unable to speak, but clung to him spasmodically, for everything seemed to swim round before her eyes.

"I am penniless. There, that proves to you I did not rob poor old Van. I want money—enough to escape over to France—to get to London first. Then I shall change my name. Don't be alarmed," he said tremblingly, as he felt Louise start. "I shall give up the name of Vine, but I'm not going to call myself des Vignes, or any of that cursed folly."

"Harry!"

"All right, dear. It made me mad to think of it all. I've come to my senses now, and I'm going over the channel to make a fresh start and to try and prove myself a man. Some day when I've done this father shall know that I am alive, and perhaps then he may take me by the hand and forgive me."

"Harry, let me send for him—let me tell him now."

"No," said the young man sternly.

"He loves you! He will forgive you and bless God for restoring you once more, as I do, my darling. Oh, Harry, Harry! My mother!"

"Hush," he whispered with his voice trembling as he held her to him and stroked her face. "Hush, sis, hush!"

"Then I may send for him?"

"No, no, no?" he cried fiercely. "I am little better than a convict. He must not, he shall not know I am alive."

"But Harry, dearest—"

"Silence!" he whispered angrily, "I came to you, my sister, for help. No, no, dear, I'm not cross; but you talk like a woman. The dear old dad would forgive me, God bless him! I know he would, just as you have, and fall on my neck and kiss me as—as—as—Ah! Lou, Lou, Lou, my girl," he cried, fighting against his emotion, "the law will not be like your love. You must help me to escape, at all events for a time."

"And may I tell him where you are gone—my father and Maddy?"

"Hush!" he cried, in so wild and strange a voice that she shrank from him. "Do you want to unman me when I have planned my future, and then see me handcuffed and taken to gaol? No; Harry Vine is dead. Some day another man will come and ask the forgiveness he needs."

"Harry!"

"But not this shivering, cowardly cur—a man, a true blameless man, whom it will take years to make. Now, then, once more, will you help me, and keep my secret?"

Louise was silent for a few moments.

"Well, never mind, you must keep my secret, for after I am gone if you said you had seen me, people would tell you that you were mad."

"I will help you, Harry, and keep your secret, dear—even," she added to herself, "if it breaks my heart."

"That's right. We've wasted too much time in talking as it is, and—"

"But Harry—Madelaine—she loves you."

He wrested himself from her violently, and stood with his hands pressed to his head. A few moments before he had been firm and determined, but the agonised thought of Madelaine and of giving her up for ever had ended the fictitious strength which had enabled him to go so far.

It was the result of his long agony shut up in that cave; and though he struggled hard he could do no more, but completely unnerved, trembling violently, and glancing wildly from time to time at the door and window, he sank at his sister's feet and clutched her knees.

"Harry, Harry!" she whispered—she, the stronger now—"for Heaven's sake don't give way like that."

"It's all over now. I'm dead beat; I can do no more."

"Then let me go for father; let me fetch him from Van Heldre's."

"Yes," he moaned; "and while you are gone I'll go down to the end of the point and jump in. This time I shall be too weak to swim."

"Harry, don't talk like that!" she cried, embracing him, as she saw with horror the pitiable, trembling state in which he was.

"I can't help it," he whispered as he clung to her now like a frightened child, and looked wildly at the door. "You don't know what I've suffered, buried alive like, in that cave, and expecting the sea to come in and drown me. It has been one long horror."

"But, Harry, dear, you are safe now."

"Safe?" he groaned; "yes, to be taken by the first policeman I meet, and locked up in gaol."

"But, Harry!" she cried, his agitation growing contagious, "I have promised. I will help you now. I'll keep it a secret, if you think it best, dear. Harry, for Heaven's sake be a man."

"It's all over now," he groaned, "so better end it all. I wish I was dead. I wish I was dead."

"But, Harry, dear," she whispered, trembling now as much as he, "tell me what to do."

"I can't now," he said; "I'm too weak and broken. All this has been so maddening that I'm like some poor wretch half-killed by drink. It's too late now."

"No, no, Harry, dear. It shall be our secret then. Up, and be a man, my brave, true brother, and you shall go and redeem yourself. Yes, I'll suffer it all hopefully, for the future shall make amends, dear. You shall go across to France, and I will study my father's comfort, and pray nightly for you."

"Too late," he moaned—"too late!"

She looked at him wildly. The long strain upon his nerves had been too great, and he was white as a sheet, and shaking violently.

"Harry, dear, tell me what to do."

"Let them take me," he said weakly. "It's of no use."

"Hush?" she said, full now of a wild desire to save him from disgrace and to aid him in his efforts to redeem the past. "Let me think. Yes; you want money."

Full of the recollection of his former appeal, she took out her keys, opened a drawer, while he half knelt, half crouched upon the carpet. She had not much there, and, whispering to him to wait, she left the room, locking him in, and ran up to her chamber.

Harry started as he heard the snap made by the lock; but he subsided again in a helpless state, and with the disease that had been hanging about waiting to make its grand attack, gradually sapping its way.

In five minutes Louise was back.

"I have not much money," she whispered hastily; "but here are my watch, two chains, and all the jewels I have, dear. They are worth a great deal."

"Too late!" he moaned as he gazed up at her piteously, and for the moment he was delirious, as a sudden flush of fever suffused his cheeks.

"It is not too late," she said firmly. "Take them. Now tell me what next to do."

"What next?" he said vacantly.

"Yes. You must not stay here. My father may return at any time. Brother—Harry—shall I get you some clothes?"

"No—no," he said mournfully. "I shall want no more clothes."

"Harry!" she cried, taking his face between her hands, and drawing it round so that the light fell upon it; "are you ill?"

"Ill? yes," he said feebly. "I've felt it before—in the wet cave—fever, I suppose. Lou, dear, is it very hard to die?"

"Oh, what shall I do?" cried the agitated girl, half frantic now. "Harry, you are not very ill?"

"Only sometimes," he said slowly, as he looked round. "I seem to lose my head a bit, and then something seems to hold me back."

"Harry!"

"Yes," he cried, starting up; "who called? You, Louy, money—give me some money."

"I gave you all I had, dear, and my jewels."

"Yes, I forgot," he said huskily, as in a moment his whole manner had changed, and with feverish energy he felt for the trinkets she had given him.

"You are ill, dear," she whispered tenderly. "Would it not be better to let me fetch our father?"

"I'd sooner die," he cried, catching her wrist. "No. He shall not know. There, I can see clearly now. That horrible weakness is always taking me now, and when it's on I feel as if I should kill myself."

"Harry!"

"Hush! I know now. We must go before he comes back."

"We?" she said aghast.

"Yes, we. I'm not fit to be alone. You must come with me, Lou, and help me. If I go alone I shall go mad."

"Oh, Harry! my darling brother."

"Yes," he cried in a hoarse whisper; "I know I shall. It's too horrible to live alone, as I've been living. You must come with me and save me—from myself—from everybody. Why do you look at me like that?"

He caught her by the shoulder, and glared at her with a long, fierce stare.

"I—I could not leave home, Harry," she said faintly.

"You must, you shall," he cried, "unless you want me to really die."

"But my father, dear?"

"Quick! write!" he said with the feverish energy which frightened her; and dragging open the blotter on a side table, he pointed to a chair.

"He is mad—he is mad," she wailed to herself, as in obedience to a will far stronger at that moment than her own, she sat down and took up pen and paper.

"Write," he said hoarsely.

"Write, Harry?"

"Yes, quick!"

In a horror of dread as she read her brother's wild looks, and took in his feverish semi-delirium, lest he should carry out a threat which chilled her, she dipped her pen and waited as, after an evident struggle with a clouding intellect, Harry said quickly:

"Dear father, I am forced by circumstances to leave home. Do not grieve for me, I am well and happy; and no matter what you hear do not attempt to follow me. If you do you will bring sorrow upon yourself, and ruin upon one I love. Good-bye; some day all will be cleared up. Till then, your loving daughter, Louise."

"Harry!" she sobbed, as he laid down the pen, and gazed at the tear-blurred paper. "You cannot mean this. I dare not—I could not go."

"Very well," he said coldly. "I told you it was too late. It does not matter now."

"Oh," she panted, "you are not reasonable. I have given you money. Go as you said and hide somewhere. You are weak and ill now."

"Yes," he said, in a voice which wrung her heart. "I am weak and ill now."

"A little rest, dear, and the knowledge that you have the means of escaping will make you more calm."

He looked at her with his eyes so full of wild anger that she half shrank from him, but his face changed.

"Poor little sis!" he said tenderly; "I frighten you. Look at me. Am I fit to go away alone? I know — I feel that at any moment I may break down and go off my head among strangers."

She looked at him wildly, and as she stood trembling there in a state of agitation which overset her generally calm balance, she read in his eyes that he was speaking the truth.

"Put that note in an envelope and direct it," he said in a slow, measured way, and mechanically, and as if for the time being his will was again stronger than hers, she obeyed him, dropped the letter on the table, and then stood gazing from it to her brother and back again.

"It's hard upon you," he said, with his hand to his head, as if he could think more clearly then, "hard upon the poor old dad. But it seems my only chance, Lou, my girl."

Father — brother — what should she do?

"I can feel it now," he said drearily. "There, I'm cool now. It's lying in that cold, wet cave, and the horrors I've gone through. I've got something coming on — had touches of it before — in the nights," he went on slowly and heavily, "p'r'aps it'll kill me — better if it does."

"No, no, Harry. Stay and let me nurse you here. We could keep it a secret from every one, and — "

"Hold your tongue!" he said fiercely. "I might live — if I went away — where I could feel — I was safe. I can't face the old man again. It would kill me. There, it's too much to ask you — what's that?"

Louise started to the door. Harry dashed to the window, and his manner was so wild and excited that she darted after him to draw him away.

"Nothing, dear, it is your fancy. There, listen, there is no one coming."

He looked at her doubtingly, and listened as she drew him from the window.

"I thought I heard them coming," he said. "Some one must have seen me crawl up here. Coming to take me — to gaol."

"No, no, dear. You are ill, and fancy all this. Now come and listen to me. It would be so wild, so cruel if I were to leave my home like this. Harry! be reasonable, dear. Your alarm is magnified because you are ill. Let me—no, no, don't be angry with me—let me speak to my father—take him into our confidence, and he will help you."

"No," he said sternly.

"Let me make him happy by the knowledge that you are alive."

"And come upon him like a curse," said Harry, as there was a tap at the door, which neither heard in the excitement of the moment, for, eager to help him, and trembling lest he should, in the excited state he was, go alone, Louise threw herself upon her knees at her brother's feet.

"Be guided by me, dearest," she sobbed, in a low, pained voice. "You know how I love you, how I would die if it were necessary to save you from suffering; but don't—pray don't ask me to go away from poor father in such a way as this."

As she spoke a burst of hysteric sobbing accompanied her words, and then, as she raised her tear-blinded eyes, she saw that which filled her with horror. Uttering a faint cry, she threw herself before her brother, as if to shield him from arrest.

Duncan Leslie was standing in the open doorway, and at her action, he took a stride fiercely into the room.

Harry's back was half turned toward him, but he caught a glimpse of the figure in the broad mirror of an old dressoir, and with one sweep of his arm dashed the light over upon the floor.

The heavy lamp fell with a crash of broken glass, and as Louise stood clinging to her brother, there was a dead silence as well as darkness in the room.

Chapter Forty Eight
The Plant Aunt Marguerite Grew

As Duncan Leslie walked up the steep path leading to the old granite house he could not help thinking of the absurdity of his act, and wondering whether Louise Vine and her father would see how much easier it would have been for him to call at Van Heldre's.

"Can't help it," he said. "The old man must think what he likes. Laugh at me in his sleeve? Well, let him. I shan't be the first man in love who has been laughed at."

"In love, man, in love! How stupid it sounds; and I suppose I am weak."

"Human nature!" he said after a pause; and he walked very fast.

Then he began to walk very slowly, as a feeling of hesitation came over him, and he asked himself whether the Vines would not feel his coming as an intrusion, and be annoyed.

"She can't be annoyed," he said half aloud. "She may think it unfortunate, but she knows I love her, and she is too true and sweet a woman to be hard upon me."

With the full intention of going boldly to the house, and trying to act in a frank, manly way, letting Louise see that he was going to be patient and earnest, he again strode on rapidly, but only to hesitate again and stop by one of the great masses of rock, which occurred here and there along the shelf-like slope cut from the side of the towering hill.

Here he rested his arms upon the shaggy stone, and stood gazing out to sea, the darkness looking wonderfully transparent and pure. From where he stood the harbour was at his feet, and he could see a spark-like light here and there in cottage or boat, and a dull glow from some open doorway on the opposite side of the estuary.

The red light at the end of the east pier sent a ruddy stain out to sea, and there was another light farther out just rocking gently to and fro, and as it caught his eye he shuddered, for it shone out softly, as did the light of the lugger on the night when Harry Vine took that terrible leap.

"Poor weak boy," said Leslie to himself. And then, "The more need for her to have one in whom she can confide; only I must be patient—patient."

He turned with a sigh, and began to walk back, for in his indecision the feeling was in him strong now that a call would be an intrusion, and that he must be content to wait. By the time he was fifty yards down the path the desire to see Louise again was stronger than ever, and he walked back to the stone, leaned over it, and stood thinking. After a few minutes he turned sharply round and looked, for he heard a heavy step as of a man approaching; but directly after, as he remained quiescent, he just made out that it was not a man's step, but that of a sturdy fisherwoman, who seemed in the gloom to resemble Poll Perrow, but he could not be sure, and forgot the incident as soon as she passed. By the time the steps had died out, Duncan Leslie's mind was fully made up; and, following the woman, he walked firmly up to the gateway, entered, and, reaching the hall door, which stood open, he rang. He waited for some time listening to a low murmur of voices in the dining-room, and then rang again. There was no reply, consequent upon the fact that Liza was at the back gate, to which she had been summoned by her mother, who had come up in trouble, and was asking her questions whose bearing she could not understand.

Leslie's courage and patience began to fail, but he still waited, and then at last changed colour, feeling the blood rush to his cheeks, for there was a peculiarity in the conversation going on in the dining-room, and it seemed to him that some one was agitated and in pain.

He turned away so as to force himself not to hear, feeling that he was an interloper, and then, in spite of himself, he returned to find that the sounds had grown louder, and as if involuntarily agitated and troubled more than he would have cared to own, he rang again and then entered the hall.

He hesitated for a few moments, and then certain from the voices that there was something strange, and divining wrongly or rightly from the tones of one of the voices—a voice which thrilled him as he stood there trembling with excitement, that the woman he loved needed help, he threw aside all hesitation, and turned the handle of the door.

The words which fell upon his ear, the scene he saw of Louise kneeling at some strange rough-looking man's feet, sent the blood surging up to his brain, rendering him incapable of calm thought, and turned the ordinarily patient deliberative man into a being wrought almost to a pitch of madness.

It did not occur to him that he was an intruder, and that he had no right to make such a demand, but taking a stride forward, he exclaimed—

"Louise! Who is this man?" as the lamp was swept from the table, and they were in darkness.

For a few moments no one spoke, and Louise stood clinging to her brother, trembling violently and at her wits' end to know what to do.

The simple way out of the difficulty would have been to take Duncan Leslie into their confidence at once; but in her agitation, Louise shrank from that. She knew his stern integrity; she had often heard of his firmness with his mine people; and she feared that in his surprise and disgust, at what seemed to her now little better than a trick played by her brother to deceive them, Leslie would turn against him and refuse to keep the secret.

On the other hand, Harry, suffering from a fresh access of dread, but now strung up and excited, placed his lips to her ear and bade her be silent on her life.

The silence was for a few moments terrible, and then Harry's breath could be heard coming and going as if he had been hunted, while Louise, in her agony of excitement, sought vainly for words that should put an end to the painful encounter.

No one moved; and in the midst of the nervous strain a sharp puff of wind came sweeping up from the sea, like the *avant-garde* of a storm, and the casement window was blown to with a loud clang.

Harry started as if he had felt that his retreat was cut off, but he kept his face averted, and dragged his rough hat down over his eyes, though the action was unnecessary, for the darkness was too great for him to be recognised.

As he started Louise clung to him, and for the moment he struggled to escape from her, but he clung to her the next instant, and quivered with fear as the silence was broken by Leslie's voice, so cold, deep, and harsh that it seemed as if a stranger was speaking.

"I suppose I have no right to interfere," he said; "but there are times when a man forgets or puts aside etiquette, and there are reasons here why I should speak. Miss Vine, where is your father?"

Louise made an effort to reply, but there was only a spasmodic catching of her breath.

"Send him away. Tell him to go," whispered Harry.

"I said, where is your father, Miss Vine?" said Leslie again more coldly.

"At—at Mr Van Heldre's," she murmured at last. "Mr Leslie—pray—"

"I am your father's friend, and I should not be doing my duty—Ah! my duty—to myself," he cried angrily, "if I did not speak plainly. Does Mr Vine know that this gentleman is here?"

"No," said Louise, in an almost inaudible voice, and in the contagion of her brother's fear she seemed to see him once more hunted down by the officers of justice; and the terrible scene on the pier danced before her eyes.

"So I suppose," said Leslie coldly.

"Send him away," whispered Harry hoarsely.

"It is not in Miss Louise Vine's power to send me away, sir," cried Leslie fiercely; and the poor trembling girl felt her brother start once more.

"You, sir, are here, by her confession, clandestinely. You are a scoundrel and a cur, who dare not show your face or you would not have dashed out that light."

Harry made a harsh guttural sound, such as might be uttered by a beast at bay.

"Who are you? I need not ask your object in coming here. I could not help hearing."

"Tell him to go away," said Harry sharply, speaking in French to disguise his voice.

"Mr Leslie, pray, pray go. This is a private visit. I beg you will go."

"Private enough," said Leslie, bitterly; "and once more I say you may think I have no right to interfere. I give up all claims that I might have thought I had upon you, but as your father's friend I will not stand calmly by and see wrong done his child. Speak out, sir; who are you? Let's hear your name, if you are ashamed to show your face."

"Tell him to go away," said Harry again.

Leslie writhed, for Aunt Marguerite's hints about the French gentleman of good descent came up now as if to sting him. This man he felt, in his blind rage, was the noble suitor who in his nobility stooped to come in the darkness to try and persuade a weak girl to leave her home; and as he thought this it was all he could do, hot-blooded, madly jealous and excited, to keep from flinging himself upon the supposed rival, the unworthy lover of the woman he had worshipped with all the strength of a man's first passion.

"I can't talk to him in his wretched tongue," cried Leslie, fiercely; "but I understand his meaning. Perhaps he may comprehend mine. No. I shall not go. I shall not leave this room till Mr Vine returns. He can answer to your father, or I will, if I have done wrong."

"Mr Leslie!" cried Louise, "You don't know what you are doing—what you say. Pray—pray go."

"When my old friend George Vine tells me I have done wrong, and I have seen you safe in his care."

"No, no. Go now, now!" cried Louise.

Leslie drew a deep breath and his heart beat heavily in the agony and despair he felt. She loved this man, this contemptible wretch who had gained such ascendency over her that she was pleading in his behalf, and trying to screen him from her father's anger.

"Mr Leslie. Do you hear me?" she cried, taking courage now in her despair and dread lest her father should return.

"Yes," he said coldly. "I hear you, Miss Vine; and it would be better for you to retire and leave this man with me."

"No, no," she cried excitedly. "Mr Leslie! You are intruding here. This is a liberty. I desire you to go."

"When Mr Vine comes back," said Leslie sternly. "If I have done wrong then no apology shall be too humble for me to speak. But till he comes I stay. I have heard too much. I may have been mad in indulging in those vain hopes, but if that is all dead there still remains too much honour and respect for the woman I knew in happier times for me to stand by and let her wrong herself by accompanying this man."

"Mr Leslie, you are mistaken."

"I am not."

"Indeed—indeed!"

"Prove it then," he cried, in stern judicial tones. "I am open to conviction. You love this man?" Louise was silent. "He was begging you to accompany him in flight." Louise uttered a low wail. "Hah!" ejaculated Leslie, "I am right."

"No, no; it is all a misapprehension," cried Louise, excitedly. "Mr Leslie, this—"

"Hold your tongue," whispered Harry hoarsely, and she moaned as she writhed in spirit.

"There are reasons why my father should not know of this visit."

"So I suppose," said Leslie sternly; "and you ask me to be a partner by giving way to a second blow to that true-hearted, trusting man. Louise Vine, is it you who are speaking, or has this man put these cruelly base words in your mouth?"

"What can I say? What can I do?" wailed Louise, wringing her hands, as with every sense on the strain she listened for her father's step.

Harry, who now that the first shock had passed was rapidly growing more calm and calculating, bent down over his sister, and whispered to her again in French to go quickly, and get her hat and mantle.

"He will not dare to stop us," he said.

Louise drew a long breath full of pain, for it seemed to be the only way to save her brother. She must go; and, taking a step or two she made for the door.

"No," said Leslie calmly, "it is better that you should stay, Miss Vine."

Harry was at her side in a moment.

"Never mind your hat," he whispered in French, "we must go at once."

"Stand back, sir!" cried Leslie, springing to the door. "Your every act shows you to be a base scoundrel. You may not understand my words, but you can understand my action. I am here by this door to keep it till Mr Vine returns. For the lady's sake, let there be no violence."

"Mr Leslie, let us pass!" cried Louise imperiously, but he paid no heed to her, continuing to address his supposed rival in calm, judicial tones, which did not express the wild rage seething in his heart.

"I say once more, sir, let there be no violence—for your own sake—for hers."

Harry continued to advance, with Louise's hand in his, till Leslie had pressed close to the door.

"Once more I warn you," said Leslie, "for I swear by Heaven you shall not pass while I can lift a hand."

At that moment, in the obscurity, Louise felt her hand dropped, and she reeled to the side of the room, as now, with a fierce, harsh sound, Harry sprang at Leslie's throat, pushed him back against the door in his sudden onslaught, and then wrenched him away.

"Quick, Louise!" he cried in French. "The door!"

Louise recovered herself and darted to the door, the handle rattling in her grasp. But she did not open it. She stood as if paralysed, her eyes staring and lips parted, gazing wildly at the two dimly-seen shadows which moved here and there across the casement frames in a curiously weird manner, to the accompaniment of harsh, panting sounds, the dull tramping of feet, heavy breathing, and the quick, sharp ejaculations of angry men.

Then a fresh chill of horror shot through her, as there was a momentary cessation of the sounds, and Leslie panted.

"Bah! then you give in, sir!"

The apparent resignation of his adversary had thrown him off his guard, and the next moment Harry had sprung at him, and with his whole weight borne him backwards, so that he fell with his head upon the bare patch of the hearthstone.

There was the sound of a terrible blow, a faint rustling, and then, as Louise stood there like one in a nightmare, she was roused to action by her brother's words.

"Quick!" he whispered, in a hoarse, panting way. "Your hat and mantle. Not a moment to lose!"

The nightmare-like sensation was at an end, but it was still all like being in a dream to Louise as, forced against her own will by the effort of one more potent, she ran up to her own room, and catching up a bonnet and a loose cloak, she ran down again.

"You have killed him," she whispered.

"Pish! stunned. Quick, or I shall be caught."

He seized her wrist, and hurried her out of the front door just as Liza went in at the back, after a long whispered quarrel with her mother, who was steadily plodding down towards the town, as brother and sister stepped out.

"What's that? some one in front?" whispered Harry, stopping short. "Here, this way."

"Harry," moaned his sister, as he drew her sidewise, and began to climb up the rough side of the path so as to reach the rugged land above.

"It is the only chance," he said hastily. "Quick!"

She followed him, half climbing, half dragged, till she was up on the granite-strewn waste, across which he hurried her, reckless of the jagged masses of rock that were always cropping up in their way, and of the fact that in three places farther along, once fenced in by stones, which had since crumbled down, were, one after the other, the openings to three disused mines, each a terrible yawning chasm, with certain death by drowning for the unfortunate who was plunged into their depths.

Chapter Forty Nine
After the Great Sorrows

"No, no, no, Mr Vine—I mean no, no, no, George Vine," sobbed Mrs Van Heldre; "I did, I know, feel bitter and full of hatred against one who could be so base as to raise his hand against my loving, forbearing husband; but that was when I was in misery and despair. Do you think that now God has blessed us by sparing his life and restoring him to us, I could be so thankless, hard and wicked as to bear malice?"

"You are very, very good," said Vine sadly.

"I wish I was," said Mrs Van Heldre, with a comic look of perplexity on her pretty, elderly countenance, "but I'm not, George, I'm a very curious woman."

"You are one of the best and most amiable creatures that ever existed," said Vine, taking her hand and kissing it.

"I try to be good-tempered and to do my best," said the little woman with a sigh, "but I'm very weak and stupid; and I know that is the one redeeming point in my character, I can feel what a weak woman I am."

"Thank God you are what you are," said Vine reverently. "If I had had such a wife spared to me all these years, that terrible catastrophe would not have occurred."

"And you, George Vine, thank God, too, for sparing to you the best and most loving daughter that ever lived. Now, now, now, don't look like that. I wanted to tell you how fond and patient John always has been with me, and Maddy too, when I have said and done weak and silly things. For I do, you know, sometimes. Ah, it's no use for you to shake your head, and pretend you never noticed it. You must."

"I hope you will never change," said Vine with a sad smile.

"Ah, that's better," cried Mrs Van Heldre. "I'm glad to see you smile again, for Louy's sake, for our sake: and now, once for all, never come into our house again, my dear old friend and brother, looking constrained. John has had long, long talks with me and Maddy."

"Yes," cried Vine excitedly. "What did he say?"

Mrs Van Heldre took his hand and held it.

"He said," she whispered slowly, "That it grieved and pained him to see you come to his bedside, looking as if you felt that we blamed you for what has passed. He said you had far more cause to blame him."

"No, no," said Vine hastily. "I do not blame him. It was fate—it was fate."

"It wasn't anything of the kind," said Mrs Van Heldre sharply; "it was that stupid, obstinate, bigoted, wrong-headed old fellow Crampton."

"Who felt that he owed a duty to his master, and did that duty."

"Oh!" sighed the little woman with a look of perplexity in her puckered-up forehead, "I told you that I was a very stupid woman. I wanted to make you more cheerful and contented, and see what I have done!"

"How can I be cheerful and contented, my good little woman?" said Vine sadly. "There, there! I shall be glad when a couple of years have gone."

"Why?" said Mrs Van Heldre, sharply.

"Because I shall either be better able to bear my burden or be quite at rest."

"George Vine!" exclaimed Mrs Van Heldre reproachfully. "Is that you speaking? Louise—remember Louise."

"Ah, yes," he said sadly, but sat gazing dreamily before him. "Louise. If it had not been for her—"

He did not finish his sentence.

"Come, my dear. John will be expecting you for a long chat. Try and be more hopeful, and don't go up to him looking like that. Doctor Knatchbull said we were to make him as cheerful as we could, and to keep him from thinking about the past. He did say, too, that we were not to let you see him much. There—"

Poor little Mrs Van Heldre looked more perplexed than ever, and now burst into tears.

"He said that? The doctor said that?"

"Yes; but did you ever hear such a silly woman in your life? To go and blurt out such a thing as that to you!"

"He was quite right—quite right," said Vine hastily; "and I'll be very careful not to say or do anything to depress him. Poor John! Do you think he is awake now?"

"No," said Mrs Van Heldre, wiping her eyes. "Maddy is with him, and she will come down directly he wakes."

At that moment there was a ring, and on the door being opened the servant announced Luke Vine.

"Hallo," he said, coming in after his usual unceremonious fashion. "How is he?"

"Very, very much better, Luke Vine," said Mrs Van Heldre. "George is going up to see him as soon as he wakes."

"George? My brother George? Oh, you're there, are you? How are you, George? How's the girl?"

"Sit down, Luke Vine."

"No, thank you, ma'am. Sit too much as it is. Don't get enough exercise."

"You shall go up and see John, as soon as he wakes."

"No, thankye. What's the use? I couldn't do him any good. One's getting old now. No time to spare. Pity to waste what's left."

"Well, I'm sure," said Mrs Van Heldre bridling. "Of all men to talk like that, you ought to be the last. I'll go up and see whether he is awake."

"Poor little woman," said Uncle Luke, as she left the room. "Always puts me in mind, George, of a pink and white bantam hen."

"As good a little woman as ever breathed, Luke."

"Yes, of course; but it's comic to see her ruffle up her feathers and go off in a huff. How's Lou?"

"Not very well, Luke. Poor girl, she frets. I shall have to take her away."

"Rubbish! She'll be all right directly. Women have no brains."

George Vine looked up at him with an air of mild reproof.

"All tears and doldrums one day; high jinks and coquetry the next. Marry, and forget all about you in a week."

"Luke, my dear brother, you do not mean this."

"Don't soap, George. I hate to be called my dear brother. Now, do I look like a dear brother?"

"I shall never forget your goodness to us over our terrible trouble."

"Will you be quiet? Hang it all, George! don't be such an idiot. Let the past be. The poor foolish boy is dead; let him rest. Don't be for ever digging up the old sorrow, to brood over it and try to hatch fresh. The eggs may not be addled, and you might be successful. Plenty of trouble without making more."

"I do not wish to make more, Luke; but you hurt me when you speak so lightly of Louise."

"A jade! I hate her."

"No, you do not."

"Yes, I do. Here's Duncan Leslie, as good a fellow as ever stepped, who has stuck to her through thick and thin, in spite of my lady's powder, and fan, and her insults."

"Marguerite has been very sharp and spiteful to Mr Leslie," said George Vine sadly.

"She's mad. Well, he wants to marry the girl, and she has pitched him over."

"Has Louise refused him?"

"He doesn't say so; but I saw him, and that's enough. Of course I know that at present—et cetera, et cetera; but the girl wants a husband; all girls do. There was one for her, and she is playing *stand off* with him. Just like woman. He! he! he! he!" He uttered a sneering laugh. "Going to marry Madge's French count, I suppose—Monsieur le Comte de Mythville. There, I can't help it, George, old lad; it makes me wild. Shake hands, old chap. Didn't mean to hurt your feelings; but between ourselves, though I've never shown it to a soul, I was rather hit upon the idea of Leslie marrying Louise."

"I had thought it possible," said George Vine, with a sigh.

"Her fault. Hang it all, George, be a man, and bestir yourself."

"I am trying, brother Luke."

"That's right, lad; and for goodness' sake put down your foot and keep Margaret in her place. Louy is soft now with trouble, and that wicked old woman will try to work her and mould her into what shape she pleases. You've had enough of Margaret."

"I have tried to do my duty by our sister."

"You've done more, my lad. Now take care that she leaves Louy alone. You don't want another old maid of her pattern in the family."

"John is awake now, George Vine," said Mrs Van Heldre, re-entering the room.

"Will you go up?"

"Yes, I'll go up," said George Vine quietly.

"Well, aren't I to be asked to see him?" grumbled Uncle Luke.

"Oh, what a strange man you are!" said Mrs Van Heldre; "you know I wanted you to go up."

"No, I don't; I know you asked me to go up. Different thing altogether."

"I did want you to go. I felt that it would cheer up poor John."

"Well, don't be cross about it, woman. Ask me again."

Mrs Van Heldre turned with a smile to George Vine, as much as to say, "Did you ever hear such an unreasonable being?"

"Rum one, aren't I, John's wife, eh?" said Uncle Luke grimly. "Good little woman, after all."

"After all!" ejaculated Mrs Van Heldre, as she followed them into the room, and then stepped back. "Too many of us at once can't be good, so I must stay down," she added with a sigh.

Crossing to the table where her bird's cage was standing, she completely removed the cover, now displaying a pink and grey ball of feathers upon the perch, her action having been so gentle that the bird's rest was not disturbed.

"Poor little prisoner!" she said gently. "There, you may wake up to-morrow morning and pipe and sing in the bright sunshine, for we can bear it now—thank God! we can bear it now."

Chapter Fifty
The Discovery

Madelaine rose as the brothers entered the room, and before coming to the bed, where Van Heldre lay rapidly mending now, George Vine took the girl's hands, looked down in her pale face, which sorrow seemed to have refined, and bent down and kissed her.

"How are you, Maddy?" said Luke Vine, gruffly; and he was going on to the bed, but Madelaine laid her hand upon his shoulder, leant towards him, and kissed him.

"Hah! yes, forgot," he said, brushing her forehead roughly with his grey beard; and then, yielding to a sudden impulse, kissing the girl tenderly, "How I do hate girls!" he muttered to himself, as he went straight to the window and stood there for a few moments.

"Poor lad!" he said to himself. "Yes, hopeless, or a girl like that would have redeemed him."

He turned back from the window.

"Room too hot and stuffy," he said. "Well, how are you, John?"

"Getting well fast," replied Van Heldre, shaking hands. "Splendid fish that was you sent me to-day; delicious."

"Humph! all very fine! Shilling or fifteen pence out of pocket," grumbled Uncle Luke.

"Get out!" said Van Heldre, after a keen look at George Vine. "Poll Perrow wouldn't have given you more than ninepence for a fish like that. It's wholesale, Luke, wholesale."

"Ah! you may grin and wink at George," grumbled Uncle Luke, "but times are getting hard."

"They are, old fellow, and we shall be having you in the workhouse, if we can't manage to get you to the Victoria Park place."

"Here, come away, George," snarled Uncle Luke. "He's better. Beginning to sneer. Temper's getting very bad now, I suppose, my dear?" he added to Madelaine.

"Terrible. Leads me a dreadful life, Uncle Luke," she said, putting her arm round Van Heldre's neck to lay her cheek against his brow for a moment or two before turning to leave the room.

"Cant and carny," said Uncle Luke. "Don't you believe her, John Van; she'll be coming to you for money to-morrow—bless her," he added *sotto voce*; then aloud, "What now?"

For Madelaine had gone behind his chair, and placed her hands upon his shoulders.

"It's all waste of breath, Uncle Luke," she said gently. "We found you out a long time ago, Louise and I."

"What do you mean?"

"All this pretended cynicism. It's a mere disguise."

"An ass in the lion's skin, eh?"

"No, Uncle Luke," she whispered, with her lips close to his ear, so that the others should not catch the words, "that is the wrong way, sir. Reverse the fable."

"What do you mean, hussy?"

"The dear old lion in the ass' skin," she whispered; "and whenever you try to bray it is always a good honest roar."

"Well, of all—"

He did not finish, for Madelaine had hurried from the room, but a grim smile came over his cynical countenance, and he rubbed his hands softly as if he was pleased. Then, drawing his chair nearer to the bed, he joined in the conversation at rare intervals, the subjects chosen being all as foreign as possible from the past troubles, till Mrs Van Heldre came softly into the room.

"I am Doctor Knatchbull's deputy," she said; "and my orders are not to let John excite himself."

"All nonsense, my dear," said Van Heldre.

"She is quite right, John," said George Vine, rising.

"Quite right," said Uncle Luke, following his brother's example. "Keep him quiet. Make haste and get well. Good night. Come, George."

He was at the door by the time he had finished his speech, and without pausing to shake hands began to descend.

Madelaine came out of the drawing-room as the old man reached the hall.

"What do you think of him?" she said eagerly.

"Going backwards—dying fast," he said shortly.

"Oh!"

"Don't be a little goose," he cried, catching her in his arms as she reeled. "We all are; especially people over fifty. Bonny little nurse. You've done wonders. Good night, my dear; God bless you!"

She returned his loving fatherly kiss, given hastily, as if he were ashamed of his weakness, and then he strode out into the dark night.

"Poor Uncle Luke!" she said softly. "I was right. He must have had some shock to change his life like this. Good night, dear Mr Vine. My dearest love to Louy."

"Good night, my darling," he whispered huskily, and the next minute he was walking slowly away beside his brother in the direction of the turning up to the granite house.

"Good night, Luke," said George Vine. "It is of no use to say come up."

"Yes, it is," said Uncle Luke snappishly. "I want to see Louy, and have a decent cup of tea."

"I am very glad," said his brother warmly. "Hah! that's right. Come more often, Luke. We are getting old men now, and it's pleasant to talk of the days when we were boys."

"And be driven from the place by Madge with her pounce-box and her civet-cat airs. You kick her out, and I'll come often."

"Poor Marguerite!"

"There you go; encouraging the silly French notions. Why can't you call her Margaret, like a British Christian?"

"Let her finish her span in peace, brother," said George Vine, whose visit to his old friend seemed to have brightened him, and made voice and step elastic. "We are crochety and strange too, I with my mollusc hobby, and you with your fishing."

"If you want to quarrel, I'm not coming up."

"Yes, you are, Luke. There, come often, and let poor Margaret say what she likes. We shall have done our duty by her, so that will be enough for us."

"Hang duty! I'm getting sick of duty. No matter what one does, or how one tries to live in peace and be left alone, there is always duty flying in one's face."

"Confession of failure, Luke," said his brother, taking his arm. "You have given up ordinary social life, invested your property, sent your plate to your banker's, and settled down to the life of the humblest cottager to, as you say, escape the troubles of everyday life."

"Yes, and I've escaped 'em—roguish trades-people, household anxieties, worries out of number."

"In other words," said Vine, smiling, "done everything you could to avoid doing your duty, and for result you have found that trouble comes to your cottage in some form or another as frequently as it does to my big house."

Uncle Luke stopped short, and gave his stick a thump on the path.

"I have done, Luke," said Vine quietly. "Come along; Louise will think we are very long."

"Louise will be very glad to have an hour or two to herself without you pottering about her. Hah! what idiots we men are, fancying that the women are looking out for us from our point of view when they are looking out from theirs for fear of being surprised, and—"

"Here we are, Luke. Come in, my dear boy."

Uncle Luke grunted.

"Oh, I don't know," he said, "it's getting late. Perhaps I had better not come in now."

"The tea will be waiting," said his brother, holding his arm lightly as he rang.

"Horribly dark for my walk back afterwards," grumbled Uncle Luke. "Really dangerous place all along there by the cliff. No business to be out at night. Ought to be at home."

"Tea ready, Liza?" said George Vine, as the door was opened, and the pleasant glow from the hall shone upon them in a way that, in spite of his assumed cynicism, looked tempting and attractive to Uncle Luke.

"Miss Louise hasn't rung for the urn yet, sir."

"Hah! that will do. Give me your hat, Luke."

"Bah! nonsense! Think I can't hang up my own hat now."

George Vine smiled, and he shook his head at his brother with a good-humoured smile as he let him follow his own bent.

"That's right. Come along. Louy dear, I've brought Uncle Luke up to tea. All dark? Liza, bring the lamp."

Liza had passed through the baize-covered door which separated the domestic offices from the rest of the house, and did not hear the order.

"Louy? Louy dear!"

"Oh! I don't mind the dark," said Uncle Luke. "Here, why don't the girl let in some air these hot nights?" he continued, as he crossed the room towards the big embayment, with its stained glass heraldic device.

Crack! Crackle!

"Hullo here! broken glass under one's feet," said Luke Vine, with a chuckle. "This comes of having plenty of servants to keep your place clean."

"Glass?"

"Yes, glass. Can't you hear it?" snarled Uncle Luke, who, as he found his brother resume his old demeanour, relapsed into his own. "There! glass—glass—glass crunching into your Turkey carpet."

As he spoke he gave his foot a stamp, with the result that at each movement there was a sharp cracking sound.

"It's very strange. Louise!"

"Oh!"

A low, piteous moan.

"What's that?" cried Uncle Luke sharply.

George Vine stood in the darkness paralysed with dread.

Some fresh trouble had befallen his house—some new horror assailed him; and his hand wandered vaguely about in search of support as a terrible feeling of sickness came over him, and he muttered hoarsely, "Louise! my child! my child!"

Luke Vine was alarmed, but he did not lose his presence of mind.

"Margaret—a fit," he said to himself, as, turning quickly, his foot kicked against another portion of the lamp-globe, which tinkled loudly as it fell to pieces.

He brushed by his brother, hurrying out into the hall, to return directly bearing the lamp which stood on a bracket, and holding it high above his head as he stepped carefully across the carpet.

"There! there!" whispered George Vine, pointing towards the fireplace, where he could see a figure lying athwart the hearthrug.

Then, as Luke held the light higher, George Vine seemed to recover his own presence of mind, and going down on one knee as he bent over, he turned the face of the prostrate man to the light.

"Duncan Leslie!" cried Uncle Luke excitedly, as he quickly set down the lamp and knelt on the other side. "Where's Louy? The poor boy's in a fit."

"No, no," whispered his brother hoarsely. "Look! look!"

Luke drew in a quick, hissing breath.

"Call Louy," he said sharply. "Tell her to bring something to bind up his head—scissors, sponge, and water."

"Has he been struck down?" faltered George Vine, with the thought of his old friend rushing to his mind.

"No, no. Don't talk. Here, your handkerchief, man," said Luke, who was far the more matter-of-fact. "A fall. Head cut. Slip on the cliff, I suppose, and he has come here for help."

Taking the handkerchief passed to him by his brother, he rapidly bound it round the place where a deep cut was slowly swelling, while George Vine dragged sharply at the bell and then ran to the door and called, "Louise! Louise."

Liza came hurrying into the hall, round-eyed and startled.

"Where is your mistress?" cried Vine.

"Miss Louise, sir? Isn't she there?"

"No. Go up to her room and fetch her. Perhaps she is with Miss Vine."

"I'll go and see, sir," said the girl wonderingly; and she ran up-stairs.

"Help me to get him on the sofa, George," said Uncle Luke; and together they placed the injured man with his head resting on a cushion.

"Now, then, I think we had better have Knatchbull. He must have had a nasty fall. Send your girl; or no, I'll go myself."

"No," said Leslie feebly; "don't go."

"Ah! that's better. You heard what I said?"

"Yes; what you said."

It was a feeble whisper, and as the brothers bent over the injured man, they could see that he was gazing wildly at them with a face full of horror and despair.

"I'll trot down and fetch Knatchbull," whispered Uncle Luke.

"No."

The negative came from Leslie, who was lying back with his eyes closed, and it was so decisive that the brothers paused.

At that moment Liza entered the room.

"She isn't up-stairs, sir. Ow!"

The girl had caught sight of Leslie's ghastly face, and she uttered an excited howl and thrust her fingers into her ears.

Leslie looked up at George Vine vacantly for a moment, and then light seemed to come to his clouded brain, and his lips moved.

"Say it again," said Vine, bending over him.

"Send—her—away," whispered the injured man.

"Yes, of course. Liza, go and wait—no; get a basin of water, sponge, and towel, and bring them when I ring."

The girl looked at him wildly, but she had not heard his words; and Uncle Luke put an end to the difficulty by taking her arm and leading her into the hall.

"Go and get sponge and basin. Mr Leslie has fallen and hurt himself. Now, don't be stupid. You needn't cry."

The girl snatched her arm away and ran through the baize door.

"Just like a woman!" muttered Uncle Luke as he went back; "no use when she's wanted. Well, how is he?"

Leslie heard the whisper, and turned his eyes upon him with a look of recognition.

"Better," he whispered. "Faint—water."

George Vine opened the cellarette, and gave him a little brandy, whose reviving power proved wonderful. But after heaving a deep sigh, he lay back with his forehead puckered.

"Hadn't I better fetch Knatchbull, my lad?" said Uncle Luke gruffly, but with a kindly ring in his voice. "Cut on the back of your head. He'd soon patch it up."

"No. Better soon," said Leslie in a low voice. "Let me think."

"Be on the look-out," whispered Uncle Luke to his brother. "Better not let Louise come in."

Leslie's eyes opened quickly, and he gazed from one to the other.

"Better not let her see you till you are better," said Uncle Luke, taking the injured man into their confidence.

A piteous sigh escaped from Leslie, and he closed his eyes tightly.

"Poor boy!" said Uncle Luke, "he must have had an ugly fall. Missed his way in the dark, I suppose. George, you'll have to keep him here to-night."

"Yes, yes, of course," said George Vine uneasily, for his ears were on the strain to catch his child's step, and her absence troubled him.

All at once Leslie made an effort to sit up, but a giddy sensation overcame him, and he sank back, staring at them wildly.

"Don't be alarmed," said George Vine kindly. "You are faint. That's better."

Leslie lay still for a few moments, and then made a fresh effort to sit up. This time it was with more success.

"Give him a little more brandy," whispered Uncle Luke.

"No; he is feverish, and it may do harm. Yes," he said to Leslie, as the injured man grasped his arm, "you want to tell us how you fell down."

"No," said Leslie quickly, but in a faint voice, "I did not fall. It was in the struggle."

"Struggle?" cried Uncle Luke. "Were you attacked?"

Leslie nodded quickly.

"Where? Along the road?"

"No," said Leslie hoarsely; "here."

"Here!" exclaimed the brothers in a breath; and then they exchanged glances, each silently saying to the other, "The poor fellow is wandering."

"There," said Leslie, "I can think clearly now. It all seemed like a dream. You must know, Mr Vine. I must tell you," he added piteously. "Mr Vine, what do you propose doing?"

"Hush!" said George Vine, laying his hand upon the young man's shoulder, "you are ill and excited now. Don't talk at present. Wait a little while."

"Wait?" cried Leslie, growing more excited. "You do not know what you are saying. How long have I been lying here? What time is it?"

"About nine," said Vine kindly. "Come, come, lie back for a few moments. We'll get some cold water, and bathe your temples."

"Man, you will drive me mad," cried Leslie. "Do you not—no, you have not understood yet. Louise—Miss Vine!"

George Vine staggered as if he had been struck, and his brother caught his arm as he stood there gasping, with his hand to his throat.

"What do you mean?" cried Uncle Luke sternly.

"I am sick and faint," said Leslie, pressing his hands to his brow, as if unable to think clearly. "I remember now. I came in to ask about Mr Van Heldre, and a stranger was with Miss Vine. I tried to stop him—till you returned. We struggled, and he threw me. I recollect no more."

"You're mad!" said Uncle Luke savagely. "Where is Louise?"

His brother caught hold of the back of a chair to support himself, and his lips moved, but no sound came.

"Yes, I can recollect it all clearly now," panted Leslie. "You must know!"

And he told them all.

They heard him in silence, devouring his words, and from time to time exchanging a hurried glance of inquiry.

"Bah!" ejaculated Uncle Luke, as the young man finished. Then, changing his manner, "Yes, of course. There, lie back, my lad, and tell us again after you've had a rest."

"No, no," cried Leslie passionately, "it is wasting time. She was forced to go. She was imploring him to let her stay when I came in, and they must be miles away by now. For heaven's sake do something before it is too late."

"A Frenchman?" said Uncle Luke eagerly.

"Yes; he spoke to her in French, as well as in English."

"And did my niece speak to him in French?"

"No; she was appealing to him in English, but he spoke at times in French."

"Do you hear this, George? Has Louise a French friend?"

"No," cried her father angrily, "it is a delusion."

"I would to heaven it were," groaned Leslie, "I would to heaven it were!"

George Vine crossed to the bell-pull, and rang sharply, repeating the summons before Liza had time to enter the room.

"When did you see your mistress last?" he said sharply.

"When I took in the lamp, sir."

Liza knew no more, and was dismissed, after staring wonderingly from one to the other.

"Stop!" cried Uncle Luke. "Go up and ask Miss Vine if my niece has been with her."

Liza returned with an answer in the negative; and as soon as they were alone, Leslie said piteously:

"You disbelieve me."

"No, no, my lad," said Uncle Luke; "we only think you are suffering from your fall, and distrust what you have, or think you have, seen."

"Think!" said Leslie angrily.

"You say some man was with my niece—a Frenchman."

"Yes; I am bound to tell you for her sake."

"It is not true," cried George Vine fiercely.

They looked at him with surprise, for he seemed transformed from the quiet, mild-looking man to one full of fierce determination as he stood there with flashing eyes.

"My daughter knew no Frenchman."

Leslie winced as if stung, for the mental suggestion was there that Louise had hoodwinked her father, and kept up some clandestine engagement with this man.

"Do you hear me?" cried Vine angrily. "I say it is not true. Mr Leslie, you have been deceived, or you have deceived yourself. I beg your pardon. You are not yourself. It seems useless to discuss this further. Luke, all this seems mysterious because we have no key to the puzzle. Pish! puzzle! it is no puzzle. Louise will be here shortly. Mr Leslie, be advised; lie still for an hour, and then my brother and I will see you home. Or, better still, let me offer you the hospitality of my house for the night."

The cloud that had obscured Leslie's brain had now passed away, leaving his mental perceptions clear, while his temper was exacerbated by the injury he had received, and by the agony he suffered on account of Louise. In place of lying back, he rose from the couch and faced George Vine, with his lips quivering and an angry look in his eyes.

"Look," he said hoarsely, "I am weak and helpless. If I take a few steps I shall reel and fall, or I would do what I tried to do before, act on her behalf. You mock at my words. You, her father, and stand there wasting time; valuable time, which, if used now, might save that poor girl from a life of misery. Do you hear me? I tell you she has gone—fled with that man. He forced her to go with threats. Do you not hear me?"

"Leslie, my lad," said Uncle Luke, "be calm, be calm."

"You are as mad and blind as he!" cried Leslie. "Heaven help me, and I am as weak as a child."

He strode towards the door, and proved the truth of his words, for he tottered, and would have fallen but for Uncle Luke.

"There, you see," he cried fiercely, "I can do nothing, and you, uncle and father, stand blind to the misery and disgrace which threaten you."

"Silence!" cried George Vine; "I can hear no more."

He turned upon Leslie fiercely.

"Your words, sir, are an insult to me, an insult to my child. I tell you I can hear no more. What you say is false. My daughter could not leave my house like this. Go, sir, before I say words which I may afterwards repent, and—and—"

"George, man, what is it?" cried Uncle Luke, as his brother's words trailed off, and he stopped suddenly in the agitated walk he had kept up to and fro while he was addressing Leslie.

There was no answer to the agitated question, for George Vine was gazing down at something beside the table, lying half covered by the dragged-aside cloth.

Whatever it was it seemed to act as a spell upon the old naturalist, whose eyes were fixed, and his whole aspect that of one suddenly fixed by some cataleptic attack.

"What is it? Are you ill?" cried Uncle Luke excitedly as he stepped forward. "Hah, a letter!"

He was in the act of stooping to pick it up, but his act seemed to rouse his brother from his lethargy, and he caught him by the arm.

"No, no," he whispered; and slowly put his brother back, he stooped and stretched out his hand to pick up the half-hidden letter.

They could see that his hand trembled violently, and the others stood watching every act, for the feeling was strong upon both that the letter which Vine raised and held at arm's length contained the explanation needed.

George Vine held the letter toward the shaded lamp, and then passed his left hand over his eyes, and uttered a hoarse sigh, which seemed as if torn from his heart.

"I—I can't read," he whispered—"eyes dim to-night, Luke. Read."

Uncle Luke's hand trembled now as he took the missive, and slowly tore open the envelope; but as he drew out the letter it was snatched from his hands by his brother, who held it beneath the lamp-shade and bent down to read.

He raised himself lip quickly and passed his hand across his eyes, as if to sweep away some film which hindered his reading, and the silence in that room was terrible as he bent down again.

A strong pang of suffering shot through Duncan Leslie as he saw the old man's lips quivering, while he read in a slow, laborious way the few lines contained in the note, and then, after once more making an effort to clear his vision, he seemed to read it again.

"George—brother—why don't you speak?" said Uncle Luke at last. George Vine looked up in a curiously dazed way. "Speak?" he said huskily; "speak?"

"Yes; is that from Louise?" He bowed his head in assent.

"Well, what does she say, man? What does it mean?" George Vine looked in his brother's eyes once more—the same curiously dazed look as if he hardly comprehended what was taking place. Then he slowly placed the note in Luke's hands.

There was no slow, dazed manner here, for the old cynic was full of excitement, and he seemed to read the note at a glance.

"Gone!" he said. "Then she has gone?"

"Yes," said his brother slowly; "she has gone."

"But this man, George—this man, Leslie. Don't stare, man, speak."

"What do you wish me to say, sir?" said Leslie, hoarsely.

"Who was he? What was he like?"

"I could not see his face, he kept it averted. I can tell you no more, sir. I tried to force him to stay till Mr Vine's return, as I before told you, and you saw the result."

"A Frenchman?"

"He spoke in French."

"George, had you any suspicion of this?"

"No."

"You never heard a word?"

"I never heard a word."

"But it must have been going on for long enough. And you knew nothing whatever?"

"And I knew nothing whatever," said George Vine, his words coming slowly and in a voice which sounded perfectly calm.

"Then you know from what black cloud this bolt has come?"

"I—I know nothing," said Vine, in the same slow, strange way.

"Then I can tell you," cried Luke, furiously. "If ever man nursed viper at his fireside, you have done this, for it to sting you to the heart. Hah!" he cried, as the door opened and Aunt Marguerite sailed in, drawing herself up in her most dignified way, as she saw who was present, and then ignoring both strangers, she turned to her brother.

"What is the meaning of these inquiries?" she said sternly. "Where is Louise?"

"Ask your own heart, woman," cried Uncle Luke, furiously. "Gone— gone with some wretched French impostor of your introduction here."

Aunt Marguerite gazed at him angrily.

"I say where is Louise?" she cried excitedly.

"Mr Leslie," said George Vine, after drawing a long breath, his sister's shrill voice having seemed to rouse him; "you will forgive a weak, trusting old man for what he said just now?"

"Forgive you, Mr Vine!"

"I was sure of it. Thank you. I am very weak."

"But Louise?" cried Aunt Marguerite.

"Read her letter. Gone!" cried Uncle Luke fiercely, as he thrust the note in the old woman's face.

"Gone!" said George Vine, staring straight before him with the curious look in his eyes intensified, as was the stony aspect of his face. "Gone! Thank God—thank God!"

"George, what are you saying?" cried Uncle Luke excitedly.

"I say thank God that my dear wife was not spared to me to see the blow that has fallen upon my home to-night."

Brother, sister, Duncan Leslie stood gazing at the silvered head, dimly-seen above the shaded lamp. The face was unnaturally calm and strange; and weak as he was, Duncan Leslie sprang forward. He had seen what was coming, and strove vainly to save the stricken man, for George Vine seemed to have been robbed of all power, and fell with a weary moan senseless at his brother's feet.

Chapter Fifty One
Broken with the Fight

"Better stop where you are, man," said Uncle Luke.

"No," said Leslie, as he stood gazing straight before him, as one who tries to see right on into the future along the vista of one's own life.

"But it is nearly one o'clock. Sit down there and get a nap."

"No. I must go home," said Leslie slowly, and in a measured way, as if he were trying to frame his sentences correctly in carrying on the conversation while thinking of something else.

"Well, you are your own master."

"Yes," said Leslie. "How is he?"

"Calmer now. He was half mad when he came to, and Knatchbull was afraid of brain fever, but he gave him something to quiet the excitement. Better have given you something too."

"What are you going to do?" said Leslie, turning upon the old man suddenly, and with a wild look in his eyes.

"Do nothing rashly," said Uncle Luke.

"But time is flying, man."

"Yes. Always is," said Uncle Luke, coolly, as he watched his companion with half-closed eyes.

"But—"

"That will do. I cannot discuss the matter to-night, my head's in a whirl. Do nothing rashly is a capital maxim."

"But we are wasting time."

"Look here, young man," said Uncle Luke, taking Leslie by the lappet of the coat. "I'm not blind. I daresay I can see as far through you as most people can. I am an old man, and at my time of life I can be calm and dispassionate, and look on at things judicially."

"Judicially?" said Leslie bitterly; "any child could judge here."

"Oh, no," said the old man; "big child as you are, you can't."

"What do you mean?"

"That you are only a big stupid boy, Duncan Leslie."

"Don't insult me in my misery, man."

"Not I, my lad. I like you too well. I am only playing the surgeon, hurting you to do you good. Look here, Leslie, you are in pain, and you are madly jealous."

"Jealous!" cried the young man scornfully, "of whom?"

"My niece—that man—both of them."

"Not I. Angry with myself, that's all, for being an idiot."

"And because you are angry with yourself, you want to follow and rend that man who knocked you down; and because you call yourself an idiot for being deeply attached to Louise, you are chafing to go after her, and at any cost bring her back to throw yourself at her feet, and say, 'Don't have him, have me.'"

"Ah!" cried Leslie furiously. "There, you are an old man and licensed."

"Yes, I am the licensed master of our family, Leslie, and I always speak my mind."

"Yes, you sit there talking, when your duty is to follow and bring your niece back from disgrace," cried the young man furiously.

"Thank you for teaching me my duty, my lad. You have had so much more experience than I. All the same, Duncan Leslie, my hot-headed Scot, I am going to sleep on it, and that's what I advise you to do. There; be reasonable, man. You know you are not in a condition for dispassionate judgment."

"I tell you any one could judge this case," said Leslie hotly.

"And I tell you, my dear boy, that it would have puzzled Solomon."

"Will you go in search of her directly?"

"Will I go out in the dark, and run my head against the first granite wall? No, my boy, I will not."

"Then I must."

"What, run your head against a wall?"

"Bah!"

"Look here, Leslie, I've watched you, my lad, for long enough past. I saw you take a fancy to my darling niece Louy; and I felt as if I should like to come behind and pitch you off the cliff. Then I grew more reasonable, for I found by careful watching that you were not such a bad fellow after all, and what was worse, it seemed to me that, in spite of her aunt's teaching, Louy was growing up into a clever sensible girl, with only one weakness, and that a disposition to think a little of you."

Leslie made an angry gesture.

"Come, my lad, I'll speak plainly and put aside all cynical nonsense. Answer me this: How long have you known my niece?"

"What does that matter?"

"Much. I'll tell you. About a year, and at a distance. And yet you presume, in your hot-headed, mad, and passionate way, to sit in judgment upon her and to treat my advice with contempt."

"You cannot see it all as I do."

"Thank goodness!" muttered Uncle Luke.

"You did not witness what I did to-night."

"No. I wish I had been there."

"I wish you had," said Leslie, bitterly.

"Now you are growing wild again. Be calm, and listen. Now I say you have known our child a few months at a distance, and you presume to judge her. I have known her ever since she was the little pink baby which I held in these hands, and saw smile up in my face. I have known her as the patient, loving, unwearying daughter, the forbearing niece to her eccentric aunt— and uncle, my lad. You ought to have said that. I have known her these twenty years as the gentle sister who fought hard to make a sensible man of my unfortunate nephew. Moreover, I have known her in every phase, and while I have openly snarled and sneered at her, I have in my heart groaned and said to myself, what a different life might mine have been had I known and won the love of such a woman as that."

"Oh, yes, I grant all that," said Leslie, hurriedly; "but there was the vein of natural sin within."

"Natural nonsense, sir!" cried Uncle Luke, angrily. "How dare you! A holier, truer woman never breathed."

"Till that scoundrel got hold of her and cursed her life," groaned Leslie. "Yes, trample on me. I suppose I deserve it."

"Yes," cried the old man, "if only for daring to judge her, when I tell you, that with all my knowledge of her and her life, I dare not. No, my lad, I'm going to sleep on it, and in the morning see if I can't find out the end of the thread, of the clue which will lead us to the truth."

"There is no need," groaned Leslie. "We know the truth."

"And don't even know who this man is. No, indeed, we do not know the truth. All right, my lad, I can read your looks. I'm a trusting, blind, old fool, am I? Very well, jealous pate but I warn you, I'm right and you're wrong."

"Would to heaven I were! I'd give ten years of my life that it could be proved."

"Give ten years of nonsense. How generous people are at making gifts of the impossible! But look here, Duncan Leslie, I'll have you on your knees for this when we have found out the mystery; and what looks so black and blind is as simple as A B C. Trash! bolt with some French adventurer? Our Louy! Rubbish, sir! Everything will be proved by-and-by. She couldn't do it. Loves her poor old father too well. There, once more take my advice, lie down there and have a nap, and set your brain to work in the sunshine not in the dark."

"No."

"Going?"

"Yes, I am going. Good night, sir."

"Good night, you great stupid, obstinate, thick-headed Scotchman," growled Uncle Luke, as he let him out, and stood listening to his retiring steps. "I hope you'll slip over the cliff and half kill yourself. There's something about Duncan Leslie that I like after all," he muttered, as he went back to the dining-room, and after a few minutes' thought, went softly up to his brother's chamber, to find him sleeping heavily from the effect of the sedative given by the doctor.

Uncle Luke stole out quietly, shook his fist at his sister's door, and then went below to sit for a while studying Louise's letter, before lying down to think, and dropping off to sleep with the comforting self-assurance that all would come right in the end.

Meanwhile Duncan Leslie had gone down the steep descent, and made his way to the foot of the cliff path, up which, with brain and heart throbbing painfully, he slowly tramped. The night was dull and cold, and as he ascended toward Luke Vine's rough cottage, he thought of how often he had met Louise on her way up there to her uncle's; and how he had often remained at a distance watching from his own place up at the mine the graceful form in its simple attire, and the sweet, earnest face, whose eyes used once to meet his so kindly, and with so trusting a look.

"Sleep on it!" he said, as he recalled the old man's words. "No sleep will ever make me think differently. I must have been mad—I must have been mad."

He had reached the old man's cottage, and almost unconsciously stopped and seated himself on the rough block of granite which was Uncle Luke's favourite spot when the sun shone.

Before him lay the sea spreading out deep and black, and as impenetrable as to its mysteries as the blank future he sought to fathom, and as he looked ahead, the sea, the sky, the future all seemed to grow more black.

His had been a busy life; school, where he had been ambitious to excel; college, where he had worked still more hard for honours, with the intention of studying afterwards for the bar; but fate had directed his steps in another direction, and through an uncle's wish and suggestions, backed by the fact that he held the mine, Duncan Leslie found himself, when he should have been eating his dinners at the Temple, partaking of them in the far West of England, with a better appetite, and perhaps with better prospects from a monetary point of view.

His had been so busy a life that the love-idleness complaint of a young man was long in getting a hold, but when it did seize him, the malady was the more intense.

He sat there upon the old, worn piece of granite, making no effort to go farther, but letting his memory drift back to those halcyon days when he had first begun to know that he possessed a heart disposed to turn from its ordinary force-pump work to the playing of a sentimental part such as had stranded him where he was, desolate and despairing, a wreck with his future for ever spoiled.

He argued on like that, sometimes with tender recollections of happy days when he had gone back home from some encounter, with accelerated pulses and a sensation of hope and joy altogether new.

He dwelt upon one particular day when he had come down from the mine to find Louise seated where he then was; and as he recalled the whole scene, he uttered a groan of misery, and swept it away by the interposition of that of the previous evening; and here his wrath once more grew hot against the man who had come between them, for without vanity he could feel that Louise had turned toward him at one time, and that after a while the memory of the trouble which had come upon them would have grown more faint, and then she would once more have listened to his suit.

But for that man—He ground his teeth as he recalled Aunt Marguerite's hints and smiles; the allusions to the member of the French *haute noblesse*; their own connection with the blue blood of Gaul, and his own plebeian descent in Aunt Marguerite's eyes. And now that the French noble had arrived, how noble he was in presence and in act! Stealing clandestinely into the house during the father's absence, forcing the woman he professed to love into obedience by threats, till she knelt at his feet as one who pleads for mercy.

"And this is the *haute noblesse!*" cried Leslie, with a mocking laugh. "Thank heaven, I am only a commoner after all."

He sat trying to compress his head with his hands, for it ached as if it would split apart. The cool night breeze came off the sea, moist and bearing refreshment on its wings; but Duncan Leslie found no comfort in the deep draught he drank. His head burned, his heart felt on fire, and he gazed straight before him into the blackness trying to make out his path. What should he do? Act like a man and cast her off as unworthy of a second thought, or rouse himself to the manly and forgiving part of seeking her out, dragging her from this scoundrel, and placing her back in her stricken father's arms?

It was a hard fight, fought through the darkness of that terrible night, as he sat there on the rock, with the wind sighing from off the sea, and the dull, low boom of the waves as they broke at the foot of the cliff far below.

It was a fight between love and despair, between love and hate, between the spirit of a true, honest man who loved once in his life, and the cruel spirits of suspicion, jealousy, and malignity, which tortured him with their suggestions of Louise's love for one who had tempted her to leave her father's home.

As the day approached the air grew colder, but Duncan Leslie's brow still burned, and his heart seemed on fire. The darkness grew more dense, and the fight still raged.

What should he do? The worse side of his fallible human nature was growing the stronger; and as he felt himself yielding, the greater grew his misery and despair.

"My darling!" he groaned aloud, "I loved you—I loved you with all my heart."

He started, alarmed at his own words, and gazed wildly round as if expecting that some one might have heard. But he was quite alone, and all was so dark right away ahead. Was there no such thing as hope for one stricken as he? The answer to his wild, mental appeal seemed to come from the far east, for he suddenly became conscious of a pale, pearly light which came from far down where sea and sky were mingled to the sight. That pale, soft light grew and grew, seeming to slowly suffuse the eastern sky, till all at once he caught sight of a fiery flake far on high, of another, and another, till the whole arc of heaven was ablaze with splendour from which the sea borrowed glistening dyes.

And as he gazed the tears rose to his eyes, and seemed to quench the burning fire in his brain, as a fragment which he had read floated through his memory:—

"Joy cometh in the morning—joy cometh in the morning."

Could joy ever again come to such a one as he? He asked the question half-bitterly, as he confessed that the dense blackness had passed away, and that hope might still rise upon his life, as he now saw that glittering orb of light rise slowly above the sea, and transform the glorious world with its golden touch.

"No, no," he groaned, as he rose to go on at last to his desolate home. "I am broken with the fight. I can do no more, and there is no cure for such a blow as mine. Where could I look for help?"

"Yes; there," he said resignedly. "I'll bear it like a man," and as he turned he rested his hand upon the rough granite wall to gaze down the path, and drew back with a curious catching of the breath, as he saw the light garments of a woman pass a great patch of the black shaley rock.

Madelaine Van Heldre was hurrying up the cliff path towards where he had passed those long hours of despair.

Chapter Fifty Two
A Strange Summons

Madelaine Van Heldre closed the book and sat by the little table gazing towards her father's bed.

Since he had been sufficiently recovered she had taken her father's task, and read the chapter and prayers night and morning in his bedroom—a little later on this night, for George Vine had stayed longer than usual.

Madelaine sat looking across the chamber at where her father lay back on his pillow with his eyes closed, and her mother seated by the bed's head holding his hand, the hand she had kept in hers during the time she knelt and ever since she had risen from her knees.

Incongruous thoughts come at the best of times, and, with the tears standing in her eyes, Madelaine thought of her many encounters with Aunt Marguerite, and of the spiteful words. She did not see why a Dutchman should not be as good as a Frenchman, but all the same there was a little of the love of descent in her heart, and as she gazed at the fine manly countenance on the pillow, with its closely-cut grey hair displaying the broad forehead, and at the clipped and pointed beard and moustache, turned quite white, she thought to herself that if Aunt Marguerite could see her father now she would not dare to argue about his descent.

The veil of tears grew thicker in her eyes, and one great drop fell with a faint *pat* upon the cover of the prayer-book as she thought of the past, and that the love in her heart would not be divided now. It would be all for those before her, and help to make their path happier to the end.

"'And forgive us our trespasses as we forgive them that trespass against us,'" said Van Heldre thoughtfully. "Grand words, wife—grand words. Hah! I feel wonderfully better to-night. George Vine acted like a tonic. I've lain here hours thinking that our old companionship would end, but I feel at rest now. His manner seemed to say that the old brotherly feeling would grow stronger, and that the past was to be forgotten."

He stopped short, and a faint flush came into his pale checks, for on opening his eyes they had encountered the wistful look in Madelaine's. He had not thought of her sufferings, but now with a rush came the memories of her confession to him of her love for Harry, on that day when she had asked him to take the young man into his office.

"My darling!" he said softly as he held out his arms; and the next moment she was folded sobbing to his heart.

No word was spoken till the nightly parting; no word could have been spoken that would have been more touching and soothing than that embrace.

Then "Good night!" and Madelaine sought the solitude of her own chamber, to sit by the open window listening to the faintly heard beat of the waves upon the bar at the mouth of the harbour. Her spirit was low, and the hidden sorrow that she had fought hard to keep down all through the past trouble had its way for the time, till, at last wearied out, she closed her window and went to bed. Still for long enough it was not to sleep, but to think of the old boy-and-girl days, when Harry was merely thoughtless, and the better part of his nature, his frank kindness and generosity, had impressed her so that she had grown to love him with increasing years, and in spite of his follies that love still lay hidden in her heart.

"And always will be there," she said softly, as she felt that the terrible end had been the expiation, and with the thought that in the future Harry Vine, forgiven, purified—the Harry of the past—would always be now the frank, manly youth she idealised, she dropped off to sleep—a deep, restful slumber, from which she started with the impression full upon her that she had only just closed her eyes. There must have been some noise to awaken her, and she sat up listening, to see that it was day.

"Yes? Did any one knock?" she said aloud, for the terror was upon her now, one which had often haunted her during the unnerving past days—that her father had been taken worse.

All silent.

Then a sharp pattering noise at her window, as if some one had thrown up some shot or pebbles. She hurried out of bed, and ran to the window to peep through the slit beside the blind, to see below in the street Liza, the Vines' maid, staring up.

"Louise—ill? or Mr Vine?" thought Madelaine, as she quickly unfastened and opened the window.

"Yes, Liza. Quick! what is it?"

"Oh, miss, I've been awake all night, and, not knowing what to do, and so I come on."

"Is Mr Vine ill?"

"No, 'm; Miss Louise."

"Ill? I'll come on at once."

"No, miss; gone," whispered Liza hoarsely; and in a blundering way she whispered all she knew.

"I'll come on and see Mr Vine," said Madelaine hastily, and Liza ran back while her blundering narrative, hastily delivered, had naturally a confusing effect upon one just awakened from sleep.

Louise gone, Mr Leslie found bleeding, Mr Vine sitting alone in his room busy over the molluscs in his aquaria! It seemed impossible. Aunt Marguerite hysterical. Everything so strange.

No mention had been made of Uncle Luke by the girl, nor yet of Leslie's departure.

"Am I still dreaming?" Madelaine asked herself as she hastily dressed, "or has some fresh terrible disaster come upon us?"

"Upon *us*," she said, for the two families seemed so drawn together that one could not suffer without thrilling the other's nerves.

"Louise gone! It is impossible!"

She said that again and again, trying all the while to be cool and think out what were best to be done. She felt that it would be better not to alarm her father by waking him at that early hour, and that she could not arouse her mother without his knowing.

She was not long in deciding.

Uncle Luke had shown during the troubles of the past how he could throw aside his eccentricity and become a useful, helpful counsellor, and it seemed the natural thing to send a message up to him, and beg him to come down. Better still, to save time, she would run up there first.

Liza had not been gone a quarter of an hour before Madelaine was well on her way, after stealing silently out of the house.

The effort to be calm was unavailing, for a wild fit of excitement was growing upon her, and instead of walking up the steep cliff path, she nearly ran.

Would Uncle Luke be at home? He was eccentric and strange in his habits, and perhaps by that time out and away fishing off some rocky point.

She scanned the rough pier by the harbour, and shuddered as the scene of that horrible night came back. But there was no sign of the old man there, neither could she see him farther away, and feeling hopeful that perhaps she would be in time to catch him, she hurried on, panting. As she turned a corner of the devious way, and came in sight of the cottage, with Leslie's house and mine chimney far up at the back, she stopped short, breathless and wondering, and with a strange reaction at work, suggesting that after all, this was some mythical invention on the part of the servant, for there, stood Duncan Leslie outside Uncle Luke's cottage awaiting her coming.

Chapter Fifty Three
Her Defender

"Miss Van Heldre!"

"Mr Leslie! That woman came to our house this morning to say—Oh, then, it is not true?"

"Yes," he said slowly; "it is all true."

"True that—that you were hurt—that—that—Oh, pray speak! Louise—Louise!"

"Gone!" said Leslie hoarsely, and, sick at heart and suffering, he leaned back against the wall.

"Gone? Louise gone? Gone where?"

Leslie shook his head mournfully, and gazed out to sea.

"Why do you not speak?" cried Madelaine. "Can you not see how your silence troubles me? Mr Leslie, what is the matter? You were found hurt—and Louise—gone! What does it mean?"

He shook his head again.

"Where is Mr Luke Vine?" cried Madelaine, turning from him quickly.

"At the house."

"Then I have come here for nothing," she cried agitatedly. "Mr Leslie, pray, pray speak."

He looked at her wistfully for a few moments.

"What am I to say?" he said at last.

"Tell me—everything."

He still remained retentive; but there was a grim smile full of pity and contempt for himself upon his lips as he said coldly—

"Monsieur de Ligny has been."

"Monsieur de Ligny?"

"The French gentleman, the member of the *haute noblesse* who was to marry Miss Vine."

Madelaine looked at him wonderingly.

"Mr Leslie," she said, laying her hand upon his arm, and believing that she saw delirium in his eyes, consequent upon his injury, her late experience having made her prone to anticipate such a sequel. "Mr Leslie, do you know what you are saying?"

"Yes, perfectly," he said slowly. "Monsieur de Ligny the French gentleman of whom Miss Marguerite so often talked to me, came last night, while Mr Vine was at your father's, and he was persuading Louise to go with him, when I interfered and said she should not go till her father returned."

"Yes?—well?" said Madelaine, watching him keenly.

"Well, there was a struggle, and I got the worst of it. That's all."

"That is not all!" cried Madelaine angrily. "Louise, what did she say?"

"Begged him—not to press her to go," he said slowly and unwillingly, as if the words were being dragged out of him.

"Yes?"

"That is all," he said, still in the same slow, half-dreamy way. "I heard no more. When I came to, the Vines were helping me, and—"

"Louise?"

"Louise was gone."

"Mr Leslie," said Madelaine gently, as in a gentle, sympathetic way she laid her hand upon his arm. "You seem to have been a good deal hurt. I will not press you to speak. I'm afraid you hardly know what you say. This cannot be true."

"Would to Heaven it were not!" he cried passionately. "You think I am wandering. No, no, no; I wish I could convince myself that it was. She is gone—gone?"

"Gone? Louise gone? It cannot be."

"Yes," he said bitterly; "it is true. I suppose when a man once gets a strong hold upon a woman's heart she is ready to be his slave, and obey him to the end. I don't know. I never won a woman's love."

"His slave—obey—but who—who is this man?"

"Monsieur de Ligny, I suppose. The French nobleman."

Madelaine made a gesticulation with her hands, as if throwing the idea aside.

"No, no, no," she said impatiently. "It is impossible, de Ligny — de Ligny? You mean that Louise Vine, my dear friend, my sister, was under the influence of some French gentleman unknown to me?"

"Unknown to her father too," said Leslie bitterly, "for he reviled me when I told him."

"I cannot do that," said Madelaine firmly; "but I tell you it is not true." ˙

"As you will," he said coldly; "but I saw her at his knees last night."

"De Ligny — a French gentleman?"

"Yes."

"I tell you it is impossible."

"But she has gone," said Leslie coldly.

"Gone? I cannot believe it. Mr Vine? He knows where?"

Leslie shook his head mournfully. "Some secret love," he said.

"Yes; Louise did nurture a secret love," said Madelaine scornfully, "and for a man unworthy of her."

"Poor girl!"

"Yes; poor girl! Shame upon you, Duncan Leslie! She may be gone for some good reason, but it is not as you say and think. Louise, my sister, my poor suffering friend, carry on a clandestine intrigue with some French gentleman? It is not true."

"You forget her aunt — the influence she has had upon the poor girl."

"I forget everything but the fact that Louise loved you, Duncan Leslie, with all her heart."

"No, no," he cried with an angry start.

"I tell you it is true," cried Madelaine. "De Ligny? — a French nobleman? Absurd! A fable invented by that poor old half-crazy woman to irritate you and scare you away."

"I might have thought so once, but after what I saw last night —"

"A jealous man surrounds all he sees with a glamour of his own," cried Madelaine. "Oh where is your reason? How could you be so ready to believe it of the truest, sweetest girl that ever lived!"

"But —"

"Don't speak to me," cried Madelaine, angrily. "You know what that old woman is with her wild ideas about birth and position. Louise, deceive her father—cheat me—elope! Duncan Leslie, I did not think you could be so weak."

"I will not fight against your reproaches," he said, coldly.

"No. Come with me. Let us go down and see Uncle Luke."

"But you really think—" he faltered.

"I really think?" she cried with her eyes flashing. "Am I to lose all faith and confidence in you? I tell you what you say is impossible."

Her words, her manner, sent flashes of hope through the darkness that haunted Leslie's spirit, and without a word he turned and walked hurriedly down with her toward the town till they reached the seat in the sheltered niche, where he had had that memorable conversation with Aunt Marguerite.

There he paused, and pointed to the seat.

"She sat there with me," he said bitterly, "and poured her poison into my ears till under a smiling face I felt half mad. I have tried so hard to free myself from their effect, but it has been hard—so hard. And last night—"

"You saw something which shook your confidence in Louise for the moment, but that is all gone now."

"I think—I—"

"I vouch for my friend's truth," said Madelaine proudly. "I tell you that you have been deceived."

Leslie was ghastly pale, and the injury he had received and the mental agony of the past night made him look ten years older, as he drew in a catching breath, and then said hastily—

"Come on, and let us find out the truth."

Chapter Fifty Four
Aunt Marguerite Finds a Friend

Uncle Luke met them at the garden gate, and took Madelaine's hands in his, drawing her towards him, and kissing her brow.

"Tell me, Mr Luke," she said quickly, "it is not true?"

"What he says is not true, Maddy," said the old man quietly.

"But Louise?"

"Gone, my dear. Left here last night. No," he continued, "we know nothing except what her letter says. She has good reason for what she has done, no doubt, but it is very terrible for my brother."

Madelaine darted a triumphant look at Leslie.

"Look here, my child," said Uncle Luke, "I am uneasy about George. Go in and see him, and if he says anything about Louy, you will side with me and take her part?"

"Do you think I could believe it of Louise?" said Madelaine, proudly.

Uncle Luke held her hand in his, patting it softly the while.

"No," he said, "I don't think you could. Go to him now. Tell him it will all be cleared up some day, perhaps sooner than we think."

"Where is he?" she said quietly.

"In his study."

She nodded her head with a confident look in her eyes, crossed the hall, and tapped at the study door.

"Come in."

The words bidding her to enter were uttered in so calm and matter-of-fact a way, that Madelaine felt startled, and Uncle Luke's words, "I am uneasy about George," came with a meaning they had not before possessed.

She entered and stopped short, for there before the open window, close to which was a glass vessel full of water, stood George Vine, busy with a microscope, by whose help he was carefully examining the structure of some minute organism, while one busy hand made notes upon a sheet of paper at his side.

His face was from her, and he was so intent upon his task that he did not turn his head.

"Breakfast?" he said quietly. "I shall not have any. Yes," he added hastily; "bring a cup of tea, Liza—no sugar, and a little dry toast."

A pang shot through Madelaine's heart, and for a few moments she strove vainly to speak.

"It is I, Mr Vine," she faltered at last in a voice she did not recognise as her own.

"Madelaine, my child!" he cried, starting and dropping his pencil as he turned. "How rude of me! so intent upon this beautiful preparation of mine here. Very, very glad to see you," he continued, as he took her hands in his. "How is your father this morning?"

"I—I have not seen him this morning," faltered Madelaine, as she gazed upon the pale, lined face before her, to note the change thereon, in spite of the unnatural calmness which the old man had assumed, "I—I came on at once, as soon as I had heard."

He drew in a long breath as if her words were cutting him. Then raising her hands to his lips he kissed them tenderly.

"Like you," he said gently, "like you, my child. There, I have nothing to say, nothing to hear."

"But dear Mr Vine," cried Madelaine, as she clung to him, and her tears fell fast, "I am sure—"

He smiled down at her lovingly, as he kissed her hand again.

"Spare me, my child," he said. "Never mention her name again."

"But, Mr Vine—"

"Hush, my dear! It is like you," he whispered. "Good, gentle and forgiving. Let the whole of the past be dead."

"But, Mr Vine, Louise—"

"Hush!" he said sternly. "There, come and sit down and talk to me. No, my dear, I had a nasty fainting attack last night, but I am not mad. You need not fear that. Let the past be dead, my child. Will you bring me some tea?"

Madelaine's face worked pitifully, as she clung to him for a few moments, and then as he resumed his place at the table, she felt that the hour was not opportune, and turned to leave the room.

At that moment there was a gentle tap at the door.

"See who that is, my child," said Vine, quietly; "and do not let me be interrupted. If it is my mother, ask him not to speak to me to-day."

Madelaine crossed quickly to the old man's side, bent over him, and kissed his forehead, before going to the door, to find Uncle Luke waiting.

"Maddy," he whispered, "tell my brother that Margaret wants to see her. Ask him if she may come in."

Madelaine took the message, and felt startled at the angry look in the old man's face.

"No," he cried peremptorily. "I could not bear to see her Maddy, my darling, you are almost like a daughter to me. You know all. Tell her from me to keep to her room, I could not trust myself to see her now."

Madelaine clung to him, with the tears gathering in her eyes. From her earliest childhood she had looked up to him as to some near relative, who had treated her as he had treated his own child—her companion, Louise; and now as she saw the agony depicted in his face, she suffered with him, and in her womanly sympathy her tears still fell fast.

"But, dear Mr Vine," she whispered, "forgive me for pressing you at such a time, but there is some mistake."

"Yes," he said sternly; and she shivered as she saw how he was changed, and heard how harsh his voice had grown. "Yes, Madelaine, my child, there has been a terrible mistake made by a weak, infatuated man, who acted on impulse, and never let his mind stray from the hobby he pursued—mine."

"Mr Vine!"

"Hush, my child, I know. You are going to say words that I could not bear to hear now. I know what I have done, I see it too plainly now. In my desire to play a kindly brother's part, I let that of a father lapse, and my punishment has come—doubly come."

"If you would only let me speak," she whispered.

"Not now—not now. I want strength first to bear my punishment, to bear it patiently as a man."

It seemed to be no time to argue and plead her friend's cause, but she still clung to him.

"Bear with me," he whispered. "I am not going to reproach you for what you have said. There, my dear, leave me now."

Madelaine sighed, and with her brow wrinkled by the lines of care, she stood watching the old man as he bent over his microscope once more, and then softly left the room.

"Well?" said Uncle Luke eagerly, as she joined him in the hall. "What does he say?"

"That he will not see her. That he could not trust himself to meet her now."

"Ah!"

Madelaine started, and turned sharply round as a piteous wail fell upon her ears.

Aunt Marguerite was standing within the dining-room door, wringing her hands, and looking wild and strange.

"I can't bear it," she cried. "I can't bear it. He thinks it is my fault. Go in and tell him, Luke. He must not, he shall not blame me."

"Let him alone for a bit," said Luke, coldly.

"But he thinks it is all my fault. I want to tell him—I want him to know that it is no fault of mine."

"Can't convince him of impossibilities," said Uncle Luke coldly.

"And you think it, too!" cried Aunt Marguerite passionately. "I will see him."

"Go up to your room and wait a bit. That's the best advice I can give you."

"But George will—"

"Say things to you that will be rather startling to your vain old brain, Madge, if you force yourself upon him, and I'll take care that you do not."

"And this is my brother!" cried Aunt Marguerite indignantly.

"Uncle Luke is right," said Madelaine quietly, speaking of him as in the old girlish days. "If I might advise you, Miss Vine."

"Miss Margue—No, no," cried the old lady, hastily. "Miss Vine; yes, Miss Vine. You will help me, my child. I want my brother to know that it is not my fault."

The old contemptuous manner was gone, and she caught Madelaine's arm and pressed it spasmodically with her bony fingers.

"You could not go to Mr Vine at a worse time," said Madelaine. "He is suffering acutely."

"But if you come with me," whispered Aunt Marguerite. "Oh, my child, I have been very, very hard to you, but you will not turn and trample on me now I am down."

"I will help you all I can," said Madelaine gravely; "and I am helping you now in advising you to wait."

"I—I thought it was for the best," sobbed the old lady piteously. "Hush! don't speak to me aloud. Mr Leslie may hear."

She glanced sharply round to where Leslie was standing with his back to them, gazing moodily from the window.

"Yes; Mr Leslie may hear," said Madelaine sadly; and then in spite of the long years of dislike engendered by Aunt Marguerite's treatment, she felt her heart stirred by pity for the lonely, suffering old creature upon whose head was being visited the sufferings of the stricken household.

"Let me go with you to your room," she said gently.

"No, no!" cried Aunt Marguerite, with a frightened look. "You hate me too, and you will join the others in condemning me. Let me go to my brother now."

"It would be madness," said Madelaine gently; and she tried to take the old woman's hand, but at that last word, Aunt Marguerite started from her, and stretched out her hands to keep her off.

"Don't say that," she said in a low voice, and with a quick glance at her brother and at Leslie, to see if they had heard. Then catching Madelaine's hand, she whispered, "It is such a horrible word. Luke said it to me before you came. He said I must be mad, and George might hear it and think so too."

"Let me go with you to your room."

"But—but," faltered the old woman, with her lips quivering, and a wildly appealing look in her eyes, "you—you don't think that?"

"No," said Madelaine, quietly; "I do not think that."

Aunt Marguerite uttered a sigh full of relief.

"I only think," continued Madelaine in her matter-of-fact, straightforward way, "that you have been very vain, prejudiced, and foolish, but I am wrong to reproach you now."

"No, no," whispered Aunt Marguerite clinging to her, and looking at her in an abject, piteous way; "you are quite right, my dear. Come with me, talk to me, my child. I deserve what you say, and—and I feel so lonely now."

She glanced again at her brother and Leslie, and her grasp of Madelaine's arm grew painful.

"Yes," she whispered, with an excited look; "you are right, I must not go to him now. Don't let them think that of me. I know—I've been very—very foolish, but don't—don't let them think that."

She drew Madelaine toward the door, and in pursuance of her helpful rôle, the latter went with her patiently, any resentment which she might have felt toward her old enemy falling away at the pitiful signs of abject misery and dread before her; the reigning idea in the old lady's mind now being that her brothers would nurture some plan to get rid of her, whose result would be one at which she shuddered, as in her heart of hearts she knew that if such extreme measures were taken, her conduct for years would give plenty of excuse.

Chapter Fifty Five
Half Converted

"Well, Leslie," said Uncle Luke, as he stood gazing at the closed door through which the two women had passed, "What do you think of that?"

"Think of that?" said Leslie absently.

"Those two. Deadly enemies grown friends. My sister will be adopting you directly, you miserable low-born Scotch pleb, without a drop of noble French blood in your veins."

"Poor old woman!" said Leslie absently.

"Ah, poor old woman! Margaret and I ought to be shut up together in some private asylum. Well, you have slept on all that?"

"No," said Leslie sadly. "I have not slept."

"You're—well, I won't say what you are—well?"

"Well?" said Leslie, sadly.

"You have come to your senses, I hope."

"Had I lost them?"

"*Pro tem*, young man. And it is a usurpation of our rights. One lunatic family is enough in a town. We're all off our heads, so you had better keep sane."

Leslie remained silently thinking over Madelaine's words.

"Look here," said Uncle Luke. "I have slept upon it, and I am cool."

"What have you learned, sir?"

"Nothing but what I knew last night—at present."

"And what do you propose doing?"

"I propose trying to act as nearly like a quite sensible man as one of my family can."

"And Mr Vine?"

"As much like a lunatic as he can. You had better take his side and leave me alone. He is of your opinion."

"And you remain steadfast in yours?"

"Of course, sir. I've known my niece from a child, as I told you last night; and she could not behave like a weak, foolish, brainless girl, infatuated over some handsome scoundrel."

"But Miss Marguerite—have you questioned her?"

"Might as well question a weather-cock. Knows nothing, or pretends she knows nothing. There, I'm going to start at once and see if I cannot trace her out. While I'm gone I should feel obliged if you would keep an eye on my cottage; one way and another there are quite a couple of pounds' worth of things up yonder which I should not like to have stolen. You may as well come down here too, and see how my brother is going on. Now then, I'll just step down to Van Heldre's and say a word before I start."

"By what train shall you go?"

"Train? Oh, yes, I had almost forgotten trains. Hateful way of travelling, but saves time. Must arrange to be driven over to catch one at mid-day. Come and see me off."

"Yes," said Leslie, "I'll come and see you off. What shall you take with you?"

"Tooth-brush and comb," grunted Uncle Luke. "Dessay I shall find a bit of soap somewhere. Now then, have you anything to say before I go?"

"There is no occasion; we can make our plans as we go up."

"We?"

"Yes; I am going with you."

Uncle Luke smiled.

"I knew you would," he said, quietly chuckling.

"You knew I should? Why did you think that?"

"Because you're only a big boy after all, Duncan, and show how fond you are of Louy at every turn."

"I am not ashamed to own that I loved her," said the young man, bitterly.

"Loved?" said Uncle Luke, quietly. "Wonder what love's like, to make a man such a goose. Don't be a sham, Leslie. You always meant to go. You said to yourself, when you thought ill of the poor girl, you would go after her and try and break the man's neck."

"Not exactly, sir."

"Well, something of the kind. And now Maddy Van Heldre has been giving you a good setting down, and showing you what a weak baby you are—"

"Has Miss Van Heldre—"

"No, Miss Van Heldre has not said a word; but your face is as plain as a newspaper, and I know what Maddy would say if anybody attacked my niece. There, what's the use of talking? You will say with your lips that Louise is nothing to you now, and that you believe she has eloped with some French scoundrel."

Leslie bit his lip and made an impatient gesture.

"While that noble countenance of yours, of which you are so proud, has painted upon it love and trust and hope, and all the big-boy nonsense in which young men indulge when they think they are only a half, which needs another half to make them complete."

"I am not going to quarrel with you," said Leslie, flushing angrily, all the same.

"No, my boy, you are not. You are coming with me, my unfortunate young hemisphere, to try and find that other half to which you shall some day be joined to make you a complete little world of trouble of your own, to roll slowly up the hill of life, hang on the top for a few hours, and then roll rapidly down. There, we have wasted time enough in talking, and I'll hold off. Thank ye, though, Leslie, you're a good fellow after all."

He held out his hand, which Leslie slowly took, and Uncle Luke was shaking it warmly as Madelaine re-entered the room.

"Well," said the old man grimly, "have you put the baby to bed?"

"Uncle Luke!" said Madelaine imploringly, "pray be serious and help us."

"Serious, my girl! I was never so serious before. I only called Margaret a baby. So she is in intellect, and a very troublesome and mischievous one. Glad to see though that my little matter-of-fact Dutch doll has got the better of her. Why, Maddy, henceforth, you'll be able to lead her with a silken string."

"Uncle Luke dear—Louise," said Madelaine imploringly.

"Ah, to be sure, yes, Louise," said the old man with his eyes twinkling mischievously. "Circumstances alter cases. Now look here, you two. I'm only an old man, and of course thoroughly in your confidence. Sort of respectable go-between. Why shouldn't I try and make you two happy?"

Leslie bit his lip, and Madelaine gave the old man an imploring look; but in a mocking way he went on:

"Now suppose I say to you two, what can be better than for you to join hands—partners for life, you know, and—"

"Mr Luke Vine!" cried Leslie sternly, "setting aside the insult to me, is this gentlemanly to annoy Miss Van Heldre with your mocking, ill-chosen jokes?"

"Hark at the hot-blooded Scotchman, Maddy; and look here how pleasantly and patiently my little Dutch doll takes it, bless her!"

He put his arm round Madelaine and held her to his side.

"Why, what are you ruffling up for in that fashion? Only a few minutes ago you were swearing that you hated Louy, and that you gave her up to the French nobleman—French nobleman, Maddy!—and I offer you a pleasant anodyne for your sore heart—and a very pleasant anodyne too, eh, Maddy? Ah, don't—don't cry—hang it all, girl, don't. I do hate to see a woman with wet eyes. Now what have you got to sob about?"

"Is this helping us?"

"No. But I'm going to, little one. I was obliged to stick something into Leslie, here. He is such a humbug. Swore he didn't care a bit for Louy now, and that he believed everything that was bad of her, and yet look at his face."

"It is impossible to quarrel with you, sir," said Leslie, with the look of a human mastiff.

"Of course it is," cried Uncle Luke. "Well, Maddy, I've converted him. He sees now that it's a puzzle we don't understand, and he is coming up to town with me to solve the problem."

"I knew he would," cried Madelaine warmly. "Mr Leslie, I am very, very glad."

"Of course, you are; and as soon as I bring Louy back, and all is cleared, Leslie shall come and congratulate us. D'ye hear, Leslie? I am going to marry Madelaine. Marry her and stop up in the churchyard afterwards," he said with a grim smile full of piteous sadness.

"Uncle Luke!"

"Well, it's right enough, my dear. At my time of life hardly worth while to make two journeys up to the churchyard. So you could leave me there and go back, and take possession of my estate."

"Louise."

"Ah, yes. I mustn't forget Louise," said the old man. "Let's see—about Margaret. Leave her all right?"

"Yes; she is more calm now."

"Did you question her, and get to know anything?"

"Nothing."

"Humph!" ejaculated the old man. "Close as an oyster, or else she doesn't know anything."

"That is what I think," said Madelaine eagerly.

"Ah, well, we are only wasting time," said Uncle Luke testily. "So now, Leslie, business. First thing we have to do is to go up to London. No; first thing, Maddy, is to run on to your house, and tell them what we are going to do. You'll have to stay here, my dear, and look after those two. Comfort George all you can; drive him with that silken thread rein of yours, and keep a good tight curb over Margaret. There, you'll manage them."

"Yes. Tell them at home I think it better to stay here now," said Madelaine earnestly. "You will send me every scrap of news?"

"Leslie and I are going to secure the wire and run ourselves in telegrams. Ready, Miner?"

"Yes."

"Then come on."

Madelaine caught Leslie's extended hand, and leaned towards him.

"My life on it," she whispered. "Louise is true."

He wrung her hand and hurried away.

"Good-bye, Uncle Luke. Be happy about them here; and, mind, we are dying for news."

"Ah! yes; I know," he said testily; and he walked away—turned back, and caught Madelaine to his breast. "Good-bye, Dutch doll. God bless you, my darling," he said huskily. "If I could only bring back poor Harry too!"

Madelaine stood wiping the tears from her eyes as the old man hurried off after Leslie, but she wiped another tear away as well, one which rested on her cheek, a big salt tear that ought almost to have been a fossil globule of crystallised water and salt. It was the first Uncle Luke had shed for fifty years.

Chapter Fifty Six
Hard Test

"Harry, dear Harry!" said Louise, as they stood together in a shabbily furnished room in one of the streets off Tottenham Court Road, "I feel at times as if it would drive me mad. Pray, pray let me write!"

"Not yet, I tell you; not yet," he said angrily. "Wait till we are across the Channel, and then you shall."

"But—"

"Louy!" he half shouted at her, "have some patience."

"Patience, dear? Think of our father's agony of mind. He loves us."

"Then the joy of finding we are both alive and well must compensate for what he suffers now."

"But you do not realise what must be thought of me."

"Oh, yes, I do," he said bitterly; "but you do not realise what would be thought of me, if it were known that I was alive. I shiver every time I meet a policeman. Can't you see how I am placed?"

"Yes—yes," said Louise wearily; "but at times I can only think of our father—of Madelaine—of Uncle Luke."

"Hush?" he cried with an irritable stamp of the foot. "Have patience. Once we are on the Continent I shall feel as if I could breathe; but this wretched dilatory way of getting money worries me to death."

"Then why not sell the jewels, and let us go?"

"That's talking like a woman again. It's very easy to talk about selling the jewels, and it is easy to sell them if you go to some blackguard who will take advantage of your needs, and give you next to nothing for them. But, as Pradelle says—"

"Pradelle!" ejaculated Louise, with a look of dislike crossing her face.

"Yes, Pradelle. That's right, speak ill of the only friend we have. Why, we owe everything to him. What could we have done? Where could we have gone if it had not been for him, and my finding out where he was through asking at the old meeting-place?"

"I do not like Mr Pradelle," said Louise firmly. "Then you ought to," said Harry, as he walked up and down the room like some caged animal. "As he says, if you go to sell the things at a respectable place they'll ask all manner of questions that it is not convenient to answer, and we must not risk detection by doing that."

"Risk detection?" said Louise, clasping her hands about one knee as she gazed straight before her.

"The people here are as suspicious of us as can be, and the landlady seems ready to ask questions every time we meet on the stairs."

"Yes," said Louise in a sad, weary way; "she is always asking questions."

"But you do not answer them?"

"I—I hardly know what I have said, Harry. She is so pertinacious."

"We must leave here," said the young man excitedly. "Why don't Pradelle come?"

"Do you expect him to-night?"

"Expect him? Yes. I have only half-a-crown left, and he has your gold chain to pledge, he is to bring the money to-night. I expected him before."

"Harry, dear."

"Well?"

"Do you think Mr Pradelle is trustworthy?"

"As trustworthy as most people," said the young man carelessly. "Yes, of course. He is obliged to be."

"But could you not pledge the things yourself instead of trusting him?"

"No," he cried, with an impatient stamp. "You know how I tried, and how the assistant began to question and stare at me, till I snatched the thing out of his hands and hurried out of the shop. I'd sooner beg than try to do it again."

Louise was silent for a few moments, and sat gazing thoughtfully before her.

"Let me write, Harry, telling everything, and asking my father to send us money."

"Send for the police at once. There, open the windows, and call the first one up that you see pass. It will be the shortest way."

"But I am sure, dear—"

"Once more, so am I. At the present moment I am free. Let me have my liberty to begin life over again honestly, repentantly, and with the earnest desire to redeem the past. Will you let me have that?"

"Of course—of course, dear."

"Then say no more to me about communicating with home."

Louise was silent gain, beaten once more by her brother's arguments in her desire to see him redeem the past.

"Harry," she said at last, after her brother had been standing with his cheek pressed against the window pane, looking down the street in search of the expected visitor.

"Well?"

"Has it ever occurred to you that Mr Pradelle is trying to keep us here?"

"Absurd!"

"No; I feel sure it is so, and that he does not want us to go away. Let me take my bracelets and necklet to one of those places where they buy jewellery or lend money."

"You?"

"Yes. Why not?"

"Are you mad?"

"No. Why should I not sell what is my own?"

"Can you not understand?" cried Harry, whose voice sounded harsh from the mental irritation which had given him the look of one in constant dread of arrest.

"No, dear, I cannot. I want to help you. I want to get away from here—to remove you from the influence of this man, so that we may, if it must be so, get abroad and then set them at rest."

"Now you are bringing that up again," he cried angrily.

"I must, Harry, I must. I have been too weak as it is; but in the excitement of all that trouble I seemed to be influenced by you in all I did."

"There, there, little sis," he said more gently. "I ought not to speak so crossly, but I am always on thorns, held back as I am for want of a few paltry pounds."

"Then let me go and dispose of these things."

"It is impossible."

"No, dear, you think of the degradation I should not be ashamed. We have made a false step, Harry, but if we must go on, let me do what I can to help you. Let me go."

"But the beggarly disgrace. You don't know what you are going to undertake."

She looked at him with her frank, clear eyes.

"I am going to help you. There can be no disgrace in disposing of these trinkets for you to escape."

"Ah! at last!" cried Harry, leaving the window to hurry to the door, regardless of the look of dislike which came into his sister's face.

"Is that Mr Pradelle?" she said shrinkingly.

"Yes, at last. No, Louy, I'm bad enough, but I'm not going to send you to the pawnbroker's while I stop hiding here, and it's all right now."

"Ah, Harry! Day, Miss Louy," said Pradelle, entering, very fashionably dressed, and with a rose in his buttonhole. "Nice weather, isn't it?"

"Look here, Vic," cried Harry, catching him by the arm. "How much did you get?"

"*Get*?"

"Yes; for the chain?"

"Oh, for the chain," said Pradelle, who kept his eyes fixed on Louise. "Nothing, old fellow."

"Nothing?"

"Haven't taken it to the right place, yet."

"And you promised to. Look here, what do you mean?"

"What do I mean? Well, I like that. Hear him, Miss Louy? What a fellow he is! Here have I got him into decent apartments, where he is safe as the bank, when if he had depended upon himself he would have taken you to some slum where you would have been stopped and the police have found you out."

"You promised to pledge those things for me."

"Of course I did, and so I will. Why, if you had been left to yourself, who would have taken you in without a reference?"

"Never mind that," said Harry, so angrily that Louise rose, went to his side, and laid her hand upon his arm. "If you don't want to help me, say so."

"If I don't want to help you! Why, look here, Miss Louy, I appeal to you. Haven't I helped him again and again? Haven't I lent him money, and acted as a friend should?"

"Why haven't you pledged that chain?" said Harry.

"Because people are so suspicious, and I was afraid. There you have the truth."

"I don't believe it," cried Harry, excitedly.

"Well then, don't. Your sister will. If you want me to bring the police on your track, say so."

In a furtive way, he noted Harry's start of dread, and went on.

"Take the chain or a watch yourself, and if the pawnbroker is suspicious, he'll either detain it till you can give a good account of how you came by it, or send for a policeman to follow you to you lodgings."

"But I am quite penniless!" cried Harry.

"Then why didn't you say so, old fellow? Long as I've got a pound you're welcome to it, and always were. I'm not a fine-weather friend, you know that. There you are, two halves. That'll keep you going for a week."

"But I don't want to keep borrowing of you," said Harry. "We have enough to do what I want. A sovereign will do little more than pay for these lodgings."

"Enough for a day or two, old fellow, and do, for goodness' sake, have a little more faith in a man you have proved."

"I have faith in you, Vic, and I'm very grateful; but this existence maddens me. I want enough to get us across the Channel. I must and will go."

"Right into the arms of those who are searching for you. What a baby you are, Harry! Do you want to be told again that every boat which starts for the Continent will be watched?"

Harry made a despairing gesture, and his haggard countenance told plainly of the agony he suffered.

"My dear Miss Louy," continued Pradelle, "do pray help me to bring him to reason. You must see that you are both safe here, and that it is the wisest thing to wait patiently till the worst of the pursuit is over."

"We do not know that there is any pursuit, Mr Pradelle," said Louise coldly.

"Come, I like that!" cried Pradelle, in an ill-used tone. "I thought I told you that they were searching for you both. If you like to believe that you can leave your home as you did without your people making any search, why you have a right to."

Harry began pacing the room, while Pradelle went on in a low, pleading way.

"Ever since Harry came to me, I thought I had done all that a friend could, but if I can do more, Miss Louy, you've only got to tell me what, and it shall be done."

"You've done your best, Prad," said Harry.

"Yes, but you don't think it. I could go and do all kinds of rash things; but I've been working to throw them off the scent, and I don't think, so far, I've done amiss. You're not taken yet."

Harry drew a long breath and glanced at door and window, as if for a way of escape.

"Come, that's better," cried Pradelle. "Take a more cheerful view of things. You want change, Harry. You've been shut up too much. Have a cigar," he continued, drawing out his case. "No? I beg your pardon, Miss Louy. Oughtn't to ask him to smoke here."

Harry shook his head impatiently.

"Yes; have one, old fellow. They're good. Take two or three; and, look here; go and have a walk up and down for an hour. It's getting dusk now."

Louise gave her brother an excited look, which did not escape Pradelle. "Let's all go," he said. "We might go along the back streets as far as the park. Do you both good."

"No, no," said Harry sharply. "I shall not go out."

"Go together, then," said Pradelle, half mockingly. "I don't want to intrude; but for goodness' sake, man, try and have a little change; it would make life move different, and you'd be more ready to take a friend's advice."

"What advice?"

"To settle down here. London's the best place in the world for hiding yourself."

"Don't talk to me any more, old fellow," said Harry. "I'm out of temper. I can't help it."

"All right, lad. I'll go now; and you get him out, Miss Louy, do. It's the best thing for him."

Harry made an impatient gesture, and threw himself in a chair.

"You shall do as you like, and I'll raise all the money for you that I can," said Pradelle, rising to go; "but take things more coolly. Good-bye, old boy."

"Good-bye," said Harry, shaking hands limply.

"Good-bye," said Pradelle, as Harry turned away to rest his aching head upon his hand.

"Miss Louy!"

He gave his head a jerk towards the door, and Louise rose and followed him.

"Come outside," he whispered. "I want to speak to you."

"Mr Pradelle can say what he has to say here."

"But it's about him."

"Well, Mr Pradelle?"

"Well, Miss Louy, I only wanted to say that some day you'll find out who is your true friend. I want to help you both. I do, on my honour."

"Your honour!" thought Louise.

"Have a little more confidence in a man if you can. I do want to help you. Good-bye."

He held out his hand, and she felt constrained to give him hers, which he held, and, after glancing hastily at Harry, raised to his lips; but the kiss he imprinted was on the yielding air, for the hand was snatched indignantly away.

"You'll know me better by-and-by," said Pradelle; and giving her a peculiar look, he left the room.

Louise stood for a few minutes gazing after him, her brow knit and her eyes thoughtful. Then, going back to where her brother sat with his head resting upon his hand, she laid hers upon his shoulder.

"Harry, dear," she said firmly, "that man is fighting against us."

"Rubbish," he cried impatiently. "You never liked Pradelle."

"Better for you if you had hated him. Harry, he is striving to keep us here."

"Nonsense! Don't talk to me now."

"I must, Harry. You must act, and decisively."

"What do you mean?"

"Either you must raise money at once, and go right from here—"

He looked up sharply.

"No, I do not mean that," she said sadly. "I will not leave you till you are fit to leave; but you must either act as I advise at once, or I shall do what I think best."

"What do you mean?"

"Write to our father to come and help us, for you are too weak and broken down to protect me."

"Louy!" he cried excitedly; "I am not so weak as you think. I will act; I will take your advice."

"And get rid of this Mr Pradelle?"

"Anything you like, Louy, only don't let them know at home—yet, and don't leave me. If you did I should break down at once."

"Then will you be guided by me?"

"Yes."

"And take these jewels yourself and raise money?"

"Yes; but it is too late now."

Louise glanced at the window, and in her ignorance of such matters half felt the truth of his words.

"Then to-morrow you will do as I wish?"

"Yes, to-morrow," he said wearily.

"Put not off until to-morrow—" said Louise softly to herself; and she stood watching her brother as he sat with bended head, weak, broken, and despairing, in the gathering gloom.

Chapter Fifty Seven
An Old Friend—or Enemy?

"Where shall we stay? I'll show you," said Uncle Luke, after giving instructions to the cabman. "My old hotel in Surrey street. Comfortable, motherly woman. No nonsense."

"And what do you propose doing?"

"Let's hear first what you propose," shouted the old man, so as to make his voice heard above the rattle of the cab windows—four-wheelers Jehu's enemies, which lose him many a fare.

"I have nothing to propose," said Leslie sadly; "only to find her."

"And I've given you twenty-four hours to think it out, including last night at Plymouth."

"My head is in a whirl, sir; I am in no condition to think. Pray suggest something."

"Hah! The old folks are useful, then, after all. Well, then, you would like to hear my plans?"

Leslie nodded.

"First, then, there is a good tea, with some meat; and while we are having that I shall send off a messenger."

"To find them?"

"No. Wait."

Leslie had found out that the best way to deal with Uncle Luke was to treat him like a conger-eel, such as they caught among the rocks about Hakemouth. Once hooked, if the fisher dragged at the line, the snaky monster pulled and fought till the line cut into the holder's hands, and sometimes was broken or the hook torn out: whereas, if, instead of pulling, the creature had its head given, it began to swim up rapidly, and placed itself within reach of the gaff. So, in spite of his fretful irritation of mind he allowed the old man to have his own way.

The result was, that before they sat down to their meal at the quiet hotel, Uncle Luke wrote a letter, which was dispatched by special messenger, after which he ate heartily; while Leslie played with a cup of tea and a piece of dry toast.

"Not the way to do work," said Uncle Luke grimly. "Eat, man; eat. Coal and coke to make the human engine get up steam."

Leslie made an effort to obey, but everything seemed distasteful, and he took refuge behind a paper till the waiter entered with a card.

"Hah! yes; show him in," said Uncle Luke. "Here he is, Leslie," he continued.

"Here who is?"

"Parkins."

"Parkins?"

"Sergeant Parkins. You remember?"

Leslie had forgotten the name, but directly after the whole scene of the search for Harry came back as the quiet, decisive-looking detective officer entered the room, nodded shortly to both, and after taking the seat indicated, looked inquiringly at Uncle Luke.

"At your service, sir," he said. "You've brought me some news about that affair down yonder?"

"No," said Uncle Luke. "I have come to see if you can help us in another way;" and he told him the object of his visit.

"Hah!" ejaculated their visitor. "Yes, that's different, sir;" and taking out a note-book, he began to ask question after question on points which seemed to him likely to be useful, till he had gained all the information he thought necessary, when he closed the book with a snap, and buttoned it up in his breast.

"Rather curious fact, sir," he said, looking at both in turn; "but I've been thinking about Hakemouth a good deal this last day or two."

"Why?" asked Uncle Luke shortly.

"I've been away all over the Continent for some time—forgery case, and that Hakemouth business has gone no farther. As soon as I got back, and was free, I wanted something to do, so I said to myself that I'd take it on again, and I have."

"Oh, never mind that now," said Leslie angrily. "Can you help us here?"

"I don't know, sir. I shall try; but I might mention to you that we think we have obtained a clue to the gentleman who escaped."

"Yes, yes," said Leslie impatiently; "but can you help us here?"

"Give me time, sir, and I'll do my best," said the sergeant. "Not an easy task, sir, you know. A needle is hard to find in a bundle of hay, and all the clue you give me is that a lady left your neighbourhood with a French gentleman. Fortunately I did see the lady, and should know her again. Good morning."

"But what are we to do?" said Leslie eagerly.

"You, sir?" said the sergeant quietly, and with a suspicion of contempt in his tone. "Oh, you'd better wait."

"Wait!" cried Leslie in a voice full of suppressed rage.

"And practise patience," muttered the man. "One moment, sir," he said aloud. "You saw this French gentleman?"

"I saw him, but not his face. Mr Vine here told you; the light was overturned."

"But you saw his figure, the man's shape?"

"Yes, of course."

"And you heard his voice?"

"Yes."

"Broken French?"

"Yes."

"Now, sir, just think a moment. I have a slight idea. French name—spoke—"

"We mentioned no name." "One minute, sir. Spoke French—brother's fellow-clerk and intimate—gentleman who went off—been staying at the house—long time in the lady's society. What do you say now to its being this Mr Pradelle?"

Uncle Luke gave the table a thump which made the tea-things rattle, and Leslie started from his seat, gazing wildly at the officer, who smiled rather triumphantly.

"Great Heavens!" faltered Leslie, as if a new light had flashed into his darkened mind.

"Of course, sir, this is only a suggestion," said the sergeant. "It is all new to me; but seems likely."

"No," said Uncle Luke emphatically, "no. She would never have gone off with him."

"Very good, gentlemen. I'll see what I can do at once."

"One moment," said Leslie as he slipped some notes into the man's hand. "You will spare neither time nor money."

"I will not, sir."

"Tell me one thing. What shall you do first?"

"Just the opposite to what you've done, gentlemen," said the officer.

"What do you mean?"

"Go down to Hakemouth by to-night's mail, and work back to town."

"I feel certain," said Leslie, "that he brought her to London to take tickets for France."

"I don't, sir, yet. But even if I did, it's a long bridge from here to Cornwall, and I might find them resting in one of the recesses. You leave it to me, sir. Good-day.

"Humph!" he added as he went out; "plain as a pikestaff. Women are womanly, and I have known instances of a woman sticking to a man for no reason whatever, except that he was a scamp, and sometimes the greater the scamp the tighter the tie. Pradelle's my man, and I think I can put my thumb upon him before long."

"No, Leslie, no. Louy wouldn't look at him. That's not the clue," said Uncle Luke.

Chapter Fifty Eight
The Needle in a Bundle of Hay

A week of anxiety, with the breaks in it of interviews with Sergeant Parkins, who had very little to communicate; but still that little was cogent.

He had been down to Hakemouth, and by careful inquiry had tracked the missing pair to Plymouth, where he had missed them. But, after the fashion of a huntsman, he made long casts round and picked up the clue at Exeter, where a porter remembered them from what sounded like an altercation in a second-class compartment, where a dark young lady was in tears, and the "gent" who was with her said something to her sharply in a foreign tongue. Pressed as to what it was like, he said it sounded as if the gent said "Taisey."

There the sergeant had lost the clue; but he had learned enough to satisfy himself that the fugitives had been making for London, unless they had branched off at Bristol, which was hardly likely.

"Come up to London," said Leslie. "Well, that is what we surmised before we applied to you."

"Exactly, sir; but I have nearly made your surmise a certainty."

"Yes, nearly," said Leslie bitterly.

"We must have time, sir. A hunter does not secure his game by rushing at it. He stalks it."

"Yes," said Uncle Luke in assent, "and of course you must be certain. This is not a criminal matter."

"No, sir, of course not," said the sergeant drily, and with a meaning in his tone which the others did not detect.

"If you are successful in finding their whereabouts, mind that your task ends there. You will give us due notice, and we will see to the rest."

"Certainly, sir; and I have men on the look-out. The bundle of hay is being pretty well tossed over, and some day I hope to see the shine of the needle among the puzzling dry strands. Good morning."

"Is that man a humbug, sir, or in earnest?"

"Earnest," replied Uncle Luke. "He proved that before."

If the occupants of the hotel room, which seemed to Leslie like a prison, could have read Sergeant Parkins' mind as he went away, they would have thought him in deadly earnest.

"Not a criminal case, gentlemen, eh?" he said to himself. "If it is as I think, it is very criminal indeed, and Mr Pradelle will find it so before he is much older. I haven't forgotten the night on Hakemouth Pier, and that poor boy's death, and I shan't feel very happy till I've squared accounts with him, for if he was not the starter of all that trouble I am no judge of men."

Chapter Fifty Nine
Pradelle is Pricked

Seeing more and more that if an alteration was to be made in their present position, the change must come from her urging, Louise attacked her brother soon after breakfast the next morning. She was fully convinced that Pradelle was determined to keep them in London for reasons of his own—reasons the bare thought of which brought an indignant flush into her cheek; and it was evident that he was gaining greater influence over his old companion, who was just now in the stage when it would be easy for one of strong mind to gain the mastery. This being so, Louise determined that hers should be the strong will, not Pradelle's. To this end she took three or four of the most likely of her jewels, making a point of carefully wrapping them up, and dwelling upon the task till she caught her brother's attention.

"What are you doing there?" he said.

"Getting ready some things upon which to raise money."

He uttered an impatient ejaculation.

"Leave them till Pradelle comes."

"No, Harry; either you or I must part with these. Who is it to be?"

"Let Pradelle take them."

"No," she said firmly. "It is time that we acted for ourselves. Will you go, or shall I?"

"But you heard what he said yesterday?"

"Yes, and I do not believe it. Come, Harry, for your own sake, for mine."

"Yes, yes; but wait."

"You forced me into this compromising position to help you escape from England."

"I could not help it."

"I am not blaming you; I only say act, or let me."

He started from his chair, and stood there swayed by the various passions which pervaded his spirit.

"Harry."

"I cannot do it."

"Then let me go."

"No, no, no!" he cried. "I am not so lost to all manly feeling as that. Here, give them to me, and let us get away."

"Yes," she said eagerly, "at once. You will go, Harry, and let us cross to-night."

He nodded his head, and without another word swept the jewels into his pocket, and made towards the door. As he laid his hand upon the lock he turned sharply and came back.

"I'm like a curse to you. Louy," he said kissing her; "but I'm going to try, and you shall guide me now."

She clung to him for a few moments, and then loosened her grasp.

"I shall be ready when you come back," she said. "We can pay these people, and it will be like breathing afresh to get away."

"Yes," he said. "But Pradelle?"

"Is our enemy, Harry. Your evil genius."

"No, no; he has been very kind."

"For his own ends. There, go."

He went off without a word; and after making the few trilling preparations necessary, Louise put on her hat and cloak, and waited impatiently for her brother's return. An hour passed, which seemed like two, and then the blood mounted to her pale cheek, and she crossed towards the door ready to admit her brother, for there was a step upon the stair. She glanced round to see if she had forgotten anything, but there was nothing to do, save to pay the landlady, and then they would be free. She threw open the door as the step paused on the landing, and then she ran back with her lips apart, and a look of repugnance and dread in her eyes.

"Mr Pradelle!"

"Yes, Miss Louy, me it is, and you don't look best pleased to see me."

As she fell back he entered and closed the door.

"My brother is out, Mr Pradelle."

He nodded, and stood smiling at her.

"You can leave any message you wish for him."

"And go? Exactly. Hah! I should like to make you think differently of me, Miss Louy. You know I always loved—"

"Mr Pradelle, I am alone here, and this visit is an intrusion."

"Intrusion? Ah, how hard you do keep on me; but I'm patient as a man can be. What a welcome to one who has come to serve you! I am only your brother's messenger, Miss Louy. He has been and done that business."

"You know?"

"Of course I know. Harry is not so hard upon me as you are. I have seen him, and he sent me on here with a cab. He wants you to join him."

"To join him?"

"Yes, at the station. He says it is not safe to come back here, and you are to join him at the waiting-room."

"He sent that message by you?"

"Yes. It's all nonsense, of course, for I think he has not so much cause to be alarmed. There is a risk, but he magnifies it. You are ready, so let's go on at once."

"Why did not my brother return? There is the landlady to pay."

"He has commissioned me to do that. I am going to see you both off, and if you'll only say a kind word to me, Miss Louy, I don't know but what I'll come with you."

"Did my brother send that message to me, Mr Pradelle?" said Louise, looking at him fixedly.

"Yes, and the cab's waiting at the door."

"It is not true," said Louise firmly.

"What?"

"I say, sir, it is not true. After what has passed between us this morning, my brother would not send such a message by you."

"Well, if ever man had cause to be hurt I have," cried Pradelle. "Why, you'll tell me next that he didn't go out to pawn some of your jewels."

Louise hesitated.

"There, you see, I am right. He has taken quite a scare, and daren't come back. Perhaps you won't believe that. There, come along; we're wasting time."

"It is not true."

"How can you be so foolish! I tell you I was to bring you along, and you must come now. Hush! don't talk, but come."

He caught her hand and drew it through his arm so suddenly that, hesitating between faith and doubt, she made no resistance; and, ready to blame herself now for her want of trust, she was accompanying him towards the door when it was opened quickly, and their way was blocked by Leslie and Uncle Luke.

Pradelle uttered an angry ejaculation, and Louise shrank back speechless, her eyes dilated, her lips apart, and a bewildering sense of confusion robbing her of the power of speech, as she realised to the full her position in the sight of those who had sought her out.

"Then he was right, Leslie," said Uncle Luke slowly, as he looked from his niece to Pradelle, and back.

"Uncle!" she cried in agony, "what are you thinking?"

"That you are my niece—a woman," said the old man coldly; "and that this is Mr Pradelle."

"Uncle, dear uncle, let me explain," cried Louise wildly, as she shivered at the look of contempt cast upon her by Leslie.

"The situation needs no explanation," said Uncle Luke coldly.

"Not a bit," said Pradelle with a half laugh. "Well, gentlemen, what do you want? This lady is under my protection. Please to let us pass."

"Yes," said Uncle Luke in the same coldly sarcastic tone of voice, "you can pass, but, in spite of everything, the lady stays with me."

"No, sir, she goes with me," said Pradelle in a blustering tone. "Come on," he whispered, "for Harry's sake."

"No," said Uncle Luke. "I think we will spare her the pain of seeing you arrested. Mr Pradelle, the police are on the stairs."

Chapter Sixty
The Dog Bites

Pradelle started back as if he had been stung. "Police?" he said. "What do you mean?"

"What a man does mean, you scoundrel, when he talks about them—to give you into custody."

"It is not a criminal offence to elope with a lady," said Pradelle with a malicious look at Leslie, who stood before the door with his hands clenched.

"Uncle!" cried Louise, whose pale face now flamed up as she glanced at Leslie, and saw that he avoided her eyes.

"You wait," he said. "I'll finish with this fellow first, and end by taking you home."

"But, uncle, let me explain."

"You'll hold your tongue!" cried Pradelle sharply. "Think what you are going to do."

"Yes, she can hold her tongue," cried Uncle Luke, "while I settle our little business, sir. Let me see. Ah! I was always sure of that."

Pradelle had thrust himself forward offensively, and in a threatening manner so near that the old man had only to dart out one hand to seize him by the throat; and quick as lightning had drawn an old gold ring from the scarf the young man wore.

"What are you doing?" roared Pradelle, clenching his fist.

"Taking possession of my own. Look here, Leslie, my old signet ring that scoundrel took from a nail over my chimney-piece."

"It's a lie, it's—"

"My crest, and enough by itself to justify the police being called up."

"A trick, a trumped-up charge," cried Pradelle.

"You must prove that at the same time you clear yourself of robbing Van Heldre."

"I—I rob Van Heldre! I swear I never had a shilling of his money."

"You were not coming away when I knocked you down with old Crampton's ruler, eh?"

Pradelle shrank from the upraised stick, and with an involuntary movement clapped his hand to his head.

"See that, Leslie!" cried the old man with a sneering laugh. "Yes, that was the place. I hit as hard as I could."

"A trick, a trap! Bah! I'm not scared by your threats. You stand aside, and let us pass!" cried Pradelle in a loud, bullying way, as he tried to draw Louise toward the door; but she freed herself from his grasp.

"No, no!" she cried widely, as with her ears and eyes on the strain she glanced at window and door, and caught her uncle's arm.

"Hah! glad you have so much good sense left. Nice scoundrel this to choose, my girl!"

"Uncle!" she whispered, "you shall let me explain."

"I don't want to hear any explanation," cried the old man angrily. "I know quite enough. Will you come home with me?"

"Yes!" she cried eagerly, and Leslie drew a breath full of relief. "No!"

The negative came like a cry of agony.

"I cannot, uncle, I cannot."

"I'll see about that," cried the old man. "Now, Leslie, ask Sergeant Parkins to step up here."

"Let him if he dares!" cried Pradelle fiercely.

"Oh, he dares," said Uncle Luke, smiling. "Call him up, for it is a criminal case, after all."

"Stop!" cried Pradelle, as Leslie laid his hand upon the door.

"Yes, stop—pray, pray stop!" cried Louise in agony; and with a wild look of horror, which stung Leslie with jealous rage. "Uncle, you must not do this."

"I'd do it if it was ten times as hard?" cried the old man.

"What shall I say—what shall I do?" moaned Louise.

"Uncle, uncle, pray don't do this. You must not send for the police. Give me time to explain—to set you right."

"Shame upon you!" cried the old man fiercely. "Defending such a scoundrel as that!"

"No, no, uncle, I do not defend this man. Listen to me; you do not know what you are doing."

"Not know what I am doing? Ah!"

He turned from her in disgust, and with a look of agony that thrilled him, she caught Leslie's arm.

"You will listen to me, Mr Leslie. You must not, you shall not, call in the police."

He did not speak for the moment, but stood hesitating as if yielding to her prayer; but the frown deepened upon his brow as he loosened her grasp upon his arm.

"It is for your good," he said coldly, "to save you from a man like that."

"I must speak, I must speak!" cried Louise, and then she uttered a wail of horror, and shrank to her uncle's side.

For as she clung to Leslie, Pradelle, with a bullying look, planted himself before the door to arrest Leslie's progress, and then shrank back as he saw the grim smile of satisfaction upon the young Scot's face.

It was the work of moments, and the action seemed like to that of one of his own country deer hounds, as Leslie dashed at him; there was the dull sound of a heavy blow, and Pradelle went down with a crash in one corner of the room.

"Mr Leslie! Mr Leslie! for pity's sake stay!" cried Louise as she made for the door; but Uncle Luke caught her hand, and retained it as the door swung to.

"Uncle, uncle!" she moaned, "what have you done?"

"Done!" he cried. "You mad, infatuated girl! My duty to my brother and to you."

"All right," said Pradelle, rising slowly. "Let's have in the police then. I can clear myself, I daresay."

"Mr Pradelle, if you have a spark of manliness in you, pray say no more," cried Louise, as, snatching herself free, she ran to him now.

"Oh, I'm not going to be made a scapegoat!" he cried savagely; but as his eyes met hers full of piteous appeal, his whole manner changed, and he caught her hands in his.

"Yes, I will," he whispered. "I'll bear it all. It can't be for long, and I may get off. Promise me—"

He said the rest of the words with his lips close to her ear.

"Your wife?" she faltered as she shrank away and crossed to her uncle. "No, no, no!"

There was a sharp rap on the panel, the door yielded, and Sergeant Parkins stepped in.

"Mr Pradelle, eh?" he said with a grim smile. "Glad to make your acquaintance, sir, at last. You'll come quietly?"

"Oh, yes, I'll come," said Pradelle. "I've got an answer to the charge."

"Of course you have, sir. Glad to hear it. Sorry to put a stop to your pleasant little game. Shall I?"

"There's no need," said Pradelle in answer to a meaning gesticulation toward his wrists. "I know how to behave like a gentleman."

"That's right," said the sergeant, who with a display of delicacy hardly to have been expected in his triumph at having, as he felt, had his prognostication fulfilled, carefully abstained from even glancing at the trembling girl, who stood there with agony and despair painted on her face.

"It ain't too late yet, Miss Louy," said Pradelle crossing toward her.

"Keep that scoundrel back, Parkins," cried Uncle Luke.

"Right sir. Now, Mr Pradelle."

"Stop a moment, can't you?" shouted the prisoner. "Miss Louy—to save him you'll promise, and I'll be dumb. I swear I will."

Louise drew herself up as a piteous sigh escaped her breast.

"No," she said firmly. "I cannot promise that, Uncle dear. I have tried to save him to the last. I can do no more."

"No," said the old man. "You can do no more."

"Mr Pradelle," she cried, "you will not be so base?"

"Will you promise?" he cried.

"No."

"Then—here, just a minute. You, Mr Luke Vine, will you give me a word?"

"No," roared Uncle Luke. "Take him away."

"Then the sergeant here will," cried Pradelle savagely. "Look here, sit down and wait for a few minutes, and you can take Harry Vine as well."

"What do you mean?" cried the sergeant roughly.

"Only that he has gone out to raise the money for a bolt to France, and he'll be back directly. Two birds with one stone."

"Only a trick, sir," said the sergeant grimly. "Now, Mr Pradelle, hansom or four-wheeler? I give you your choice."

"Four-wheeler," said Pradelle, with a sneering laugh.

"My poor brother!" moaned Louise, as she made a clutch at the air, and then sank fainting in her uncle's arms.

"You scoundrel! to speak like that," cried Uncle Luke fiercely.

"Here, what do you mean?" said the sergeant.

"What I said. He wasn't drowned. Harry was too clever for that."

Click—Click!

A pair of handcuffs were fastened to his wrists with marvellous celerity, and he was swung into a chair.

"I don't know whether this is a bit of gammon, Mr Pradelle," said the sergeant sharply, "but I never lose a chance."

He paid not the slightest heed to the other occupants of the room, but ran to the window, threw it open, and called to some one below but only his last words were heard by those inside.

"Quick! first one you see, and I'll give you a shilling."

The sergeant closed the window and crossed to Pradelle.

"If it's a trick it will do you no good. You see, to begin with, it has brought you those."

"I don't care," said Pradelle, glowering at Uncle Luke. "It will take some of the pride out of him, and I shan't go alone."

"It is a trick, sergeant. Take the scoundrel away."

"Must make sure, sir. Sorry for the lady, but she may have been deceived that horrible night, and there's more in this than I can understand. Your friend be long, sir?"

"Mr Leslie? I expected him back with you."

"Mr Leslie went on out into the street, sir. Here, I have it. He has been in hiding down your way, and came up with the lady there."

"That's it, sergeant, you're a 'cute one," said Pradelle with a laugh.

"Who has been in hiding?"

"Your nephew, sir. I see it all now. What a fool I've been."

"My nephew!—Not dead?"

"Harry—brother!" moaned Louise. "I could do no more. Ah!"

Uncle Luke fell a-trembling as he caught the half-insensible girl's hand, gazing wildly at the sergeant the while.

"Look here, Pradelle, no more nonsense. Will he come back?"

"If you keep quiet of course. Not if he sees you."

"Ah!" ejaculated the sergeant, crossing to the door as he heard a step; and hurrying out he returned directly with a constable in uniform.

"Stop!" he said shortly, and he nodded to the prisoner. "Very sorry, Mr Vine, sir," he then said; "but you must stay here for a bit. I am going down to wait outside."

"But Parkins!" cried Uncle Luke, agitatedly, "I cannot. If this is true—that poor boy—no, no, he must not be taken now."

"Too late, sir, to talk like that," cried the sergeant. "You stop there."

"Yes," said Pradelle, as the door closed on the sergeant's retiring figure; "pleasant for you. I always hated you for a sneering old crab. It's your time to feel now."

"Silence, you scoundrel!" cried Uncle Luke, fiercely. "She's coming to."

Uncle Luke was wrong, for Louise only moaned slightly, and then relapsed into insensibility, from which a doctor who was fetched did not seem to recall her, and hour after hour of patient watching followed, but Harry did not return.

"The bird has been scared, sir," said Parkins, entering the room at last. "I can't ask you to stay longer. There's a cab at the door to take the lady to your hotel."

"But are you sure—that—my poor boy lives?"

"Certain, sir, now. I've had his description from the people down below. I shall have him before to-night."

"L'homme propose, mais—"

Five minutes later Louise, quite insensible, was being borne to the hotel; Mr Pradelle, to an establishment offering similar advantages as to bed and board, but with the freedom of ingress and egress left out.

Chapter Sixty One
Diogenes Discovers

"Blame you, my dear? No, no, of course not. Then you knew nothing about it till that night when he came to the window?"

"Oh, no, uncle, dear."

Louise started up excitedly from the couch at the hotel upon which she was lying, while the old man trotted up and down the room.

"Now, now, now," he cried piteously, but with exceeding tenderness as he laid his hand upon her brow, and pressed her back till her head rested on the pillow. "Your head's getting hot again, and the doctor said you were not to be excited in any way. There, let's talk about fishing, or sea-anemones, or something else."

"No, no, uncle dear, I must talk about this, or I shall be worse."

"Then for goodness' sake let's talk about it," he said eagerly, as he took a chair by her side and held her hand.

"You don't blame me then—very much."

"Well, say not very much; but it's not very pleasant to have a nephew who makes one believe he's dead, and a niece who pretends that she has bolted with a scampish Frenchman."

"Uncle, uncle," she cried piteously, "You see it has been a terrible upset for me, while as to your poor father—"

"But, uncle, dear, what could I do?"

"Well, when you were writing, you might have said a little more."

"I wrote what poor Harry forced me to write. What else could I say?"

"You see, it has upset us all so terribly. George—I mean your father—will never forgive you."

"But you do not put yourself in my place, uncle. Think of how Harry was situated; think of his horror of being taken. Indeed, he was half mad."

"No; quite, Louy; and you seem to have caught the complaint."

"I hardly knew what I did. It was like some terrible dream. Harry frightened me then."

"Enough to frighten any one, appearing like a ghost at the window when we believed he was dead."

"I did not mean that, uncle. I mean that he was in a terrible state of fever, and hardly seemed accountable for his actions. I think I should have felt obliged to go with him, even if he had not been so determined."

"Ah! well, you've talked about it quite enough."

"No, no; I must talk about it—about Harry. Oh! uncle! uncle! after all this suffering for him to be taken after all! The horror! the shame! the disgrace! You must—you shall save him!"

"I'm going to try all I know, my darling; but when once you have started the police it's hard work to keep them back."

"How could you do it?"

"How could I do it?" cried the old man testily. "I didn't do it to find him, of course; but to try and run you to earth. How could I know that Harry was alive?"

"But you will not let him be imprisoned. Has he not suffered enough?"

"Not more than he deserves to suffer, my child; but we must stop all that judge and jury business somehow. Get Van Heldre not to prosecute."

"I will go down on my knees to him, and stay at his feet till he promises to spare him—poor foolish boy! But, uncle, what are you going to do? You will not send word down?"

"Not send word? Why, I sent to Madelaine a couple of hours ago, while you lay there insensible."

"You sent?"

"Yes, a long telegram."

"Uncle, what have you done?"

"What I ought to do, my child, and bade her tell her father and mother, and then go and break it gently to my brother."

"Uncle!"

"There, there, my dear, you said I ought to put myself in your place; suppose you put yourself in mine."

"Yes, yes, uncle, dear; I see now; I see."

"Then try and be calm. You know how these difficulties sometimes settle themselves."

"Not such difficulties as these, uncle. Harry! my brother! my poor brother!"

"Louy, my dear child!" said the old man, with a comical look of perplexity in his face, "have some pity on me."

"My dearest uncle," she sobbed, as she drew his face down to hers.

"Yes," he said, kissing her; "that's all very well, and affectionate, and nice; but do look here. You know how I live, and why I live as I do."

"Yes, uncle."

"To save myself from worry and anxiety. I am saving myself from trouble, am I not? Here, let go of my hand, and I'll send off another message to hasten your father up, so as to set me free."

"No, uncle, dear, you will not leave me," she said, with a pleading look in his eyes.

"There you go?" he cried. "I wish you wouldn't have so much faith in me, Louy. You ought to know better; but you always would believe in me."

"Yes, uncle, always," said Louise, as she placed his hand upon her pillow, and her cheek in his palm.

"Well, all I can say is that it's a great nuisance for me. But I'm glad I've found you, my dear, all the same."

"After believing all manner of evil of me, uncle."

"No, no, not quite so bad as that. There; never mind what I thought. I found you out, and just in the nick of time. I say, where the dickens can Leslie be?"

"Mr Leslie!"

Louise raised her face, with an excited look in her eyes.

"Well, why are you looking like that?"

"Tell me, uncle—was he very much hurt, that night?"

"Nearly killed," said the old man grimly, and with a furtive look at his niece.

"Uncle!"

"Well, what of it? He's nothing to you. Good enough sort of fellow, but there are thousands of better men in the world."

Louise's brow grew puckered, and a red spot burned in each of her cheeks.

"Been very good and helped me to find you; paid the detective to hunt you out."

"Uncle! surely you will not let Mr Leslie pay."

"Not let him? I did let him. He has plenty of money, and I have none—handy."

"But, uncle!"

"Oh! it pleased him to pay. I don't know why, though, unless, like all young men, he wanted to make ducks and drakes of his cash."

Louise's brow seemed to grow more contracted.

"Bit of a change for him to run up to town. I suppose that's what made him come," continued the old man; "and now I've found you, I suppose he feels free to go about where he likes. I never liked him."

If Uncle Luke expected his niece to make some reply he was mistaken, for Louise lay back with her eyes half-closed, apparently thinking deeply, till there was a tap at the door.

"Hah! that's Leslie," cried the old man, rising.

"You will come back and tell me if there is any news of Harry, uncle," whispered Louise. Then, with an agonised look up at him as she clung to his hands, "He will not help them?"

"What, to capture that poor boy? No, no. Leslie must feel bitter against the man who struck him down, but not so bad as that."

The knock was repeated before he could free his hands and cross the room.

"Yes, what is it?"

"That gentleman who has been to see you before, sir," said the waiter, in a low voice.

"Not Mr Leslie? He has not returned?"

"No, sir."

"I'll come directly. Where is he?"

"In the coffee-room, sir."

Uncle Luke closed the door and recrossed the room, to where Louise had half risen and was gazing at him wildly.

"News of Harry, uncle?"

"Don't know, my dear."

"You are keeping it from me. That man has taken him, and all this agony of suffering has been in vain."

"I'd give something if Madelaine were here," said Uncle Luke. "No, no; I am not keeping back anything. I don't know anything; I only came back to beg of you to be calm. There, I promise you that you shall know all."

"Even the worst?"

"Even the worst."

Louise sank back, and the old man descended to the coffee-room, to find Parkins impatiently walking up and down.

"Well?"

"No, sir; no luck yet," said that officer.

"What do you mean with your no luck?" cried Uncle Luke angrily. "You don't suppose I want him found?"

"Perhaps not, sir, but I do. I never like to undertake a job without carrying it through, and I feel over this that I have been regularly tricked."

"What's that to me, sir?"

"Nothing, sir; but to a man in my position, with his character as a keen officer at stake; a great deal. Mr Leslie, sir. Has he been back?"

"There, once for all, it's of no use for you to come and question me, Parkins. I engaged you to track out my niece; you have succeeded, and you may draw what I promised you, and five-and-twenty guineas besides for the sharp way in which you carried it out. You have done your task, and I discharge you. I belong to the enemy now."

"Yes, sir; but I have the other job to finish, in which you did not instruct me."

"Look here, Parkins," said Uncle Luke, taking him by the lapel of his coat, "never mind about the other business."

"But I do, sir. Every man has some pride, and mine is to succeed in every job I take in hand."

"Ah! well, look here; you shall succeed. You did your best over it, and we'll consider it was the last act of the drama when my foolish nephew jumped into the sea."

"Oh, no, sir. I—"

"Wait a minute. What a hurry you men are in. Now look here, Parkins. I'm only a poor quiet country person, and I should be sorry for you to think I tried to bribe you; but you've done your duty. Now go no farther in this matter, and I'll sell out stock to a hundred pounds, and you shall transfer it to your name in the bank."

Parkins shook his head and frowned.

"For a nest egg, man."

"No, sir."

"Then look here, my man; this is a painful family scandal, and I don't want it to go any farther, for the sake of those who are suffering. I'll make it two hundred."

"No, sir; no."

"Then two hundred and fifty; all clean money, Parkins."

"Dirty money, sir, you mean," said the sergeant quietly. "Look here, Mr Luke Vine, you are, as you say, a quiet country gentleman, so I won't be angry with you. You'll give me five hundred pounds to stop this business and let your nephew get right away?"

Uncle Luke drew a long breath.

"Five hundred!" he muttered. "Well, it will come out of what I meant to leave him, and I suppose he'll be very glad to give it to escape."

"Do you understand me, sir? You'll give me five hundred pounds to stop this search?"

Uncle Luke drew another long breath.

"You're a dreadful scoundrel, Parkins, and too much for me; but yes, you shall have the money."

"No, sir, I'm not a dreadful scoundrel, or I should make you pay me a thousand pounds."

"I wouldn't pay it—not a penny more than five hundred."

"Yes, you would, sir; you'd pay me a thousand for the sake of that sweet young lady up-stairs. You'd pay me every shilling you've got if I worked you, and in spite of your shabby looks I believe you're pretty warm."

"Never you mind my looks, sir, or my warmth," cried Uncle Luke indignantly. "That matter is settled, then? Five hundred pounds?"

"Thousand would be a nice bit of money for a man like me to have put away against the day I get a crack on the head or am shot by some scoundrel. Nice thing for the wife and my girl. Just about the same age as your niece, sir."

"That will do; that will do," said Uncle Luke stiffly. "The business is settled, then."

"No, sir; not yet. I won't be gruff with you, sir, because your motive's honest, and I'm sorry to have to be hard at a time like this."

"You dog!" snarled Uncle Luke; "you have me down. Go on, worry me. There, out with it. I haven't long to live. Tell me what I am to give you, and you shall have it."

"Your—hand, sir," cried the sergeant; and as it was unwillingly extended he gripped it with tremendous force. "Your hand, sir, for that of a fine, true-hearted English gentleman. No, sir; I'm not to be bought at any price. If I could do it I would, for the sake of that poor broken-hearted girl; but it isn't to be done. I will not insult you, though, by coming here to get information. Good-day, sir; and you can write to me. Good-bye."

He gave Uncle Luke's hand a final wring, and then, with a short nod, left the room.

"Diogenes the second," said Uncle Luke, with a dry, harsh laugh; "and I've beaten Diogenes the first, for he took a lantern to find his honest man, and didn't find him. I have found one without a light."

Chapter Sixty Two
Uncle Luke Turns Prophet

"Why doesn't Leslie come?" said Uncle Luke impatiently, as he rose from a nearly untasted breakfast the next morning to go to the window of his private room in the hotel, and try to look up and down the street. "It's too bad of him. Here, what in the world have I done to be condemned to such a life as this?"

"Life?" he exclaimed after a contemptuous stare at the grimy houses across the street. "Life? I don't call this life! What an existence! Prison would be preferable."

He winced as the word prison occurred to him, and began to think of Harry.

"I can't understand it. Well, he's clever enough at hiding, but it seems very cowardly to leave his sister in the lurch. Thought she was with me, I hope. Confound it, why don't Leslie come?"

"Bah! want of pluck!" he cried, after another glance from the window. "Tide must be about right this week, and the bass playing in that eddy off the point. Could have fished there again now. Never seemed to fancy it when I thought poor Harry was drowned off it. Confound poor Harry! He has always been a nuisance. Now, I wonder whether it would be possible to get communication with him unknown to these police?"

He took a walk up and down the room for a few minutes.

"Now that's where Leslie would be so useful; and he keeps away. Because of Louy, I suppose. Well, what is it? Why have you brought the breakfast back?"

"The young lady said she was coming down, sir," said the chambermaid, who had entered with a tray.

"Stuff and nonsense!" cried the old man angrily. "Go up and tell her she is not to get up till the doctor has seen her, and not then unless he gives her leave."

The maid gave her shoulders a slight shrug, and turned to go, when the door opened, and, looking very pale and hollow-eyed, Louise entered.

Uncle Luke gave his foot an impatient stamp.

"That's right," he cried; "do all you can to make yourself ill, and keep me a prisoner in this black hole. No, no, my darling, I didn't mean that. So you didn't like having your breakfast alone? That'll do; set it down."

The maid left the room, and Louise stood, with her head resting on the old man's breast.

"Now, tell me, uncle, dear," she said in a low voice, and without looking up, "has poor Harry been taken?"

"No."

"Hah!"

A long sigh of relief.

"And Mr Leslie? What does he say?"

"I don't know. He has not been here since he left with me yesterday."

"And he calls himself our friend!" cried Louise, looking up with flushing face. "Uncle, why does he not try to save Harry instead of joining the cowardly pack who are hunting him down?"

"Come, I like that!" cried Uncle Luke. "I'd rather see you in a passion than down as you were last night."

"I—I cannot help it, uncle; I can think of only one thing—Harry."

"And Mr Leslie, and accuse him of hunting Harry down."

"Well, did he not do so? Did he not come with that dreadful man?"

"To try and save you from the French scoundrel with whom he thought you had eloped."

"Oh, hush, uncle, dear. Now tell me, what do you propose doing?"

"Nothing."

"Uncle!"

"That's the best policy. There, my darling, I have done all I could this morning to help the poor boy, but—I must be plain—the police are in hot pursuit, and if I move a step I am certain to be watched. Look there!"

He pointed down into the street.

"That man on the other side is watching this house, I'm sure and if I go away I shall be followed."

"But while we are doing nothing, who knows what may happen, dear?"

"Don't let's imagine things. Harry is clever enough perhaps to get away, and now he knows that we have found out the truth, you will see that he is not long before he writes. I want Leslie now. Depend upon it the poor fellow felt that he would be *de trop*, and has gone straight back home."

Louise uttered a sigh full of relief.

"You scared him away, my dear, and perhaps it's for the best. He's a very stupid fellow, and as obstinate—well, as a Scot."

"But knowing Harry as he does, uncle, and being so much younger than you are, would it not be better if he were working with you? We must try and save poor Harry from that dreadful fate."

"Oh, I don't know," said Uncle Luke slowly. "There, have some tea."

Then rising from his seat, he rang, and going to the writing-table sat down; and while Louise made a miserable pretence of sipping her tea, the old man wrote down something and gave it to the waiter who entered.

"Directly," he said; and the man left the room.

"Yes, on second thoughts you are quite right, my dear."

Louise looked up at him inquiringly.

"So I have telegraphed down to Hakemouth for Leslie to come up directly."

Louise's eyes dilated, and she caught his arm.

"No, no," she whispered, "don't do that. No; you and I will do what is to be done. Don't send to him, uncle, pray."

"Too late, my dear; the deed is done."

Just then the waiter re-entered.

"Telegram, sir."

Louise turned if possible more pale.

"Tut—tut!" whispered Uncle Luke. "It can't be an answer back. Hah! from Madelaine."

"*Your news seems too great to be true. Mr George Vine started for town by the first train this morning. My father regrets his helplessness.*"

"Hah! Come. That's very business-like of George," said the old man. "Louy, my dear, I'm going to turn prophet. All this trouble is certain to turn in the right direction after all. Why, my child?"

She had sunk back in her chair with the cold, dank dew of suffering gathering upon her forehead, and a piteous look of agony in her eyes.

"How can I meet him now!"

The terrible hours of agony that had been hers during the past month had so shattered the poor girl's nerves, that even this meeting seemed more than she could bear, and it called forth all the old man's efforts to convince her that she had nothing to fear, but rather everything to desire.

It was a weary and a painful time though before Louise was set at rest.

She was seated in the darkening room, holding tightly by the old man's hand, as a frightened child might in dread of punishment. As the hours had passed she had been starting at every sound, trembling as the hollow rumbling of cab-wheels came along the street, and when by chance a carriage stopped at the hotel her aspect was pitiable.

"I cannot help it," she whispered. "All through these terrible troubles I seem to have been strong, while now I am so weak and unstrung—uncle, I shall never be myself again."

"Yes, and stronger than ever. Come, little woman, how often have you heard or read of people suffering from nervous reaction and—thank God!" he muttered, as he saw the door softly open behind his niece's chair, and his brother stand in the doorway.

"I did not catch what you said, dear," said Louise feebly, as she lay back with her eyes closed.

Uncle Luke gave his brother a meaning look, and laid his niece's hand back upon her knees.

"No; it's very hard to make one's self heard in this noisy place. I was only saying, my dear, that your nerves have been terribly upset, and that you are suffering from the shock. You feel now afraid to meet your father lest he should reproach you, and you can only think of him as being bitter and angry against you for going away, as you did; but when he thoroughly grasps the situation, and how you acted as you did to save your brother from arrest, and all as it were in the wild excitement of that time, and under pressure—"

"Don't leave me, uncle."

"No, no, my dear. Only going to walk up and down," said the old man as he left his chair. "When he grasps all this, and your dread of Harry's arrest, and that it was all nonsense—there, lie back still, it is more restful so. That's better," he said, kissing her, and drawing away. "When, I say, he fully knows that it was all nonsense due to confounded Aunt Margaret and her noble Frenchmen, and that instead of an elopement with some scoundrel, you were only performing a sisterly duty, he'll take you in his arms—"

Uncle Luke was on the far side of the room now, and in obedience to his signs, and trembling violently, George Vine had gone slowly towards the vacated seat.

"You think he will, uncle, and forgive me?" she faltered, as she lay back still with her eyes closed.

"Think, my darling? I'm sure of it. Yes, he'll take you in his arms."

A quiet sigh.

"And say—"

George Vine sank trembling into the empty chair.

"Forgive me, my child, for ever doubting you."

"Oh, no, uncle."

"And I say, yes; and thank God for giving me my darling back once more."

"Forgive me! Thank God for giving me my darling back once more! Louise!"

"Father!"

A wild, sobbing cry, as the two were locked in each other's arms.

At that moment the door was closed softly, and Uncle Luke stood blowing his nose outside upon the mat.

"Nearly seventy, and sobbing like a child," he muttered softly. "Dear me, what an old fool I am."

Chapter Sixty Three
Leslie Makes an Announcement

It was a week before the London doctor said that Louise Vine might undertake the journey down home; but when it was talked of, she looked up at her father in a troubled way.

"It would be better, my darling," he whispered. "You shrink from going back to the old place. Why should you, where there will be nothing but love and commiseration?"

"It is not that," she said sadly. "Harry!"

"Yes! But we can do no more by staying here."

"Not a bit," said Uncle Luke. "Let's get down to the old sea shore again, Louy. If we stop here much longer I shall die. Harry's safe enough somewhere. Let's go home."

Louise made no more opposition, and it was decided that they should start at once, but the journey had to be deferred on account of business connected with Pradelle's examination.

This was not talked of at the hotel, and Louise remained in ignorance of a great deal of what took place before they were free to depart.

That journey down was full of painful memories for Louise, and it was all she could do to restrain her tears as the train stopped at the station, which was associated in her mind with her brother, and again and again she seemed to see opposite to her, shrinking back in the corner by the window nearest the platform, the wild, haggard eyes and the frightened furtive look at every passenger that entered the carriage.

The journey seemed interminable, and even when Plymouth had been reached, there was still the long slow ride over the great wooden bridges with the gurgling streams far down in the little rock ravines.

"Hah!" said Uncle Luke cheerily, "one begins to breathe now. Look."

He pointed to the shadow of the railway train plainly seen against the woods, for the full round moon was rising slowly.

"This is better than a gas-lamp shadow, eh, and you don't get such a moon as that in town. I've lost count, George. How are the tides this week?"

Vine shook his head.

"No, you never did know anything about the tides, George. Always did get cut off. Be drowned some day, shut in under a cliff; and you can't climb."

They rode on in silence for some time, watching the moonlight effect on the patches of wood in the dark hollows, the rocky hill slopes, and upon one or another of the gaunt deserted engine-houses looking like the towers of ruined churches high up on the hills, here black, and there glittering in the moonlight, as they stood out against she sky.

These traces of the peculiar industry of the district had a peculiar fascination for Louise, who found herself constantly comparing these buildings with one beyond their house overlooking the beautiful bay. There it seemed to stand out bold and picturesque, with the long shaft running snake-like up the steep hillside, to end in the perpendicular monument-like chimney that formed the landmark by which the sailors set vessels' heads for the harbour.

But that place did not seem deserted as these. At any time when she looked she could picture the slowly moving beam of the huge engine, and the feathery plume of grey smoke which floated away on the western breeze. There was a bright look about the place, and always associated with it she seemed to see Duncan Leslie, now looking appealingly in her eyes, now bitter and stern as he looked on her that night when Harry beat him down and they fled, leaving him insensible upon the floor.

What might have been!

That was the theme upon which her busy brain toiled in spite of her efforts to divert the current of thought into another channel. And when in despair she conversed with father or uncle for a few minutes, and silence once more reigned, there still was Duncan Leslie's home, and its owner gazing at her reproachfully.

"Impossible!" she always said to herself; and as often as she said this she felt that there would be a terrible battle with self, for imperceptibly there had grown to be a subtle advocate for Duncan Leslie in her heart.

"But it is impossible," she always said, and emphasised it. "We are disgraced. With such a shadow over our house that could never be; and he doubted, he spoke so cruelly, his eyes flashed such jealous hatred. If he had loved me, he would have trusted, no matter what befel."

But as she said all this to herself, the advocate was busy, and she felt the weakness of her case, but grew more determinedly obstinate all the same.

And the train glided on over the tall scaffold-like bridges, the treetops glistened in the silvery moonlight, and there was a restful feeling of calm in her spirit that she had not known for days.

"No place like home," said Uncle Luke, breaking along silence as they glided away from the last station.

"No place like home," echoed his brother, as he sought for and took his child's hand. "You will stop with us to-night, Luke?"

"Hear him, Louy?" said the old man. "Now, is it likely?"

"But your place will be cheerless and bare to-night."

"Cheerless? Bare! You don't know what you are talking about. If you only knew the longing I have to be once more in my own bed, listening to wind and sea. No, thank you."

"But, uncle, for to-night, do stay."

"Now, that's unkind, Louy, after all the time you've made me be away. Well, I will, as a reward to you for rousing yourself up a bit. One condition though; will you come down to-morrow and talk to me while I fish?"

She remained silent.

"Then I don't stop to-night."

"I will come to-morrow, uncle."

"Then, I'll stop."

The train glided on as they watched in silence now for the lights of the little town. First, the ruddy glow of the great lamp on the cast pier of the harbour appeared; then glittering faintly like stars, there were the various lights of the town rising from the water's edge right up to the high terrace level, with the old granite house—the erst peaceful, calm old home.

The lights glittered brightly, but they looked dim to Louise, seen as they were through a veil of tears, and now, as they rapidly neared, a strange feeling of agitation filled the brain of the returned wanderer.

It was home, but it could never be the same home again. All would be changed. A feeling of separation must arise between her and Madelaine. The two families must live apart, and a dark rift in her life grow wider as the time glided on, till she was farther and farther away from the bright days of youth, with little to look forward to but sorrow and the memory of the shadow hanging over their home.

"Here we are," cried Uncle Luke, as the train glided slowly alongside the platform and then stopped. "Got all your traps? George, give me my stick. Now, then, you first."

The station lamps were burning brightly as Louise gave her father her hand and stepped out. Then she felt blind and troubled with a strange feeling of dread, and for a few moments everything seemed to swim round as a strange singing filled her ears.

Then there was a faint ejaculation, two warm soft arms clasped her, and a well-known voice said, in a loving whisper:

"Louise — sister — at last?"

For one moment the dark veil over her eyes seemed to lift, and like a flash she realised that Madelaine was not in black, and that resting upon a stick there was a pale face which lit up with smiles as its owner clasped her to his breast in turn.

"My dearest child! welcome back. The place is not the same without you."

"Louy, my darling!" in another pleasant voice, as kisses were rained upon her cheek, and there was another suggestion of rain which left its marks warm.

"He would come, George Vine;" and the giver of these last kisses and warm tears did battle for the possession of the returned truant. "Maddy, my dear," she cried reproachfully, and in a loud parenthesis, "let me have one hand. He ought not to have left the house, but he is so determined. He would come."

"Well, Dutch doll, don't I deserve a kiss?" cried old Luke grimly.

"Dear Uncle Luke!"

"Hah, that's better. George, I think I shall go home with the Van Heldres. I'm starving."

"But you can't," cried the lady of that house in dismay; "we are all coming up to you. Ah, Mr Leslie, how *do* you do?"

"Quite well," said that personage quietly; and Madelaine felt Louise's hand close upon hers spasmodically.

"Leslie! you here?" said George Vine eagerly.

"Yes; I came down from town in the same train."

"Too proud to be seen with us, eh?" said Uncle Luke sarcastically, as there was a warm salute from the Van Heldres to one as great a stranger as the Vines.

"I thought it would be more delicate to let you come down alone," said Leslie gravely.

George Vine had by this time got hold of the young man's hand.

"My boy—Harry?" he whispered, "have you any news?"

"Yes," was whispered back. "Let me set your mind at rest. He is safe."

"Cut where? For Heaven's sake, man, speak!" panted the trembling father as he clung to him.

"Across the sea."

Chapter Sixty Four
Harry's Message

"Do you wish me to repeat it? Have you not heard from your father or your uncle?"

"Yes; but I want to hear it all again from you. Harry sent me some message."

Leslie was silent.

"Why do you not speak? You are keeping something back."

"Yes; he gave me a message for you, one I was to deliver."

"Well," said Louise quickly, "why do you not deliver it?"

"Because Harry is, in spite of his trouble, still young and thoughtless. It is a message that would make you more bitter against me than you are now."

Louise rose from where she was seated in the dining-room, walked across to the bay window, looked out upon the sea, and then returned.

"I am not bitter against you, Mr Leslie. How could I be against one who has served us so well? But tell me my brother's message now."

He looked at her with so deep a sense of passionate longing in his eyes, that as she met his ardent gaze her eyes sank, and her colour began to heighten.

"No," he said, "I cannot deliver the message now. Some day, when time has worked its changes, I will tell you word for word. Be satisfied when I assure you that your brother's message will not affect his position in the least, and will be better told later on."

She looked at him half wonderingly, and it seemed to him that there was doubt in her eyes.

"Can you not have faith in me?" he said quietly, "and believe when I tell you that it is better that I should not speak?"

"Yes," she said softly, "I will have faith in you and wait."

"I thank you," he said gravely.

"Now tell me more about Harry."

"There is very little to tell," replied Leslie. "As I went down-stairs that day, I found him just about to enter the house. For a moment I was startled, but I am not a superstitious man, and I grasped at once how we had all been deceived, and who it was dealt me the blow and tripped me that night; and in the reaction which came upon me, I seized him, and dragged him to the first cab I could find."

"I was half mad with delight," continued Leslie, speaking, in spite of his burning words, in a slow, calm, respectful way. "I saw how I had been deceived that night, who had been your companion, and why you had kept silence. For the time I hardly knew what I did or said in my delirious joy, but I was brought to myself, as I sat holding your brother's wrist tightly, by his saying slowly:—

"'There, I'm sick of it. You can leave go. I shan't try to get away. It's all over now.'"

"He thought you had made him a prisoner?"

"Yes; and I thought him a messenger of peace, who had come to point out my folly, weakness, and want of faith."

Louise covered her face with her hands, and he saw that she was sobbing gently.

"It was some time before I could speak," continued Leslie. "I was still holding his wrist tightly, and it was not until he spoke again that I felt as if I could explain."

"'Where are you taking me?' he said. 'Is it necessary for Mr Leslie, my father's friend, to play policeman in the case?'

"'When will you learn to believe and trust in me, Harry Vine?' I said.

"'Never,' he replied bitterly, and in the gladness of my heart I laughed, and could have taken him in my arms and embraced him as one would a lost brother just returned to us from the dead.

"'You will repent that,' I said; and I felt then that my course was marked out, and I could see my way."

Louise let fall her hands, and sank into a chair, her eyes dilating as she gazed earnestly at the quiet, enduring man, who now narrated to her much that was new; and ever as he spoke something in her brain seemed to keep on repeating in a low and constant repetition:

"He loves me—he loves me—but it can never be."

"'Where am I taking you?' I said," continued Leslie. "'To where you can make a fresh start in life.'" And as Louise gazed at him she saw that he was looking fixedly at the spot upon the carpet where her brother had last stood when he was in that room.

"'Not to—'

"He stopped short there; and I—Yes, and I must stop short too. It is very absurd, Miss Vine, for me to be asked all this."

"Go on—go on!" said Louise hoarsely.

Leslie glanced at her, and withdrew his eyes.

"'Will you go abroad, Harry, and make a new beginning?' I said.

"Poor lad! he was utterly broken down, and he would have thrown himself upon his knees to me if I had not forced him to keep his seat."

"My brother!" sighed Louise.

"I asked him then if he would be willing to leave you all, and go right away; and I told him what I proposed—that I had a brother superintending some large tin mines north of Malacca. That I would give him such letters as would ensure a welcome, and telegraph his coming under an assumed name."

"And he accepted?"

"Yes. There, I have nothing to add to all this. I went across with him to Paris, and, after securing a berth for him, we went south to Marseilles, where I saw him on board one of the Messageries Maritimes vessels bound for the East, and we parted. That is all."

"But money; necessaries, Mr Leslie? He was penniless."

"Oh, no," said Leslie smiling; and Louise pressed her teeth upon her quivering lip.

"There," said Leslie, "I would not have said all this, but you forced it from me; and now you know all, try to be at rest. As I told Mr Vine last night, I suppose it would mean trouble with the authorities if it were known, but I think I was justified in what I did. We understand Harry's nature better than any judge, and our plan for bringing him back to his life as your brother is better than theirs. So," he went on with a pleasant smile, "we will keep our secret about him. My brother Dick is one of the truest fellows that ever stepped, and Harry is sure to like him. The climate is not bad. It will be a complete change of existence, and some day when all this trouble is forgotten he can return."

"My brother exiled; gone for ever."

"My dear Miss Vine," said Leslie quietly, "the world has so changed now that we can smile at all those old-fashioned ideas. Your brother is in Malacca. Well, I cannot speak exactly, but I believe I am justified in saying that you could send a message to him from this place in Cornwall, and get an answer by to-morrow morning at the farthest, perhaps to-night. You father at one time could not have obtained one from Exeter in the same space."

"There," he continued quietly, "you are agitated now, and I will say good-bye. Is not that Madelaine Van Heldre coming up the path? Yes, unmistakably. Now, let us bury the past and look forward to the future—a happier one for you, I hope and pray. Good-bye."

He held out his hand, and she looked at him wonderingly.

"Good-bye?"

"Well, for a time. You are weak and ill. Perhaps you will go away for a change—perhaps I shall. Next time we meet time will have softened all this trouble, and you will have forgiven one whose wish was to serve you, all his weakness, all his doubts. God bless you, Louise Vine! Good-bye!"

He held out his hand again, but she did not take it. She only stood gazing wildly at him in a way that he dared not interpret, speechless, pale, and with her lips quivering.

He gave her one long, yearning look, and, turning quickly, he was at the door.

"Mr Leslie—stop!"

"You wished to say something," he cried as he turned toward her and caught her outstretched hand to raise it passionately to his lips. "You do not, you cannot, say it? I will say it for you, then. Good-bye!"

"Stop!" she cried as she clung to his hand. "My brother's message?"

"Some day—in the future. I dare not give it now. When you have forgiven my jealous doubts."

"Forgiven you?" she whispered as she sank upon her knees and held the hand she clasped to her cheek—"forgive me."

"Louise! my darling!" he cried hoarsely as he caught her up to his breast upon which she lay as one lies who feels at peace.

Seconds? minutes? Neither knew; but after a time, as she stood with her hands upon his shoulders gazing calmly in his eyes, she said softly—

"Tell me now; what did Harry say?"

Leslie was silent for a while. Then, clasping her more tightly to his breast, he said in a low, deep voice—

"Tell Louy I have found in you the truest brother that ever lived; ask her some day to make it so indeed."

There was a long silence, during which the door was pressed slowly open; but they did not heed, and he who entered heard his child's words come almost in a whisper.

"Some day," she said; "some day when time has softened all these griefs. Your own words, Duncan."

"Yes," he said, "my own."

"Hah!"

They did not start from their embrace as that long-drawn sigh fell upon their ears, but both asked the same question with their eyes.

"Yes," said George Vine gravely as he took Leslie's hand and bent down to kiss his child, "it has been a long dark night, but joy cometh in the morning."

Chapter Sixty Five
Uncle Luke has a Word

John Van Heldre sat in his office chair at his table once more after a long and weary absence, and Crampton stood opposite scowling at him.

The old clerk had on one of his most sour looks when Van Heldre raised his eyes from the ledger he was scanning, and he made no remark; but looking up again he saw the scowl apparently intensified.

"What's the matter, Crampton? Afraid I shall discover that you have been guilty of embezzlement?" said Van Heldre, smiling.

"Not a bit," said the old clerk, "nor you aren't either."

"Then what is the meaning of the black look?"

"Oh, nothing—nothing!"

"Come, out with it, man. What's the matter?"

"Well, if you must know, sir, I want to know why you can't keep quiet and get quite well, instead of coming muddling here."

"Crampton!"

"Well, I must speak, sir. I don't want you to be laid up again."

"No fear."

"But there is fear, sir. You know I can keep things going all right."

"Yes, Crampton, and show a better balance than I did."

"Well then, sir, why don't you let me go on? I can manage, and I will manage if you'll take a holiday."

"Holiday, man? why it has been nothing but one long painful holiday lately, and this does me good. Now, bring in the other book."

Crampton grunted and went into the outer office to return with the cash-book, which he placed before his employer, and drew back into his old position, watching Van Heldre as he eagerly scanned the pages and marked their contents, till, apparently satisfied, he looked up to see that Crampton was smiling down at him.

"What now?"

"Eh?"

"I say what now? Why are you laughing?"

"Only smiling, sir."

"Well, what have I done that is ridiculous?"

"Ridiculous? Why I was smiling because it seemed like the good old times to have you back busy with the books."

"Crampton, we often say that my old friend is an eccentric character, but really I think Luke Vine must give place to you."

"Dessay," said Crampton sourly. "You go on with these accounts. Look half way down."

Van Heldre did look half way down, and paused.

"Five hundred pounds on the credit side, per the cheque I wrote for Mr Luke Vine—why, what's this?"

"Ah! that's what you may well say, sir. Refused to take the money, sir. I'm sure I'm not so eccentric as that."

"But you never mentioned it, Crampton?"

"Yes, I did, sir, with my pen. There it is in black and white. Better and plainer than sounding words: and, besides you weren't here."

"But this is absurd, Crampton."

"That's what I told him, sir."

"Well, what did he say?"

"That I was an old fool, sir."

"Tut—tut—tut!" ejaculated Van Heldre; "but he must be paid. I can't let him lose the money."

"What I told him, sir. I said we couldn't let him lose the money."

"What did he say to that?"

"Called me an old fool again much stronger, sir. Most ungentlemanly— used words, sir, that he must have picked up on the beach."

"I hardly like to trouble him directly he is back; but would you mind sending up to Mr Luke Vine, with my compliments, and asking him to come here."

"Send at once, sir?"

"At once."

"Perhaps before I leave the office, sir, I might as well call your attention to a communication received this morning."

Van Heldre looked enquiringly at his old clerk.

"It's rather curious, sir," he said, handing a letter, which he had been keeping back as a sort of *bonne bouche* for the last piece of business transacted that morning.

"Never presented yet?" said Van Heldre, nodding his head slowly.

"They must have known I stopped the notes directly," said Crampton with a self-satisfied smile.

"I had hoped that the whole of that terrible business had been buried for good."

"So it had, sir," grunted Crampton; "but some one or another keeps digging it up again."

Van Heldre made no reply, so Crampton left the office, sent off a messenger, and returned to find his employer seated with his face buried in his hands, thinking deeply, and heedless of his presence.

"Poor George!" he said aloud. "Poor misguided boy! I wish Crampton had been—"

"I'm back here," said Crampton.

"Ah! Crampton," said Van Heldre starting, "sent off the message?"

"Yes, sir, I've sent off the message," said the old man sternly. "Pray finish what you were saying, sir. Never mind my feelings."

"What I was saying, Crampton? I did not say anything."

"Oh, yes, you did, sir; you wished Crampton had been—what, sir— buried too, like the trouble?"

"My good fellow—my dear old Crampton! surely I did not say that aloud."

"How could I have heard it, sir, if you hadn't? I only did my duty."

"Yes, yes, of course, of course, Crampton. Really I am very, very sorry."

"And only just before I left the room you were complaining about people digging up the old trouble."

"Come, Crampton, I can deny that. I apologise for thinking aloud, but it was you who spoke of digging up the old trouble."

"Ah! well, it doesn't matter, sir. It was my birthday just as you were at your worst. Seventy-five, Mr Van Heldre, sir, and you can't be troubled with such a blundering old clerk much longer."

"My dear Crampton—"

"May I come in?" followed by three thumps with a heavy stick.

Crampton hurried to the outer office to confront Uncle Luke.

"Met your messenger just outside, and saved him from going up. How much did you give him? He ought to pay that back."

"Oh, never mind that, Luke. How are you?"

"How am I?"

"Yes. Getting settled down again?"

"How am I? Well, a little better this morning. Do I smell of yellow soap?"

"No."

"Wonder at it. I spent nearly all yesterday trying to get off the London dirt and smoke. Treat to get back to where there's room to breathe."

"Ah, you never did like London."

"And London never liked me, so we're even there. Well," he continued after a pause filled up by a low muttering grunt, "what do you want? You didn't send for me to come and tell you that I had caught a cold on my journey down, or got a rheumatic twinge."

"No, no, Luke, of course not."

"Nice one, 'pon my word!" muttered Crampton.

"Well, what is it?"

Crampton moved toward the door, his way lying by Uncle Luke; but just as he neared the opening, the visitor made a stab at the wall with his heavy stick, and, as it were, raised a bar before the old clerk, who started violently.

"Bless my heart, Mr Luke Vine!" he cried; "what are you about? Don't do that."

"Stop here, then. Who told you to go?"

"No one, sir, but—"

"How do I know what he wants. I may be glad of a witness."

"Oh, yes! You need not go, Crampton," said Van Heldre. "Sit down, Luke."

"No, thankye. Sit too much for my health now. Come; out with it. What do you want? There is something?"

"Yes, there is something," said Van Heldre quietly. "Look here, my dear Luke Vine."

"Thought as much," sneered the old man. "You want to borrow money, *my dear* Van Heldre."

"No; I want to pay money, Luke Vine. It seems that you have returned that five hundred pounds to Crampton."

"What five hundred pounds?"

"The money you—there, we will not dwell upon that old trouble, my dear Luke. Come; you know what I mean."

"Oh, I see," said the old man with much surprise. "That five hundred pounds. Well, what about it?"

"How could you be so foolish as to return my cheque?"

"Because you didn't owe me the money."

"Nonsense, my dear fellow! We are old friends, but that was entirely a business transaction."

"Yes, of course it was."

"Five hundred pounds were stolen."

"Yes, and I was all right."

"Exactly. Why should you suppose it was your money?"

"Suppose? Because it was mine—my new Bank of England notes."

"How do you know that?"

"Never mind how I know it, and never mind talking about the money I didn't lose."

"But you did, Luke Vine, and heavily. Of course I am going to refund you the money."

"You can't, man."

"Can't?"

"No; because I've got it safely put away in my pocket-book."

Van Heldre made an impatient gesticulation.

"I tell you I have. The same notes, same numbers, just as you laid them all together."

"Nonsense, man! Come, Luke Vine, my dear old friend, let me settle this matter with you in a business-like way; I shall not be happy till I do."

"Then you'll have to wait a long time for happiness, John," said Uncle Luke, smiling, "for you are not going to pay me."

"But, my dear Luke."

"But, my dear John! you men who turn over your thousands are as careless as boys over small amounts, as you call them."

"Oh, come, Mr Luke Vine, sir," said Crampton sturdily; "there's no carelessness in this office."

"Bah! Clerk!" cried Uncle Luke. "Careful, very. Then how was it the money was stolen?"

"Well, sir, nobody can guard against violence," said Crampton sourly.

"Yes, they can, you pompous old antiquity. I could. I'm not a business man. I don't have ledgers and iron safes and a big office, but I took care of the money better than you did."

"My dear Luke Vine, what do you mean?" cried Van Heldre, after giving Crampton a look which seemed to say, "Don't take any notice."

"Mean? Why, what I said. You people were so careless that I didn't trust you. I had no confidence."

"Well, sir, you had confidence enough to place five hundred pounds in our house," said Crampton gruffly.

"Yes, and you lost it."

"Yes, sir, and our house offered you a cheque for the amount, and you sent it back."

"Of course I did. I didn't want my money twice over, did I?"

"Is this meant for a riddle, Luke?" said Van Heldre, annoyed, and yet amused.

"Riddle? No. I only want to prick that old bubble Crampton, who is so proud of the way in which he can take care of money, and who has always been these last ten years flourishing that iron safe in my face."

"Really, Mr Luke Vine!"

"Hold your tongue, sir! Wasn't my five hundred pounds—new crisp Bank of England notes—in your charge?"

"Yes, sir, in our charge."

"Then, why didn't you watch over them, and take care of 'em? Where are they now?"

"Well, sir, it is hard to say. They have never been presented at any bank."

"Of course they haven't, when I've got 'em safe in my pocket-book."

"In your pocket-book, sir?"

"Yes. Don't you believe me? There; look. Bit rubbed at the edges with being squeezed in the old leather, but there are the notes; aren't they? Look at the numbers."

As the old man spoke he took a shabby old pocket-book from his breast, opened it, and drew out a bundle of notes held together by an elastic band, and laid them on the office table with a bang.

"Bless my heart!" cried Crampton excitedly, as he hastily put on his spectacles and examined the notes, and compared them with an entry in a book. "Yes, sir," he said to Van Heldre; "these are the very notes."

"But how came you by them, Luke Vine?" cried Van Heldre, who looked as much astounded as his clerk.

"How came I by them?" snarled Uncle Luke. "Do you think five hundred pounds are to be picked up in the gutter. I meant that money, and more too, for that unfortunate boy; and the more careless he was the more necessary it became for me to look after his interests."

"You meant that money for poor Harry?"

"To be sure I did, and by the irony of fate the poor misguided lad sent his companion to steal it."

"Good heavens!" ejaculated Van Heldre, while Crampton nodded his head so sharply that his spectacles dropped off, and were only saved from breaking by a quick interposition of the hands.

"And did the foolish fellow restore the money to you?" said Van Heldre.

"Bah! no! He never had it."

"Then how —"

"How? Don't I tell you I watched — hung about the place, not feeling satisfied about my property, and I came upon my gentleman just as he was escaping with the plunder."

"And —" exclaimed Crampton excitedly.

"I knocked him down — with that ruler, and got my money out of his breast. Narrow escape, but I got it."

"Why did you not mention this before, Luke Vine?"

"Because I had got my money safe — because I wanted to give clever people a lesson — because I did not want to see my nephew in gaol — because I did not choose — because — Here, you Crampton, give me back those notes. Thankye, I'll take care of them in future myself."

He replaced the notes in the case, and buttoned it carefully in his breast.

"Luke, you astonish me," cried Van Heldre.

"Eccentric, my dear sir, eccentric. Now, then, you see why I returned you the cheque. Morning."

Crampton took out his silk pocket-handkerchief, and began to polish his glasses as he gazed hard at his employer after following Uncle Luke to the door, which was closed sharply.

"Poor Harry Vine!" said Van Heldre sadly. "Combining with another to rob himself. Surely the ways of sin are devious, Crampton?"

"Yes," said the old man thoughtfully. "I wish I had waited till you got well."

"Too late to think of that, Crampton," said Van Heldre sadly. "When do you go to Pradelle's trial?"

"There, sir, you've been an invalid, and you're not well yet. Suppose we keep that trouble buried, and let other people dig it up, and I'll go when I'm obliged. I suppose you don't want to screen him?"

"I screen him?"

"Hah!" ejaculated the old clerk, who began rubbing his hands, "Then I'm all right there. I should like to see that fellow almost hung—not quite."

"Poor wretch!"

"Know anything about—eh?"

"Harry Vine? Not yet. Only that he has escaped somewhere, I hope for good."

"Yes, sir, I hope so too—for *good*."

Chapter Sixty Six
Tried in the Fire

After, as it were, a race for life, the breathless competitors seemed to welcome the restful change, and the sleep that came almost unalloyed by the mental pangs which had left their marks upon the brows of young and old. And swift tides came and went with the calms and storms of the western coast, but somehow all seemed to tell of rest and peace.

It was a year after Victor Pradelle had been placed in what Sergeant Parkins facetiously termed one of her Majesty's boarding schools, under a good master, that John Van Heldre wrote the following brief letter in answer to one that was very long, dated a month previous to the response, and bearing the post-mark of the Straits Settlements:—

"Harry Vine,—I quite appreciate what you say regarding your long silence. I am too old a man to believe in a hasty repentance forced on by circumstances. Hence, I say, you have done wisely in waiting a year before writing as fully as you have. George and Luke Vine have always been to me as brothers. You know how I felt toward their son. I say to him now you are acting wisely, and I am glad that you have met such a friend as Richard Leslie.

"Certainly; stay where you are, though there is nothing to fear now from the law, I guarantee that. The years soon roll by. I say this for all our sakes.

"As to the final words of your letter—one of my earliest recollections is that of my little hands being held together by one whom you lost too soon in life. Had your mother lived, your career might have been different. What I was taught as my little hands were held together, I still repeat: 'As we forgive them that trespass against us.' Yes. Some day I hope to give you in the flesh that which I give you in the spirit now—my hand."

Six more years had passed before a broad-shouldered, bronzed, and bearded man—partner in the firm of Leslie and Vine, Singapore and Penang—grasped John Van Heldre's hand, and asked him a question to which the old merchant replied: "Yes, all is forgiven and forgotten now. If you can win her; yes."

But the days glided on and the question was not asked. Uncle Harry was constantly on the beach or down on the rocks with the two little prattling children of Duncan Leslie and his wife, and Uncle Luke, who seemed much the same, was rather disposed to be jealous of the favour in which the returned wanderer stood; but he indulged in a pleasant smile now and then, when he was not seen, and had taken to a habit of stopping his nephew on the beach at unexpected times, and apparently for no reason whatever.

The question was not asked, for Aunt Marguerite, who had taken to her bed for the past year, was evidently fading fast. As Dr Knatchbull said, she had been dying for months, and it was the state of her health which brought her nephew back to England, to find his old sins forgotten or forgiven, a year sooner than he had intended.

By slow degrees the vitality had passed from the old woman step by step, till the brain alone remained bright and clear. She was as exacting as ever, and insisted upon her bed being draped with flowers and lace and silk, and her one gratification was to be propped up, with a fan in one nerveless hand and a scent-bottle in the other, listening to the reading of some old page of French history, over which she smiled and softly nodded her head.

One day Harry was down near the harbour talking to Poll Perrow, whose society he often affected, to the old woman's great delight, when Madelaine Van Heldre came to him hastily.

"Is anything wrong?" he asked excitedly.

She bowed her head, and for the moment could not speak.

"Aunt Marguerite?"

"Yes. I was reading to her, and you know her way, Harry; half mockingly she was telling me that I should never gain the pure French accent, when she seemed to change suddenly, and gasped out your name. Louy had not gone home; I was relieving her, as I often do now, and she is with her aunt. Leslie has gone to fetch Mr Vine, who is down on the shore with Uncle Luke."

A few minutes later Harry was in the old lady's room, the doctor making way for him to approach the bed, about which the rest of the family were grouped.

"There," she said sharply, "you need not wait. I want to speak to Harry."

He bent down to place his arm beneath the feeble neck, and she smiled up at him with the ruling passion still strong even in death, and her words came very faintly; but he heard them all.

"Remember, Harry, the hope of our family rests on you. We are the des Vignes, say what they will. Now marry—soon—some good, true woman, one of the *Haute Noblesse*."

"Yes, aunt, I will."

An hour later she was peacefully asleep.

"Closed in death," said Harry Vine as he laid his hand reverently across the withered lids; "but her eyes must be open now, father, to the truth."

There was to be a quiet little dinner at Leslie's about a fortnight later, and after a walk down through the churchyard, the party were going up the steep cliff path. Leslie and his handsome young wife were on ahead; the old men coming slowly toiling on behind as Harry stopped with Madelaine in the well-known sheltered niche.

They stood gazing out at the sea, stretching as it were into infinity, and as they gazed they went on with their conversation, talking calmly of the quaint old lady's prejudices and ways.

"Did you hear her last words?" said Harry gravely.

"Yes."

The look which accompanied the answer was frank and calm. It seemed to lack emotion, but there was a depth of patient truth and trust therein which told of enduring faith.

"She would have me marry soon—some good, true woman, one of the *Haute Noblesse*."

"Yes; it would be better so."

"I have loved one of the *Haute Noblesse* for seven years as a weak, foolish boy—seven years as a trusting man—and she has not changed. Maddy, is my reward to come at last?"

As Madelaine placed her hands calmly in those extended to her she seemed without emotion still; but there was a joyous light in her brightening eyes, and then a deep flush suffused her cheeks, as two words were spoken by one of the trio of old men who had slowly toiled up toward where they stood.

"Thank God?"

It was George Vine who spoke, and the others seemed to look "*Amen.*"